Strategic Management

Strategic Management
A Multi-Perspective Approach

Edited by

Mark Jenkins
and
Véronique Ambrosini

palgrave

First published 2002 by
PALGRAVE
Houndmills, Basingstoke, Hampshire RG21 6XS and
175 Fifth Avenue, New York, N.Y. 10010
Companies and representatives throughout the world

PALGRAVE is the new global academic imprint of
St. Martin's Press LLC Scholarly and Reference Division and
Palgrave Publishers Ltd (formerly Macmillan Press Ltd).

ISBN 0-333-73900-0 hardback
ISBN 0-333-73901-9 paperback

This book is printed on paper suitable for recycling and made from fully
managed and sustained forest sources.

A catalogue record for this book is available from the British Library.

Library of Congress Cataloging-in-Publication Data
Strategic management : a multi-perspective approach / edited by Mark Jenkins,
Véronique Ambrosini.
    p. cm
  Includes bibliographical references and index.
  ISBN 0-333-73900-0 (cloth) — ISBN 0-333-73901-9 (pbk.)
  1. Strategic planning. 2. Industrial management. I. Jenkins, Mark, 1959–
II. Ambrosini, Véronique.
HD30.28 .S72927 2002   2001058507
658.4′012—dc21

10   9   8   7   6   5   4   3   2   1
11   10   09   08   07   06   05   04   03   02

Printed and bound in Great Britain by
Antony Rowe Ltd, Chippenham, Wiltshire

Contents

Acknowledgements

We would like to acknowledge the contribution of a number of individuals that have supported us throughout this project. First of all, we would like to express our gratitude to Professor Cliff Bowman for his invaluable input in the early stages of this book. We would also like to thank all the authors for their co-operation, hard work and patience. Finally we are indebted to Margaret Hamer and Alison Southgate for their detailed work in finalising the manuscript.

MARK JENKINS
VERONIQUE AMBROSINI

Notes on the Contributors

The editors

Mark Jenkins is Professor of Competitive Strategy and Director of the DBA programme at Cranfield School of Management. Prior to joining Cranfield he worked for the Lex Service Group and Massey Ferguson Tractors Ltd. His teaching focuses on the areas of competitive strategy, knowledge management and innovation. His consulting activities reflect these specializations where he has worked throughout Europe, the USA and in parts of the Far East and Middle East. In addition to his work at Cranfield he has been a visiting Professor in Strategic Management at the University of Colorado and has contributed to the MBA programme at Warwick Business School. He is currently researching the role of knowledge and innovation in the development of Formula One motorsport. He has published and presented a wide range of work in the areas of strategy and marketing. He is a founding editor of the *Journal of Marketing Practice*, a member of the editorial review board for the *European Journal of Marketing* and is author of *The Customer-Centred Strategy* (1997).

Véronique Ambrosini joined Cranfield in April 1994, prior to which she was an Assistant Manager working for McDonald's Restaurants. She holds an MBA from the University of Birmingham and studied for her first degree at the ISEG, a French business school. She is now a Research Fellow in Strategic Management, with a PhD from the Cranfield School of Management. Her research interests include the resource-based theory of the firm, tacit knowledge, organizational routines and competitive advantage. She has had article, published in the *Journal of Management Studies*, the *British Journal of Marketing*, the *European Management Journal* and the *Journal of General Management*.

The contributors

Nardine Collier joined the Strategic Management Group at Cranfield in 1998, prior to which she worked at a public relations consultancy as an Account Executive for a number of national companies. She holds a BA (Hons) in Business Administration form DeMontfort University. She is now a Research Assistant in Strategic Management, working with Professor Mark Jenkins. In 2000 she also enrolled as a part-time PhD student.

Philip Davies teaches strategic management in an international context, strategic change and organizational politics, post-acquisition integration and alliance management, strategic consultancy and leadership. He works with international companies mainly in the pharmaceutical, engineering, aerospace and high technology sectors, and is experienced in working with senior managers from different cultures. He has also worked with government and not-for-profit organisations, and is on the Board of the Cranfield Trust. Prior to joining Cranfield he was the Human Resources Director of a National Health Service Hospital and a British Army Intelligence Corps officer with service in Hong Kong, Germany, Northern Ireland and Cyprus. He has a first degree in Modern History from Exeter College, Oxford University and an MBA from Cranfield.

Steve Floyd is a Cizik Professor of Strategic Technology Management at the University of Connecticut, where he teaches Strategy and the Management of Innovation and Technology. His research on strategy-making processes, corporate entrepreneurship and technological innovation has been published in such journals as *Academy of Management Review, Strategic Management Journal, Journal of Management, Organizational Studies, Journal of Management Information Systems, Entrepreneurship: Theory and Practice* and *Academy of Management Executive.* Professor Floyd also serves on several editorial boards and participates actively in the Strategic Management Society and the US Academy of Management. Professor Floyd is co-author (will Bill Wooldridge) of *The Strategic Middle Manager* (1996) and *Building Strategy From the Middle* (2000). The ideas in these books are the basis for on-going research and consulting conducted on both sides of the Atlantic. His current research and writing focuses on developing and managing strategic initiatives within large complex organizations.

Royston Greenwood is Associate Dean (Research) at the School of Business, University of Alberta, and the Telus Professor of Strategic Management. His research, which has appeared in the *Academy of Management Journal, Academy of Management Review,* and *Organization Studies,* focuses upon the management practices of professional service firms using the theoretical lens of institutional theory. Currently he is examining the dynamics of change in highly institutionalized fields, with especial reference to the concept of theorization. He is on the editorial board of *Organization Science* and the *Journal of Management Inquiry,* and is associate editor of *Strategic Organization.*

Gerard P. Hodgkinson is Associate Dean for Research and Professor of Organizational Behaviour and Strategic Management at Leeds University Business School, The University of Leeds UK. A Fellow of the British Academy of Management and a Fellow of the British Psychological Society, his principal research interests centre on the psychological analysis of strategic management processes, especially cognitive processes in strategic decision making and business competition. His work has appeared in a range of scholarly international journals including *Strategic Management Journal, Journal of Management Studies, Journal of Occupational and Organizational Psychology, Organization Studies* and *Human Relations.* Professor Hodgkinson is co-author (with Paul R. Sparrow) of *The Competent Organization: A Psychological Analysis of The Strategic Management Process* (forthcoming). He has also published a number of chapters in edited volumes, including 'Cognitive

Processes in Strategic Management: Some Emerging Trends and Future Directions', in N. Anderson, D.S. Ones, H. K. Sinangil and C. Viswesvaran (eds), *Handbook of Industrial, Work and Organizational Psychology* (2001). He is Editor-in-Chief of the *British Journal of Management* and a Consulting Editor of the *Journal of Occupational and Organizational Psychology*. A practising Chartered Occupational Psychologist, he has conducted numerous consultancy assignments across a wide range of private and public sector organizations.

David J. Jeremy is Professor of Business History in the Business School, The Manchester Metropolitan University. His *Transatlantic Industrial Revolution: The Diffusion of Textile Technologies between Britain and America, 1790–1830s* (1981) received the Dexter Prize of the Society for the History of Technology and the John H. Dunning Prize of the American Historical Association. At the LSE he edited the *Dictionary of Business Biography* (6 vols, 1984–86). He is the author of *Capitalists and Christians: Business Leaders and the Churches in Britain, 1900–1960* (1990); *Artisans, Entrepreneurs, and Machines* (1998), and *A Business History of Britain, 1900–1990s* (1998). Currently he is working on an historical study of boardroom culture and governance with special reference to the North West of England. His work has been funded by the Leverhulme Trust and the Economic and Social Research Council.

Gerry Johnson is Professor of Strategic Management at the University of Strathclyde Graduate School of Business. After graduating from University College, London, he worked for several years in management positions in Unilever and Reed International before becoming a Management Consultant. He taught at Aston University Management Centre, where he obtained his PhD and Manchester Business School before joining Cranfield School of Management in 1988, where he remained until taking up his current appointment in 2000. Professor Johnson is co-author of Europe's best selling strategic management text book *Exploring Corporate Strategy* (6th edition, 2001) and co-editor of a book series which develops themes in that text. He is also author of *Strategic Change and the Management Process*, editor of *Business Strategy and Retailing, the Challenge of Strategic Management*, and *Strategic Thinking*, author of numerous papers on Strategic Management and a member of the editorial board of the *Strategic Management Journal*. His research work is primarily concerned with processes of strategy development and change in organizations. He also works extensively as a consultant at a senior level on issues of strategy development and strategic change with UK and international firms and public sector organizations.

Stephen Regan is Lecturer in Managerial Economics at Cranfield School of Management. Prior to joining Cranfield he was Senior Lecturer in Economics at Anglia Polytechnic University and Visiting Lecturer at Birmingham University. His research interests are in the interaction between firm behaviour and regulation. He acts as a consultant in the public sector and in privatized utilities. He has published mostly in the area of international business and public policy. Stephen has a BA and an MBA from Warwick University.

Séan Rickard studied economics at the London School of Economics and Birkbeck College, London and has an MBA from Cranfield School of Management. Prior to joining the Economics Group at Cranfield in 1994 he worked as a business economist and from 1987 was Chief Economist with the National Farmers' Union, Europe's largest trade association. As Chief Economist and Head of the NFU's European and Economics Department, Séan directed research into – and commented publicly on – a wide range of issues relating to the agricultural and food industries in the UK and the European Union. Key areas of expertise are agricultural policy, (food) supply chain relationships, world trade relationship and the European Union. Séan has been a member of a number of prominent UK and EU committees and working parties, including the influential CBI's Economic Trends Committee. Since joining Cranfield he has been a member of the Minister of Agriculture's Think Tank on future agricultural and rural policy, and an employers' representative on the Agricultural Wages Board. Séan wrote the present government's agricultural manifesto and is currently an academic adviser to the government. He is an experienced public speaker and appears regularly on radio and television. In addition to lecturing and research he is retained as a consultant by a number of international companies and trade associations.

Steven Sonsino is a Fellow of the Centre for Management Development at London Business School and is Director of one of the School's flagship General Management programmes. His research interests focus on senior executives in complex organizations, and specifically their use of language in sensemaking and sensegiving. He is the author of numerous conference papers and is currently researching a book on new leadership theories.

Pauline Weight is Lecturer in the Strategic Management Group. Also, she is Director of the Full-time MBA Programme and Director of the Executive Programme Developing Deliverable Strategies. She teaches strategy, leadership and change management, and consults in the area of improving personal and team effectiveness. Her work includes the design and delivery of in-company senior management development programmes. Pauline's research degree focused on identifying links between organizational structure and performance in the NHS. Her doctoral research focused on the role of professionals in senior management. Pauline has had a varied career, mostly in the public sector. In the NHS she progressed her career through finance, administration and general management, leaving as a Unit General Manager in 1990.

1 Strategy as Multi-Perspectives

Mark Jenkins, Véronique Ambrosini and Nardine Collier

None of the contributors to this book can claim to be dyed-in-the-wool 'strategists', we have all arrived in this domain by following varied paths across other occupations, disciplines and functional areas. However it is also fair to say that most of those who teach, research and practice strategic management have travelled along similarly eclectic paths. The variety of backgrounds among those working in the area of strategic management is indicative of a domain that is essentially driven by particular kinds of issues and problems rather than any specific doctrine. Strategy can therefore be seen not as a discipline or a function or even a tool kit, but as an agenda: a series of fundamental questions and problems that concern organizations and their successful development. Whether it be Chester Barnard's (1938) review of the role of the individual executive in the strategy of the organization, Igor Ansoff's (1965) focus on strategic analysis for the purpose of decision making, Henry Mintzberg's (1994) energetic and eloquent critiques of the adoption of formal planning processes, Andrew Pettigrew's (1985) work on developing our understanding of strategic change or Colin Eden and Fran Ackerman's (1998) more contemporary view of strategy as a journey of organizational regeneration, they are all important contributions to the field of strategic management in that they are all concerned with addressing questions about the future performance of organizations.

If we define strategy as a particular kind of agenda, then the imperative is to address these questions and problems by whatever means we have at our disposal. Organizations are some of the most complex phenomena studied in the social sciences, and whilst it may be convenient for academics to see strategy from a unitary perspective when conducting research, this complexity means we have to embrace any approach that can add to our ability to refine, develop and address some of these strategic questions. It also underlines the converse issue that if we restrict ourselves to a unitary perspective we can never adequately explore such questions.

In addition to requiring a range of perspectives, the strategy agenda is concerned with a number of levels. Whilst strategic management is concerned with the success of the 'organization', in order to address this it also has to consider the context or environment in which the organization performs, and the individuals whose actions help shape the performance of the organization. These three levels are summarized in Figure 1.1.

1

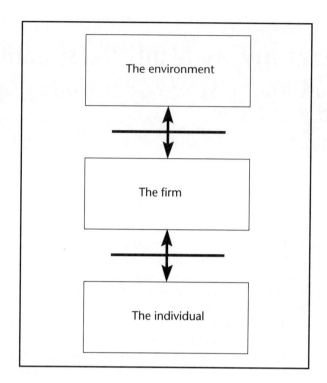

FIGURE 1.1   *The three core levels of analysis of strategic management*

If we start with an organization, then this has to be placed within some kind of environment. A review of this environment needs to consider competing firms, influential stakeholders, competing technologies and regulatory influence, all of which may affect the nature of strategic issues. The second level concerns individual firms and how they operate, the ways in which resources and know-how are combined to create a coherent organization. It is also about the uniqueness of firms and the basis up on which they compete. The third level, and arguably the most important one that strategic management needs to consider, is the role of the individual. This role in developing, engaging and enacting strategy is central to the nature of the process. Each of these levels interact and combine to create a dynamic set of ideas that form the basis of strategic management – none is sufficient on its own but each is necessary, and in our view each draws on differing perspectives to illuminate important aspects and qualities. The final point is that the strategy agenda requires us to move between these three basic levels constantly, and to understand the dynamics between the levels as well as exploring each one in depth. Clearly it requires a more sophisticated approach than simply applying the same lens to look at different levels of analysis. For example the dynamics of technological change may require a different perspective than would an assessment of the motivations of a member of the R & D team, but both may be essential to exploring the strategic issues raised by technological change.

In addition to recognizing the importance of diversity and the need for multiple perspectives and different levels of analysis, it is important to clarify areas of commonality. If we frame strategy as an agenda then we need to be clear about the kinds of issues and questions that are of relevance to this agenda. We propose seven key categories of strategic issues, related to the three levels described above – context, competing, corporate, competences, culture, change and control, (the 7 Cs):

- *Context* covers the issues concerned with an organization's external environment: how the external environment is perceived, how it is scanned, what the organization can do to control it and to change it. It also refers to industry and market structure, and strategic groups.
- *Competing* deals with how organizations gain customers, how they identify their competitors and how they outperform them. It is also about the competitive strategies organizations can implement to achieve sustainable advantage, and about cooperation and collaboration.
- *Corporate* strategy typically addresses the multibusiness context and therefore deals with questions such as alliances, diversification, mergers, globalization and corporate parenting, to cite just a few.
- *Competences* deals with issues concerning the organization's resources, such as skills, know-how, organizational knowledge, routines, competences and capabilities, the role of these in the organization and the part they play in generating competitive advantage. It also deals with issues such as the transferability and imitability of resources.
- *Culture* is about the organization's internal environment. It includes the role of organizational culture, its importance and its influence on the staff. It can also be about how culture is created or changed and how staff members perceive organizational culture.
- *Change* concerns the types of change an organization can implement, and how change can take place or be constrained. This category deals with the reasons for change, the change process and the possible outcomes of change programmes.
- *Control* is about organizational structure, power relationships and the way managers control what is happening in their organization. This category involves the role of managers in the organization, and the extent to which managers can 'manage' what is happening inside organizations and know what is happening around them.

If we apply these seven categories of commonality in strategic issues to six of the seminal teaching texts in the field of strategic management we can account for most of the chapters in these books (Table 1.1).

The seven categories therefore seem to provide a common theme across strategy texts as well as, we believe, the contributions in this book. They are there to provide a reference point when considering how these differing perspectives may inform particular areas of strategic management. Clearly in some cases the perspective may not address a certain category; this is of course important in itself as it emphasizes the partial nature of any perspective, but it can also indicate how different aspects of the field have to draw on different

Table 1.1 Seven categories of strategic issues

	Exploring Corporate Strategy Johnson and Scholes (1999)	Strategic Management Dess and Miller (1993)	Strategy de Wit and Meyer (1998)	Strategic Management Hill and Jones (1998)	Strategic Management Thompson and Strickland (1993)	Contemporary Strategy Analysis Grant (1991)
Context: Environmental analysis Global	(3) Porter PEST	(7) Strategic management (SM) at the international level (2) Porter's Global analysis methods	(8) Industry life cycle Industry context (10) Global	(8) Global environment Entry mode Alliances (3) Porter's Strategy groups Industry life cycle stages	(3) Industry analysis Competitive analysis	(2) Environmental analysis Industry analysis Porter's Competitive analysis (11) Strategy in global industry
Competing: Competitive strategy Business level	(6) Types of competitive strategy (7) Strategic development	(4) Sources of competitive advantage Life cycles	(3) Plans SM processes (5) SBU strategy Competitive strategy PIMS	(6) Market segmentation Generic strategy Strategic groups Life cycles	(5) Generic strategy	(5) Sources of competitive advantage Types of strategy (6) Cost advantage (7) Differentiation advantage
Corporate: Parenting Development	(5) Corporate governance	(6) Diversification Ethics Acquisition	(7) Network alliances (11) Organizational purpose Governance Stakeholders (6) Corporate strategy Value of parent	(10) Portfolio analysis Acquisition Joint venture Turnaround (2) Stakeholders Governance Ethics (9) Corporate strategy Integration Diversification Alliances	(7) Diversification Turnaround Retrench Multinational	(12) Diversification – competitive advantage (13) Managing diversified organizations PIMS

Competence: Internal analysis Functional competence	(4) Value chain analysis SWOT Critical success factors	(3) S & W Value chain Information systems (4) Value chain (5) SM at function Kaizen	6) Core competences Business portfolio	(4) Sources of competitive advantage Value chain Sustaining competitive advantage Sources of core competence (5) Economies of scale Innovation TQM	(4) SWOT Cost analysis (8) Techniques for diversification Growth/share Life cycle	(3) Segment analysis (4) Analyzing resources Value chain (6) Value chain
Culture: Functional competence	5) Cultural context Purpose of organization	(11) Leadership Ethics Culture – development	(9) CEOs Leadership	(12) Organizational culture Rewards (13) Match organizational structure to strategy	(9) Implementation and culture	
Change: Strategy change Implementation	(11) Managing strategic change Types and process	(8) McKinsey Integration	(4) Kaizen Paths to change	(14) Need for and evaluation of change		
Control: Control systems Structure	(9) Structure Organizational configuration (10) Resource allocation Control – influences	(9) Dimension of structure Links to strategy (10) Control Evaluation	(9) Systems	(11) Role of structure Differentiation: vertical/horizontal (12) Systems Implementation Rewards	(9) Creating organizational structure Budgets Reward	

Note:
Figures in brackets refer to individual chapters in each of these respective books.

sets of ideas in order to further understanding. Table 1.2 summarizes some of the key aspects raised in each perspective in terms of how they fit with the seven categories of strategic issues.

Our argument, therefore, is that because strategic management is distinct from other management fields it has to adopt a multi-perspective approach in order to address the complex demands of the strategy agenda. This complexity arises from the need for questions that address different levels of analysis and different dynamics relating to organizations and their strategies. One of the real challenges in an undertaking of this kind is to bring differing and often irreconcilable perspectives together in a way that allows the reader to contrast and compare. We are therefore particularly grateful to the contributors to this book for both endeavouring to restrict their creativity through the use of a common framework and endeavouring to make connections with and relate their perspective to other areas that inform strategic issues. We believe that this book is just the start of the process of drawing together contrasting perspectives in the area of strategy.

We have attempted to structure the book in a way that will make it understandable and accessible to the reader. Naturally there are many different ways in which it could have been structured and we continue (probably at this very moment) to reflect on the numerous alternatives we could have adopted. However, short of creating an interactive book in which the reader designs the sequence of chapters, or indeed changes the sequence of chapters to suit a particular agenda, we have committed ourselves to a format that distinguishes between the three levels outlined in Figure 1.1. We do not see these perspectives as exhaustive, but as indicative and reasonably complete. We are sure that there are many more approaches that could be included in a text on multiple perspectives on strategy, and perhaps in a future edition we shall be able to introduce further perspectives to add to the breadth of the material offered.

This is not a book that should be read from cover to cover in the sequence laid out. There are several ways of using it. The most straightforward approach is to use it as a means of understanding a particular perspective on strategy. But there are other routes around the material. You may be interested in exploring one of the 7 Cs in more depth, in which case you might want to dip into several chapters and read the sections on, say, 'culture' or 'competing' from various perspectives. Alternatively you could investigate perspectives that appear to be contradictory, and compare and contrast them. The tension between markedly different views may provoke some new insights.

In order to help the reader connect to the issues raised by a particular perspective, most of the chapters include an illustrative case study. These are designed to raise a series of practical questions that can be addressed by the perspectives in question. We hope you will find the book stimulating – and controversial! Strategy is an exciting field of study, dealing as it does with fundamental issues of organization. We believe that by getting inside the various dimensions, by broadening the range of perspectives that can be brought to bear on strategy, we can generate a richer picture of organizations, their environment and individuals' contribution to their success.

TABLE 1.2 Reviewing the 7 C's

	Context	Competing	Corporate	Competence	Culture	Change	Control
Part 1: The Environment							
Chapter 2: Industrial organization economics	Market environment driven by demand and supply dynamics	Competition defined by economic structure of an industry	Primarily a business level perspective	Emphasizes similarity amongst firms, i.e. that there are no unique competences	Assumes that firms are homogeneous, profit-maximizing entities	Emphasizes the static analysis of firms and the struggle to deal with the dynamics of change	Control is equated with economic power: price-setting power
Chapter 3: Institutional theory	Main focus stems from the institutionalized nature and regularity role of the environment	Competition is viewed similarly within organizational fields	Emphasis on achieving legitimization and corporate parenting	The similarity between organizations is focused on, and competences are identified in the taken-for-granted practices and structures of the organization	Culture is bounded in the taken-for-granted assumptions, beliefs and practices of the organization	Change can be viewed as a deviation from the norm; however when it does occur it is incremental and within the bounds of what is taken for granted	Control mechanisms and structures are set to implement their strategy
Chapter 4: Business history	Emphasis on external environment and how it changes and influences firms	Emphasis on how ways of competing change over time	Emphasis on how dominant corporate strategies change over time	Emphasis on changes in managerial and organizational skills over time	Emphasis on how different types of cultures emerge over time	Emphasis on how companies change their structure over time	Emphasis on how different control systems are used in different time periods

TABLE 1.2 *continued*

	Context	Competing	Corporate	Competence	Culture	Change	Control
Part 2: *The Firm* Chapter 5: Game theory	Context is defined as a group of competitors (strategic group)	Emphasizes the competitive dynamics between individual firms	Multiple games in multiple businesses	'Rational' game playing	Culture is only covered through the concept of reputation	Games may change over time in order to ensure overall victory	Control is exerted through the control of information
Chapter 6: Transaction cost economics	The context is linked to the types of transaction cost: it is associated with the person making the transaction, or those associates with the technology of the transaction	Competition within an industry is dependent on its structural characteristics	Correct choice of institutional architecture means that the organization should be able to enter a specific market	Based on the ability of managers to control resources	Culture is defined as the organization's honesty, whether altruistic, selfish or self-interested	Managing change is regarded as part of the organization's architecture. This is related to managing human resources	Emphasis on the role of owners versus managers and how managers manage and control resources on behalf of the owner
Chapter 7: Resource-Based view of the firm	Emphasis on the internal environment rather than the external	Competitive success is due to resources which are valuable, rare, inimitable and non-substitutable	Emphasis on related diversification and internal growth	Emphasis on internal competences that are rare, imperfectly imitable, imperfectly mobile and valuable	Emphasis on culture as source of competitive advantage	Emphasis on how different change is	Focus on controlling versus possessing resources, and the ability to capture value

Chapter 8 Military strategy	The environment in which the military campaign takes place	Competing is about how, when, where and why to fight. Emphasis on planning	Emphasis on gaining consensus about the goals	Competences are threefold: tactical, operational and strategic	Culture is the glue holding military forces together – culture creates a world separate from the civilian world	Change is directed – leadership is key	Control is exercised through orders, culture and behaviour
Part 3: The Individual							
Chapter 9: Managerial and organizational cognition	Analysis of strengths and weaknesses from the individual's perspective. Environments are subjective worlds 'enacted' by managers	Competition is defined by the mental models of managers	Corporate logic can be seen as a particular cognitive map that combines business units in order to share synergies	Cognitive mapping is used to identify an organization's core competences	Focuses on the culturally embedded aspects of the organization, and how culture is manifested through individual sense-making	Key individuals' and group's cognitive inertia acts as a barrier to change	Emphasis on managers' control processes being based on judgements and heuristics rather than rational processes
Chapter 10: Role theory	Context shifts from internal to external environment	Emphasis on enacting strategy throughout the organization	Relies on operating in an international or global environment	Competences are embedded in the role employees in the organization undertake	The role played out by individual reflect the culture and culture affects role performance	Main emphasis on creating motivation for and ownership of change, with a focus on behaviour at the level of the individual	Role clarity is seen as a control mechanism, it provides clear lines of accountability

TABLE 1.2 *continued*

	Context	Competing	Corporate	Competence	Culture	Change	Control
Chapter 11: Leadership	Emphasis on the environment and how different leadership styles suit different types of environment, and on how complex the internal and external environments are	Emphasis on managing both people and the environment	Creating cohesion across business and corporate governance	Styles and competences of the leader	Culture is about how leaders can influence and manage it	How to stay ahead of the game (change in environment) and how change should take place	Leadership styles influence approaches and levels of control
Chapter 12: Entrepreneurship	Emphasis on how the environment is an area in which opportunities are to be identified	Emphasis on innovation and risk taking	Corporate 'intrapreneurship', a subset of the entrepreneurial perspective	Emphasis on individual characteristics of the entrepreneur and the ability to recognize and exploit opportunities	Emphasis on how culture supports entrepreneurial behaviour	Emphasis on change as a constant phenomenon	Emphasis on controlling to obtain support and inspire people through different control systems

References

Ansoff, H. I. (1965) *Corporate Strategy: An Analytic Approach to Business Policy for Growth and Expansion* (New York: McGraw-Hill).

Barnard, C. I. (1938) *The Functions of the Executive* (Cambridge, Mass.: Harvard University Press).

Eden, C. and F. Ackermann (1998) *Making Strategy: The Journey of Strategic Management* (London: Sage).

Mintzberg, H. (1994) *The Rise and Fall of Strategic Planning* (New York: Prentice-Hall).

Pettigrew, A. M. (1985) *The Awakening Giant: Continuity and Change in ICI* (Oxford: Basil Blackwell).

Part 1
The Environment

Part 1
The Environment

2 Industrial Organization Economics
Séan Rickard

Basic principles

The economics of industrial organizations – or, as it is more widely referred to, industrial organization (IO) economics – is a branch of microeconomics that seeks to theorize and explain the economic behaviour of firms, both as individual entities and within their industry groups. To describe IO as a branch of microeconomics is to risk seriously undervaluing the role that IO plays in applied microeconomics. The theory of the firm and the theory of consumer behaviour are the twin foundations of microeconomics and IO is central to understanding the economic behaviour of firms. It interprets economic behaviour widely, ranging from the internal organization of the firm – how its processes and its relationships with customers and suppliers generate the conditions for cost minimization – through to dynamic, strategic interactions between small groups of firms. In essence IO seeks to explain how individual firms develop and grow, and as such it provides the microeconomic foundations of strategic management.

Case study

The situation

The situation is a private meeting between two senior executives operating in an industrial sector that is characterized by a small number of rivals, where the success of strategic decisions depends to a large extent on subsequent decisions taken by commercial rivals. The broadsheet sector of the UK newspaper industry is a classic example of a differentiated oligopoly. In September 1993 Rupert Murdoch, the multimillionaire owner of News International, reduced the cover price of *The Times* from 45p to 30p. For a paper that was probably already making a loss this was a bold step. By his action Murdoch was risking the explosion of a price war. The conversation that follows is a fictional discussion between two senior News International executives, Andy McFee and Dale Wildgoose Jr. The two executives were meeting early on 23 June 1994, the day on which the *Daily Telegraph* slashed its cover price from 48p to 30p – some ten months after the cut in *The Times* cover price.

The conversation

Andy: I don't know what Conrad [the owner of the *Daily Telegraph*] is up to. Doesn't he realize the Boss [Rupert Murdoch] means business? This will spark a real price war.

Dale: Hey, just calm down Andy. We should have known this was coming once the *Telegraph*'s sales fell below a million and Conrad reduced his shareholding. Seems the Boss miscalculated when he concluded that Conrad would be constrained by the impact of a price war on the *Telegraph*'s stockmarket valuation.

Andy: I suppose we should be thankful he waited ten months. His sitting on the fence has enabled our daily sales to rise 22 per cent and in the process the addition of 80 000 daily sales has done wonders for our unit costs by more fully utilizing our presses.

Dale: Yeah, and don't forget the benefit of those extra sales for advertising revenue. The Boss's action means that *The Times* is now breaking even, and that's a big improvement on the losses we were making.

Andy: Well, I'm worried. We have succeeded so far by taking sales from the other broadsheets. But how can we hold onto our market share with the *Telegraph* costing 30p? This is all going pear-shaped.

Dale: Relax will you. The Boss seems to know what he's doing. You know he has ordered that we cut *The Times* cover price to 20p tomorrow?

Andy: Oh no! Then it really is a fight to the death. We'll be making losses from tomorrow.

Dale: There you go again. That's the trouble with you Brits. Always looking on the dark side. Yeah, it's going to be a rough for a few weeks, maybe months, but look at it from our point of view. We have first mover advantage. We have gained market share. Conrad now has the additional handicap of having to win back readers who have switched and, you know, price isn't everything. Look at the way we've revamped *The Times* – more sport, more features. It's less stuffy, more appealing. We altered the product to make it more attractive to a wider range of English people.

Andy: When push comes to shove its all on the price. And we can't make money on daily sales of 450 000 and a cover price of 20p. You're just not facing up to the implications of a price war, and you're overlooking . . .

Dale: For god's sake Andy cool it. Yeah, price is important, but it's not the only consideration. The *Guardian*'s cover price is still 50p and its daily sales are more or less unchanged. That shows the value of a clearly differentiated product and a loyal readership.

Andy: I was going to say that you're overlooking the cost of newsprint. Our suppliers say costs are going to rise massively in the coming months. Up 50 per cent was their estimate. This price war could not have come at a worse time. We are bound to lose sales and despite the Boss's deep pocket he won't fund a cover price of 20p for long if newsprint costs rise 50 per cent. You know him. If he isn't winning he'll cut and run.

Dale: I don't think you know the Boss. In fact, at times you seem out of step with the aggressive competitive culture he has introduced. He's a gambler, but he's also a tactician who seems to have an intuitive grasp of the economics of business. You've spent the last fifteen minutes worrying about costs. Yeah sure, in this business volume lowers unit costs but it's demand, not unit costs, that will get our profits up. With daily sales of almost one million the economics of Conrad's operation are more impressive than our 450 000 daily sales. But the Boss has a target of one million daily sales and I think he'll get there.

Andy: What one million daily sales! Are you mad? You know that the UK market is about three million – ignoring *The Scotsman* – and even if we drive *The Independent* out of business we can only realistically expect to pick up a proportion of their 300 000 sales. In my view the Boss was lucky that Carsberg [Sir Bryan Carsberg, director of the Office of Fair Trading] threw out *The Independent*'s claim that we were engaged in predatory pricing.

Dale: Predatory pricing: no one can make that stick. No one in their right mind could conclude that that was our game. The Boss knows as well as anyone that there will always be some rich guy prepared to buy a newspaper so that he has a vehicle for pushing his views on the government. No Andy, the world has changed, people are more price conscious, success now depends on being able to offer both a distinctive product and a low price.

Andy: Are you telling me that the Boss is indifferent to the presence of say *The Independent*?

Dale: Yep. He has his sights set on another market. He knows, like you, that the traditional broadsheet market is probably limited to three million and declining, but unlike you Brits he doesn't have any of the class hang-ups. It was his reading of the downward trend in broadsheet sales and the competition from alternative news sources that prompted him to act. The name of his game is to find the price at which *The Times* becomes an alternative to middle-class tabloids. Not so much the top people's paper as the people's paper. If he can get a hold on that market we are talking of a million daily sales.

Issues

This conversation raises a number of issues that are the subject matter of IO. By the end of this chapter we will have shown how IO has developed a body of theory to help explain the economics of Rupert Murdoch's strategic behaviour. The following issues arise from the case study.

- Only firms with market power (for example producers of differentiated products) have the ability to alter their prices.
- If the market is in decline, firms must choose between falling sales or cutting price.
- If the market is supplied by a small number of players (that is, it is an oligopoly) the success of a price-cutting strategy by an individual firm – in terms of revenue and profits – will depend on the reactions of rivals.
- In an oligopolistic market the implementation of a price-cutting strategy by an individual firm will always result in an increase in sales, but to succeed in increasing profits the strategy must also result in an increase in demand, as customers switch from the now more expensive rival offerings.

- The influence of structure on the nature of the competitive rivalry between firms with market power is not dominant – other factors, such as contestability and the organizational culture and competences of the individual firms, are arguably of greater importance.
- The skills of an individual firm's workforce and the ability of its managers to exercise discretion over their use are crucial to the firm's competitive process.
- Competition is a dynamic process that combines innovation with organizational knowledge and routines to produce a product whose value is hard for rivals to replicate.

Key contributions

The origin of industrial economics

The school of IO is a relative newcomer to the science of economics. As a discipline in its own right it can be traced back to the 1930s and the publication of a number of seminal papers that addressed deficiencies in the traditional microeconomic approach to the firm. The traditional approach to explaining the process of production started with the founding father of modern economics, Adam Smith (1776). He was primarily concerned to identify the 'laws' governing the relationship between production and value rather than the behaviour of individual firms. He set down the foundations of the approach, including the productive benefits of specialization and the central role of profits in bringing together the factors of production – labour, land and capital. However it was left to Jean-Baptiste Say (1803) to provide an explanation of how these factors of production were to be organized or managed. He did so by means of his concept of the entrepreneur: the so-called fourth factor of production.

Following Smith, economists throughout the nineteenth century were concerned to explain what firms should do rather than what they actually did do. Towards the end of that century the views of Smith and his 'classical' successors were superseded by those of the emerging neoclassical school, who identified markets, rather than production methods, as the determinant of value. Most importantly they recognized that markets were driven by individual demand arising from the exercise of free choice. However this insight into individual behaviour did not spread to the supply side. At the turn of the century one of the giants of the neoclassical school, Alfred Marshall (1890), was writing of the 'representative firm' rather than the behaviour of the individual firm.

Defining competition

Neoclassical economists were not blind to the fact that in practice individual firms had distinctive characteristics, but this empirical fact was viewed as no more than a stage on the path to 'perfect competition'. The deductive theory of perfect competition had many contributors but was ultimately refined by Knight (1921) in the early years of the twentieth century. Under perfect competition, industries are characterized by an atomistic structure and homogeneous products. That is, they are assumed to consist of a very large number of relatively small firms, each of whose output is perfectly substitutable for that of the other firms. These two conditions ensure that no one firm can influence the market price by altering its level of output. The theory also requires that firms should be able freely to enter and exit the industry, and that all the firms in the industry have the same knowledge and technology. One consequence of these highly restrictive conditions is that the demand by these firms for resources, for example labour, will eventually result in the equalization of costs across the industry.

These restrictive assumptions allowed the construction of the now familiar 'perfect competition' model (Figure 2.1). The analysis is static in the sense that it relates to one production period, say one month. The horizontal price line, P_0, reflects the neoclassical ideal that the individual firm should be a price taker, that is, unable to influence the market price by changing its level of output. Within the production period the firm's choice of inputs is restricted – for example the number of machines available is fixed – and consequently changes in the level of output will cause unit production costs to vary. This is the justification for the well-known, U-shaped, short-run average cost curve (SRAC). Most importantly, average costs are defined to include 'normal' profits, that is, the level of profit that is just sufficient to give an entrepreneur the incentive to invest capital in the enterprise.

The firm's unit costs are represented in Figure 2.1 by $SRAC_0$ and market demand is such that for output Q_0 the price is raised above the firm's average costs, generating 'superprofits', represented on a per unit basis by the vertical distance BA. For the neoclassical school this is not a stable equilibrium. As entrepreneurs are assumed to be profit maximizers, a price in excess of average costs will attract new entrants to the industry. Consequently in successive production periods the number of firms in the industry will rise. These new entrants will increase the market supply, which in turn will depress the market price (P_1), and their additional demand for resources will raise the costs of production for all firms in the industry, represented by a vertical upward shift in the average cost curve ($SRAC_1$). Thus Figure 2.1 incorporates two production periods: the current period, where superprofits AB are being generated; and a future production period, where firms in the industry have achieved equilibrium at point C. When the price falls to P_1 and unit costs rise to $SRAC_1$ our representative firm's profits have been reduced to a 'normal' level and market entry is no longer an attractive proposition for entrepreneurs. Thus point C becomes the neoclassical ideal of economic efficiency: the exercise of consumer choice has determined the market price, unit production costs for this level of output are at their lowest possible level, and profits are reduced to the minimum necessary to produce Q_B.

The importance of scale

The theoretical elegance of the neoclassical theory of the firm – with its emphasis on correct logical deductions from precise assumptions in order to determine conclusions – has ensured that it remains one of the most powerful models of economic behaviour. But whatever its merits the theory suffers a number

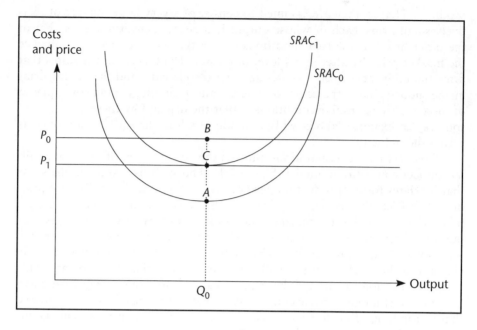

FIGURE 2.1   *The perfect competition model*

of major failings. As well as not recognizing differences between actual firms, its ability to explain how and why firms grow is severely limited. The nearest the neoclassical school came to explaining growth was in distinguishing between the short run and the long run. The long run is defined as that period over which the entrepreneur's choice of resources is unrestricted, and therefore the scale and combination of resources that will deliver the lowest unit costs can be chosen.

Of particular relevance for strategy is the influence of scale, and the neoclassical school identified the inverse relationship between increasing scale of production and unit production costs. The reasons for the inverse relationship are many: construction costs generally rise at a slower rate than the increase in productive capacity; scale can minimize waste by enabling increased utilization of specialized resources; and scale increases bargaining power with suppliers and customers. The relationship between average production costs and the scale of output is generally known as economies of scale and is illustrated in Figure 2.2.

Economies of scale augmented the neoclassical theory of the firm by providing an explanation for the growth of the firm; namely the desire to lower unit production costs, as represented by points A and B. In the first production period the firm plans to produce output Q_0; in the second it plans to achieve scale economies and produce output Q_1. The curve that is drawn to envelop the short-run cost curves associated with these points is the long-run average cost curve (LRAC). The LRAC therefore defines the lowest unit production cost boundary as the firm's scale of production rises. However the neoclassical school was forced to argue that at some scale of production diseconomies set

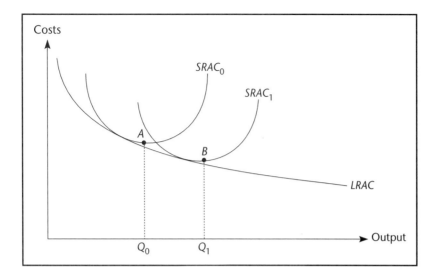

Long-run costs   *FIGURE 2.2*

in, causing the LRAC to start rising. Thus the LRAC was also assumed to be U-shaped because without this assumption, in the neoclassical paradigm, there were no limits to the size of firms.

It is obvious from the foregoing that the perfect competition model could not explain why, within an industry, different firms display varying rates of growth and different scales of production. The theory owed nothing to empiricism; it was a triumph of theory over empirical fact and, as we have seen, relied on a long list of restrictive assumptions. The purpose was not to explain the many examples that deviated from the model but rather to use correct, logical deductions from precise assumptions to determine absolute rules or laws. The approach could be justified on the ground that it demonstrated how unfettered competition could bring about the efficient allocation of resources so that consumer demands were satisfied at the lowest possible price. The essence of the neoclassical economists' approach to the firm was to set out the conditions for achieving this ideal. Deviations from the ideal were recognized as possible – indeed the neoclassical school developed a profit maximizing model for a pure monopoly – but could only be temporary exceptions if all firms had the same information on prevailing technologies and the prices of inputs. Real world factors such as advertising and product differentiation had no place in the neoclassical model of the firm. Under the model of perfect competition the only strategy open to a entrepreneur was to minimize the costs of production.

Links to strategy

The first major challenge to the neoclassical, perfect competition, approach to the firm was contained in the seminal paper by Sraffa (1926), who noted that in practice firms generally refrain from further expansion not because it will cause unit costs to rise but because it will require an unacceptable fall in price. This is completely at odds not only with the idea of the firm being a price taker, but also with the reliance on a rising LRAC to limit firm size. Sraffa argued that firms generally face downward sloping demand curves; that is, they have some degree of market power and can therefore influence the prices they charge. His contribution is summarized in Figure 2.3, which combines a downward sloping demand curve with a firm's cost curves. Sraffa pointed out that a firm operating at point A – charging price P_0 and selling quantity Q_0 – will have to lower the price of its product in order to increase output. In the short run it cannot go beyond B without making a loss, and in the long run it cannot go beyond point C unless it engineers a rise in demand, as represented by a rightward shift in the demand curve. Thus demand limits the size of a firm even if it benefits from economies of scale.

Sraffa's short article – just 15 pages – paved the way for two of the most important antecedents of IO, namely the theories of oligopolistic competition and monopolistic competition. Both theories were developed in the 1930s and both were attempts to acknowledge the influence of a downward sloping demand curve on the behaviour of firms. Although the monopolistic competition model preceded the oligopolistic model we shall start with the latter as it provides a more straightforward explanation of the impact of demand on strategic behaviour.

A market that is supplied by a small number of sellers is described as having an oligopolistic structure. These sellers may produce a homogeneous product (for example oil) or a differentiated product (for example newspapers). In such markets each seller is likely to have a degree of market power and therefore the power to influence sales by altering price. Even in markets with larger numbers of sellers, product differentiation can mean that a firm faces strong competition from only a limited number of competitors. Such a 'local' oligopoly will tend to generate the same competitive interdependence as in an industry comprising only a few firms.

Figure 2.4 illustrates perhaps the best known attempt, if elementary textbooks are any guide, to explain oligopolistic competition within the neoclassical paradigm; the so-called kinked demand curve (Sweezy, 1939). The main motivation for Sweezy's model was the empirical evidence that oligopolists rarely seemed to compete on price despite their ability to alter price. He set out to demonstrate (as summarized in Figure 2.4), why 'competition amongst the few' was unlikely to involve price competition. The firm's costs are represented in the short run by $SRAC$ and in the long run by $LRAC$. The firm is earning supernormal profits at price P_0 since price is above unit production costs. Starting at point A, suppose our firm contemplates raising its price to P_1 – seen as the 'profit maximizing price'. According to Sweezy the firm's rivals are likely to respond by leaving their prices unchanged, and consequently our firm will suffer a fall in demand as its customers switch to rivals with cheaper products. This is represented by the leftward shift in demand from D_0 to D_1, bringing the firm to point B.

Alternatively the firm may contemplate reducing its price to, say, P_2 in the expectation of an increase in demand (represented by D_2) if its rivals do

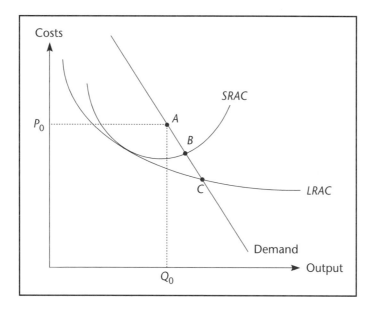

Demand and firm size   *FIGURE 2.3*

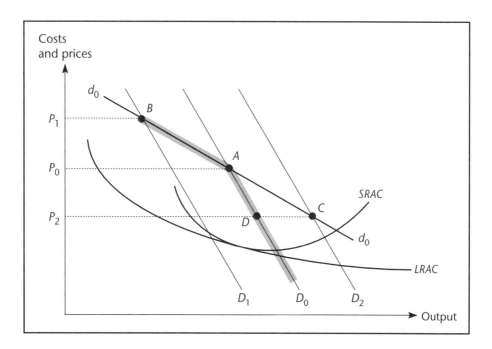

The kinked demand curve   *FIGURE 2.4*

not respond. But the reasoning underlying the kinked demand curve is that the firm's rivals are likely to respond in kind and match the price cut in order to protect their market shares. Hence for our oligopolist the increase in sales resulting from a price cut to P_2 is likely to be point D, not point C. Thus the line d_0d_0 shows the downward sloping demand curve facing the firm at point A *if no other competing firm changes its price*. D_0D_0 shows the demand curve facing the firm if competing firms change their prices in proportion. Because the model determines that the firm's rivals will respond differently depending on whether the price is raised or lowered the oligopolist faces a kinked demand curve, arrived at by joining points B, A and D. The kinked demand curve illustrates an important point: the strategic advantage of reducing price depends on achieving a rise in demand. As the likelihood of a rise in demand is minimized by the high probability that rivals will match a price cutting strategy, the kinked demand curve model provides an explanation of the empirical rarity of price competition between oligopolists.

The main motivation for Chamberlin's (1933) monopolistic competition model was empirical evidence of a world in which firms competed with differentiated products. As the theory allows individual firms discretion over their products' characteristics and the ability to alter the price, this implies a downward sloping demand curve. The essence of the monopolist competition model is set out in Figure 2.5. Because Chamberlin's model assumes that a large number of firms are competing for market share, each firm behaves as though it faces the *ceteris paribus* demand curve, d_0d_0 – that is, it assumes its rivals will not respond (see Figure 2.4 for the derivation of this). If all firms lower their prices together, each firm moves down D_0D_0. With free entry and a price above $SRAC$, firms will enter the market, attracted by supernormal profits. As the number of producers rises the demand for an individual firm's differentiated product declines because consumers have more alternatives to choose from – this is represented by a leftward shift in both D_0D_0 and d_0d_0.

The limit of this leftward shift is represented by D_1D_1, which passes through point A, where the P_1Q_1 combination generates only normal profits. Once supernormal profits have been competed away, new entry to the market ceases. Therefore point A appears to be the point of equilibrium for a firm operating under conditions of monopolistic competition. To the delight of the neoclassical school, Chamberlin's model implied an equilibrium with excess capacity – it seemed to confirm the neoclassical dictum that any departure from perfect competition would result in inefficiency. Chamberlin's 'famous' conclusion of excess capacity is derived from the fact that at equilibrium unit production costs are being held above their minimum short-run (represented by point B) and long-run levels. In the absence of product differentiation higher output could be achieved at lower cost.

Context

Both the monopolistic competition model and the oligopolistic model were rapidly absorbed into the economics literature, possibly reflecting the profession's unease about its reliance on an ideal model of perfect competition that did not appear to have much in common with the environment in which most

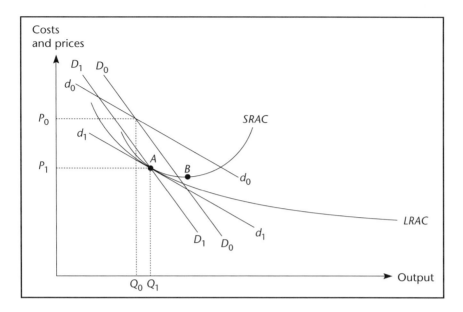

Monopolistic competition FIGURE 2.5

senior managers operated. The importance of the models from the perspective of strategy is that they necessarily focused attention on the market environment facing the firm. By placing the firm in context it opened the door to the empirics of competitive behaviour, and in so doing it raised a host of contextual issues, which are now the substance of IO.

By recognizing that most firms attempt to produce differentiated products, Chamberlin was forced to introduce the concept of the 'competing group' (now more generally known as the strategic group); that is, the firms in the group produce products that are close – but not identical – substitutes for each other. But such products might be physically very dissimilar, for example hot water bottles and electric blankets, and therefore a firm's main competitors may not all be in the same industry. This raises enormous difficulties as the competitive group is not easily defined: substitutability between products is not capable of clear definition and the limits of the competing group become an empirical matter.

The introduction of product heterogeneity seriously compromised Chamberlin's model. In this model cost curves must include selling costs, for example advertising expenditure, and as the units of output are physically dissimilar the unit costs will vary. The logic of these assumptions is that competing firms do not face the same LRAC curves. Figure 2.5 is therefore seriously flawed – a point that seems to have escaped the authors of many economic text books. In short, Chamberlin's bold attempt to establish a more empirically based economic model of the firm was compromised by the logical inconsistency of combining a downward sloping demand curve – derived from product heterogeneity – with uniform costs derived from a homogeneity model.

The kinked demand curve model has also attracted criticism. First, many oligopolists produce differentiated products, thus the points raised above on costs are equally applicable. Second, like the monopolistic competition model it is a static analysis in the neoclassical tradition; neither model provides an explanation of how the starting price is arrived at – any price between unit costs (SRAC) and the monopoly price can be the starting point. Third, there is no allowance for a possible relationship between the starting price and costs. Ironically both the oligopolist and monopolist competition models fail in the very area they were designed to address; namely empirical relevance. Both models lack predictive power. It has been shown that virtually no predictions emerge from these models (Archibald, 1961). They are incapable of providing even qualitative – let alone quantitative – predictions of the firm's price, output and capacity utilization following a change in market demand and/or costs.

The significance of both Sweezy's and Chamberlin's models to the development of IO are the issues they raised rather than their attempted solutions. Both models raised the contextual issue of market structure – the number of sellers, competing groups – as the determinant of performance in terms of prices, selling costs and profits. Both models switched attention from the 'representative' to the individual firm. In so doing they opened up strategic issues such as how to differentiate, which product variant to produce and what price to charge. The lasting contribution of both models is that they formed the platform upon which one of the major developments of IO was built; namely the structure–conduct–performance (SCP) paradigm (Bain, 1956). The SCP model postulates crucial relationships between the number and size distribution of firms in a market and their competitive behaviour and consequential performance. The famous SCP paradigm marked a shift from the deductive theoretical reasoning of the neoclassical school, in which both Chamberlin's and Sweezy's models were founded, to the empirical approach of the new IO school.

According to the SCP paradigm rivalry can take many forms, including pricing, product design and promotional strategies, plant investment, R & D, innovation and legal tactics. This conduct delivers market performance, which is manifested in productivity, allocative efficiency, product variety, innovation and profits. Thus the SCP paradigm emphasizes the causal flow from the context of industry structure to conduct and strategic behaviour to the individual performance of firms (Figure 2.6).

Competences

The SCP paradigm gave rise to a decade or more of cross-sectional empirical analysis to test the model's many propositions. But by the 1970s there was growing dissatisfaction with the premise inherent in the SCP model that market structure was exogenously determined; for example the size and number of competing firms were determined by the scope for economies of scale, which in turn was determined by current technology (Viner, 1952). Research indicated that market structure could also be endogenous; that is, the conduct and performance of firms in the industry was also an important influence on structure. For example mergers directly affected the size and distribution of firms, ad-

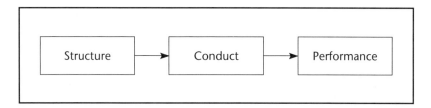

The structure–conduct–performance paradigm   FIGURE 2.6

vertising and innovation could raise entry barriers and predatory pricing could force competitors out of the market – in essence behaviour that directly or indirectly raised the costs of entry into a market also influenced structure. The idea that resources controlled by established firms could form the basis of entry barriers and that therefore market structure could be the result of deliberate measures (that is, conduct) taken by established firms was alien to the SCP paradigm.

Economists in the field began to draw a distinction between innocent and strategic entry barriers. Innocent entry barriers arose where technology required entry on a very large scale in order to achieve unit production costs that would make the new entrant's selling price competitive, for example oil refining. In contrast strategic entry barriers were created by the competences of established firms that through their control of industry resources sought to limit competition from new entrants. For example they may have established their products in their customers' preferences, forcing a new entrant to incur very costly promotion costs in order to overcome the advantage of the established firm. Once incurred such costs were sunk – that is, unrecoverable – thereby forcing the new entrant to contemplate the exit costs if the entry proved unsuccessful.

The inability to explain market structure was only one of the causes of dissatisfaction with the SCP paradigm. Like Chamberlin's and Sweezy's models the model rested firmly on the neoclassical approach to the firm. Namely, noncooperative behaviour by firms was typically assumed: producers and consumers all had the same information, and preferences and current technology were taken as being exogenous, that is, uninfluenced by the behaviour of the firms. The SCP model ignored the wealth of empirical evidence showing that individual firms were very heterogeneous in their competences.

Of significance for the area of strategic management was the growing recognition that individual firms, or rather their senior managers, could influence both market structure and the nature of competitive rivalry. This inevitably began to focus attention on the competences of individual firms. The IO school was coming to realize that the resource endowments of individual firms, for example the skills of its workforce and the ability of managers to exercise discretion over their use, were of crucial importance. If competitive behaviour was to be explained this necessitated a much sharper focus on individual firms.

Competences fall into a number of categories: superior technological know-how, organizational excellence, exceptional human resource management, trusting relationships with stakeholders, and financial expertise (see Chapter 4 for a more detailed discussion). The idea that each firm is unique can be traced back to Penrose's (1959) resource-based approach to the firm. This approach acknowledges that firms have similar physical resources – such as labour, machines and so on – but the services they can generate from these resources depend on accumulated experience and learning. Thus the ability to exploit opportunities effectively varies from firm to firm. This insight began to gain momentum, and by the 1970s the IO school was beginning to focus on the behaviour of individual firms – particularly the discretionary behaviour of senior managers – in order to understand and explore the link between market structure and individual firms' behaviour and performance.

Culture

As early as the 1930s, descriptive studies of firms, particularly the giant ones, showed that senior managers exercised discretion over prices, output and advertising (Chandler, 1962). This led the empirical school to become even more sceptical about the neoclassical assumption that the pursuit of profit maximization explained the behaviour of firms. It also encouraged the development of alternative theories of the firm. These alternative models of the firm essentially represented an attempt to understand the process of decision making within firms by analyzing the internal environment in which decisions were made. If we define culture as 'a complex set of values, belief assumptions and symbols that define the way in which a firm conducts its business' (Barney, 1986) then this branch of IO was in effect researching the influence of a firm's culture.

These alternative approaches to the theory of the firm can be divided into two schools; the management and behavioural schools. Strictly speaking, much of the subsequent research into these alternative approaches fell outside the scope of IO and would more properly be located within managerial and/or organizational economics. But the links between these separate schools became increasingly blurred. The IO literature now includes the *transaction cost* approach, which focuses on the organization as a means of allocating resources (see Chapter 4). It also includes the managerial approach, which focuses on non-profit-maximizing objectives and the way in which such objectives are formed as a means of understanding the strategic behaviour of individual firms.

The management school developed from attempts to assess the impact on firms of the separation of ownership and day-to-day operations by salaried managers (Beale and Means, 1932). The recognition of managerial discretion has given rise to a vast IO literature on theories of managerial motivation and control. The most frequently argued view of the management school is that firms' behaviour depends on the objectives of senior managers as a group and that this group's motives sparing from a desire for income, status and power, subject to constraints, for example profits on managerial discretion. Good examples are Baumol's (1958) sales maximization model and Oliver Williamson's (1964) expense preference model.

The behavioural approach to decision making within the firm attempts to integrate economics and organizational theory (Cyert and March, 1963). At its most general level this approach argues that the firm is a coalition of individuals, some of whom are organized into groups. This gives rise to goal conflicts and the assumption that firms do not maximize anything; instead people normally *satisfice* – managers aspire to reach a satisfactory level of profit that is achievable, rather than striving for the maximum (Simon, 1959).

These alternative approaches to the firm have in common the objective of explaining the interaction of individual, organizational and strategic behaviour. The IO literature has focused in particular on two pricing strategies that reflect the senior managers' culture: predatory pricing and price leadership. Predatory pricing arises when a firm decides to sacrifice profits in the short term in order to drive a rival out of the market, the intention being to increase the firm's market power and hence its ability to set prices to achieve a supernormal profit. Predation is now illegal as its longer-term objective is to reduce rather than enhance competition. As a strategy it is the product of a particularly aggressive if not ruthless management culture. Dominant-firm price leadership is a strategy that arises from a risk averse management culture. Setting the level of the market's prices provides a degree of stability for those managers with the discretion to effect such a policy, but price leadership comes at the cost of some erosion of market share (Yamawaki, 1985).

Competing

The SCP paradigm forms the basis of what is perhaps the best known model of competitive strategy, namely Michael Porter's five forces model (Porter, 1980). Porter's model – shown in Figure 2.7 – is essentially structuralist, attributing the nature of competition to five key forces: rivalry, entry barriers, substitute products, relationships with suppliers, and relationships with customers. The model arose from the SCP paradigm but is considerably more complex in that it recognizes that competitive strategies vary according to whether the industry is emerging, mature or declining. But there is no theory of the organization in the model, and hence no guidance on the competitive contribution of horizontal, vertical and diversified strategies. In Porter's own words, 'competition in an industry is rooted in its underlying economic structure' (ibid.). Not surprisingly this approach added little to the issue of endogeneity outlined above.

This lack of organizational perspective necessarily limits Porter's model to the level of the business unit rather than the corporation. The model suggests that the business unit attains a sustainable competitive advantage – that is, sustained profitability – from a superior market position, such as offering highly differentiated products or producing at lower unit costs than those of rivals. But Porter is silent on the organizational structures and resources needed to achieve this superior position.

At about the time Porter was setting out his five forces model William Baumol's (1982) concept of contestable markets was casting doubt on the idea that structure could shed much light on competitive rivalry. Baumol argued that markets are contestable if a potential entrant has access to the same technology and resources as incumbents and is able to salvage the capital costs of entry upon exit (that is, there are no sunk costs). In such a situation there is the constant threat of entry and this forces existing firms to minimize their production costs and resist the temptation to raise prices to achieve supernormal

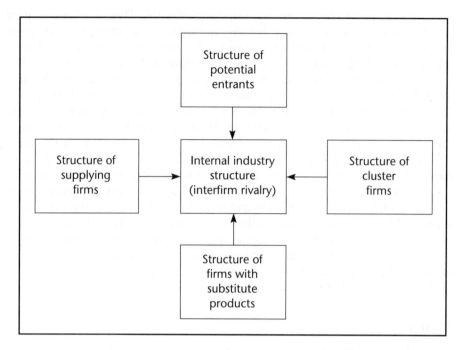

FIGURE 2.7   *Forces driving competition (adapted from Porter, 1930)*

profits. Thus conduct in contestable markets is not determined by market structure. Under such conditions the need to deter entry is the main influence on performance. Baumol's theory of contestable markets was just one of a number of significant developments in the field of IO at the start of the 1980s that attempted to explain industrial structure endogenously. Other seminal contributions showed how innovation (Dasgupta and Stiglitz, 1980) and product improvement (Shaked and Sutton, 1983) – that is, competences – could influence market structure.

It would however be wrong to describe Porter's contribution to IO as that of a structuralist empiricist. His models and writing are powerful because of their attention to empirical detail and their focus on the benefits of exploiting interrelationships with buyers and suppliers – developed in more detail in Porter's (1985) concept of the value chain. In this Porter links competitive strategy to another developing IO trend: organizational economics, and in particular the role of transaction costs. Transaction cost economics developed from a seminal article by Ronald Coase (1937) and is discussed in more detail in Chapter 6.

The significance of transaction cost economics for IO is its contribution to understanding how firms might achieve competitive advantage by means of vertical integration – producing a good or service internally rather than relying on the market – or forming close, longer-term, trusting relationships with stakeholders, for example the workforce, suppliers and customers (Kay, 1993). Transaction cost analysis qualifies the SCP paradigm and its acceptance of the neoclassical view that unfettered markets always deliver the best value in terms of price and quality.

While the SCP paradigm dominated the IO literature until the 1980s it was not without its critics, principally the neo-Austrian school. The Austrian approach to competition ignored structural issues, for example oligopoly, and concentrated instead on the dynamic progress. For the Austrians the major issue was the competitive process itself, a 'voyage of exploration into the unknown, an attempt to discover new ways of doing things better than they have been done before' (Hayek, 1945). The Austrian view of competition clashed head-on with the neoclassical view of profits. For the neoclassicists, supernormal profits were evidence of the exploitation of market power – consumers were forced to pay a price that was higher than the cost of production – and as such represented a loss of efficiency. For the Austrians, supernormal profits encouraged entrepreneurs to seek out new ideas, to be innovative and hence to improve welfare.

Corporate strategy

Noted above under culture was the development of an overlap between three separate approaches – IO theories, organizational economics and managerial economics – to explain the relationship between managerial discretion and strategy. IO has studied the role of managerial discretion with the aid of *game theory*, which provides a tool to analyze discretionary strategic decision making by senior managers. Game theory can be traced back to the 1940s (Neumann and Morgenstein, 1944) and is considered in detail in Chapter 5. The game theoretic approach brought to IO a focus on strategic moves by firms, particularly at the corporate level. Game theory, as applied by IO, has two basic themes: reputation and commitment strategies. Reputation describes stakeholder beliefs about the behaviour of a firm, for example a belief by customers in the firm's integrity, and this links directly to corporate behaviour.

One of game theory's major contributions to corporate strategy is the insight that if strategic actions are to work they must influence the beliefs of those whose behaviour it is designed to influence. The strategic move, if it is to influence the actions of rivals, must be credible and have a lasting effect on cost or demand conditions such as investment in capacity, R & D, advertising or product development. Strategic moves of this kind require irreversible commitment and these considerations have led to a greater appreciation of the importance of sunk costs (as opposed to fixed costs) (Sutton, 1992). In many settings what matters is the degree to which costs are irrecoverable – that is, sunk – rather than the relationship between unit costs and output, that is, economies of scale.

Game theory sheds light on the interactions between competitors. For example in oligopolistic markets the pricing and output decisions of individual firms have a direct impact on rivals' returns. In such a situation a major consideration for a firm considering a strategic decision is the likely response of a rival. This leads on to the role of signalling. If one firm has more information than its rival – a situation of asymmetric information – the rival will be forced to make inferences from its competitor's behaviour. Hence there is an incentive for the more informed rival to engage in strategic signalling, which may be manifested in limit pricing – holding prices lower than might otherwise be the case – and predatory pricing – cutting prices so that a loss is incurred (Roberts, 1986).

This analysis of move and countermove might better be described as the study of the dynamics of corporate competition. Paradoxically Chamberlin (1929) was one of the first economists to draw attention to the interdependence of oligopolist markets. We saw in the kinked demand curve model that for the individual firm the profitability of changing price depends on rivals' reactions. The essence of such interdependence is that it provides an incentive for various types of cooperative behaviour – including tacit collusion – between corporate decision makers. In the absence of a binding agreement between two firms not to reduce prices, both will be tempted to engage in 'tacit' collusions, subject to their management culture (Tirole, 1993).

Change

Perhaps one of the greatest failings of the IO models founded upon the neoclassical approach was their emphasis on 'static' analysis. Positions of equilibrium were compared and analyzed but the path between the two points of equilibrium was ignored. This major omission was highlighted by Schumpeter as early as the 1940s, when he observed that the competition that mattered was 'the competition from the new commodity, the new technology, the new source of supply, the new type of organization . . . competition which commands a decisive cost or quality advantage' (Schumpeter, 1942). For Schumpeter the process of change involved invention, innovation and diffusion. The neoclassical model's assumption of perfect information cannot explain the processes of invention and innovation, or indeed change in general.

After Schumpeter some 40 years elapsed before IO utilized the emerging evolutionary economics to help identify characteristics of firms and markets that were likely to generate invention, innovation and growth. Research in this area has generally concentrated on attempting to integrate concepts such as organizational knowledge and routines to Schumpeter's concept of dynamic competition (Nelson and Winter, 1982). As a branch or subset of IO, evolutionary economics emphasizes the inevitability of mistaken decisions in an uncertain world. The relevance of this approach to IO and strategy is its inevitable concern with technological change and its implications for firms and managers exposed to such change. Evolutionary economics has brought to the fore a framework in which firms compete primarily through a struggle to improve or innovate. In this process a firm's managers have only a partial understanding of the opportunity set. Organizational capabilities are based on routines that are not explicitly comprehended and therefore cannot be easily replicated even when observed. In this respect evolutionary economics has brought IO back to one of its founding principles, namely an emphasis on empiricism rather than hypothetical sets of alternative theories.

The first IO models to deal explicitly with change focused on the growth of firms. Over the years models to explain the growth of firms have become numerous in the IO literature. Most owe something to Marris (1963), whose theory integrates both supply and demand elements. This basic model produced a stream of subsequent research covering areas such as firm growth and profit maximization (Williamson, 1966), growth through vertical integration (Williamson, 1971), and the influence of finance on growth performance (Heal and Silberston, 1972). Central to much of the work on the growth-maximizing firm is the threat of takeover. Takeovers, however, are also a means by which firms can grow. Empirical studies suggest that up to a third of the growth of UK firms has been achieved through acquisition (Aaronovitch and Sawyer, 1975). A continuing debate concerns the impact of market structure on the incentive to innovate. The traditional view is that only firms with a degree of market power have the incentive and resources to exploit innovation. But this viewpoint has been successfully challenged, at least to the extent that a competitive environment provides more incentive for patenting (Arrow, 1962).

Control

Much of IO seeks to explain control both without and within the firm. It was explained above how dissatisfaction with the SCP paradigm caused economists working in the field to question the way in which firms set about controlling their external environment. We have also observed how oligopolistic interdependence encourages the avoidance of price competition and a willingness to act together, even in the absence of formal collusion, to exploit the profit opportunities afforded by barriers to entry (Hay and Morris, 1991).

This work has resulted in the individual firm emerging as the central player. The developments outlined above mean that individual firms can no longer be viewed as passive units. Rather they are active players that take strategic decisions with the purpose of controlling their competitive business environment in order to earn higher profits. But we have also discovered that IO cannot provide a general solution as to how a firm might achieve this objective. Pricing, product differentiation, investment in physical capacity, R & D and advertising are all tools to be used in this process of control: of key interest to IO research is how organizations reach decisions on the use of these tools and how competition between firms influences these decisions.

The elevation of the individual firm to centre stage has necessarily focused attention on the discretion afforded to senior managers to formulate and carry out strategic objectives. The dispersion of shareholdings make it unlikely that the owners of the capital can exercise tight control. Organizational structures and managerial compensation systems offer a degree of control, but there is little reason or evidence to suggest that these constraints can do more than place limits on the extent to which managers pursue their strategic objectives. The relationships involved are very complicated and require the integration of economics and organizational theory; the more they are explored the more complex these models become, reducing their generality and the provision of testable predictions.

Another area of control concerns public policy. By means of explicit regulatory intervention, government agencies can exercise a great deal of control over the behaviour of firms. The array of possible policy instruments is large, and not surprisingly a substantial area of IO is devoted to identifying appropriate policies. Cost, investment, prices and output can all be influenced by taxes and subsidies. The government might act to increase the amount of information available to firms and use legislation to keep market structures conducive to competition. This area of public control has encouraged the integration of IO and law and prompted a vast body of empirical literature on antitrust actions (Scherer and Ross, 1990).

Tools and techniques

It was noted above that the introduction of the SCP paradigm gave rise to a decade or more of empirical analysis to test the model's many propositions. The reason for this was only partly the model's proposition; arguably of equal importance was the fact that the introduction of the SCP model coincided with the arrival of computers. Computers made the complicated calculations inherent in multiple regression considerably easier. Thus, suddenly, economists in the field could use the power of multiple regression to test statistically the relationships between market structure, conduct and performance. Multiple regression allowed in principle for the influence of explanatory factors (seller concentration, entry barriers, level of demand and so on) to be separately identified and their impact on, say, profits to be measured. Armed with such a powerful tool, it is perhaps not surprising that the SCP paradigm held sway for so long. With the benefit of hindsight it appears that the opportunities for empirical analysis provided by the computer outweighed the development of rigorous theoretical support.

The next significant tool was game theory, and in particular multiperiod game theory, which enabled IO to analyze the dynamics of competitive behaviour (Shapiro, 1986). Multiperiod game theory models have shed light on 'tacit' collusion, demonstrating that any cheating by a firm in one period can, if detected, be punished in subsequent periods by non-cooperative behaviour by the rest of the oligopolist group. This work suggests that tacit collusion normally causes profits (that is, performance) to rise above the non-cooperative level, which supports the neoclassical analysis of oligopolistic markets. But with game theory the outcome is the result of rigorous analysis of the interactions involved (that is, the process), rather than interpolation between fully competitive and monopolistic behaviour. Repeated games bring a dynamic aspect to the static approach of traditional IO models. Indeed the successes of game theory in IO are largely due to the fact that game theory provides a language and techniques for modelling dynamic, competitive interactions (Kreps, 1990). As will be discussed more fully in Chapter 5, game theory as a tool allows a focus on the process of rivalrous behaviour rather than just the outcome, and in doing so it explicitly allows for uncertainty and the transaction costs associated with a lack of or asymmetric information.

Ironically, given that empirical relevance was such a driving force for the founding fathers of IO, game theory is a highly theoretical tool and has taken IO to new heights of mathematical elegance and obscurity. The pendulum is now swinging back, and many of the hypotheses that arose from the theoretical contributions of the 1980s are now the subject of empirical analysis. Statistical analysis, and in particular regression analysis, has a key role to play but researchers are increasingly augmenting their statistical studies with detailed case studies, controlled experiments in laboratories (particularly appropriate for testing theoretical game theory developments) and evidence from antitrust cases (Scherer, 1988).

The search is on to derive robust general predictions that can only be revealed by empirical studies. In this respect the wheel has turned full circle. As in the 1930s, economists are turning to empirics to resolve the many questions raised by the game theoretic approach to multiperiod, limited information models. But thanks to the burst of theorizing in the 1980s researchers now have a far richer understanding of 'behaviour' within markets and firms. Over the coming years we are likely to see the emergence of a number of robust predictions that will provide policy makers with a better understanding of the interaction between the power of individual firms and economic welfare.

Case study revisited

Armed with the foregoing we can now return to Andy and Dale. Andy was expressing a classic IO stance: for an oligopolist, to engage in price cutting is to invite retaliation from rivals. The effect of this, according to the traditional view, will be a general reduction in prices with only a small increase in sales, and hence a fall in revenue and profits (see Figure 2.4). But the classic conclusion may not always hold. Dale was voicing an appreciation of the fact that Rupert Murdoch's price cutting strategy was likely to prove an exception to the SCP rule.

Demand is crucially important to profits and longer-term growth. If *The Times*' rivals were to find it difficult to match the price cut then *The Times* would enjoy an increase in demand – in terms of Figure 2.4, sales would go from A to C. And there were good reasons why *The Times* had to take such drastic action and why there was a high probability that its rivals would find it difficult to respond in kind.

The market for broadsheet newspapers – after something of a renaissance in the 1980s – was declining. As sales fell, each publisher was pushed up his cost curve (see Figure 2.2). Falling sales also reduced advertising revenue, so the inevitable result was the pincer action of falling revenue and rising per unit costs on profits – or one suspects in the case of *The Times* in 1993, growing losses. In this situation, unless action was taken it would only be a matter of time before *The Times* would have to exit the market or be taken over by a new owner who was either prepared to subsidize further losses or was confident about reversing *The Times*' flagging performance.

Even so, to cut price is to risk a price war, and at this point the culture and management style of *The Times* would have had a crucial influence on the decision. Rupert Murdoch's willingness to take risks and to compete hard would have been decisive. Oligopolistic interdependence and game theory suggests that *The Times*' managers would have done their best to anticipate their rivals' response. The timing was fortuitous. The *Telegraph* was a publicly quoted company and its share price would have plummeted if investors had believed a price war was looming. *The Independent* was already in financial difficulties and the *Guardian* had just taken over the *Observer* and was therefore financially stretched. In this situation Murdoch was able to engage in non-cooperative behaviour. He gambled, correctly, that the *Telegraph* would not immediately respond and *The Times* was likely to enjoy an undisputed first mover advantage.

As *The Times* was believed to be making a loss (its accounts are lost inside News International) it was perhaps inevitable that Murdoch would be accused of predatory pricing – taking a profit sacrifice in order to drive a rival out of the market. But falling sales meant that he had to take action and the competition authorities would always prefer a price cut to tacit collusion and a rise in price across the market in such a situation. An important game theory conclusion is that strategic actions must be credible. After ten months of falling sales the *Telegraph* was forced to respond. When Conrad Black reduced the price of the *Telegraph*, Murdoch's immediate reaction was to cut the price of *The Times*. Although this worried Andy it was the correct response. It sent a signal to Black that Murdoch meant business and if he wanted to risk a price war he was going to get one. Within three months the price of *The Times* and the *Telegraph* were raised – the price war was over. By that time, whether by design or default, Murdoch had reaped a real benefit from his aggressive behaviour: by lowering the price of *The Times* to a level below that of the tabloids he had attracted a large number of new consumers into the broadsheet market. Murdoch's action had substantially increased demand, but not so much by taking sales from rivals as by widening the market. Five years later *The Times* had more than doubled its daily sales.

References

Aaronovitch, S. and M. C. Sawyer (1975) 'Mergers, Growth and Concentration', *Oxford Economic Papers*, vol. 27, pp. 136–55.

Archibald, G. C. (1961) 'Chamberlin versus Chicago', *Review of Economic Studies*, vol. 24, pp. 9–28.

Arrow, K. (1962) *Economic Welfare and the Allocation of Resources for Invention in Rate and Direction of Inventive Activity*, (Cambridge, Mass.: NBER).

Bain, J. (1956) *Barriers to New Competition* (Cambridge, Mass.: Harvard University Press).

Barney, J. B. (1986) 'Organisation Culture: Can it be a source of sustained competitive advantage?', *Academy of Management Review*, vol. 11, pp. 656–65.

Baumol, W. (1958) 'On the Theory of Oligopoly', *Economica*, vol. 25, pp. 187–98.

Baumol, W. (1982) 'Contestable Markets: An Uprising in the Theory of Industrial Structure', *American Economic Review*, vol. 72, pp. 1–15.

Berle, A. and G. Means (1932) *The Modern Corporation and Private Property* (New York: Macmillan).

Chamberlin, E. H. (1929) 'Duopoly Value Where Sellers are Few', *Quarterly Journal of Economics*, vol. 43, pp. 63–100.

Chamberlin, E. H. (1933) *The Theory of Monopolistic Competition* (Cambridge, Mass.: Harvard University Press).

Chandler, A. D. (1962) *Strategy and Structure* (Cambridge, Mass.: MIT Press).

Coase, R. H. (1937) 'The nature of the firm', *Economica*, vol. 4, pp. 386–405.

Cyert, R. and J. March (1963) *A Behavioural Theory of the Firm* (Englewood Cliffs, NJ: Prentice-Hall).

Dasgupta, P. and J. Stiglitz (1980) 'Industrial Structure and the Nature of Innovative Activity', *Economic Journal*, vol. 90, pp. 266–93.

Hay, D. A. and D. J. Morris (1991) *Industrial Economics and Organization* (Oxford: Oxford University Press).

Hayek, F. (1945) 'The use of knowledge in society', *American Economic Review*, vol. XXXV, no. 4, pp. 519–30.

Heal, G. and A. Silberston (1972) 'Alternative Managerial Objectives: An Explanatory Note', *Oxford Economic Papers*, vol. 24, pp. 137–50.

Kay, J. (1993) *Foundations of Corporate Success* (Oxford: Oxford University Press).

Knight, F. (1921) *Risk, Uncertainty and Profit* (New York: Houghton Mifflin).

Kreps, D. M. (1990) *Game Theory and Economic Modelling* (Oxford: Oxford University Press).

Marris, R. (1963) 'A Model of the Managerial Enterprise', *Quarterly Journal of Economics*, vol. 77, pp. 185–209.

Marshall, A. (1890) *Principles of Economics* (London: Macmillan).

Nelson, R. and S. Winter (1982) *An Evolutionary Theory of Economic Change* (Cambridge, Mass.: Ballinger).

Neumann, J. von and O. Morgenstein (1944) *Theory of Games and Economic Behaviour* (Princeton, NJ: Princeton University Press).

Penrose, E. (1959) *The Theory of the Growth of the Firm* (Oxford: Oxford University Press).

Porter, M. E. (1980) *Competitive Strategy: Techniques for Analysing Industry and Competitors* (New York: Free Press).

Porter, M. E. (1985) *Competitive Advantage: Creating and Sustaining Superior Performance* (New York: Free Press).

Prais, S. J. (1976) *The Evolution of Giant Firms in Britain* (Cambridge: Cambridge University Press).

Roberts, J. A. (1986) 'Signalling Model of Predatory Pricing', in D. J. Morris (ed.) *Strategic Behaviour and Industrial Competition* (Oxford: Oxford University Press).

Say, J.-B. (1803) 'Traité d'Economie Politique', cited in Alexander Wray, *The Development of Economic Doctrine* (London: Longmans, Green, 1948).

Scherer, F. M. (1988) 'Review of The Economics of Market Dominance', *International Journal of Industrial Organization*, vol. 6, pp. 517–18.

Scherer, F. M. and D. Ross (1990) *Industrial Market Structure and Economic Performance* (Boston, Mass.: Houghton Mifflin).

Schumpter, J. (1942) *Capitalism, Socialism and Democracy* (New York: Harper and Row).

Shaked, A. and J. Sutton (1983) 'Natural Oligopolies', *Econometrica*, vol. 51, pp. 1469–83.

Shapiro, C. (1986) 'Theories of Oligopolistic Behaviour', in R. Schmalensee and R. Willig (eds), *Handbook of Industrial Organisation* (Amsterdam: North-Holland).

Simon, H. A. (1959) 'Theories of Decision Making in Economics and Behavioural Science', *American Economic Review* vol. , pp. – .

Smith, A. (1776) *An Inquiry into the Nature and Causes of the Wealth of Nations* (London: Strahan and Cadell).

Sraffa, P. (1926) 'The Laws of Return Under Competitive Conditions', *Economic Journal*, vol. 36, pp. 535–50.

Sutton, J. (1992) *Sunk Costs and Market Structure* (Cambridge, Mass.: MIT Press).

Sweezy, P. (1939) 'Demand Under Conditions of Oligopoly', *Journal of Political Economy*, vol. 47, pp. 568–73.

Tirole, J. (1993) *The Theory of Industrial Organisations* (Cambridge, Mass.: MIT Press).

Viner, J. (1952) 'Cost Curves and Supply Curves', in J. Viners, *Readings in Price Theory* (Homewood, Ill.: Irwin).

Williamson, J. (1966) 'Profit, Growth and Sales Maximization', *Economica*, vol. 33, pp. 1–66.

Williamson, O. E. (1964) *The Economics of Discretionary Behaviour* (Englewood Cliffs, NJ: Prentice-Hall).

Williamson, O. E. (1971) 'The Vertical Integration of Production: Market Failure Considerations', *American Economic Review*, vol. 51, pp. 112–23.

Yamawaki, H. (1985) 'Dominant Firm Pricing and Fringe Expansion: The Case of the US Iron and Steel Industry 1907–1930', *Review of Economics and Statistics*, vol. 67, pp. 429–37.

3 Institutional Theory Perspective
Gerry Johnson and Royston Greenwood

Basic principles

The arguments put forward in most books on strategic management are typically based on two core assumptions. The first is that the world of the manager – the external and internal environment of organizations – is an objective reality capable of examination and analysis. The second and linked assumption is that managers themselves behave in an essentially rational analytic way to make sense of that world. Institutional theory is not based on these assumptions but on the concept of *social construction*. The assumptions here are different. They are that the external and internal world of organizations is that which is subjectively understood or perceived by people in those organizations, influenced by social norms and expectations; and that when we perceive our world in a particular way we behave accordingly, and consequently help create a world in line with our perceptions.

The basic principles of institutional theory are summarized below and the rest of the chapter shows how these relate to some of the main issues in strategic management.

- Organizations are not autonomous agents seeking to maximize economic opportunities but are set within a social web of norms and expectations that constrain and shape, often in subtle ways, managerial choice. Choosing strategies is not an unfettered act but is constrained by these social prescriptions.
- Social prescriptions are transmitted to organizations through such agencies as the state, professional institutes and other carriers of ideas and beliefs about appropriate managerial conduct.
- By conforming to social prescriptions, organizations secure approval, support and public endorsement, thus increasing their 'legitimacy'.
- Social prescriptions may become 'taken for granted' (that is, institutionalized) and thus very difficult to change or resist.
- Conformity to social prescriptions rather than attendance to the 'task environment' (for example markets) may adversely affect efficiency and other economic measures of performance, but may improve long-term chances of survival.
- Because similar organizations experience similar social expectations they conform to the same prescriptions and thus adopt similar strategies and managerial arrangements. This is the process of 'isomorphism'.

Case study

The situation

Quill, Dipstick and Gold (QDG) is one of the world's major accountancy firms. With its origins in the nineteenth century, QDG now has over 5000 partners worldwide, with some 600 in the UK alone. Its initial business was auditing, but it now offers many professional services, including tax and financial advice, corporate recovery, management consultancy, information systems and so on.

Edward Gray, the senior partner in the UK practice of QDG, is having dinner with a number of his fellow partners in a private dining room at the firm's central London office. Last week Edward attended a meeting of the QDG international board, where the topic was the increasing global development of accountancy firms. He has called this meeting to seek the views of three influential senior UK partners as to how he should respond to questions posed at last week's meeting.

Around the table are two long-established partners from the audit practice, Paul Madeley and Alan Clarke. Both joined the firm from university, one from Oxford and the other from Cambridge, both became partners in their early 30s and both have over 20 years' experience as partners. They each have clients whose billings with QDG run into many millions of pounds. They are powerful men in the firm, not least because of the client business they control, but also because of their reputation in the wider accountancy profession, where they are seen as leading authorities. Each has also represented the profession on government committees of inquiry. Also at the meeting is Michael Jones, who is relatively new to QDG and, unlike the others, is not an accountant – he heads up the UK consultancy arm of QDG, having been recruited from a senior position in a specialist strategy consultancy firm.

Edward Gray explains the background to the meeting. At the international board meeting the preceding week the international chairman of QDG argued strongly that the firm was at risk of being left behind in the global development of accountancy firms. Hitherto most accountancy firms had been content to organize themselves along national lines. There were big national practices such as those in the US, the UK, Germany, France and so on; and there were practices in smaller countries. The larger practices in particular had a great deal of local autonomy and had developed their own services to a considerable extent according to local need. International cooperation did take place but it was largely down to the personal contacts of partners across the world.

However in the last few years a number of significant changes had taken place, one of the biggest being the opening up of Eastern Europe to the market economy. Business enterprises were being established, and many of QDG's biggest clients were moving into Eastern Europe. It was not clear how this region would develop or what the needs of business would be: it was felt there would be a major need for accountancy and consultancy services, and the professional services infrastructure in such countries was minimal compared with the West. It was also known that two of the major competitors of QDG had recently merged, the main purpose of which was to pursue a more structured global development of their operations. The effect on QDG was to relegate the firm to the third rather the second largest accountancy firm in the world.

The conversation

Edward Gray: The view being put forward last week was that unless we recognize the need to move towards a more global form of business, QDG could not only lose out on potential business in a big way, especially in developing economies and Eastern Europe, but also could lose its position as one of the leading accountancy firms in the world. The fact is that our competitors are moving this way, so we have to. The implication is that we can't carry on doing things the way we have in the past. Last week's meeting came to this view pretty much unanimously. The discussion was then about how QDG might do this. They are the issues I would like us to discuss this evening.

Paul Madeley: There is no doubt at all of the huge need for the sort of services we can offer in Eastern Europe. There are increasing signs that governments there will insist on standards of practice that their own infrastructure cannot meet. But they have real difficulties; for example, there is often no real concept of what profit means, let alone how to measure it. If a market economy is to be developed, the need for the sort of services we can provide is high. We should also remember that our own clients will expect a consistent level of service from us as they move into these countries. It is, however, a major challenge which none of the firms really fully understands. There are major problems, not least the number of people that will be required, which is enormous. Where will we find experienced partners and senior personnel prepared to work in these countries?

Alan Clarke: I agree about the need but I am concerned. Our professional standards simply have to be met. I hear what is said about the needs of Eastern Europe for example; but we do have to be very careful that things are done properly. I have heard the suggestion that we crash-train people. This just will not do. It is not possible to churn out accountants overnight; and standards would most certainly be compromised if we did try to do so. Presumably none of us would be happy to see the firm driven by a market opportunity at the expense of our standards. There is also another issue we should not forget. Our business is based on personal relationships and trust; this must not be compromised in the name of 'global integration'.

[This is an argument that Michael Jones has heard before. He recognizes that QDG's reputation in the field of accountancy and financial advice is of a very high order and should not be jeopardized. He is also persuaded that personal relationships with clients, often at a very senior level, are indeed important to QDG. However he thinks that the problem they face is more challenging than has so far been expressed.]

Michael Jones: You must forgive me if I do not have the same experience as some of you around this table. I approach this as something of an outsider. But it does seem to me that, whilst the imperative for global development is undeniable, there is a further challenge. All our competitors will be driving in the same direction. They will all be going global; they will all be pitching for business with the same sorts of potential clients; they will all be offering the same sort of services and promising the same high standard of service. They will all build their business by trying to cultivate the same sort of personal relationships at the same sort of level in these businesses and with governments as they have in the West. They will be exporting Western accountancy, building their firms around audit, accountancy and information services. Where is the difference? I suggest that to achieve any sort of advantage over the competition we need to start thinking about how we might do things differently from others. That suggests to me that we need to think beyond the obvious. I can see the way this discussion might go. In order to invest in Eastern Europe we need the resources to do so; to do that we need to merge with some other organization – another of the big five or six perhaps – and then we need to pool resources to provide the same sort of services as the others will be doing. But that is the way everyone will be thinking. Can I suggest we might think about a different strategy. For example we might want to think about the constraints of a partnership. If we became a public company, for example, we could raise the sort of investment we require, maybe. Second, what about merging with someone else other than an accountancy firm. What about one of the major consultancies for example. After all that is where growth opportunities lie.

Alan Clark: I really do think we have to be careful about our responses to all this. We are not talking here about an opportunity to make money; we are talking here about fundamental change to an economic system. A number of colleagues from other firms – and from the legal profession – met with government representatives a month or so ago. They, like us, see as the main concern the development of an infrastructure to handle fundamental changes to the economies of countries in Eastern Europe. This is about the development of proper systems in such countries. It is also something we need to cooperate with others on, not least to make sure that there are compatible standards in accounting. I might also add that it is important to ensure such standards from the point of view of our own clients. They will be operating there and will expect the same quality of service they receive elsewhere in the world. I do not see how any of this can be helped by changing the partnership structure. It is an arrangement that has served us well for almost a hundred years. In any case, even if we wished to, it is no easy matter: the partners are owners of the firm; why would they wish to change that? Apart from anything else partners have invested huge amounts of intellectual capital and time in becoming a partner; 12 or 15 years for most of them. Can I ask, Edward, what was being proposed last week?

Edward Gray: [Gray explains that the feeling the previous week was that the international partnership is overly dependent on national firms at the expense of international coordination; overly concerned with discipline-based organization around audit, taxation and so on at the expense of coordination across discipline boundaries; and overly reliant on the personal relationships and contacts between partners, often based on years of working together, as distinct from finding ways of working with individuals and teams of the highest calibre from anywhere in the world.] In short what is being looked for is a more internationally coordinated firm, with less emphasis on national boundaries, more interdisciplinarity, an effective client management system and a recognition that we need to be rather less reliant on who knows whom and rather more able to draw on the very best of our people when we need them. To do all that major investment is needed in the international firm.

Michael Jones: You seem to be saying Edward, that what is needed is a more managed firm. By client management system I assume you mean we have to market ourselves effectively. I agree with that and, as you know, I have long argued that it makes sense to do so across boundaries. For example with regard to consultancy there is a great need for international coordination on this; a global consultancy division would make a lot of sense in a world which is globalizing. And it may well be that the same would apply for other services we provide.

Paul Madeley: It seems to me that there is a risk here of jumping to an answer before we really discuss the problem. Structures can be fads. We may not have the right sort of structure, but jumping from what we have to international divisions of some sort may equally not be right. For example I could equally argue that we have an unparalleled network of personal relationships throughout the world which we have been building and nurturing for decades. This is the basis of the trust we have with our clients. What we have to do is strengthen this and we might well be able to use modern technology and modern communications.

Alan Clarke: Can I also repeat my previous comments. The problem with these sorts of ideas is that, almost by definition, they weaken the nature of the partnership. The key people become the specialist managers. What then is the role of the partner? If we are not very careful we end up with the situation where professional managers are managing the very people who own the firm. There is a real risk that we end up with diminished standards.

Edward Gray: We all recognize the problems of change, not least in a firm like ours. However there comes a time when the forces for change are so powerful that we may have to accept that incremental change is just not possible any longer; or at least, if it is, it may lead to our demise. This was the major concern raised in the discussion last week.

[At this point the meeting is interrupted. Edward Gray's personal assistant arrives carrying a telephone. He suggests that, bearing in mind the theme of the meeting, his boss might wish to take the call. Edward Gray listens with an expression rather more of resignation than surprise. It is a call from his counterpart in another major firm. He has arrived back from a meeting with his international associates in which the possibility of a merger with QDG has been discussed. He wonders if Edward Gray would care to meet to discuss the idea.]

Issues

The following issues, arising from the case study, can usefully be informed by understanding institutional theory. They are considered later in this chapter in the section on links to strategy.

- What is the definition of success for an accountancy firm? Is this to do with financial performance and market share; or is it more to do with its standing in the community; or both? What are bases for such definitions?

- Do partnerships have particular competences? How similar are these to those in other firms?
- Is the idea of competitive advantage and competitive strategy appropriate to an accountancy firm?
- Why is entry to Eastern Europe so important to QDG? Is this because of external pressures, because of its own reputation and standing, because clients expect it or because other firms are doing it?
- How might QDG reconcile the potential conflict between maintaining standards and moving quickly? What do you think it will do?
- What are the problems of strategic change that might exist in a firm like QDG?

Key contributions

Origins of institutional theory

The starting point for contemporary institutional theory was the 1977 publication of Meyer and Rowan's 'Institutionalized organizations: formal structure as myth and ceremony'. This paper had a significant impact on the world of academia, but little apparent impact on the world of practice. Strategic management theory has been dominated by perspectives in which organizational strategies and structures are deemed effective if deliberately aligned to the requirements and challenges of the task environment (by which institutional theorists mean the sources of inputs – supplies, labour and so on – and markets). The role of top management is conceptualized as understanding and ensuring that alignment. Meyer and Rowan's work, however, ran counter to this view of managers as essentially seizing market opportunities and outwitting potential competitive threats.

Meyer and Rowan argue two things. First, organizations are confronted with pressures emanating from arenas other than the task environment. Specifically, organizations use strategies, structures and practices that are socially expected of them. For example accounting firms organize themselves as professional partnerships and are active in socially anticipated ways: they support university education, comment studiously and seriously on government tax policies, and project accounting as a rigorous science with strong ethical underpinnings. Using such structures and practices meets with social approval (that is, confers legitimacy on the organization) and increases the likelihood that external constituents will assist the organization (for example by conferring grants and resources, favourably appraising them publicly and so on). Meyer and Rowan define these pressures of social expectation as arising from the 'institutional environment'. In the case of accounting, the institutional environment incorporates professional institutions, agencies of the state (for example the SEC), important interest groups and the media.

In one sense Meyer and Rowan could be seen as merely raising a set of pressures through which managers have to navigate. In fact they go further and suggest that these institutional pressures often come to be taken for granted; that is, managers do not choose to conform, they simply do conform because alternatives are not recognized. Hence accounting firms are organized as partnerships, perform certain services (large firms always provide assurance services), support certain community activities and behave in accordance with prescriptions of how professionals behave. They do so because that is how accounting firms are expected to behave. In the same way it would be almost unthinkable for a business school not to have an MBA degree and not to teach accounting, strategy and marketing.

Social expectations may run counter to the pursuit of efficiency. That is, an organization might be *less* efficient as a consequence of meeting institutional expectations. Giving financial support to universities or 'worthwhile' public causes, or simply spending time serving on community or government committees, increases costs and thus reduces efficiency. Meyer and Rowan's key point is that all organizations are embedded within an institutional as well as a task environment and the model of managers as autonomous actors is simply not validated by empirical observation. On the contrary, managers are constrained by socially derived norms and expectations that contain assumptions about their organizational world and about appropriate conduct.

The idea that organizations are embedded in institutional as well as task contexts does not mean they experience the same balance of pressures. On the contrary, as shown in Figure 3.1 the relative intensity of institutional and market pressures differs by type of industry. Most strategic management perspectives implicitly assume that organizations reside in the top right quadrant, that it is the pursuit of efficiency and competitive advantage that predominates. Institutionalists, on the other hand, stress the several possible locations in the diagram, and that even where task pressures are paramount, institutional residues still occur.

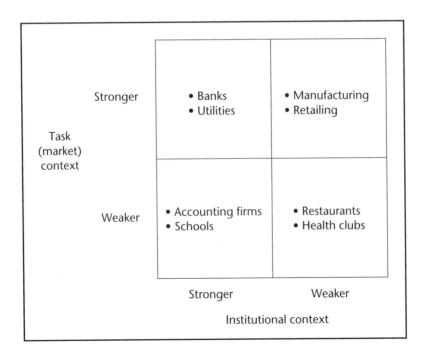

(adapted from Scott, 1987: 126)   *FIGURE 3.1*

Meyer and Rowan's second point is that the possible contradiction between institutionalized expectations and organizational efficiency sometimes leads organizations to engage in the 'decoupling' of formal structures from actual work practices. That is, organizations adopt structures and practices that are aligned with institutional prescriptions but are deliberately distanced from how work is actually performed. Conformity is thus 'ceremonial' rather than substantive. For example, accounting work is portrayed as a rigorous science, concealing the essential subjectivity that actually occurs; senior executives may debate the strategy of their organization energetically in meetings without translating such rhetoric into action; and fads of management will be subscribed to as they come and go.

An important difference between Meyer and Rowan's focus and most other perspectives on strategic management is that they are intrigued by the *similarity* of organizational practices. Their focus is on how social pressures that occur at the level of an industry (or organizational field, as the institutionalists prefer)[1] apply equally, or roughly so, to all organizations within that industry/field and thus 'cause' organizations to converge on similar strategies and structures. Instead of the rational-actor model, in which the manager dispassionately analyzes the external world and makes competitive choices, Meyer and Rowan's world consists of actors who, wittingly or otherwise, acquiesce collectively to the expectations of the institutional setting. This homogenization of organizational practices is known as *institutional isomorphism*, the process by which organizations facing similar pressures come to resemble one another in the pursuit of social legitimacy.

Meyer and Rowan's thesis draws heavily on the social constructionist account of reality (Berger and Luckman, 1967; Zucker, 1977, 1987). Collective beliefs are seen as emerging from repeated interactions between organizations. Organizations develop categorizations (or typifications) of their exchanges, which achieve the status of objectification and thus constitute social reality. Organizations behave in accordance with this socially constructed reality because to do so reduces ambiguity and uncertainty. Shared understandings of appropriate practice permit ordered exchanges. Over time, however, these shared understandings, or collective beliefs, become reinforced by regulatory processes involving state agencies and professional bodies, which normatively and/or coercively press conformity upon constituent communities. Regulatory processes thus both disseminate and reproduce the coded prescriptions of social reality. Deviations from such prescriptions cause discomfort and trigger attempts to justify (that is, legitimize) specific departures from the social norm (Elsbach, 1994; Lamertz and Baum, 1998).

The notion that communities of organizations develop collective beliefs about the dynamics of industry (or field) circumstances and about the appropriate strategic responses for competing successfully within them is not unique to institutional thinking. Huff (1982) and Spender (1989) were early reporters of these phenomena. More recently Porac *et al.* (1989) and Abrahamson and Fombrun (1994) have discussed how organizational actors in the same industry develop similar understandings of the dynamics of their competitive circumstances and evolve shared views of basic strategies ('recipes' in Spender's terms) for coping.

Elaborations

Meyer and Rowan's (1977) work sparked considerable theoretical and empirical activity. Two works in particular were to exert considerable influence: Tolbert and Zucker (1983) and DiMaggio and Powell (1983).

Tolbert and Zucker

Tolbert and Zucker (1983) examined the spread of personnel reforms in local government in the US between 1880 and 1930. Their work uncovered possible stages in the process of institutionalization not only in the public sector but also in the market sector. (This process was subsequently elaborated in Tolbert and Zucker, 1996.) According to Tolbert and Zucker there is a preinstitutionalization stage characterized by experimentation as organizations seek to align themselves to their task environment in such a way as to gain a competitive advantage. As the success of particular experiments (for example new strategies, products, technologies or structures) becomes known, other organizations copy them. The motive for doing so is to become more competitive. (Up to this point Tolbert and Zucker are entirely consistent with strategic choice theory.) But as more and more organizations adopt the same practices, mimicry occurs – not because the new practices are expected to bring economic advantage, but because the practice has attained the status of being the 'appropriate' or 'right' way to do something. Adoption has become not the outcome of calculated intent, but the product of social beliefs and expectations. Importantly, organizations that adopt the new practice in this semi-institutionalized stage are *knowingly* adopting the innovation. Other studies have found similar mimetic effects. For example Westphal *et al.* (1997) tracked the adoption of total quality management (TQM) practices across 2700 US hospitals and showed that early adopters customized TQM practices, whereas later adopters did not.

According to Tolbert and Zucker (1983) full institutionalization occurs only when a practice becomes taken for granted; that is, the practice (strategy, structure or whatever) comes to be regarded as *the* way of doing things. The practice is uncritically adopted and alternatives become literally unthinkable. In Meyer and Rowan's (1977) terms, 'institutionalization' has occurred because practices take on 'a rulelike status'. For example the way in which we speak of the functions of business – 'marketing', 'production', 'research and development' – is taken for granted. In Western businesses the concept of profit is taken for granted, and as seen in the case study above it is very likely to be assumed that it should be similarly taken for granted elsewhere.

Tolbert and Zucker's (1983) contribution is particularly important because it fundamentally challenges the notion of unrestricted human agency in strategic decision making. That is, on the full institutional stage managers behave as they do *unwittingly*, with strategic choice being shaped and determined by taken-for-granted solutions. Even in the semi-institutional stage, in which managers take action knowingly, they are constrained by expectations of appropriate conduct. Strategic choice, to the institutionalist, is less a calculated act than a normatively constrained and often habitual effect.

The key point is that managers are not 'free' decision makers. They do exercise choice, but not unfettered choice. Social pressures circumscribe the available choices. Strategic choice is shaped by recipes and historically legitimated practices that inform the sector generally and individual organizations in particular. These socially coded prescriptions may be more intense in some decision areas than others and more intense in some industries than others (note Figure 3.2 above). But strategic choice is directed by institutional prescriptions.

DiMaggio and Powell

DiMaggio and Powell (1983) have identified three mechanisms by which institutional isomorphism can occur: *coercive*, *mimetic* and *normative* processes. Coercive mechanisms occur as a result of actions by agencies such as the state or regulatory bodies, upon which collectivities of organizations are dependent. For example Slack and Hinings (1995) show how sports organizations have transformed their governance arrangements in order to maximize opportunities for state funding.

Normative mechanisms stem primarily from professionalization. DiMaggio and Powell (1983) draw attention to the processes by which occupational groups socialize members into codes of conduct and behaviour, and sustain compliance, by means of career-long training, the monitoring of behaviour, disciplinary action and acts of ceremonial celebration. The professions – such as accounting, law and medicine – figure as exemplary sites of these processes. Professional firms and professionals behave in similar ways because of the essentially normative pressures promulgated by the profession and its constitutive agencies. Thus accounting firms do what they do and organize themselves as they do because the professional community determines that they will do so.

Mimetic mechanisms occur primarily in circumstances of ambiguity and uncertainty, when managers copy organizations that are perceived to be more successful and more legitimate. Hence, for example, the spread of megamergers, which have affected all the largest accounting firms.

DiMaggio and Powell's tripartite classification has sparked considerable empirical inquiry. But there are two other, albeit secondary, themes in their seminal contribution. First, they identify the agencies that operate within the institutional context: the state, the professions and exemplary organizations that act as role models. By drawing attention to these agencies, DiMaggio and Powell have sharpened the difference between the task and institutional contexts and clarified how the two might be studied. As a consequence, later scholars have explicitly examined how state agencies and professional institutes are instrumental in monitoring and reinforcing institutional definitions of appropriate conduct.

The second subtheme in DiMaggio and Powell's paper picks up the difficult notion of structuration, which refers to the process whereby institutionalized structures shape action and behaviour, and are themselves recreated and reproduced by those actions and behaviours. That is, the existing structures and relationships within an organizational field first act to shape the behaviour of the organizations within that field. Accounting firms are thus affected by the practices of the professional institute and the expectations of clients and other accountants. In this way the structure of the field shapes behaviour (action). But the very act of conforming serves to amplify those structures. Action thus drives structure, modifying its form. Accounting firms join in the actions of the professional institute, thus elaborating and supporting its role. Interaction amongst members of the field becomes more formalized. Relationships, roles and responsibilities become more sharply defined and thus more bound within the field's network. Hence although the structure of the field shapes behaviour, that behaviour in turn clarifies the structure, reinforcing its constraining presence.

DiMaggio and Powell are thus emphasizing the dynamic of reproduction. Institutional structures *arise from* social interaction, serve to *constrain* those interactions and are then *reproduced by* those interactions. Institutionalists do not insist that all actors and organizations are equally or completely subjected to institutional expectations. Responses can and do vary. Nevertheless in its early forms institutional theory was associated with the idea of inertia and stability. Institutionalized practices, almost by definition, were seen as enduring. Change was treated as unusual. By uncovering the taken-for-granted rules of conduct, institutional theorists emphasized the stability and resistance to change of much strategic behaviour.

Other work

In the two decades since Meyer and Rowan's classic 1977 paper, much empirical and theoretical work has appeared under the rubric of institutional theory. This will be touched on in the next section but fuller reviews are provided elsewhere (for example Powell and DiMaggio, 1991; Scott, 1995). To date most studies have been content to show the occurrence of institutional effects rather than their consequences. However it is worth commenting on two studies that have examined the link between institutional alignment and organizational performance, which is a relatively neglected part of institutional theory.

Baum and Oliver (1991) studied whether child-care organizations have a better chance of survival if they have links to agencies with a high social legitimacy. The argument is that organizations can obtain social support by reflected legitimacy: for example a child-care agency licensed by the state, run in association with a church or as a not-for-profit organization will have greater legitimacy. Baum and Oliver found that institutional linkages of this form 'play a very significant role in reducing the likelihood of organizational mortality' (ibid., p. 213). Oliver (1997) also studied construction companies to establish whether organizations with good relationships with institutional and/or task agencies are more successful (in terms of profits and control of construction costs). She found that institutional relationships are correlated with performance but much less so than task relationships, especially under tight market circumstances. However profitability is significantly affected by the strength of institutional relationships under conditions of regulatory stringency.

Links to strategy

How, then, do the concepts of institutional theory help us to understand issues to do with strategy and strategic management? This will be discussed here and the case study of QDG will be used to illustrate the discussion.

It is worth starting by re-emphasizing the importance of the 'taken for granted' and social pressures as underpinning a good deal of what follows; this itself can be illustrated with regard to accountancy. A good deal of the discussion in the case study is about the need for excellence of service, defined in terms of professional standards. This is taken for granted, indeed is the *raison d'être* of accountancy firms. In turn, the way in which the firms operate reinforces this. The established professional institutions lay down the norms and exert regulatory pressure to conform; there are university courses that educate people in the application of those norms and provide a supply of labour; and there are professional examinations that test the suitability of individuals to practice. There has developed an organizational field in which the parties involved (universities, financial directors, partners in firms and so on) take all this as given and behave according to the prescribed norms. Moreover the clients of accountancy firms behave in ways that conform to and consolidate the system. It is perhaps no coincidence that many of the financial directors of large corporations are themselves chartered accountants who have worked for or been partners in those firms, and we can see from the case study that the intention is now to export their norms, practices and standards to other areas of the world. This is all on the unquestioned assumption that the norms, standards and practices have a 'rightness' in themselves.

Context

As explained above, the traditional emphasis in the strategy literature has been on what institutional theorists would call the task environment. Institutionalists, on the other hand, have emphasized the institutionalized nature and regulatory role of the environment. The environment is conceived of in terms of forces such as government or other regulatory bodies that impose rules and codes of practice with which organizations have to comply. These rules and regulations may be to do with how services are provided or what services are required. For example an audit is required by law; similarly businesses require advice on navigating taxation law. Other regulatory agencies include professional bodies that lay down standards and require conformity to particular practices, for example the training and examination required to become a chartered accountant and the terms and conditions imposed on those who seek to practice within that profession. The institutional world for accountants, then, is an example of one that is highly regulated.

The case study also provides a good example of how the environment can be considered in terms of both 'real', objective opportunities and institutionally defined opportunities. Objectively, entry to Eastern Europe is important to QDG for several reasons. First, it has to serve its global clients wherever those clients go. Competitive (task) pressures are making accountancy firms nervous that they will lose clients if they cannot offer them the kinds of service and breadth of geographical coverage that clients demand. But the case study also reveals strong institutional pressures for entering Eastern Europe. Accountancy firms are expected to play their part in developing Western economic institutions in the former communist bloc. The larger accountancy firms would find it difficult to resist the expectations of the professional associations, their accounting colleagues and government agencies. Moreover refusal to go would attract adverse publicity. So even though the larger firms might lose money in Eastern Europe there are good institutional reasons for moving into this arena. There is also the perceived need for the regulation of firms operating in such markets and the consequent real or assumed demand for services such as accountancy. The assumption at QDG is that the same sort of services are needed as are provided in the West by the same sort of firms. It is very likely that governments in Eastern Europe also believe that such services will provide the sort of institutionalized legitimacy of capitalism they wish to convey. Indeed if these economies want to do business with the West they may have to conform to the institutionalized expectations of Western economies and governments with regard to appropriate forms of accounting. It is of course quite likely that QDG and other accountancy firms are actively promoting this concept not so much out of self-interest but because they genuinely believe it to be necessary.

Objectively, of course, it may be appropriate to question whether the sorts of rules, regulations and standards of the West in economic terms are necessarily appropriate for Eastern Europe. However the important thing to stress here is that from an institutional point of view it should not be expected that such objective questioning would arise. To take one example in the case study, Paul Madeley points out that there is no concept of what profit means or how to measure it. Implied in this comment is that there is an objectively 'right' way of doing this; and that this is laid down by the accountancy standards of the Western world.

There is another way in which institutional theorists conceive of the nature of the environment and which applies to firms such as QDG. Institutionalists see the environment as consisting of a web of transactions within a network of participating organizations, all of which have a common understanding of the form those transactions should take. This is the idea of the organizational field. It is taken for granted that accountancy firms work with banks and law firms, for example. Indeed they refer business from one to the other. It is taken for granted that business corporations need auditors and that auditors carry out their work in particular ways.

In the case study, Alan Clarke in particular reflects this. He sees QDG as a professional service firm interacting with other such firms, and in many respects acting as an agent of regulatory bodies such as the government to ensure that proper services are provided. It is evident from the conversation that the same sort of institutional environment is expected to be transposed to Eastern Europe. In this sense the environment becomes bounded by the organizational field and the nature of the transactions in it. There are of course dangers here: there could be entrants who do not accept the orthodoxy of this, who seek to behave in different ways. For example AMEX provides accountancy services in the US, and its entry was not expected by the established firms when it happened.

It is important to stress, then, that whilst the strategic management literature tends to emphasize markets and competition, institutionalists emphasize institutional environments and the conformity to taken-for-granted norms and practices within those environments that endow organizations – in this case QDG – with legitimacy and standing. This is quite evident in the case discussion. The main concern of Clark and Madeley, in particular, is with such legitimacy within their organizational field. To some extent all organizations are faced with these conflicting environments. For QDG the institutional environment is particularly important; but it is also faced with a market environment that it is finding increasingly intrusive. In other organizations the market environment might be especially significant but there will still be institutional pressures to conform and behave in a legitimate fashion. So for example a manufacturing firm faced with significant market pressures also has to conform to the institutional environment represented by the accountancy profession, as well as that of banks, financial institutions, the government, society and so on.

Competences

Much of the literature on strategic management emphasizes the idea of competitive advantage underpinned by core competences unique to an organization. Institutional theorists, however, tend to emphasize the similarity between organizations rather than their distinctiveness. Accountancy firms are similar, banks are similar, universities are similar and so on. The extent to which this is so does of course vary. Some organizations are much more 'institutionalized' than others. How, then, in this context do we conceive of competences? There are various ways in which institutional theory can provide different perspectives on this.

First, there is the overarching caveat that the very idea of competences has become institutionalized. Managers in organizations, reinforced by academics in strategic management, may talk as though competences are real and bestow competitive advantage when in fact there may be little evidence of this. In accountancy firms, for example, it may be very difficult indeed to pin down core competences that really do result in differentiation. For example all accountancy firms claim to offer advantages to their clients by virtue of industry specialization, and all are beginning to claim to offer 'seamless global services'. But these are not distinctive differences. All firms are making the same claim. This does not mean that the partners in an accountancy firm (or any other firm) will not talk about competences as though they are real, especially as the language of competition starts to prevail. Talk of competences can, then, be seen as symbolic rhetoric bestowing social approval (legitimacy) upon those using it. However as Meyer and Rowan (1977) argue, the rhetoric may be decoupled from what actually goes on.

There is, however, an institutional view that argues that competences lie within the very institutionalized nature of organizations. Competences are likely, in this sense, to exist within the taken-for-granted practices and structures of organizations. For example it might be argued that some organizations are better able to legitimate themselves within their organizational field than others.

They may, for instance, have established a better reputation for whatever reason, they may have some figurehead who is especially recognized within the field or they may have developed ways of working that are regarded especially highly within that field. There is evidence in the case study, or at least in the comments by Alan Clark, that QDG is trying to position itself as an influential force in government circles in respect of the development of Eastern Europe. This could conceivably be extended, such that representatives of the firm take a seat on commissions of government bodies that are especially influential. Indeed in the accountancy profession, representation on government and professional bodies is especially welcomed, as is sponsorship of charities and other 'good works'. These could all be regarded as 'responses' from the resource-based perspective (see Chapter 4).

There is of course a problem here. It could be that an organization will become over-reliant on aspects which it regards as competences but which over time become counterproductive. It could be that QDG is facing this problem. It prides itself on being a highly esteemed accountancy firm following rigorous professional codes of practice. But what if the nature of accountancy changes in the face of global development? Might that mean that the inherited legitimacies/competences of QDG become its very downfall (see the section on culture below)?

Partnerships have particular competences. They are structures that house highly professionalized workforces and are able to harness the energy and enthusiasm of idiosyncratic individuals. But there is another, more subtle competence. Partnerships typically deal with work that requires the application of standardized, prototype solutions to client situations – for example an audit is required to conform to a specified format and standards. However, because the client's situation is never entirely standardized the prototypical solution has to be modified. The professional exercises judgement when making such modifications. The partnership format also provides for decentralization, thus enabling prototype modification to occur, subject to subtle controls (mentoring, collegial appraisal, values and cultural norms) to ensure the modification is in accordance with high professional standards.

Culture

There are similarities between what institutional theorists say and the stance they take, and that taken by those who write about organizational cultures. In particular both emphasize the importance of taken-for-granted assumptions, beliefs and practices in organizations. However institutionalists observe and emphasize commonalties *across* organizations. They argue that even if there are differences between organizations, the similarities are greater than the differences. To take an example in the accountancy profession, the idea that partnership is the appropriate form of governance structure is, or at least has been until recently, taken as given, and this is supported by all manner of cultural norms. There is the ritual appointment to partnership, preceded by the ritualized indoctrination of new recruits into the firm to ensure they comply with the sort of behaviour expected of them if they aspire to become partners. There is the primacy of partners themselves in terms of their power, the status they are afforded, the sort of stories told about them and the way in which they dominate the organization, notwithstanding formal structures and controls. This is not unique to QDG; it applies to all firms of accountants to a greater or lesser extent.

The more such a culture becomes embedded – is taken as *the* basis of the way in which the organization works – the more it is likely to result in the incremental development of strategy. Strategy is constrained by culture: the organization's environment is seen through the lens of such assumptions and norms and decisions are delimited by them. This much is illustrated by the QDG case. The assumptions underlying Alan Clark's responses and probably subscribed to by Paul Madeley are very similar to those outlined above. Clark and Madeley are uneasy with the language and ideas of Michael Jones, who comes from a different institutional environment with different assumptions and ways of looking at a situation. It is likely that any strategies developed will be compatible with those assumptions, and highly unlikely that decisions will be taken that mean competing solely in terms of market opportunity or that fundamentally challenge the structure of the partnership and the way in which the firm works. Of course, since these dominant assumptions and norms are to be found in accountancy firms in general, similar strategies will be developed; hence the isomorphism that institutionalists have observed.

Competing

Inherent in the notion of strategic management is the exercise of managerial choice over competitive strategy and the bases of competition. Institutional theorists argue differently. They suggest that the rules of competition are similar within organizational fields. For example, professional service firms such as accountancy and law firms were not allowed to solicit business or advertise until quite recently. Indeed many professionals would prefer not to see themselves as a business in a competitive sense at all, but as offering services of a high professional standard. Similarity, then, is more marked than difference: accountancy firms offer similar services, seek to enhance those services in similar ways, build relationships with clients in particular ways and so on. Competitive behaviour is constrained by conventions of acceptable professional conduct in the market place. Not conforming to these norms would be frowned upon even if competitive advantage might be achieved; hence Clark and Madeley's unease when Michael Jones raised the notion of striving for competitive advantage through differentiation.

This is not to say that members of such firms might not employ the rhetoric of competition, and perhaps increasingly so. They might talk as though choices can be made about real differences that will bestow real advantages. However the tendency is to conform to the norms rather than search for real advantages. The institutionalist's emphasis on mimicry seems more appropriate as a descriptor of what happens than the more usual portrayals of managers as autonomous captains of their enterprise. Far from seeking to be different, organizations seek to be similar to others. This is especially the case where organizations face uncertainty and ambiguity – arguably as the accountancy profession does with regard to Eastern Europe. So the partners in QDG feel obliged to enter Eastern Europe, partly to service their clients (and thus avoid losing them) and partly to meet professional expectations. They also feel the need to become more integrated globally, again because of pressure from clients but also because other firms are doing so. These developments pose challenges to traditional conceptions of how the partnership format should be operated. The pressures of the market place and of the institutional context can thus coincide (over Eastern Europe) or conflict (over the partnership format). The institutionalist might predict that in such circumstances QDG will indeed develop in Eastern Europe and more globally, but is likely to try to preserve the partnership structure and the relative independence of the partners despite strategic and structural imperatives not to do so.

Institutional theorists emphasize the faddish nature of much strategic behaviour. For example in the 1980s the emphasis was on finding suitable markets in which to compete. This was the result of the marketing orthodoxy of the time and, more specifically, Porter's (1980) work on the competitive forces at play in markets. In the 1990s the emphasis swung towards core competences that were unique to the organization and upon which competitive advantage could be built. In the 1980s everyone was sure of the wisdom of the former; in the 1990s they became convinced of the wisdom of the latter. Since at any one time everyone seems to have been convinced of the wisdom of one or the other, there was a general uniformity about the very bases of and questions being asked about competitive strategy. Again institutional theorists emphasized conformity for the purpose of creating legitimacy.

It should of course be noted that the very rules of competing differ according to institutional context. For example in the US there is a much stronger emphasis on litigation than in many other parts of the world; while in the Middle East and parts of Africa, what would be regarded in the West as bribery is common place. Cooperative behaviour rather than competition is emphasized a good deal more in the public sector. It would therefore be wrong to suggest that the type of competition discussed conventionally in the strategy literature is necessarily the norm.

Corporate strategy

Among private sector organizations there are 'coercive rules' about acting to meet shareholders' expectations. Arguably, however, whilst there is ceremonial and rhetorical conformity to this, the evidence is that managers do not behave in this way. To take one example: managers in the US and UK often argue that the apparent short-termism of organizations is because investors take a short-term perspective. Actually there is rather more evidence that short-termism results from organizations using (institutionalized) measures of performance that are short term or historical in nature and encourage managers to take a short-term view. Return on sales and return on capital employed are typical measures used. Neither encourage a long-term, shareholder-benefit view of investment decisions.

The notion of institutionalization at the corporate level has other dimensions. For example the role of the corporate board is institutionalized and prescribed by law, as is the role of executive and non-executive directors. However the form taken by boards is not determined solely by regulations.

There are strong normative pressures for conformity at work here, as shown, for example, by the networks of boards of directors in which one executive holds a non-executive position in another company (an issue explored further in the following chapter). Arguably this is all about ensuring conformity of behaviour among such organizations. There is certainly considerable evidence that interlocking directorates are a key mechanism by which mimetic behaviour occurs.

It is also worth noting that the role of corporate executives, at the highest level of organizations, is explicitly about achieving legitimization. Having 'respected' figures on a board provides the organization with legitimacy (this is particularly important for charities). Such senior executives spend a good deal of time ensuring that their organizations are perceived as legitimate by the public, the government and the press.

A further aspect of corporate strategy is 'parenting'. An important question is the extent to which the corporate parent actually understands and empathizes with its business units, particularly in respect of operating across institutional boundaries. This might be one of the reasons why holding companies have problems. A holding company may have businesses as diverse as manufacturing, retailing and financial services. These are very different sorts of organization, and arguably of different institutional forms. It has to be asked whether a corporate parent can relate to these different sorts of business. Corporations with a disparate mix of businesses do not perform well in terms of share price. Arguably this is because financial analysts and investors operating under their own conventions and assumptions cannot make sense of them. It is worth noting here that economists would make the same observation about the difficulties faced by holding companies.

Mimicry is certainly evident at the corporate level. The 1970s was an era of diversification; the 1980s was an era of delayering and cost cutting; and the 1990s was an era of demerger and break-up as large corporations sought to get back to their 'core businesses'. Any one of these corporate moves might make sense at any time, but institutionalists would point out that all corporations seem to do the same thing at the same time. Haveman (1993) discusses how organizations in the US savings and loans industry (equivalent to building societies in the UK) followed successful fellow organizations into new markets. The choice of new markets was governed by the number of successful firms already in those markets: firms entered those markets which were already occupied. Hence Haveman identifies the occurrence of isomorphism within that industry via the mechanism of mimetic behaviour. Haunschild and Miner (1997) have also observed mimetic behaviour in the investment banking industry, specifically in terms of how corporations choose investment bankers to advise them on acquisitions. The authors found that under conditions of ambiguity and uncertainty mimicry is particularly salient.

So the prediction for QDG is that it will indeed enter Eastern Europe and is very likely to develop into a global partnership, and this will have just as much to do with mimicry as it will with debate in the boardroom.

Change

It was noted earlier that fully institutionalized behaviours are literally taken for granted and operate with 'rulelike status'. And there is no doubt that institutionalized practices exist. But not all organizations comply with normative expectations, either fully or in part. This has led to an interest in understanding the extent to which, and how, organizations deviate from the prevailing norms. There are several explanations from an institutional perspective.

One argument is that change is inevitable. The discussion above on culture and process made the point that change in organizations tends to occur incrementally; or to put it another way, change tends to happen within the bounds of what is taken for granted. Faced with pressures for change, managers typically minimize the extent to which they are faced with ambiguity and uncertainty by looking for that which is familiar. However, here lies an explanation of more fundamental change too. Over time it is likely, perhaps inevitable, that such incremental change may not address the necessities of the task, not least the market environment. This can give rise to the sort of strategic drift shown in Figure 3.2. The organization's strategy imperceptibly moves away from the forces at work in its task environment. This may not be detected for a long period of time; after all the organization may still be successful since it is doing what it knows how to do well. Eventually, however, its performance will suffer in some way. It may eventually die of course, or it may go through some major transformational change. This is intimated by Edward Gray in the case study. He is suggesting that there comes a time when transformational change is inevitable. He may, however, find it difficult to convince his colleagues that that time has now come.

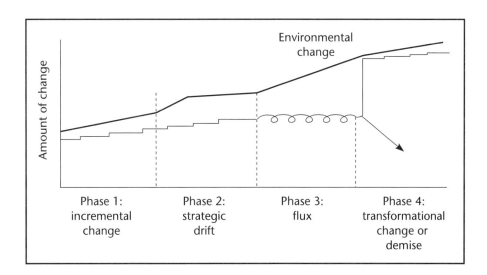

Patterns of strategy development   *FIGURE 3.2*

Oliver (1992) argues that contrary to early statements of the enduring nature of institutional rules, their power may dissipate over time if they are not actively reproduced and reinforced. This suggests that change can be understood in terms of the interplay, even contest, between prevailing institutional norms, reinforced by ritual and practice and the incursion of competing norms, ideas and expectations. There are clues as to how such competing norms may develop.

Greenwood and Hinings (1996), for example, show how and why shifts in the task and/or institutional environment may trigger changes within organizations. They analyze how the incidence of radical change varies across institutional sectors, in particular the extent to which they are more or less insulated from ideas and practices in other sectors. Over time organizations may become more 'permeable', for example many accountancy firms are focusing less on auditing and becoming more multidisciplinary. They are also placing less emphasis on the primacy of the partners and more on conventional management, with some of the partners playing more of a managerial role. Arguably, as this occurs they become more open to influences from outside the profession and therefore are more likely to change. This effect may increase if outsiders are brought into the organization, as happened, for example, with Michael Jones in the QDG case.

Greenwood and Hinings also assert that the incidence of radical change varies within sectors because of variation in the intraorganizational dynamics of particular organizations. Thus accounting firms vary in their development of tax and management consulting as structurally recognized practice areas, and in the importance they place on ideas that appeal to these occupational communities. The greater the range of occupations and experiences inside a firm, the more likely it is that new ideas will emerge and prompt change. Firms that are homogeneous are likely to interpret ideas in the same way, whereas firms containing diverse professional groups will generate debate because of multiple interpretations.

Change, then, may take place because of conflict between institutional norms within organizations. To some extent this seems to be what is happening at QDG. Michael Jones is approaching the problem from one set of institutional norms and his colleagues from another. Arguably Edward Gray is beginning to see the world rather more in Michael Jones's terms than those of his colleagues. This again emphasizes the importance of outsiders and 'mavericks'. Change is to do with the ability of an organization to break out of the prevailing institutional boundaries. New chief executives are sometimes appointed specifically for this purpose. It is argued that the role of the main board is to identify just when an organization needs an injection of new ideas. Institutionalists have observed, however, that when an organization recognizes the need for change it often imports recipes from elsewhere, rather than seek custom-made solutions.

A further explanation of change has to do with bending the rules. For most of the time people in organizations conform to the generally accepted 'rules of the game'. However they may sometimes consciously or unconsciously bend, manipulate or defy the norms. Or it may be that someone, perhaps one of the outsiders mentioned above, might consciously seek to use the accepted rules of the game but to his or her own ends. An example in a partnership might be that someone like Michael Jones may seek to build up allies by trying to introduce new partners from commercial organizations.

Institutionalists also point to the way in which management consultants carry change within and across populations of organizations. They transfer practices from one organization to another, but imperfectly so. In this respect they are agents of imperfect mimicry. As a consequence minor changes may simultaneously occur within an institutional field. Overall convergence around a given model might be the general trend, but imperfect mimicry can lead to incremental variation.

Overall, institutionalists stress the extent to which change is dependent on conformity to or challenge of institutional norms. They place less emphasis on the idea that change can be caused by intellectual persuasion exerted through some formal process. Indeed they might argue that such processes are themselves rituals within institutions.

Control

The received wisdom in strategic management is that 'structure follows strategy'. In other words organizations set their strategy and then determine the appropriate control and structure to implement that strategy. However, as we can see with QDG, structure is often a manifestation of institutional norms. A partnership is not a partnership because of the strategy it is following. It is the structural form accepted in that professional arena as the way things are done.

Similarly the idea that organizational controls are formed in order to measure important aspects of strategy is received wisdom in the strategy literature. But institutionalists argue that controls and measures are often manifestations of institutional norms. For example it is quite likely that QDG's control system emphasizes the same measures used in other accountancy firms. Such firms often place considerable importance, for example, on what is known as 'billable hours' – the amount of time individuals spend on fee-earning work for clients. This measure is emphasized not because of the strategy of the organization but because an accepted sign of success is the fee-earning capacity of individuals, and arguably because part of the ritual preparation for partnership is keeping junior members of the organization busy. The same point can be made about other types of organization. A popular measure of performance in private sector organizations is return on capital employed. Yet it is difficult to justify this objectively as a sound means of assessing the strategic health of a business since better returns must result from low-value assets (for example depreciated plant) than from investment in more costly new assets. Such measures have, however, become institutionalized measures of control.

Again mimicry and isomorphism occurs with regard to structures and control. The seminal study by Chandler (1962) shows how structural forms such as divisionalization, once developed, have become common across communities of firms, and Palmer *et al.* (1993) have demonstrated the role of interlocking directorates in spreading the adoption of this organizational form. And of course the whole field of HR systems is highly institutionalized and regulated through professional institutions that lay down quite precise norms, leading to conformity in such practices.

Other structural practices that have spread across organizations without necessarily being connected to strategy include total quality management (TQM) (see Westphal *et al.*, 1997) matrix structures (Burns and Wholley, 1993) and accounting procedures.

Note

1. Institutionalists use the term 'field' because it is broader than 'industry'. Industry usually covers a set or population of organizations producing similar products or services (for example accounting firms or car manufacturers). The 'field', however, would look not just at the producers, but also at key suppliers, customers and, critically, *regulatory agencies*.

Further Reading

Powell, W. W. and P. J. DiMaggio (1991) *The new institutionalism in organizational analysis* (Chicago, Ill.: University of Chicago Press).

Scott, W. R. (1995) *Institutions and organizations* (Thousand Oaks, CA: Sage).

Tolbert, P. S. and L. G. Zucker (1996) 'The institutionalization of institutional theory', in S. Clegg, C. Hardy and W. R. Nord (eds), *Handbook of Organization Studies* (London: Sage), pp. 175–90.

References

Abrahamson, E. and C. J. Fombrun (1994) 'Macro-cultures: Determinants and consequences', *Academy of Management Review*, vol. 19, pp. 728–55.

Baum, J. A. and C. Oliver (1991) 'Institutional linkages and organizational mortality', *Administrative Science Quarterly*, vol. 36, pp. 187–218.

Berger, P. L. and T. Luckmann (1967) *The social construction of reality* (New York: Doubleday Anchor).

Burns, L. R. and D. R. Wholley (1993) 'Adoption and abandonment of matrix management programs: Effects of organizational characteristics and inter-organizational networks', *Academy of Management Journal*, vol. 36, no. 1, pp. 106–38.

Chandler, A. D. (1962) *Strategy and structure: Chapters in the history of the industrial enterprise* (Cambridge, Mass.: MIT Press).

DiMaggio, P. J. and W. W. Powell (1983) 'The iron cage revisited: Institutional isomorphism and collective rationality in organizational fields', *American Sociological Review*, vol. 48, pp. 147–60.

Elsbach, K. D. (1994) 'Managing organizational legitimacy in the California cattle industry: The construction and effectiveness of verbal accounts', *Administrative Science Quarterly*, vol. 39, pp. 57–88.

Greenwood, R. and C. R. Hinings (1996) 'Understanding radical organizational change: Bringing together the old and the new institutionalism', *Academy of Management Review*, vol. 21, no. 4, pp. 1022–54.

Haunschild, P. R. and A. S. Miner (1997) 'Modes of interorganizational imitation: The effects of outcome salience and uncertainty', *Administrative Science Quarterly*, vol. 42, pp. 472–500.

Haveman, H. A. (1993) 'Follow the leader: Mimetic isomorphism and entry into new markets', *Administrative Science Quarterly*, vol. 38, pp. 564–92.

Huff, A. S. (1982) 'Industry influences on strategy reformulation', *Strategic Management Journal*, vol. 3, pp. 119–31.

Lamertz, K. and J. A. C. Baum (1998) 'The legitimacy of organizational downsizing in Canada: An analysis of explanatory media accounts', *Canadian Journal of Administrative Sciences*, vol. 15, pp. 93–107.

Meyer, J. W. and B. Rowan (1977) 'Institutionalized organizations: Formal structure as myth and ceremony', *American Journal of Sociology*, vol. 83, pp. 340–63.

Oliver, C. (1992) 'The antecedents of deinstitutionalization', *Organization Studies*, vol. 13, pp. 563–88.

Oliver, C. (1997) 'The influence of institutional and task environment relationships on organizational performance: The Canadian construction industry', *Journal of Management Studies*, vol. 34, no. 1, pp. 99–124.

Palmer, D. A., P. D. Jennings and X. Zhou (1993) 'Late adoption of the multidivisional form by large U.S. corporations: Institutional, political, and economic accounts', *Administrative Science Quarterly*, vol. 38, pp. 100–31.

Porac, J., H. Thomas and C. Baden-Fuller (1989) 'Competitive groups as cognitive communities: The case of the Scottish Knitwear Manufacturers', *Journal of Management Studies*, vol. 26, pp. 397–415.

Porter, M. E. (1980) *Competitive Strategy* (New York: The Free Press).

Powell, W. A. and P. DiMaggio (eds) (1991) *The new institutionalism in organizational analysis* (Chicago, Ill.: University of Chicago Press).

Scott, W. R. (1987) *Organizations: Rational, natural and open systems* (Englewood Cliffs, NJ: Prentice-Hall).

Scott, W. R. (1995) *Institutions and organizations* (Thousand Oaks, CA: Sage).

Slack, T. and C. R. Hinings (1995) 'Isomorphism and organizational change', *Organization Studies*, vol. 15, pp. 803–28.

Spender, J. C. (1989) *Industry recipes* (Oxford: Basil Blackwell).

Tolbert, P. S. and L. G. Zucker (1983) 'Institutional sources of change in the formal structure of organizations. The diffusion of civil service reform, 1880–1935', *Administrative Science Quarterly*, vol. 28, no. 1, pp. 22–39.

Tolbert, P. S. and L. G. Zucker (1996) 'The institutionalization of institutional theory', in S. Clegg, C. Hardy and W. R. Nord (eds) *Handbook of Organization Studies* (London: Sage), pp. 175–90.

Westphal, J. D., R. Gulati and S. M. Shortell (1997) 'Customization or conformity? An institutional and network perspective on the content and consequences of TQM adoption', *Administrative Science Quarterly*, vol. 42, pp. 366–94.

Zucker, L. G. (1977) 'The role of institutionalization in cultural persistence', *American Sociological Review*, vol. 42, pp. 726–43.

Zucker, L. G. (1987) 'Institutional theories of organizations', *Annual Review of Sociology*, vol. 13, pp. 443–64.

4 Business History Perspective
David J. Jeremy

This Chapter commences with an outline of the Chandler thesis, the dominant paradigm for explaining the historical development of business strategy in an international context. It then rehearses a number of the major criticisms of the thesis. The bulk of the chapter presents an historical overview of the strategies pursued in UK business.

The Chandler thesis

The most persuasive analysis of the historical development of business strategy is that pioneered by Alfred Chandler at the Harvard Business School (HBS). Although the subject of business history commenced at Harvard in 1927 and numerous historical case studies were used to buttress the case study method of teaching management for which the HBS became famous, it was not until 1948 that Harvard business historians shifted their attention from the individual business or business leader to generic themes. The first subject to attract a great deal of research effort was entrepreneurship. The Research Centre in Entrepreneurial History was established in 1948 and flourished for a decade. Arthur Cole was its 'leading spirit' but its inspiration came from Joseph Schumpeter, former Austrian minister of finance and renowned economics professor at Harvard from 1932 until his death in 1950. Among those associated with the centre were Douglass North, David Landes and Alfred Chandler. After the centre was dissolved in 1958, and with it the hope of establishing an entrepreneurial paradigm for business history, the initiative was taken up by Alfred Chandler. Almost single-handedly, he shifted the focus of business historians from entrepreneurs to organizations. He did so by moving from entrepreneurs to managers, and from the milieu of heroic capitalists (or robber barons, depending on your viewpoint) to the administrative core of the managerial revolution. His three volumes, *Strategy and Structure* (1962), *The Visible Hand* (1977) and *Scale and Scope* (1990), began respectively with case studies of a clutch of American firms, advanced to larger American samples, and then encompassed international comparisons. Chandler became 'a founder of the organizational school of American historians' (John, 1997: 171).

Chandler perceived an historical pattern to the emergence of the bureaucratic firm and its managerial hierarchies. Technical change in the nineteenth century (particularly factory production and the railways) widened markets, created mass demand and drove the transition from craft to mass production. First movers (entrepreneurs in the UK and the US, bank-guided managements in Germany) made three-pronged investments in manufacturing, marketing and management, initially in order to gain economies of scale. By the early twentieth century three broad developments were clear. In the US and in Germany corporate managerial hierarchies ran the largest firms. In the UK family-run firms remained dominant. Secondly, although the first movers, by making their three-pronged investments, raised barriers to entry against challengers, challengers nevertheless appeared. Sometimes the challengers invoked government aid (for example antitrust legislation in the US), sometimes they exploited shifts in resource markets (for example with the opening of new oil fields in the US and the Middle East) and sometimes they took advantage of new technologies (for example the early car manufacturers rivalled the locomotive builders). Changes in fashion offered challengers fresh opportunities (for example, the post-Victorian departure from heavy and prolonged mourning rituals, or the post-1960 teenage markets). Elsewhere challengers found niches (for example in the supply of oil drilling bits, hunting knives or artists' pigments). Thirdly, as the volume of activities rose, large firms reduced their costs by removing more and more transactions from outside suppliers and assigning them to units of their own. This achieved economies of scale, scope and transactions. Administrative coordination (by hierarchies of managers within one firm) replaced market coordination (by arrays of firms comprising a market).

Chandler (1962: 13) defines strategy as 'the determination of the basic long-term goals and objectives of an enterprise, and the adoption of courses of action and the allocation of resources necessary for carrying out these goals'. An early corporate strategy was horizontal integration, taking over rivals in the same industry. Such a strategy reinforced reorganization along functional lines. To achieve further production economies and increase market share, American firms possessing new technology in the 1870s and 1880s pursued vertical integration strategies, effected by the use of holding company structures. Diversification strategies in the early twentieth century, again driven by new technologies and changing markets, led after 1918 to the multidivisional structure (the M-form) (Box 4.1).

Box 4.1   The M-form

The M-form was pioneered in the US in the first two decades of the twentieth century. In essence it solved the big organizations' dilemma of centralized versus decentralized control.

At E. I. du Pont de Nemours & Co., the century-old gunpowder firm in Delaware, a managerial crisis in 1902 led to changes that eventually provided a new model for big business structures. Faced with the death or ageing of the previous generation, several young du Pont cousins, some trained in engineering and experienced in the management of steel and railway companies, decided to centralize the administration under an executive committee, giving each member two responsibilities: one for the company as a whole, the other for a functional department (three in manufacturing, plus sales, engineering and development). At the same time they pursued a strategy of vertical integration.

This structure, which with some modifications continued at du Pont until

1917, had two weaknesses: flows of materials and information responded slowly to fluctuations in demand; and top managers still concerned themselves with day-to-day issues. Wartime exposed these weaknesses and led to the decision to change from a functionally based structure to a product-based structure. Thus product divisions were created when the new organization was settled in 1921. Each product division had its own functional staff, was run by middle managers and supervised by top managers in the general office (headquarters). The multidivisional corporation, the M-form, had arrived.

In the same year a similar restructuring was independently effected at General Motors by Alfred Sloan and others. Standard Oil adopted the multidivisional format in 1925–27. At Sears Roebuck, the big American retailer, a variant of the M-form was developed in the 1930s and 1940s. Between 1921 and 1960 the new structure spread throughout the US, most rapidly in the electrical, motor vehicle and chemical industries. In some industries, such as rubber and petroleum, it was partially adopted. It was rejected in the metals and materials industries, such as steel, where executives preferred strong centralization with functional departments as a means of establishing control over highly capitalized plant.

The great advantage of the M-form was that it offered ways of overcoming managerial diseconomies of scale.

In his third magnum opus, *Scale and Scope* (1990), Chandler draws international comparisons between the competitive managerial capitalism of the US, the personal capitalism of the UK and the cooperative managerial capitalism of Germany. Concentrating on the 200 largest enterprises in each of the three nations between the 1880s and 1940s, he argues that the core dynamic was organizational capabilities ('physical facilities and human skills') nurtured by managerial hierarchies. The UK, Chandler maintains, was the least effective in developing a form of managerial capitalism, as many features of UK business apparently testified. The UK had relatively fewer large firms able to achieve economies of scale, scope and transactions. British entrepreneurs failed to make (or to make large enough) the critical triple investment in manufacturing, marketing and management in the capital-intensive industries of the second industrial revolution (metals, machinery, industrial chemicals and oil). They invested too little and too slowly in distribution. They recruited smaller managerial hierarchies. They were slow to adopt the M-form. In many firms the founder's family dominated management, either by recruiting a few salaried managers or by forming federations of small family-managed firms. The consequences of this pattern, alleges Chandler, were detrimental. Firms were starved of investment. Instead of exploiting their own resources to maintain output and prices, UK firms looked outside themselves to sources of market power such as patents, advertising and collusion. Foreign competitors entered and won UK markets relatively easily. The growth rates of the UK's large firms were much lower than those of American enterprises.

This evolutionary, historical and organizational model had a powerful appeal. Chandler's work won prizes (including a Pulitzer) and gained the respect of economists and management specialists as well as historians. To date it has remained the dominant, though now questioned, paradigm among business historians.

Lazonick (1986) has augmented Chandler's thesis. Using the case of the Lancashire cotton industry, he concludes that institutional rigidities lay at the root of the UK's relative industrial decline (as measured by economic growth rates and relative to the US, France, Germany and other states following the UK's example of industrialization). A prime illustration of these rigidities, Lazonick believes, was the persistence of the family firm. Family-run and controlled business, he argues, prevented the reorganization of British industry along American lines. The result was 'a prolonged technological backwardness and industrial decline' (ibid.: 45).

At the level of organizational strategy alone, Chandler's thesis has received weighty confirmation. The shift towards diversification and the M-form was traced in the USA after 1940 (Rumelt, 1974). Most recently, another substantial analysis of the collective behaviour of large firms has identified a similar shift in European business in the period 1970–1993 (Whittington and Mayer, 2000).

Criticisms of the Chandler thesis

Chandler's thesis has provoked numerous criticisms. Here only some of the broadest are outlined.

- The assumption that managerial capitalism is optimally achieved by following the American path is confounded by the case of Japan (Fruin, 1992, 1998).
- A model in which firms have only three organizational strategies (horizontal integration, vertical integration and diversification) overlooks the possibility of other organizational strategies, such as locational strategies (local, regional, national and multinational) (Dunning, 1993; Jones, 1996).
- The focus on organizational strategies neglects competitive market strategies (Porter, 1985, 1990), technological strategies (Pavitt, 1980; Porter, 1985; Hounshell and Smith, 1988; Campbell-Kelly, 1989; Jeremy, 1994), labour strategies (Gospel, 1992), financial strategies (Ingham, 1984; Capie and Collins, 1992), culture-shaping strategies (Kanter, 1983; Hofstede, 1991; Hampden-Turner and Trompenaars, 1993) and even ethical (or unethical) strategies (Jeremy, 1990; Tweedale and Jeremy, 1999).
- Big business in the US, in ownership and also in control, has to some degree remained in the hands of the descendants of founding families, such as the Du Ponts (the family from which Chandler himself is descended!), Mellons, Rockefellers and many more (Lundberg, 1968; Burch, 1972; Rubinstein, 1980). Whether this has been any greater than in the UK is not always easy to tell because of intermarriage and nominee shareholdings, but the most wealthy British businessmen were more modest in their presumptions and ambitions than their American counterparts (Rubinstein, 1981).
- The participation of family dynasties in business leadership (Chandler's personal capitalism) has not been confined to the UK. Among the industrialized

states it has been present in France and Germany (Cassis, 1997) and pre-1940s Japan (Morikawa, 1992).

- Family business, as the Chinese in South-East Asia have demonstrated, can be highly successful business (Church, 1990; Rose, 1995; Weidenbaum and Hughes, 1996).
- Big business in the UK has not been as inferior in performance as Chandler supposed. As measured by return on capital employed and longevity of firm, the UK's largest firms have been much more profitable and enduring than their counterparts in France and Germany between 1900 and the 1980s (Cassis, 1997).
- The Chandler thesis, predicated on competitive forms of capitalism, does not readily fit the experience of Japan, the second largest economy of the late twentieth century. Between the 1880s and the 1930s the zaibatsu (a group of diversified businesses owned exclusively by a single family or extended family) built up multi sector businesses spanning all industries except cotton and railways. The Mitsubishi zaibatsu even adopted a divisional structure in 1908 (Morikawa, 1992). Since 1945, when the old zaibatsu were broken up under the Allied Occupation, Japanese business has been characterized by competitive strategies and cooperative structures (Fruin, 1992). Three structures have been identified by Fruin: firms that act strategically, focal factories and networks. Firms may be enterprise groups, the heirs of the zaibatsu, controlling a core of major subsidiaries from all sectors (for example Mitsui, Mitsubishi and Sumitomo); or they may be the heads of vertical chains in a single industry (for example Toyota in motor vehicle manufacturing). Focal factories, which emerged between the wars, developed multifunction capabilities exploiting economies of scope in a variety of ways. They appeared widely across Japan in the postwar period. Networks linked big businesses with small businesses and core firms with subcontractors. Toyota, for example, in twenty years developed three tiers of suppliers totalling 35 768 firms by 1977. While strategies between dominant firms are based on competition, a great deal of cooperation is admissible in the furtherance of those strategies (Hirschmeier and Yui, 1981; Morikawa, 1992; Fruin, 1992; Wada, 1994).
- The big business model fails to capture the behaviour of small businesses. Here Scranton (1997) has illuminated the historical strategies of smaller American firms in the nineteenth-century, which flourished by pursuing strategies of flexibility, specialization and niche marketing.
- As history, Chandler's international comparisons fail to engage locality and local phenomena, particularly history, culture and institutions, that is, how business systems and firms are embedded (Fruin, 1998; Farnie *et al.*, 2000).

In effect the Chandler model is too limited and too limiting when applied across space and time. To be fair to Chandler, he has tried to update his thesis by collaborating extensively across nations (Chandler *et al.*, 1997), but this too has been severely faulted (Fruin, 1998).

The historical development of strategy in business : the UK case

Looking back it is often easier to find evidence of the results of strategic planning than of the *ex ante* planning stages. Short-run opportunism and intuitive action are therefore hard to disentangle from adherence to long-formulated boardroom schemes. Another complication is that the goals of corporate managers have changed over time.

Business strategies are not made in a vacuum. Invariably they have been formed in response to changes in markets (for materials, land, labour, capital, product goods and services, both domestic and international), in technology (of both products and production methods) and in institutions (primarily the state and the legal frameworks it imposes on business). Here, to facilitate an historical analysis of strategic management in the UK, the last two centuries or so can be divided into four periods largely according to growth patterns and wider business environments (Maddison, 1991). The broadest strategies that have been most widely followed by large and successful businesses are then considered.

Strategic management in the UK's early industrial age, ca. 1770 to the 1840s

During these decades the UK emerged as the world's first industrial nation. In the expanding industries of coal, iron, cotton, wool, shipping and railways the technologies of steam power, mechanical engineering and factory organization were exploited by hosts of mostly small and all intensely competitive firms aiming at regional, national and international markets.

The dominant forms of firm ownership were the single proprietor or the partnership. Apart from the agricultural estate, the vast majority of firm owners were also the firms' managers. As with all capitalist enterprises, and throughout all four periods under review, an abiding strategic goal was the maintenance and increase of profits. In this early industrial period, distinguished by highly competitive industries (where no single firm could influence pricing), profitability was sought in lowered unit costs of production. The most alert industrialists realized that unit costs fell when advantage could be taken of growth in size and capacity. Economies of scale (increases in productive capacity that lowered unit production costs) could be realized in a variety of ways. All of them involved substantial investment and difficulty in withdrawing, and therefore careful initial calculation (incipient strategic planning) before being undertaken.

Technological and organizational strategies

The most radical strategic choice for securing economies of scale was offered by the new textile technology of the late eighteenth century. It was not merely a set of new machines but machines with far-reaching organizational implications, as Marx observed in *The Poverty of Philosophy* (quoted in McLellan, 1980: 40). This was the factory. The modern factory arrived in 1771 when

Richard Arkwright (1732–92) set up his first cotton-spinning system in a rented, water-driven mill in Cromford, Derbyshire. By the time he died there were about 300 cotton factories of this kind in Britain. By 1835 three quarters of them were driven by steam engines.

The textile factory became a model for all manner of subsequent factories, and a major tool of strategic management. It exploited several cost-cutting devices. Primarily it demonstrated the power of concentrating both capital (machinery) and labour (workers) at a single site, in contrast to the 'putting out' system in which itinerate merchants distributed raw materials but found the efficiency and honesty of home workers difficult to control. Secondly, the factory utilized to the full the division and specialization of machines and workers, the principle that Adam Smith, father of modern economics, explicated at the beginning of his *Wealth of Nations* (1776). Thirdly, the machines in the factory were arranged according to sequence of production, allowing a logical and relatively rapid flow of materials between machines. Finally, in contrast to putting out, the factory required fewer and less-skilled workers per process per unit of output.

Few of these cotton factories were large. Of the nearly 350 cotton factories (an underestimate) in the UK in 1818, employing nearly 60 000 people, fewer than 10 employed more than 600 per factory. These large mills cost as much as £4500 in the 1790s (Fitton and Wadsworth, 1958: 195–6, 210). The number of factories was always less than the number of firms. Some firms were relatively large. By 1833 Samuel Greg & Co. had an empire of five mills on five different sites between Styal in north Cheshire and Lancaster. Together they employed 2000 people. Since in the previous 18 years four mills had been added to the original Quarry Bank Mill at Styal, either newly built or acquired, and since the additional investment amounted to over £70 000 in fixed capital and over £50 000 in floating capital, some very large and long-term strategic decisions were clearly being made (Rose, 1986: 40).

Layout strategies

A plant, such as a textile factory, on a cramped site could be improved by purchasing adjacent land and rearranging the processing rooms and machinery. The early nineteenth century saw the proliferation of factories. Given the long-windedness of the legal system in the transfer of property, long-term perspectives were frequently demanded. Thus John and Thomas Clark, woollen manufacturers of Trowbridge in Wiltshire, began acquiring land in the centre of the town for new factory premises in 1814. Not until 1821 did they pay off the £2300 price of the site. Subsequently, and at intervals related to the trade cycle, they enlarged and added other premises until 1840 (Beckinsale, 1951: xxvi–xxvii).

Labour management strategies

Much less quantifiable, because returns on investment were intangible, was the labour strategy of paternalism. Its proponents were few. No more than 40 or 50 paternalists among 4800 factory owners, thousands of mine owners, and tens of thousands of workshop operators in the early 1840s exerted little more than a demonstration effect on industry as a whole (Roberts, 1979: 183). However the likes of the Strutts, Gregs, Ashworths and Ashtons believed it paid to be a considerate employer. Driven by the old concepts of the aristocratic ethos and the Calvinist code, they extended fatherly care towards their workers in the provision of housing, schools, churchers and shops. In return, housing rentals made regular profits, and employee loyalty and motivation to work were strengthened. So too was the willingness to accept the new industrial discipline (Ure, 1835: 343–52; Pollard, 1965: 197–206).

Location strategies

Another prominent strategy in this early industrial period related to geography. New technology, especially the steam engine, liberated industry from riparian sites, attracting industry to the coalfields. Adopting the steam engine was a strategy that extended across all industries where entrepreneurs sought regular and cheaper power sources. More differentiated, and therefore requiring a more deliberate choice, was a decision to gravitate towards or into a particular industrial district. Before the eighteenth century industry was widespread across the country, though some districts, because of their geology and the presence of raw materials, were known for their industrial specialization. For example ironworks were found on the wooded Sussex weald, and regional woollen industries were located in Kent, the West of England and Yorkshire.

Industrialization reshaped the country's industrial districts as entrepreneurs sought proximity to raw materials, coastal ports or transportation networks. Another kind of locational strategy also lowered costs by enhancing the possibility of specialization: moving into a new industrial district in order to develop a specialized skill and a niche market. The markets and trades of the City of London, the Lancashire cotton industry and the Sheffield steel and cutlery trades were good examples of what later became the phenomenon of clustering. Between them the host of small firms in these districts were securing economies of scale (external economies), chiefly from specialization and division of labour. In Sheffield 'it would be impossible to trace the manufacturing history of a knife without following it to other workshops in Sheffield. . . . Each class of manufacturers is so dependent on the others, and there is such a chain of links connecting them all, that we have found it convenient to speak of Sheffield as one huge workshop for steel goods' (1844 description, quoted in Tweedale, 1995: 50).

Strategic management in the UK's Victorian industrial ascendancy, 1840s to 1914

This second period saw the UK at the height of its international power and prestige. In 1914 nearly a quarter of the world's land surface and population were ruled by the British Empire and London was the world's financial centre. A third of the UK workforce was employed in manufacturing. The UK's merchandise exports equalled a fifth of its gross national product, and its share of world exports stood at 28 per cent. Railway networks increased flows and volumes of traffic, widening markets in the UK, Europe, the US and elsewhere.

Chemical and steel technologies, pioneered in Europe and the US as well as the UK, brought down the cost of fundamental materials. In the last decades of the period the generation of electricity and diesel and petrol engines offered more flexible power sources. However other states were catching up in the race for economic growth, protecting their infant industries with tariff barriers: first France, the US and the German states; then Sweden, Japan and Russia (Rostow, 1960).

Collectively, businesses both responded and contributed to these broad changes. In the UK capitalist enterprise was unleashed to a new height by the arrival of freely available limited liability for joint-stock companies. Legislation (Companies Acts, consolidated in 1862) established the most permissive regime for company formation in Europe (Cottrell, 1980: 52). By the 1880s family firms were increasingly being converted into limited companies, both public and private. In 1918, of the 66 000 registered companies, 50 000 were private companies enjoying greater freedom and opacity than their public counterparts.

The impact of the joint-stock limited liability company is hard to overstate, though its effectiveness depended on the development of complementary and sophisticated capital markets – the London and provincial stock exchanges in the UK. On the one hand limited liability facilitated the ready concentration of a multitude of capitals and the possibility of creating really large capitalist enterprises. On the other hand it allowed exhausted entrepreneurs or their unsuited heirs and assignees to move out of management without surrendering the power and profits of ownership. This division of ownership and control opened the way for a new class of professional managers and the 'managerial revolution' of the twentieth century. What strategies did late-nineteenth-century owner–managers and early professional managers deploy in domestic and world markets?

Organizational strategies

Foreign exemplars spurred British industrialists to take up horizontal merger as a means of gaining fresh economies of scale. In Germany price-fixing cartels, of which there were six before 1870 but over 350 by 1900, were rapidly converted into syndicates with centralized marketing arrangements between 1897 and 1914 (Clapham, 1928: 311). In the US the federal government's Sherman Antitrust Act of 1890 was circumvented by the holding company device, and between 1897 and 1903 2800 business firms merged (Chandler, 1977: 332). Not surprisingly, as British industrialists watched their German and American rivals with growing awe, if not fear, a wave (the first) of mergers swept through UK industry in the 1890s and early 1900s.

Leading exponents of merger were the railway companies and the banks, especially in the last decade of the nineteenth century. Most aggressive between 1890 and 1906 were the Great Western Railway, which acquired 51 small railway companies in its territory; Barclays Bank, which was involved in 29 mergers, including the formative consolidation of 1896, when 15 mostly Quaker banks joined together; and Lloyds Bank, which acquired 28 other banking firms. However the largest horizontal mergers were negotiated in the textile industry, where there were thousands of small firms – more than 2000 in cotton manufacturing in 1913. The resultant giants included the Fine Cotton Spinners' & Doublers' Association (31 constituent firms in 1898), the Calico Printers' Association (46 manufacturing and 13 merchanting firms in 1899), and the Bleachers' Association (53 firms in 1900).

Implementation of these mergers met with mixed success. The railways, with their geographical divisional structures, line-and-staff management and statistical and financial techniques, as well as their nigh-military culture, did much better than the textile firms, which in some cases took years to overcome organizational indigestion.

While most mergers before the First World War were horizontal integrations (involving firms in the same industry), the big steelmakers, having already integrated backwards to secure their ore supplies, responded to the Anglo-German arms race by integrating forwards to secure shipbuilding and armaments orders. The Sheffield firms Vickers, John Brown and Cammells purchased shipbuilding firms at Barrow, on the Clyde and on the Mersey respectively (Tweedale, 1995: 122–7).

The trend towards ever larger size was viewed perceptively in 1907 by Henry Macrosty, a Fabian on the staff of the LSE. On the one hand he condemned 'the most oppressive American trust or German Kartell'. On the other hand, having surveyed the move in manufacturing towards horizontal and vertical integration, and in retailing the spread of price-fixing associations, he observed, 'So far as can be seen the great amalgamations are the best instruments of production yet devised, and to break them up into their original components would be foolish if it were not in most cases impossible' (Macrosty, 1907: 344–5).

Technological strategies

Most technical inventions were small and incremental. Relatively few were 'blockbusters', and when they were they underpinned a new technological system or part of it, such as the electric lamp and commercial electricity generation (Hughes, 1983). Technological advantage was short-lived (the life of a UK patent was 14 years) and when it had commercial potential it required a large capital investment to create the appropriate technological system. By the 1890s the days of the heroic inventor looked *passé*. As the German chemical industry demonstrated, research and development (R & D) was most efficiently conducted in heavily resourced corporate laboratories staffed by teams of scientists and technicians but directed by management towards commercial objectives.

In the UK manufacturers were slow to follow the German (and then the American) example. Firms were more haphazard in their pursuit of novel technical solutions. Thus the key discoveries and inventions in the manufacture of cheap steel were made by a professional and independent inventor (Bessemer), an electrical engineer and manufacturer (K. W. Siemens), a manufacturer–metallurgist (Pierre Martin), an ironworks chemist (Gilchrist) and a police court clerk (Thomas). Yet a single fundamental machine could endow its possessors with a huge competitive advantage. The American-invented Bonsack cigarette-making machine had propelled Wills of Bristol to dominance in the cigarette market by the beginning of the twentieth century (Alford, 1973).

Marketing strategies

The mass markets created by population growth, urbanization and rail and shipping networks, and supplied by the mass production techniques of the factory, called for new marketing strategies. Producing goods and services was one thing, winning market share was another. From the 1870s legal protection for trademarks and names, combined with cheap and more pictorial newspapers, handed producers a powerful marketing tool: branding. Branding simultaneously won customer loyalty and acted as a barrier to entry to the market by competitors. Most rewardingly it could yield enormous value added. Initially it was extensively used in the consumer goods industries where, due to the rising standard of living, demand was rising fastest: soap, tobacco, confectionery, jam, matches, soft drinks and textiles were branded. Where product quality could be upheld by technology and property rights by the courts, branding proved to be a very lucrative strategy, as numerous examples testify: William Lever's 'Sunlight' soap, Wills's 'Wild Woodbine' cigarettes, Cadbury's 'Dairy Milk' chocolate, Schweppes' 'Fountain' table waters, to name but a few. Unified mass marketing remained a compelling strategy for suppliers of consumer markets until the 1930s and beyond.

Labour management strategies

A report to the Board of Trade on Wages in 1891 recorded that labour costs varied, according to industry, between 20 per cent and 80 per cent of total production costs, but were mostly over 50 per cent (UK, Parliamentary Papers, 1890–91, c. 6535). In downturns of the trade cycle (running for eight to ten years, peak to peak) labour was easier to cut than the fixed costs of plant and machinery. However from the late 1880s unskilled labour followed the example of skilled workers in organizing themselves into trade unions to resist employers' unilateral demands, even when the employers were enlightened paternalists. In response employers increasingly organized themselves. In cotton spinning, for example, employers' associations in the North West of England covered 40 per cent of machine capacity in 1892, rising to 64 per cent in 1914 (McIvor, 1996: 63). Their objective, their strategy, was to keep trade unions out of the firm. Yet these trade associations were fiercely autonomous, and to that extent weak. Where employers did recognize unions they preferred to negotiate wages and conditions at the regional or national level, rather than within the plant or the firm, where employer solidarity was less easily mobilized.

Location strategies

In the last decade or two of the nineteenth century, industrialists in export markets were increasingly burdened by overseas tariff barriers and turned in growing numbers to a fresh locational strategy: the multinational enterprise. By 1914 about 30 per cent of the UK's national wealth was invested in overseas assets. Of this, 35 per cent (or £1340 million, current) was in the form of foreign direct investment – mines, factories, railway, gas, electricity and tramway undertakings. For example, of the UK's 100 largest employers in 1907, 62 were in manufacturing and at least eight of these had one or more foreign factories. The eight were Lever Brothers (soap), John Brown & Co. (steel and shipbuilding), Sir W. G. Armstrong Whitworth & Co. (shipbuilding and armaments), Vickers Sons & Maxim (shipbuilding and armaments), the Metropolitan Amalgamated Railway Carriage & Wagon Co., the Fine Cotton Spinners' & Doublers' Association (cotton spinning), J. & P. Coats (thread manufacturers) and the Bradford Dyers' Association (dyeing) (Jones, 1986: 21; Jeremy, 1990: 420–4).

Strategic management in disrupted and contracting international markets, 1914 to the 1940s

The third period, 1914 to the 1940s, was characterized by disrupted and contracting global markets. The First World War (1914–18) left the UK burdened by debt and the US as the world's banker. Many of the UK's export markets were lost, chiefly cotton textiles, coal and shipbuilding. Tariff walls and other protectionist measures dramatically shrank world trade, especially after the international financial collapse triggered by the Wall Street stockmarket crash of 1929: by 1935 world trade had fallen to a third of its 1929 level. Unemployment in the UK between 1921 and 1938 only once edged below 10 per cent. On the other hand the new technology industries, electrical goods, chemicals and motor vehicles flourished in the Midlands and South East of England. In this situation the widely perceived strategic objective was survival, the means was rationalization.

Organizational rationalization strategies

Rationalization in the first place meant the creation of larger, more efficient corporate structures that were better able to challenge international competition. As Prime Minister Stanley Baldwin told a meeting in Birmingham in 1925, 'you often hear men's leaders to-day speaking about the necessity for rigorous efficiency' (Baldwin, 1925: 46). In practice this meant forming horizontal mergers in which excess capacity was eliminated and less efficient firms were closed. There were numerous examples of the trend. The country's 120 railway companies were merged into just four large ones in 1922–23. Though not in international markets, transport costs of course had an impact on the value added of all manufacturing firms. In 1926, under pressure from German and American competition, four of the largest chemical firms (Nobels, Brunner, Mond, the British Dyestuffs Corporation and, the weakest of the four, United Alkali) merged to form Imperial Chemical Industries, with a workforce of 47 000 in the UK and markets around the world. New economies of scale could be reaped, not least through the concentration of R & D in dedicated research laboratories on the German model.

By the late 1920s, and especially after the financial crisis triggered by the Wall Street crash, some of the UK's older industries were in such a parlous state that the Bank of England's governor, Montagu Norman, decided to intervene. Able to mobilize very large capital resources (much from the clearing banks), in 1929 he formed a company under the aegis of the Bank of England: the Bankers' Industrial Development Company (BIDC). The BIDC offered investment capital for rationalization schemes, especially in the old industries suffering from international competition. The Lancashire Cotton Corporation was set up to integrate (and mostly close) 96 firms with ten million spindles in coarse cotton spinning. In shipbuilding, ailing firms on the Clyde were sold to Lithgows. In steel, several vertical combinations were formed, such as the English Steel Corporation and the Lancashire Steel Corporation. Although only a relatively small proportion of UK industry was subjected to organizational rationalization, Norman and the Bank of England orchestrated most of what was achieved (Payne, 1979; Tolliday, 1987).

Shrinking world markets, the very mixed fortunes of UK industry, the widely held perception of the need for rationalization, Norman's interventions: all helped to promote a second wave of mergers after the First World War that continued until the early 1930s (Hannah, 1983). This wave, like the earlier one, affected a small cluster of industries, some using new technology (food, chemicals, electrical engineering), others in the doldrums because of their old technology (shipbuilding, cotton). This time fewer firms were involved in most of the individual mergers and rapid growth was more easily absorbed. Furthermore most of the mergers were consolidations, not acquisitions. They also involved horizontal integration, rather than vertical integration or diversification. All of this suggests that relatively cautious growth strategies were being followed.

However size presented obstacles as well as opportunities. Diseconomies of scale (the reverse of economies) were encountered sooner or later. Two organizational structures checked these diseconomies. The holding company, familiar in the US in the late nineteenth century, was introduced to the UK in 1896 when Emile Garcke, a German immigrant and electrical engineer, formed the British Electric Traction Co. This offered the chance to diversify, assuming that the functional departments at the holding company headquarters were strong enough to monitor subsidiary boards and prevent strategic blunders.

A more important means of implementing scale strategies was the multi-divisional structure. Pioneered by Du Pont in the US at the end of the First World War, the M-form permitted nigh-autonomous operating divisions to flourish in an entrepreneurial but not unrestrained fashion. Strategic oversight and profit monitoring were exercised through a headquarters general staff (under the main board of directors) and interlocking directors spanning the main board and the boards of the subsidiaries/divisions. It was adopted by Nobel Industries and then its offspring ICI, but gained ground very slowly in the rest of UK industry, for the reasons noted below (Chandler, 1962; Channon, 1973; Reader, 1975).

Of great importance was the alternative strategy to merger as a means of securing market share: cartel arrangements. Price fixing agreements were utilized in the eighteenth century, for example in copper mining (Newell, 1998). Resale price maintenance spread among small businesses in the 1890s. Depression and shrinking markets between the wars gave impetus to cartelization. By 1938 resale price maintenance covered 30 per cent of consumers' expenditure. By 1960, shortly before the long demise of price fixing, 2240 restrictive agreements were recorded by the Registrar of Restrictive Trading Agreements (Jefferys, 1954; Hall, 1962: 453).

Technological rationalization strategies

The other side of rationalization was technological in character. It had two aspects: the hardware and the software of production. The former entailed use of the specialized machinery for and methods of interchangeable manufacture pioneered in the US federal armouries before the American Civil War (1861–65) and subsequently transferred to American consumer goods manufacture (sewing machines, reapers, clocks, bicycles, motorcars). These new machine tool technologies of the 1880s and 1890s then spread to the UK. They were unevenly resisted in the engineering trades, where foremen and fitting techniques survived into the First World War and beyond (Zeitlin, 1983, 1985; Hounshell, 1984). However, as the rejection of Fordism (high wages in return for high effort on a mechanized assembly production line) by UK car manufacturers in the 1920s showed, British employers were often less happy than their employees with American production methods (Lewchuk, 1987).

Without investment in the hardware of the mechanized office the multidivisional structure could not have overcome diseconomies of scale. The telephone and typewriter were well-established before 1914 and other devices appeared between the wars. The comptometer or calculating machine and the punched card accounting machine, both pioneered in the US, were increasingly adopted in the UK before the First World War. Hollerith tabulating machines, for example, recorded, sorted and tabulated data by means of a punched card system (Campbell-Kelly, 1989). Sir Herbert Austin welcomed the Powers Four range of machines (another American product) as 'representing the triumph of the Punched Hole . . . There is no system of book-keeping, and no method of costings, which they cannot carry out with unexampled speed, efficiency and economy' (quoted Campbell-Kelly, 1989: 72).

The 'software (workplace relations, from a labour strategy viewpoint), devised in the US and unevenly adopted in the UK between the wars, was 'Taylorism' or 'scientific management'. Briefly, F. W. Taylor, a Philadelphia-born engineer, wanted to give managements more control over the work process. He believed this could be done through the analysis, measurement, codification and costing of shop floor tasks. His ideas emerged in the 1890s and were published in a collective work, *Principles of Management*, in 1911. They met a very mixed reception in the US and the UK. A variant of Taylorism, the Bedaux system, was being used in about 250 UK firms by 1939, including ICI, Lucas and Huntley & Palmer (Littler, 1983; Nelson, 1995).

Location rationalization strategies

Strategies for overseas expansion were well recognized before 1914, as already discussed. In the 1920s and 1930s, which witnessed international markets in postwar chaos later torn by communist and fascist tyrannies, it was remarkable that UK industrialists preserved their faith in foreign direct investment. They did so, although their share of global FDI slipped a little from 45 per cent to 40 per cent between 1914 and 1938 (Jones and Schroter 1993: 10). There was some shift from Europe to Empire, although one survey of 448 UK multinational enterprises in 58 countries before 1939 found that movement was from underdeveloped to developed regions (Nicholas, 1991). In pursuance of these strategies, UK management performance left much to be desired. The monitoring of foreign subsidiaries tended to be spasmodic and disruptive, rather than regular, methodical and constructive. The training of managers despatched from the UK was conducted on-the-spot and was blinkered by Western cultural norms, vigorously upheld in expatriate social life.

At home, location strategies prompted several developments. In the motor industry manufacturers gravitated to the West Midlands in search of external economies from the Birmingham and Black Country metal trades (Allen, 1959; Thoms and Donnelly, 1985; Church, 1995). ICI made huge investments at Billingham on the Tees, first in ammonia synthesis (for fertilizer production), then, when the global fertilizer market collapsed in the wake of the Wall Street crash, in oil-from-coal technology (which in the late 1930s had military as well as commercial significance) (Reader, 1975). In the steel industry the Clyde-based firm Stewarts & Lloyds exhibited the most dramatic location strategy. With some support from the Bank of England and the BIDC, the company's wily chairman, Allan Macdiarmid, built a new steelworks at Corby in Northamptonshire in 1933–34, replacing obsolete capacity. In the face of Montagu Norman's strong disapproval he then expanded steel production and moved into the league of integrated steel and tube manufacturers (Tolliday, 1987).

Other strategies

Throughout these difficult decades British industrialists maintained their older labour market strategies. Marketing strategies likewise remained dedicated to unified mass marketing techniques, as exemplified by branding, reinforced by Resale Price Maintenance.

Strategic management in expanding and then uncertain global markets, 1950s to the present

The fourth period, from the early 1950s to the present, started with a golden age for global economic growth, but in 1973 growth began to falter. After the Second World War (1939–45) the Anglo-American allies developed international economic structures aimed at economic stability and market freedom. The largely abandoned gold standard (finally discarded by the UK in 1931) was replaced by stabilized exchange rates, settled under the Bretton Woods Agreements of 1944. The old protectionist barriers were progressively dismantled in a series of trade liberalizations negotiated under the General Agreement on Tariffs and Trade. War-torn economies, especially those of West Germany and Japan, were rebuilt. Aeroplanes, telecommunications and television vastly widened market opportunities after the 1950s.

However, the consequent expansion of world trade was curbed by the oil price shocks of 1973 and 1979. Even before the oil shocks the altered growth rates and trading patterns of the advanced Western economies strained the Bretton Woods arrangements to breaking point. In the early 1970s fixed exchange rates were abandoned and currencies were allowed to float. The UK, struggling to attain growth rates comparable to its Western European and American rivals (to say nothing of Japan), had earlier devalued the pound sterling (in 1949 and 1967). A new ethos in the UK arrived when the Conservatives, led by Margaret Thatcher, were elected to government in 1979. Nationalized industries (established mostly by Clement Attlee's Labour government in the five years after 1945) were privatized. Trade union powers were checked. Uncompetitive firms and industries, mainly in manufacturing, were allowed to shrivel and disappear without state aid. The UK's growth rates began to overtake those of rivals in the European Union, which the UK joined in 1973. West Germany was hampered by its reunification with East Germany after the collapse of the Soviet bloc in 1989–90. The US was hampered by budget deficits, a high national debt, high internal interest rate policies and Japanese and Asian competition.

In this period the strategic objectives of business were related to growth. Growth was measured by means of the national accounts (commenced in the 1940s) which allowed comparison with international rivals. Growth, rather than dividends, was a major concern for professional corporate managers – to meet both politically devised and firm-level targets, growth strategies depended on the old search for economies of scale and means of raising productivity.

Organizational strategies

Chandler (1990) argues that UK business was handicapped by excessive reliance on family firms, rather than professional managerial hierarchies and complementary multidivisional structures. As a consequence, he suggests, there was a record of starved investment, reluctance to diversify, reliance on barriers against newcomers and loss of markets at home and abroad to foreign competitors. While his interpretation has been challenged from numerous directions (for example John, 1997; Jeremy, 1998) it is clear that UK firms were slow to adopt new organizational structures. In 1950 less than 13 per cent of very large UK firms had a multidivisional structure. In 1960 still only 30 per cent were utilizing the M-form. However in the 1960s and 1970s it was adopted very quickly and some 72 per cent of the largest UK corporations were using it by 1970, compared with 86 per cent in the US in 1967 (Channon, 1973: 68–70, 86). In part this delay reflected a lag in the provision of management training. Whereas the first business schools and the MBA were established in the US at the end of the nineteenth century, the UK's first business schools (in Manchester and London) were not founded until 1965 (Wilson, 1992).

Adoption of the M-form was associated with a third merger wave, the largest thus far in real terms, which lasted from 1956 until about 1973 (Hannah, 1983). It embraced several and very different strategic motives. One was the old motive of rationalization. To this end the government imposed on aircraft manufacturers the necessity of merger, which produced the British Aircraft Corporation in 1960 (Gardner, 1981). Another motive was defensive, aimed at combating foreign competition. For this purpose, motor manufacturers went through the series of mergers that formed the British Motor Corporation in 1968 (Church, 1995). A further motive was to salvage what remained of old industry, hence the mergers in textiles, with Courtaulds and ICI fighting over the scraps (Blackburn, 1993). Some mergers were offensive, designed to seize global as well as domestic opportunities. GEC's takeover of Associated Electrical Industries and then English Electric in 1967–68, for which Arnold Weinstock of GEC secured government backing, was of this sort (Jones and Marriott, 1970). Over the course of the third merger wave and beyond, the number of conglomerate mergers increased, rising from 12 per cent in 1965–69 to 35 per cent in 1978–81 (Gourvish, 1996: 238). This implied a strategy of diversification. Given the earlier examples (primarily ICI), the presence of American multinationals in the UK and the strong postwar American influence on UK business, it was not surprising that many of the new corporate boards 'discovered' the M-form.

However mergers were more often unsuccessful than successful, according to one study (Meeks, 1977) The same study found that in most cases profits began to decline twelve months after the merger. The unhappy attempt by Guinness to diversify from drink into confectionery, general trading, plastics, film finance, leisure and holiday villages in the 1970s is just one documented case (Guinness, 1997). Greater corporate growth arose from internal sources (Meeks, 1977).

One of the last big business bastions of family networks and family firms was the City of London, particularly in the case of merchant banks and the Stock Exchange. In 1986 the Big Bang (the liberalization of financial markets) ushered in foreign giants such as Salomon Brothers and Goldman Sachs from New York and Nomura and Daiwa from Tokyo. The less energetic or less competent firms sold up and their partners retired, the proceeds funding swimming pools all over Surrey and villas from the South of France to the Caribbean (Reid, 1988).

Strategy within the nationalized industries

Chandler's strictures relate only to large private enterprises, mostly before 1940. Since then UK business has been characterized not only by industrial capitalism but also by state capitalism. In 1955 the nationalized industries employed just over 10 per cent of the UK workforce. What can be said about strategy within these huge businesses? On the one side it was fettered by ministerial political intervention, by changing and sometimes conflicting purposes imposed alternately by Labour and Conservative governments (for example social welfare in the 1940s, profit seeking in the 1960s, anti-inflation instruments in the 1970s), and by the interposition of Whitehall bureaucracies. On the other side (and judged by pre-existing conditions and the nationalized industries' own targets) some nationalized industries did well, others much less well.

Of the latter, railways suffered from the prolongation of steam power and delays in electrification. Even so, their war-torn infrastructure was rebuilt. Coal, with 1000 firms and 1500 collieries in 1947, was turned into a merged, divisionalized and modernized enterprise that reached its long-term targets in output and productivity within a decade. It was, however, burdened by loans from the Treasury to fund its modernization programme. In electricity, power generation was spread across three fuels (coal, oil and nuclear energy) and power supplies were abundant, compared with 1947.

The big success story was gas. The Gas Council started in 1949 with 609 local gas undertakings, all making their own gas from coal. At that time the long-term prospects looked gloomy. A national grid was regarded as wholly uneconomic in the 1940s. As coal prices rose in the 1950s, electricity threatened to take over from gas. However the discovery in 1965 of natural gas under the North Sea transformed the industry's prospects. A national gas grid was built in ten years (1967–77) and the industry was restructured, with a shift from manufacturing to distribution. These were remarkable achievements in view of the politicized, bureaucratic and unpredictable nature of state involvement in the nationalized industries (Ashworth, 1991).

Technological strategies

A long-term strategic approach paid off both in specific technology projects and on a broad technological front. In the nationalized gas industry the realization that coal gas would be uneconomic in the future led the Gas Council to invest in a consolidated research organization and then a range of projects aimed at finding improved extraction processes and substitutes. The research, especially on domestic burners, smoothed the way when undertaking the conversion to North Sea gas of some 35 million appliances (Williams, 1981: 121–31, 180–2).

On the broad front the most pervasive and transforming technology was the computer. In the early 1940s it did not exist; in 1995, 24 per cent of UK households had one. The first computers emerged from wartime research on code breaking. They performed complex scientific calculations and in-putting and out-putting the data did not take long. In industry it was the reverse: in-putting and out-putting data took a very long time and the calculations were routine, involving stock, receipts, wages and the like. In 1954 the wage calculations for the 30 000 employees of J. Lyons & Co., the caterers and food manufacturers, took 6.5 hours on the computer, compared with 55 man-weeks of clerical effort previously (Hendry, 1987).

Desk-sized, commercially profitable machines (with transistors rather than valves) arrived in the late 1950s. By the early 1960s computers were beginning to spread into the business world. In 1964 there were 1000 in the UK, compared with 22 000 in the US. Costing £15 000 (the cheapest in 1963) they could only be afforded by big firms. The vice-chairman of Lloyds Bank told his shareholders in early 1965, 'Our West End Computer Centre was established in 1963 and in the autumn of 1964 we opened another Centre in the City. At these two Centres we are now accounting for over 100 000 accounts and additional branches are being added every week' (*The Times*, 13 February 1965). To overcome the old problem of spotting winners on such a broad front and such a rapidly innovating technology as the computer, firms had to depreciate rapidly and search for integrated systems with as much compatibility and security as possible.

Multinational strategies

Between 1945 and the early 1960s UK multinational activity abroad concentrated on the high per capita income Commonwealth countries. The break-up of the British Empire helped to divert multinational investment into Western Europe and the US. By 1981 nearly 80 per cent of UK foreign direct investment was in the developed economies, with food, drink, tobacco, chemicals and electrical engineering predominating (Shepherd *et al.*, 1985: 10, 63). Curiously, UK multinationals have been more successful abroad than at home. One view is that they have always pursued market size and growth (Panic, 1982). Another is that they tend to be best at exploiting Porter's 'diamond of competitive advantage' (Jones, 1994: 201, 1996: 207).

Firms in high technology sectors exploited their science-based competitive advantage by distributing their R & D facilities around the world close to high-income markets, particularly the US, Japan and Western Europe. ICI in chemicals, Zeneca (demerged from ICI in 1992) in bioscience and Glaxo-Wellcome in pharmaceuticals were cases in point. Yet even the biggest UK retailers were now seeking overseas investments. In 1993 the chairman of Marks & Spencer, Sir Richard Greenbury, reported that 12.4 per cent of the group's turnover came from store sales in Europe, the US, Hong Kong and Japan (annual report).

Marketing strategies

In the twentieth century American marketing techniques began to cross the Atlantic. The innovative J. Walter Thompson Company opened its first UK agency after the First World War, not least to handle the accounts of incoming American multinationals. Grounded on the statistically based techniques of market testing, more American advertising firms came to the UK in the 1950s. They dominated professional marketing in the early television age and until the 1980s, when the brothers Charles and Maurice Saatchi turned the advertising world upside down. Both American and British marketing professionals advocated segmented marketing. A few UK companies, led by Unilever and Rowntree, had adopted strategies of market research and segmented mass marketing in the 1930s.

By the 1960s it was widely agreed that generic marketing had lost its force. The marketing of capital goods remained a much more discreet and personal business than the marketing of consumer goods. Significantly, marketing specialists such as the ill-starred Ernest Saunders of Guinness were moving up through the ranks of UK boardrooms here and there to replace accountants as CEOs. Their impact on strategic management has yet to be assessed (Fidler, 1981: 101; Tedlow and Jones, 1993; Jeremy, 1998: 467–96).

Labour strategies

Labour management impinges on workplace relations, employment relations (covering wages and conditions of work) and industrial or management–union relations (Gospel, 1992). Attention to all three has engaged strategic managements. In the 1970s and 1980s managements' failure to command the workplace, as in the car industry, newspaper printing and the docks, led to the collapse or removal of firms and industries. Employment relations have been concerned with managing internal (within the company) and external markets, the latter acting as a safety valve in cyclical depressions. Until the 1930s the main employment relations strategies were bureaucratic management of internal labour markets, as in the railway companies and the Post Office; old-style paternalism, as found at Lever Brothers in Port Sunlight; and the rational personnel managements set up by Quaker employers such as Cadburys and Rowntrees. After the Second World War a new approach, personnel management, pioneered by Elton Mayo and others (not least in the Hawthorne experiments), crossed the Atlantic and strongly influenced early management consultants such as Urwick, Orr & Partners. At the level of industrial relations, strategies depended on markets, technologies, governments and personalities in both firms and trade unions.

In retrospect it can be seen that industrial relations passed through a number of phases. The expansive economic climate of the late 1950s to the early 1970s strengthened the bargaining power of workers *vis-à-vis* employers. Conversely, high unemployment related to slowing growth in world markets in the 1970s and 1980s (as in the 1920s and 1930s) encouraged workplace conflict, which in turn prompted anti-union legislation, making it easier for managements to assert their right to manage. In the 1980s the upgrading of the workforce, not least as a result of the economy's structural shift from manufacturing to services since the 1970s, meant that new approaches to labour relations were necessary. Personnel management was transmuted into human resource management. The empowerment of workers became the shibboleth of the late 1980s. New communications technology permitted new work patterns such as teleworking and the virtual office (as at British Airways, Heathrow) (*The Times*, 20 July 1998). These and other factors have caused unionization to recede to the 1940s' level. Managements now search for labour strategies that are appropriate to the skill levels of their employees, rather than maintaining traditional conflictual attitudes and techniques. In this respect the impact of incoming Japanese multinationals has been very important.

Location strategies

The retailers that dominated the consumer revolution in the second half of the twentieth century resoundingly demonstrated the merits of alert location strategies. The soaring standard of living from the late 1950s unleashed a boom in consumer demand. To meet this demand the multiples concentrated on price, quality and ranges of goods that would capture large segments of the mass market. Most successful were the multiples that responded to the changing family structure and work patterns, increasing geographical mobility, population shifts away from city centres and changing tastes in food, clothing, household products and body care.

The first successful self-service store was opened in 1948 by the Portsea Island Co-op, but the cooperatives failed to maintain the lead. The big grocery multiples, led by Sainsbury and Tesco, were quick to exploit the supermarket trolley and the motorcar, and then the computer. Following the American example, stores were built in out-of-town locations, where property and rates were cheaper. The first out-of-town superstores were built in 1967. By 1971 there were 25, rising to 327 in 1981 and 2966 in 1994. Some department stores, such as the John Lewis Partnership, set up business in what looked increasingly like American-type out-of-town shopping malls. Slowest to adapt were the coops, where democratic tradition and amateurism conflicted with entrepreneurial efficiency and professionalism (Jeremy, 1998: 353–68).

Conclusion

The business historian's view of strategic management, based on a wide range of firms and industries, is that generic organizational strategies such as those explored by Chandler (1962, 1977, 1990), emphasizing integration and diversification, have to be complemented by strategic activities in other business functions. Attention has been paid to technology, multinational investment, marketing, labour and location, as well as organization. Nothing direct has been said about culture or ethics or corporate governance, areas of the firm where strategic policies have also been applied. Nor has the impact of privatization been considered. Here, for the business historian, the jury is still out. In contrast to other investigators of management, the business historian's approach is inclined towards case studies as well as generalizations from those studies. As stated at the outset, it is rare for business records to be sufficiently full and open for the historian to observe the unfolding formation and implementation of a particular strategy. As seen here, inference is a major conceptual tool.

Appendix

The development of strategic management may be viewed through a variety of lenses. The foregoing chapter has set out within a chronological framework a number of strategies conceptually derived from classical economics. Table 4A.1 in the Appendix suggests additional strategic approaches some conceptually inspired by a competitive advantage framework. The matrix by no means exhausts the analytical possibilities.

Table 4A.1 Historical dimensions of the elements of strategic management in the UK

Dimension	1770–1840s	1840s–1914	1914–1940s	1950s–1970s	1970s–1990s
Context (external to firm)	Industrialization; high growth rates in leading sectors such as cotton	International economic leadership challenged by US, Germany and France after 1870	Two world wars and global economic depression in between. Old UK industries (cotton especially) in decline	International economic expansion. Shift from old to new manufacturing industries, 1920s–1950s. Nationalization of major industries in the 1940s	Shift from manufacturing to services, 1950s–1990s. Deindustrialization (decline of manufacturing base) from 1970s. Privatization, 1980s–1990s
Culture (managerial, within the firm)	Former landowners, merchants and craftsmen become new industrialists. They create cultures either of oppressive and exploitative individualism or, rarely, of paternalism based on the aristocratic ethos and the Calvinist code	Spread of paternalism. Also self-help. Individualism bolstered by Darwin and survival of the fittest principle. Military managerial ethos in the railway companies	Merit-based management, following the growing separation of ownership and management, especially from the 1880s. Increasing rationalization of welfare schemes, e.g. on the railways	Americanization of management via Marshall Aid schemes and US multinationals	Erosion of corporate loyalty and new managerial individualism
Competences (within the firm)	Management through accumulated experience, learning by doing or apprenticeship	Technical management handbooks from the 1930s. Engineering apprenticeship or accountancy training prepared many for management	Professionalization of management via specialized societies. Accountancy and engineering still the main managerial skills	Engineering apprenticeship or accountancy training still the main preparation for management. More rarely economics or engineering degrees provided managerial competences. Business schools after 1965; also undergraduate business degrees following expansion of higher education after the Robbins Report (1963)	The rise of MBA-instilled competences

continued table 4A.1

Dimension	1770–1840s	1840s–1914	1914–1940s	1950s–1970s	1970s–1990s
Competitive advantage, sources of	By technical innovation, usually aimed at saving labour costs. Pursuit of economies of scale	Continued search for economies of scale. From 1890s, through merger	Rationalization (American technology plus horizontal integration plus removal of inefficient firms). Merger in 1920s followed by spread of cartels and collusive trading agreements	Ascendancy of giant firms: nationalized industries, multinationals, multidivisional corporations	Organizational knowledge embodied in individuals, team and technology
Change in organizational structures	Single-unit, single-product, single-location firms	Multi-unit, multiproduct or service, multilocation firms, e.g. chemical manufacturers, railway companies	Holding companies	Spread of the multidivisional firm	Globalization
Controls, managerial	Factory model: one or two layers of line management	Railway model: geographical divisions, line-and-staff control, cost accounting	Scientific management Taylorism and its variant, the Bedaux system)	Multidivisional corporation, with directors interlocking divisions under central corporate head office. Managerial science, derived from WW2 maths-based techniques	Matrix, franchise, virtual office Japanese methods, culture-based
Corporate alliances	Informal collusion between firms	Multinational enterprises and market-sharing agreements from 1880s. Mergers (mostly horizontal): on railways from the 1840s, in manufacturing from the 1890s	Horizontal and, increasingly, some vertical mergers	Mergers: aiming at vertical integration and, increasingly, diversification	Global alliances

Note:
For further consideration of most of these elements see Jeremy (1998).

Further reading

Hannah, L. (1983) *The Rise of the Corporate Economy*, 2nd edn (London: Methuen).

Jeremy, D. J. (1998) *A Business History of Britain, 1900–1990s* (Oxford: Oxford University Press).

Kirby, M. W. and M. B. Rose (eds) (1994) *Business Enterprise in Modern Britain from the Eighteenth to the Twentieth Century* (London: Routledge).

Schmitz, C. J. (1993) *The Growth of Big Business in the United States and Western Europe, 1850–1939* (London: Macmillan).

Supple, B. (ed.) (1977) *Essays in British Business History* (Oxford: Clarendon Press).

Wilson, J. F. (1995) *British Business History, 1720–1994* (Manchester: Manchester University Press).

References

Alford, B. W. E. (1973) *W.D. & H.O. Wills and the Development of the UK Tobacco Industry, 1786–1965* (London: Methuen).

Allen, G. C. (1959) *British Industries and Their Organization* (London: Longmans).

Ashworth, W. (1991) *The State in Business, 1945 to the mid-1980s* (London: Macmillan).

Baldwin, S. (1925) *Peace and Goodwill in Industry* (London: George Allen & Unwin).

Beckinsale, R. P. (ed.) (1951) *The Trowbridge Woollen Industry as Illustrated by the Stock Books of John and Thomas Clark, 1804–1824* (Devizes: Wiltshire Archaeological Society).

Blackburn, J. A. (1993) 'The British Cotton Textile Industry since World War II: The Search for a Strategy', *Textile History*, vol. 24, no. 2, pp. 235–58.

Burch, P. H. Jr (1972) *The Managerial Revolution Reassessed: Family Control in America's Large Corporations* (Lexington, Mass.: D.C. Heath).

Campbell-Kelly, M. (1989) *ICL. A Business and Technical History* (Oxford: Clarendon Press).

Capie, F. and M. M. Collins (1992) *Have the Banks Failed British Industry?* (London: Institute of Economic Affairs).

Cassis, Y. (1997) *Big Business: The European Experience in the Twentieth Century* (Oxford: Oxford University Press).

Chandler, A. D. Jr (1962) *Strategy and Structure: Chapters in the History of the American Industrial Enterprise* (Cambridge, Mass.: MIT Press).

Chandler, A. D. Jr (1997) *The Visible Hand: The Managerial Revolution in American Business* (Cambridge, Mass.: Harvard Belknap Press).

Chandler, A. D. Jr (1990) *Scale and Scope The Dynamics of Industrial Capitalism* (Cambridge, Mass.: Harvard Belknap Press).

Chandler, A. D. Jr, F. Amatori and T. Hikino (eds) (1997) *Big Business and the Wealth of Nations* (Cambridge: Cambridge University Press).

Channon, D. F. (1973) *The Strategy and Structure of British Enterprise* (London: Macmillan).

Church, R. (1990) 'The Limitations of the Personal Capitalism Paradigm', *Business History Review*, vol. 64, no. 4, pp. 703–10.

Church, R. (1995) *The Rise and Decline of the British Motor Industry* (Cambridge: Cambridge University Press).

Clapham, J. H. (1928) *The Economic Development of France and Germany, 1815–1914* (Cambridge: Cambridge University Press).

Cottrell, P. L. (1980) *Industrial Finance, 1830–1914: The Finance and Organization of English Manufacturing Industry* (London: Methuen).

Dunning, J. H. (1993) *The Globalisation of Business: The Challenge of the 1990s* (London: Routledge).

Elbaum, B. and W. Lazonick (1986) *The Decline of the British Economy* (Oxford: Clarendon Press).

Farnie, D. A., T. Nakaoka, D. J. Jeremy, J. F. Wilson and T. Abe (eds) (2000) *Region and Strategy in Britain and Japan: Business in Lancashire and Kansai, 1890–1990* (London: Routledge).

Fidler, J. (1981) *The British Business Elite. Its Attitudes to Class, Status and Power* (London: Routledge & Kegan Paul).

Fitton, R. S. and A. F. Wadsworth (1958) *The Strutts and the Arkwrights, 1758–1830. A Study of the Early Factory System* (Manchester: Manchester University Press).

Fruin, W. M. (1992) *The Japanese Enterprise System: Competitive Strategies and Co-operative Structures* (Oxford: Clarendon Press).

Fruin, W. M. (1998) 'To Compare or not to Compare: Two Books that Look at Capitalist Systems across Centuries, Countries and Industries', *Business History Review*, vol. 72, no. 1, pp. 123–36.

Gardner, C. (1981) *British Aircraft Corporation. A History* (London: Batsford).

Gospel, H. (1992) *Markets, Firms and the Management of Labour in Modern Britain* (Cambridge: Cambridge University Press).

Gourvish, T. (1996) 'Beyond the Merger Mania: Merger and De-merger Activity', in Richard Coopey and Nicholas Woodward (eds), *Britain in the 1970s: The Troubled Economy* (London: UCL Press).

Guinness, J. (1997) *Requiem for a Family Business* (London: Macmillan).

Hall, M. (1962) 'The Consumer Sector', in G. N. W. Worswick and P. H. Ady (eds) *The British Economy in the Nineteen-Fifties* (Oxford: Clarendon Press).

Hampden-Turner, C. and F. Trompenaars (1993) *The Seven Cultures of Capitalism: Value Systems for Creating Wealth in the United States, Britain, Japan, Germany, France, Sweden and the Netherlands* (New York: Doubleday).

Hendry, J. (1987) 'The Teashop Computer Manufacturer: J. Lyons, Leo and the Potential and Limits of High-Tech Diversification', *Business History*, vol. 29, no. 1, pp. 73–102.

Hirschmeier, J. and T. Yui (1981) *The Development of Japanese Business, 1600–1980* (London: George Allen & Unwin).

Hofstede, G. (1991) *Cultures and Organizations: Software of the Mind* (New York: McGraw-Hill).

Hounshell, D. A. (1984) *From the American System to Mass Production, 1800–1932. The Development of Manufacturing Technology in the United States* (Baltimore, MD: Johns Hopkins University Press).

Hounshell, D. A. and J. K. Smith (1988) *Science and Corporate Strategy: Du Pont R&D, 1902–1980* (Cambridge: Cambridge University Press).

Hughes, T. P. (1983) *Networks of Power: Electrification in Western Society, 1880–1930* (Baltimore, MD: Johns Hopkins University Press).

Ingham, G. (1984) *Capitalism Divided? The City and Industry in British Social Development* (London: Macmillan).

Jefferys, J. B. (1954) *Retail Trading in Britain, 1850–1950* (Cambridge: Cambridge University Press).

Jeremy, D. J. (1990) *Capitalists and Christians: Business Leaders and the Churches in Britain, 1900–1960* (Oxford: Clarendon Press).

Jeremy, D. J. (1994) *Technology Transfer and Business Enterprise* (Aldershot: Edward Elgar).

John, R. H. (1997) 'Elaborations, Revisions, Dissents: Alfred D. Chandler, Jr's The Visible Hand after Twenty Years', *Business History Review*, vol. 71, no. 2, pp. 151–200.

Jones, G. (ed.) (1986) *British Multinationals: Origins, Management and Performance* (Aldershot: Gower).

Jones, G. (1994) 'British Multinationals and British Business since 1850', in Kirby and Rose (eds), *Business Enterprise in Modern Britain*.

Jones, G. (1996) *The Evolution of International Business. An Introduction* (London: Routledge).

Jones, G. and H. G. Schroter (1993) *The Rise of the Multinationals in Continental Europe* (Aldershot: Edward Elgar).

Jones, R. and O. Marriot (1970) *Anatomy of a Merger: A History of GEC, AEI, and English Electric* (London: Jonathan Cape).

Kanter, R. M. (1983) *The Change Masters: Corporate Entrepreneurs at Work* (London: Unwin).

Lazonick, W. (1986) 'The Cotton Industry', in Elbaum and Lazonick.

Lewchuk, W. (1987) *American Technology and the British Motor Industry* (Cambridge: Cambridge University Press).

Littler, C. (1983) 'Taylorism in Britain in the Interwar Years', in Howard Gospel and Craig Littler (eds), *Managerial Strategies and Industrial Relations* (London: Heinemann).

Lundberg, F. (1968) *The Rich and the Super-Rich* (London: Nelson).

Macrosty, H. W. (1907) *The Trust Movement in British Industry: A Study of Business Organisation* (London: Longmans, Green).

Maddison, A. (1991) *Dynamic Forces in Capitalist Development: A Long-Run Comparative View* (Oxford: Oxford University Press).

McIvor, A. J. (1996) *Organised Capital: Employers' Associations and Industrial Relations in Northern England, 1880–1939* (Cambridge: Cambridge University Press).

McLellan, D. (1980) *The Thought of Karl Marx: An Introduction*, 2nd edn (London: Macmillan).

Meeks, G. (1977) *Disappointing Marriage: A Study of the Gains from Merger* (Cambridge: Cambridge University Press).

Morikawa, H. (1992) *Zaibatsu: The Rise and Fall of Family Enterprise Groups in Japan* (Tokyo: Tokyo University Press).

Nelson, D. (1995) *Managers and Workers: Origins of the Twentieth-century Factory System in the United States, 1880–1920*, 2nd edn (Madison, Wis.: University of Wisconsin Press).

Newell, E. (1998) 'The Irremediable Evil: British Copper Smelters' Collusion and the Cornish Mining Industry, 1725–1865', in Kristine Bruland and Patrick O'Brien (eds), *From Family Firms to Corporate Capitalism: Essays in Business and Industrial History in Honour of Peter Mathias* (Oxford: Clarendon Press).

Nicholas, S. (1991) 'The Expansion of British Multinational Companies: Testing for Managerial Failure', in James Foreman-Peck (ed.), *New Perspectives on the Late Victorian Economy: Essays in Quantitative Economic History, 1860–1914* (Cambridge: Cambridge University Press).

Panic, M. (1982) 'International Direct Investment in Conditions of Structural Disequilibrium: UK Experience since the 1960s', in J. Black and J. Dunning (eds), *International Capital Movements* (London: Macmillan).

Pavitt, K. (ed.) (1980) *Technical Innovation and British Economic Performance* (London: Macmillan).

Payne, P. L. (1979) *Colvilles and the Scottish Steel Industry* (Oxford: Clarendon Press).

Pollard, S. (1965) *The Genesis of Modern Management: A Study of the Industrial Revolution in Great Britain* (London: Edward Arnold).

Porter, M. E. (1985) *Competitive Advantage: Creating and Sustaining Superior Performance* (New York: Free Press).

Porter, M. E. (1990) *The Competitive Advantage of Nations* (London: Macmillan).

Reader, W. J. (1975) *Imperial Chemical Industries: A History*. Vol. 2. *The First Quarter Century, 1926–1952* (London: Oxford University Press).

Reid, M. (1988) *All-Change in the City: The Revolution in Britain's Financial Sector* (Basingstoke: Macmillan).

Roberts, D. (1979) *Paternalism in Early Victorian England* (New Brunswick, NJ: Rutgers University Press).

Rose, M. B. (1986) *The Gregs of Quarry Bank Mill: The Rise and Decline of a Family Firm, 1750–1914* (Cambridge: Cambridge University Press).

Rose, M. B. (ed.) (1995) *Family Business* (Aldershot: Edward Elgar).

Rostow, W. W. (1960) *The Stages of Economic Growth: A Non-Communist Manifesto* (Cambridge: Cambridge University Press).

Rubinstein, W. D. (1980) *Wealth and the Wealthy in the Modern World* (London: Croom Helm).

Rubinstein, W. D. (1981) *Men of Property: The Very Wealthy in Britain since the Industrial Revolution* (London: Croom Helm).

Rumelt, R. P. (1974) *Strategy, Structure and Economic Performance* (Cambridge Mass.: Harvard University Press).

Scranton, P. (1997) *Endless Novelty: Specialty Production and American Industrialisation, 1865–1925* (Princeton, NJ: Princeton University Press).

Shepherd, D., A. Silberston and R. Strange (1985) *British Manufacturing Investment Overseas* (London: Methuen).

Tedlow, R. S. and G. Jones (eds) (1993) *The Rise and Fall of Mass Marketing* (London: Routledge).

Thoms, D. and T. Donnelly (1985) *The Motor Car Industry in Coventry since the 1890s* (London: Croom Helm).

Smith, A. (1776; new edn 1937) *An Inquiry into the Nature and Causes of the wealth of Nations*, ed. E. Cannan (New York: Modern Library).

Tolliday, S. (1987) *Business, Banking, and Politics: The Case of British Steel, 1918–1939* (Cambridge, Mass.: Harvard University Press).

Tweedale, G. (1995) *Steel City: Entrepreneurship, Strategy, and Technology in Sheffield, 1743–1993* (Oxford: Clarendon Press).

Tweedale, G. and D. J. Jeremy (1999) 'Compensating the Workers: Industrial Injury and Compensation in the British Asbestos Industry, 1930s–60s', *Business History*, vol. 41, no. 2, pp. 102–20.

UK Parliamentary Papers (1890–91) *Report to the Board of Trade on the Relation of Wages in Certain Industries to the Cost of Production*, vol. LXXVIII, c. 6535.

Ure, A. (1835) *The Philosophy of Manufactures or an Exposition of the Scientific, Moral, and Commercial Economy of the Factory System in Great Britain* (London: Charles Knight).

Wada, K. (1994) 'Inter-Firm Relationships between Toyota and Its Suppliers in a Historical Perspective', in T. Yuzawa, *Japanese Business Success: The Evolution of a Strategy* (London: Routledge).

Weidenbaum, M. and S. Hughes (1996) *The Bamboo Network: How Expatriate Chinese Entrepreneurs Are Creating a New Economic Superpower in Asia* (New York: Free Press).

Whittington, R. and M. Mayer (2000) *The European Corporation: Strategy, Structure, and Social Science* (Oxford: Oxford University Press).

Williams, T. I. (1981) *A History of the British Gas Industry* (Oxford: Oxford University Press).

Zeitlin, J. (1983) 'The Labour Strategies of British Engineering Employers, 1890–1922', in Howard Gospel and Craig Littler (eds), *Managerial Strategies and Industrial Relations* (London: Heinemann).

Zeitlin, J. (1985) 'Engineers and Compositors: A Comparison', in R. Harrison and J. Zeitlin (eds), *Divisions of Labour: Skilled Workers and Technological Change in Nineteenth Century England* (Brighton: Harvester).

Part 2
The Firm

5 Game Theory and Strategy

Stephen Regan

Basic principles

Game theory is a set of tools for answering questions about how economic agents will react when what they do affects the actions of others. For instance in an industry where there are only a few firms, all of which can observe each other's behaviour, how will these firms take each other's reactions into account when formulating their strategies? Questions such as 'Can we use pricing to increase our sales without causing a price war?' or 'Can we defend our market against a potential new entrant?' are the sorts of question game theory seeks to address.

Game theory is thus the theory of how firms (and others) *interact* rather than act. There are a great many models of such interactive choices in game theory, and many interesting theories about how firms in particular solve such problems.

Case study

The situation

The board of directors of Sheffield Readymix Ltd are considering whether to reduce the firm's production capacity for ready mixed concrete. The date is October 1997, and the local market has two principal producers: Sheffield Readymix and Rotherham Concrete. Rotherham Concrete has roughly twice the market share of Sheffield Readymix. Prices are falling due to declining demand – more and more builders are able to mix their own concrete on site using portable mixing machines. This gives them lower costs and full control over when the mix is made, which greatly improves the cost effectiveness of mixing on site.

The current projection is that the demand for readymix will fall by 5 per cent per year, on average, for the foreseeable future, making it difficult for both Sheffield Readymix and Rotherham Concrete to maintain the same level of capacity without cutting prices. They both know this, and they both know the other knows it.

The conversation

Laurence Anthony is the sales director of Sheffield Readymix. He is concerned about maintaining sales in the declining market. He has asked for a meeting with the finance director, Annabel Grace, who is concerned about the profitability of aggressive price cutting to gain market share in a declining market. Derek Anderson, the MD of the company, is also present.

Laurence: For the last eight quarters our sales have declined steadily at about 1½ per cent quarter on quarter, and yet we have maintained price. As a result our unit costs are rising since we are spreading our fixed overheads over reduced volumes. What I want to know is, why doesn't it make sense to cut prices, and get the volume we need to keep costs down? A 1 per cent cut in price will bring about a 2 per cent increase in demand for our products in this market, which will lead to reductions in unit costs and an improvement in margins.

Annabel: That would be true if we could be sure that Rotherham Concrete won't react. If they do, then we will just have started a price war, and we will effectively be slitting our own throats. With their volume they could flood the market and force us out of business very quickly.

Derek: So what's your strategy, Annabel?

Annabel: I think the name of the game here is to stay in the market as long as possible, and that means both us and Rotherham Concrete co-operating to keep margins as high as possible, for as long as possible.

Laurence: But our costs are rising, our volumes are falling, and we are just not reacting. It seems irresponsible not to try to be competitive. At the moment we are just allowing our business to run itself into the ground. If you want to keep us in business as long as possible, surely we have to find a way of forcing Rotherham Concrete out of the market.

Derek: Laurence has got a very strong point – surely there has to come a time when we try to force Rotherham out, and wouldn't it be better to do it sooner rather than later? If we cut price now, we have the reserves to sustain losses for a while, and we also have the chance of forcing out our main rival sooner. This would give us longer to run the industry after their exit if we were to win the price war. The longer we have the industry to ourselves, the more money we make.

Laurence: I completely agree with Derek. I think we have to take a long-term, strategic view and manage our own contraction. We could have several years of profitable monopoly if we force Rotherham out now, or a couple of years of bleeding to death jointly if we don't. I don't see the logic of trying to maximize short-term gains. If we start a price war we make short-term losses, but in the long term, more profits.

Annabel: I hear what you both say, but I still think we shouldn't forget the likely reactions of Rotherham to our actions. It is not immediately obvious that we would gain from a price war, so there is a risk. I don't like taking risks I don't have to. I've prepared a spreadsheet, which I'd like you to look at. [Annabel clicks open the Excel File on her PC, and turns the screen so that her two colleagues are able to see the display below.]

Laurence: So what's your point, Annabel?

Annabel: We don't have to start a price war to force Rotherham out – we can wait them out. They'll have gone by January 2002 anyway. If I know this, then they do to. We don't have to do anything. A price war would just waste both our and their resources.

		Sheffield alone	Rotherham alone	Rotherham and Sheffield together
		Net profit per cubic metre (% return on sales)		
Date				
2001	January	9	6	2
	July	8	5	1
2002	January	7	4	0
	July	6	3	−1
2003	January	5	2	−2
	July	4	1	−3
2004	January	3	0	−4
	July	2	−1	−5
2005	January	1	−2	−6
	July	0	−3	−7
2006	January	−1	−4	−8
	July	−2	−5	−9

Derek: I don't see why they *have* to leave in January 2002. Surely if they start a price war, and force us out, they can make profits right through to January 2004.

Annabel: Quite right Rotherham *have* to leave by January 2004 – even if they force us out before then. That means they know we can make profits of 6 per cent on sales, cumulatively, that is, an average of 2 per cent per half year from January 2004 to July 2006, after they have left, if we hang on.

Derek: Which means they know we know we can cover any losses we make by sharing the market with them right back to July 2002.

Annabel: So if we *are* still there in July 2002, they know they can't force us out after that, so they would do better to leave. In fact they may leave in January 2002, because they'll just be covering costs for the first half of next year.

Derek: So we can expect to treble our return on sales, starting sometime in 2002, if we keep our capacity as it is.

Laurence: Doesn't this make a price war even more certain? Won't they have to force us out before they start to make a loss in July 2002?

Annabel: I don't think that makes sense. They should be able to see that the value of the industry is greater to us than it is to them. Thus if they start a price war they won't change our relative positions – they'll just turn the industry into a loss-making one quicker. This will just force their own exit faster than we would force them out without a price war. They know we won't want to start a price war – since it will reduce our overall profits – neither we nor they can benefit by making a single penny of losses here, and neither of us has to. They know that, we know that, and we have to believe they'll play the game in the way we see it.

Laurence: I think I'll phone their sales director for a round of golf this week.

Annabel: You do that. I hear he plays a good game. Maybe you should let him win!

The issues

This conversation reveals the importance of certain key ideas from game theory, applied to a business problem:

- *Understanding the game*: Annabel is able to calculate various *moves* or strategies available to each of the two players. She has identified the *payoffs* in each of the potential strategy profiles in each time period from now to the end of the game for each of the players.
- *Reasoning strategically*: effectively this means designing strategies based on your assessment of your opponents' best responses to each of your potential strategies. Your best response to their best response is the correct strategy for both of you. In the language of game theory, it is the *equilibrium*[1] of the game. One of the main insights from game theory is that there is always *at least one* equilibrium strategy.

Key contributions

The origins of game theory

Game theory was first developed by John von Neumann and Oskar Morgenstern, who in 1944 published a pathbreaking book called *Theory of Games and Economic Behaviour*. Von Neumann was a mathematician, although the term does not begin to cover the immense contribution he made to modern thought in a great number of areas. He was a pure mathematician but worked in theoretical physics with the community at Princeton University that included the greatest concentration of scientists in the twentieth century, such as Einstein, Nils Bohr, Richard Feynman and others. He built computers, designed logistics systems for the Pacific War, and his and Morgenstern's[2] game theory was the first successful attempt to develop a mathematical theory for human behaviour. Basically von Neumann and Morgenstern's idea was that in many areas of human activity (including business) people solve problems rather like the way in which they solve problems when they play games – they decide what to do on the basis of what they think others will do, including making decisions aimed at influencing what others do. If mathematics could solve these game type problems, then it would go a long way towards illuminating human behaviour. This is what game theory has been doing ever since 1944.

The initial applications of game theory were in military strategy, where it was used to design optimal battlefield strategies. For instance in order to predict the best strategies for antisubmarine surveillance it is important to get in inside the mind of your rival. This is exactly what game theory does, and hence its popularity during the Cold War.

The greatest uptake of game theory since the 1950s has been in economics, where it has revolutionized the way in which economists model oligopoly to study rivalry between large firms. Game theory is also popular with biologists, who use it to study interactions between animals and have developed successful models of everything from optimal foraging behaviour for baboons to the distribution of tongue lengths in bees.[3]

Game theory is beginning to make inroads into strategic management, as economists develop more insight into the practical applications of their previously rather theoretical models. We shall now look at the key principles of game theory as it has been applied to strategic management.

The key principles of games

Conflict and cooperation

A central insight from game theory that is of great value to managers is that there are always two sides to every game. In one dimension, all the players have come together to achieve some shared goal (in business, to create value). For instance even in warfare there is often a subtle cooperative agenda underneath the most bloody encounter, without which the two sides would not be able to structure their interactions.

However as well as cooperation there is also a degree of competition in every game. Once the shared objective of the game is achieved there is tremendous pressure for each contributor to that objective to make certain that he or she walks away with the biggest possible share of whatever is created. Thus games that appear to be highly cooperative (such as family interactions) are often highly competitive; while games that appear to be purely competitive (such as warfare or business competition) are often played in subtly cooperative ways.

In business both aspects of the game have to be played as well as possible. You have to cooperate *and* compete to succeed in business. This has been captured by two game theorists who led the way in applying the subject to business: Adam Brandenberger and Barry Nalebuff, who use a strategy tool they call the value net (this will be discussed in the section on tools and techniques).

This chapter defines game theory as the economic theory of strategic *behaviour* and the economic theory of strategic *rationality*. Implicit in this is an economic definition of what a strategy is: *choice in an interdependent context*. It is about how to act and how to think about your rival's actions. Game theory is about getting inside the mind of your rivals. What could be more powerful in business strategy than this? Thus game theory is the theory of interdependent choice behaviour and the theory of what is rational in such a context. The reason for this insistence on the twin meaning of game theory is that solution concepts in games depend crucially on equilibria in both beliefs (rationality) and actions (behaviour). (As can be seen in the Sheffield Readymix conversation above, Annabel does not just act strategically, she also thinks strategically.)

The economic theory of strategic behaviour

The remit of game theory as the theory of strategic behaviour in business is not narrowly defined (for instance as interfirm rivalry) but extends widely, for instance it includes managerial behaviour inside firms, regulation by government, and industrial relations bargaining between employers and employees, to name but a few of the more common strategic problems where game theory has been useful. Since many of these problems involve choices made by an individual within an organization or actions by institutions outside the organization, then game theory includes more than corporate strategy: it might be described as a general theory of strategy, including competitive, corporate and cooperative strategy.

Also, the methodology of game theory is mathematically based and thus forces the strategist to be more explicit about the nature of the relationships being modelled and then to abide by those relationships. Informal conjecture about how one rival *may* respond to another is not what game theory does; game theory quite rigorously reduces the possible sets of actions the players can reasonably be expected to demonstrate. In the immense complexity of business, game theory provides a useful simplicity.

What is a game?

There are two ways to represent a game: the strategic form and the extensive form. The strategic form is a simpler, reduced form that shows the players, their strategies and their payoffs, with each player taking one side of a matrix (Figure 5.2, page 98).

A game in extensive form is a richer representation and makes use of a device called a game tree (Figure 5.1). This shows not only the players, the strategies and the payoffs, but also the order of the moves in the game and the information each player has about the game at each point in time. It is also able to represent the game as a sequence of smaller games (subgames). The game in extensive form (the game tree) should be the preferred tool for business strategists due to its greater detail.

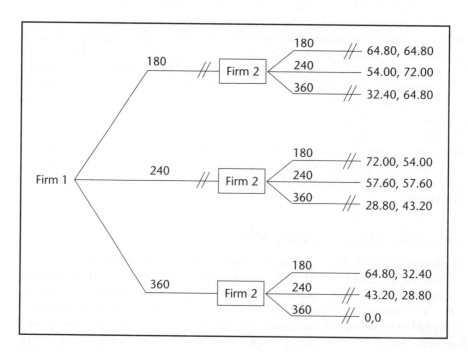

FIGURE 5.1 *The water melon game: an example of extensive form games*

In Figure 5.1, firm 1 and firm 2 are producers of water melons. Each has three strategies (choices) – a low output strategy (180 melons supplied), a medium output strategy (240 melons) and a high output strategy (360 melons). There are two players, each with three choices and thus $3 \times 3 = 9$ potential outcomes, represented by the branches of the (game) tree on the extreme right-hand side. The numbers at the ends of each of the nine branches are the payoffs to each player from that combination of strategies. The first number is firm 1's payoff, and the second is firm 2's payoff. These payoffs represent dollars of profit resulting from that particular outcome. The numbers on the branches leading to the right are the strategies of each player. Thus if firm 1 produces 180 melons and firm 2 produces 180 melons, then these firms get $64.80 of profits each. In this game firm 1 gets to move first, and firm 2 moves second. What game theory allows us to do is to:

- Model the strategic situation in the way we have just done. We have identified the players, their strategies, their move orders and their payoffs. Already we have evolved a useful way of structuring the strategic problem.
- Game theory also allows us to solve the game. This means we can predict the most rational way to play the game, which could be very useful.

To see how good you are at strategy, before we work out the answer using game theory, answer the following questions:

- Will firm 1 be better off to move first, or will firm 2 benefit by being able to watch what firm 1 does?
- Who will walk away from this game with the highest pay off?

Now let us see if you were right. We solve this sort of (extensive) game by a method known as foldback. We work out what firm 2 will do first, and then work back to firm 1's best strategy after that.

If firm 2 is faced with the three choices at the top of the tree – that is, the three strategies that are responses to firm 1 producing 180 – then firm 2 will produce 240, since this gives it a profit of $72.00, which is higher than the $64.80 it will get by producing either 180 or 360. We show this by blocking off the two strategies it does not choose with oblique strokes (Figure 5.1).

If firm 2 is put into the middle node it will choose 240 for the same reason (although it will receive less profit, since in this case firm 1 will produce more and this extra volume will suppress market prices and thus profits).

If firm 1 chooses 360, then firm 2 will maximize profits by producing a low volume (180).

We then 'fold back' to consider which strategy firm 1 and firm 2 will actually adopt. We assume that firm 1 has correctly drawn the game tree (or that it intuitively understands the game tree as we have drawn it). So firm 1 knows that only three outcomes matter. It has to choose between profits of $54.00 (along the track 180/240), $57.60 (240/240) or $64.8 (360/180). This means it will choose 360, which gives it the highest payoff ($64.80) and firm 2 will choose 180. Hence the payoffs will be $64.80 profit to firm 1 and $32.40 to firm 2.

Thus in answer to the questions asked above: firm 1 is better off by moving first – there are first mover advantages in this game; and firm 1 makes twice as much profit as firm 2.

You may be upset by this logic. Imagine you are firm 2, why don't you just tell firm 1 that unless it produces no more than 240, you will produce 360? If it agrees and produces 240, you will produce 240. The total payoffs will be higher, and you may even promise that you will reimburse firm 1 with the difference between \$57.60 and \$64.80 – this still leaves you with \$50.40,[4] which is significantly more than the \$32.40 you will get without such a deal.

If this is the way you have been thinking then you are to be commended, because (1) this is exactly the way in which many firms react strategically in such a situation (for instance this is the way OPEC has run the world oil industry since 1973 – restricting output and sharing the higher profits amongst the players); (2) this sort of cooperative behaviour between players is where state of the art game theory has been working for some time; and (3) the next game we look at, the prisoners' Dilemma (Figure 5.2), shows exactly how such agreements (known as cartels) tend to break up.[5]

| | | Player B | |
		Cooperate	Defect
Player A	Cooperate	3,3	0,4
	Defect	4,0	1,1

FIGURE 5.2   *The prisoners' dilemma*

The story behind the game is as follows. Two spies are caught behind enemy lines. They are given the chance to turn each other in (defect from each other) or to stick to their previous agreement not to do this (cooperate with each other). Their payoffs reflect these moves. If player A cooperates and B defects, player A will be shot (payoff zero) and B will be released to spy for the captor. If A cooperates and B cooperates they will both be treated as civilians and given a light prison sentence. B's payoff will be identical to A's. If they both defect they will be tortured for further information. The payoffs here are in utilities, which are numerical representations of happiness. In business applications we often look at the payoffs in terms of profit, but the principle is the same – the number games we are looking at represent the satisfaction each player has with that outcome. By convention, the first number in a cell represents the payoff to the player on the left (player A in this case) and the second number represents the payoff to the player on top (player B).

Here the best strategy for B is to defect (no matter what A does), and thus to defect is the dominant strategy for B. However this is only the case if B is unable to make a deal with A (rather like the cartel in the previous game), in which case B may prefer to choose to cooperate if he or she can be sure that A will also cooperate. This deal-making type of game theory is known as cooperative game theory, and it includes an extra dimension to non-cooperative game theory since it makes B's strategy dependent not only on what A does, but also on B's beliefs about the A. This means that solution concepts (equilibria) are much more uncertain in cooperative game theory, but such cooperative behaviour and the modelling of beliefs are fundamental to corporate strategy problems such as entry deterrence or structuring a joint venture.

If A cooperates, then B gets a payoff of 4 if he defects, but only 3 if he co-operates. So he maximizes his payoffs if he defects whenever A cooperates. What makes this a dominant strategy is that B should defect even if A does not co-operate since he gets a payoff of zero when he cooperates and A defects, and a payoff of 1 if he defects when A defects. So he will defect. In this sense to defect is better than to cooperate for B in all cases, and is thus his dominant strategy. Whatever the equilibrium of this game, B will employ his dominant strategy, and thus we have an outcome where at least one player defects. The other player knows this, and this knowledge greatly simplifies the game for her. (It may not greatly please her, but it certainly does simplify matters).

The game's solution thus unfolds as rational sets of calculations between players about their best response to the other's possible actions. At a deeper level, we have seen that notions such as dominance also allow us to understand how the other player *should* play the game, rather than just how he or she might. This is quite deep reasoning, and helpful since it allows you to calculate how you must play the game. It is a theory of strategy (if strategy means choice).

Here the grim logic of the game is that to cooperate is *never* chosen, it is irrational to cooperate for the reasons outlined above. This gives a particu-larly gloomy view of the value of rationality (so defined), since clearly human beings cooperate at least as much as they defect. Most biologists suggest that the combination of large brain and intense cooperation is what is most unique about human beings, and the basis of our success as a species. Many read-ers would probably opt to cooperate in the prisoners' dilemma and believe that their fellow players would do so too.

Solutions to games

A game in strategic form: matching pennies Players A and B independently choose whether to turn a coin heads up or tails up. If the outcome is heads-heads, or tails-tails, player A gets player B's coin. The entries in the cells of the payoff matrix represent this. If the outcome is heads-heads or tails-tails, then player A scores +1 and player B scores −1 (Figure 5.3). This makes these

FIGURE 5.3   *Matching pennies game*

outcomes zero sum (since −1 + 1 = 0). The game is symmetrical, meaning that heads-tails or tails-heads gives player B + 1 and player A − 1. The first entry in each cell is player A's payoff from that strategy profile and the second is B's payoff.

This game is a zero sum game since the players' payoffs sum to zero for each of the outcomes. In other words the game does not add value. In corporate strategy we may often be interested in value-adding games (positive sum) and value-destroying games (negative sums).

You may like to conjecture what you *should* do in a game of this type if you were player A. Your preferred outcome is head-heads or tails-tails. Actually the best you can do is flip the coin and play whichever face lands up. Anything else will let B beat you if he or she adopts the headflipping strategy. Can you see why? Note here that the rational strategy is to leave it to chance – there are many (more realistic and complex) games in business where leaving it to chance works well. The example below is a game in extensive form that relates to a business situation.

In many cases the players will wish to hide their future intentions from each other, and game theory gains much as a methodology if it is able to model such behaviour in a systematic way. When a player chooses a given strategy with certainty, say because it is a dominant strategy, then the agent is said to have a *pure* strategy. However, when the probability of a strategy is less than 1, then the agent is said to have a mixed strategy, since there is a more than zero chance that he or she will play another strategy. This adds an extra problem for the other player(s). Matching pennies (see above) is an example of a game where each player's best strategy is mixed: to play heads and tails randomly, with a 50 per cent chance of each.[6] Game theory is beginning to find out how to apply such models to highly uncertain business problems, for instance in order to solve risk management problems.

Conclusions

This section has attempted to show some of the main features of game theory as it exists today in economics. Its conclusions are that game theory is a new and disciplined language for a range of strategy problems. This language offers the strategist a range of modelling options when confronted with the facts of a particular industry. For instance zero or variable sum games, one shot or repeated games, and pure or mixed strategy games. This classification system gives access to sets of tools that have been developed specifically to solve these problems. We shall explore these in the next section.

The second major conclusion of this section is that game theory is beginning to shed light on what is rational. The analysis of *strategic rationality* is finally beginning to bridge the gap between the ideal 'rational economic man' and the actual, boundedly rational corporate men and women who populate the real world. This project has hardly begun, but it offers a promising role for game theory in understanding business problems.

Game theory in strategy

Game theory is a very general tool with wide applicability in many areas. It has entered the language of strategic management through the application of economic theory to the problems managers face. In particular game theory is widely used to analyze not only the behaviour of managers within firms, but also the structure of firms themselves and the nature of relationships between firms (for example the types of contract or alliance firms might agree with each other). Beyond this, game theory has made significant contributions to the understanding of a very wide range of problems, such as in biology, political science, military strategy and psychology, to name just the main ones. Given the broad range of fields where game theory has been applied it would be surprising if it was absent from the range of tools we use to understand strategic management. We shall now apply game theory to a number of real problems faced by strategic managers.

Context: game theory's application to the competitive structure of the US car industry in the early 1980s

Game theory has been employed as a device to analyze the business environment from a strategic group perspective. The advantage of game theory is its ability to show which forces are able to determine the number and size of strategic groups, and – out of the whole range of possible strategic groups – which will be viable and which not for which firms, and how long the strategic groups will last.

The implication here is that this sort of analysis can identify those strategies which are likely to have long-term viability. For instance the reorientation of the US car manufacturers in the 1980s in response to the entry of Japanese producers can be analyzed via game theory. Broadly, the strategic variables upon which firms competed in this context were cost, quality and innovation. Ford was average in quality, high in cost and average in innovation. General

Motors had chosen/evolved an average cost. The development of the industry was as follows:

1. The strategic group that Ford was in was not feasible (efficient in the game theoretic sense), in that the strategy it was playing was dominated by other strategies. This was evidenced by the fact that Ford's performance was declining in relation to that of GM. However it is not obvious that it should have sought to reduce costs, since another 'strategy move' might have been preferable in a game theory context (for example to improve quality and maintain cost, or to improve innovation and reduce cost).
2. The arrival of Japanese producers was characterized as the opening up of a new strategic group (low cost, average innovation, high quality).
3. Ford responded with a high-cost, high-innovation, high-quality strategy. General Motors went for low cost, high quality and low innovation (that is, its previously average innovation was now below average, due to the strategy moves by both the Japanese and Ford).

The result was that General Motors' new strategy was no longer efficient but Ford's was, in that its performance began to improve in terms of profits. The Japanese strategy was also dominant.

Thus what game theory could do for a firm such as Sheffield Readymix in respect of analyzing its market context would be to identify potentially viable long-term positions, by allowing it to predict with more confidence the likely responses of its rivals to any strategy it adopts. This is virtually what Annabel managed to do in the discussion at the start of this chapter. The approach could be taken further, for instance if the company chose to expand into home insulation, game theory would indicate the likely response of incumbent firms in the new market.

Culture: game theory and human behaviour

Rationality has a central place in economics in the sense that explanations of phenomena are regarded as part of mainstream economics if they make contact with some version of the theory of rational choice. One complaint often made about game theory by strategists is that it idealizes perfectly rational behaviour.

Managers want practical tools that are based on realistic assumptions about the way the world works, and if game theory asserts that every decision is made by ideally rational individuals, most managers with experience of how decisions are actually made will question the extent of its potential contribution. So we have to ask, what can game theory, or economics for that matter, add to our understanding of a boundedly rational world? To put it at its most extreme, can game theory help us to understand the emotional and passionate nature of real people and real decisions. The answer is a very emphatic yes!

For instance one variant of game theory is known as drama theory, which suggests that in many contexts the best thing you can do is to indicate that you will not act in your own best interests. For example there is a famous game called Chicken, which is central to the James Dean film *Rebel without a Cause*. In this film two young men agree to get in their cars and drive towards a cliff – the first person to swerve away from the cliff will be the chicken and the other will be the winner. Such games are an important part of display behaviour amongst young men. When we analyze these games, the result is usually that the two men never actually meet and the game never takes place. The real game occurs during the weeks before the car race takes place, when the players play out roles that are designed to intimidate the other into not turning up. Much modern military strategy is of this type, deriving from cold war experience, where the occurrence of an actual battle would be seen as failure.

Thus game theory can be seen as an important way of understanding all sorts of interactions between players that are designed to influence the emotions of the other players. The emotional element is not always as negative as this, for instance game theory has been used to model the dynamics of relations between lovers as they establish trust with each other (deterrence models, on the other hand, are very good for modelling divorce). In the Sheffield Readymix example, think about the script and the drama of the interactions, think about what game was really being played between the players. In the game within the game, is it not the case that Annabel won and Laurence lost? Could Laurence have lost the argument and still won the game? What if Laurence had deliberately provoked Annabel into losing her temper? How could he have done this?

One outcome of this concern with the interaction between games and the emotions of the players is the definition of what is strategically rational. For instance when we assume that all players are equally rational we might use a concept known as the 'transparency of reason', which is the notion that any player who arrives at a conclusion about a game has arrived at the same conclusion as all the other players, and they know this and he knows they know. However this kind of outcome is very close to a deterministic notion of rationality: it excludes players from arriving at different conclusions, and even from believing in the possibility of different conclusions being arrived at by others. This is clearly nonsense! So where do we go with this notion of rationality?

Whether or not this transparency of reason is empirically true is not the key question, although it is certainly a very strong one. Two of the many weaker versions that suggest themselves are: (1) all players are rational, but not all believe others to be rational; and (2) not all players are rational, but they believe they are and that others are.

The point is that these non-transparent notions of rationality may be closer to the actual nature of rationality than the idealized common-knowledge version above, and may thus attract the interest of the corporate strategy community. Game theory is the ideal tool for exploring the logical possibilities for these different notions of strategic reason, and this would seem to be a project that parallels some of the interest in the cognitive aspects of strategy. All we are saying here is that if you are going to play a game you have to make assumptions about the degree of rationality and emotion the other players will bring to the game, and play accordingly.

Competing

Signalling, broadly defined as communication between players, is an important concept in game theory. It is not an entirely new concept: for instance there are strong similarities between signalling and what Porter (1985) describes as building a competitor profile, but the analysis in game theory is slightly different. Here a player has private information about her or his own preferences (players are assumed to know their own preferences), but makes this information available to the other players by the signals she or he makes. The value to the agents of information on the other agents' true type is immense, since it allows them to make a better choice about their own actions, and thus agents have a strong incentive to form beliefs about each other.

There are models that consider what this concept means for organizations in terms of reputation building within and between them. For instance if I believe that firm A is unaggressive then I will exclude from my assumptions any potentially aggressive strategies (that is, I will assign a low probability to their likely occurrence and act accordingly). However firm A may be much better off if I do not believe this, since its best strategy may be to threaten aggression so that it will cause me to act in a way favourable to it. For instance if it wants to keep me out of its market by threatening aggression it will attempt to develop a reputation for aggressiveness, and the best way to do this is by signalling.

Signalling comes in three types. The least sophisticated is called 'cheap talk' and is just what it says it is: you make promises and threats that you have no intention of keeping. For instance cheap talk in the Sheffield Readymix case would occur if Rotherham Concrete phoned its rivals and said it intended to stay in the market for at least five more years. This is a threat, and the assumption is that when faced with having to carry out the threat (that is, lose money) it will back off. Therefore cheap talk generally means promising to do things you are never likely to do.

The two other types of signalling are reputation and commitment. The difference between reputation and cheap talk can be summed up by the phrase 'actions speak louder than words'. Here signalling constitutes repeatedly acting in a certain way. For instance in a supply chain relationship both parties have a lot to gain by acting cooperatively, and they signal that they are like this to other potential contractors by refusing to damage their existing relationship (even though there may be a short-term gain).

Commitment involves making your signal irrevocable. For instance if you want to defend your market share you might sign contracts with all your customers to guarantee you will match any other price they are offered. If these are legally binding and automatic, so that you have no choice but to honour them, then you have made a commitment. Commitment is a very deep signal, since it involves relinquishig your freedom to choose further action should something happen to trigger the commitment. This can be applied to the problem of entry deterrence, modelled as a game (Figure 5.4: 'Prey' means predatory price to drive the rival out, share means to accommodate entry and share the market with the new rival).

In this game, with a finite number of potential entrants, *share* strictly

	Entrant	
	Enter	No entry
Share	2,2	5,1
Prey	0.0	5,1

Incumbent (row label)

The entry deterrence game   FIGURE 5.4

dominates *prey* when there is incomplete information. The entrants know this and will thus enter (if there are no other barriers). However the incumbent also knows this and will therefore act to affect the entrants' beliefs, perhaps by cutting price in response to other threatening behaviours – the only thing that will convince the entrants not to enter is a belief that the incumbent is irrational; that is, that he or she does not know (what is common knowledge) that he or she should not cut prices. A nice variant of this is that entrants may look at the reputation-building behaviour as a sign of weakness, and thus interpret it as a sign they should enter the industry and compete against the very firm that is acting aggressively.

This has led to a Dr Strangelove[7] version of the entry deterrence game. When reputation is not enough to deter entry, then a higher level of signalling is to make an irrevocable commitment to act in a certain way if the entrant comes into the market. The Dr Strangelove deterrent is the construction of a doomsday machine – a machine that automatically detonates the industry from the moment a competitor enters. Such a strategy, tying one's hands in advance, is referred to as commitment – a promise to act in certain ways in the future.

A common version of the doomsday machine is limit pricing. This involves making a commitment to supply a quantity of output from now until far into the future, the consequence of which is a commitment to drive down price whenever an entrant comes into the market. This effectively means that the incumbent firm commits itself to destroying both its profits and those of the entrant, and thus the entrant will be deterred insofar as it believes in the commitment of the incumbent. The incumbent's only problem is to make the commitment irrevocable. This might be done by signing contracts with suppliers (for example take or pay contracts) or by building a new plant with heavy fixed costs that will provide the capacity to produce output at very low marginal cost if a new entrant comes in. This is risky, but it happens, for instance large steel producers sign such contracts with major car producers.

Cooperative strategy

Perhaps the highest profile contribution of game theory to corporate strategy has been in the area of cooperative strategy (Brandenburger and Nalebuff, 1995). The branch of game theory known as cooperative game theory deals with situations where the players are able to communicate with each other (this is sometimes known as bargaining theory, which better describes the behaviour it models). It is important to note that not all bargaining is cooperative – thus bargaining theory could be used to analyze highly competitive games (zero sum) as well as less hostile ones. Cooperative strategy is best thought of as a positive sum game, or as turning a zero sum game into a positive one, using the techniques of game theory.

Barry Nalebuff (1991, 1993; Brandenberger and Nalebuff, 1995) uses such game theory in precisely this way in his consultancy activities. The examples he uses are relationships between banks and their customers, where the pay-offs to the customers can be altered by the banks (by changing their tariffs) in such a way that it rewards behaviour that the banks want the customers engage in. Both the banks and the customers benefit.

The same logic is applied to relationships with competitors. For instance the General Motors credit card enables customers to build up a discount of $7000 off General Motors cars, thus locking in customers and allowing the company to maintain prices. In response Ford elected to introduce its own card and keep its prices high by locking in customers, rather than trying to pick up General Motors' non-card customers by means of price cutting. The ramifications of such tactics are felt in the banking industry, the members of which lose out to this cooperative strategy but are unable to alter the game within the industry, which is bounded by the cooperative players, to everyone's benefit.

The modern theory of strategic alliances is largely based on such models.

Change and control

Information asymmetries involve limits to the information set of one player *vis-à-vis* another. These limits are of two kinds: incomplete information and imperfect information. *Incomplete information* is where one player does not know what the preferences of the other player are (but he does know his own). The other player's preference function defines her *type*, and lack of knowledge about her type involves lack of knowledge about what her payoffs are to any given outcome. *Imperfect information* is where one of the players (at least) is unable to observe all of the actions of the other players. Information asymmetries are central to problems of agency, and thus control.

Within this informational architecture a great deal of modelling of the effects of information asymmetries can be done. For instance it is possible to model situations where players forget their own past decisions, which opens up some interesting possibilities for strategy theorists: for instance when the player is a senior management team that loses one or more of its key members during the game.

One important group of incomplete information games are those concerned with signalling. In such games players form beliefs about other players, and they update these after each round of the game. Signalling is where one player acts to affect the beliefs of the other.

This kind of thinking is in line with a lot of the ideas on bounded rationality that permeate the strategy literature. With bounded information, even complete rationality produces indeterminate choices. Does this not admit the possibility that the adoption of rules of thumb may be as good as any other choice of rule?

When information is imperfect rather than incomplete, the principal can observe the outcomes of the agent's actions (such as profits) but not the actions themselves (such as effort or skill). The agency problem is to avoid over-or under-rewarding agents for their actions. Game theory is well suited to this analysis, since the agent is inclined to signal (bluff) the poorly informed principal, and this behaviour is well modelled within games of asymmetric information. Mechanism design is a branch of information economics that uses game theory to force agents to reveal this information, and thus to restore the principal's control over the agent, for example control over the worker by the manager, or of the manager by the shareholder.

Tools and techniques derived from game theory

Several well-known game theorists have attempted to produce practically relevant strategic tools for business managers. These have had limited success, largely because business problems are often much more complex than the stylized situations economists analyze using games. For instance business games are free-wheeling affairs that do not have a clear starting or ending point, where the strategies are often very difficult to describe (because they are so numerous) and where players are able to enter or leave the game at will. One way of capturing this is with the value net, a tool developed by Barry Nalebuff and Adam Brandenburger (1996). Their basic premise is that strategic behaviour is an attempt to change the nature of the game to one you are more likely to win. However it is better for players to choose the right game, rather than the right strategies in a game.

The value net

The value net (Figure 5.5) is a way of identifying the players in a game. The vertical axis represents the transactors. The horizontal axis represents players who are interactors rather than transactors; that is, they influence the outcome for everybody in the game, but no money changes hands. These interactors are of two types: those who sell outputs or buy inputs in competition with the competitors, and those who sell outputs and buy inputs in a way that adds value to the competitors' selling and buying activities. For instance when two airline companies buy aircraft from Boeing they complement each other's purchases since they both have the possibility of lowering costs via the economies of scale they generate. An airline and a hotel company are complementary in relation to their customers, since each one's product enhances the value of the other's. Two airlines may be complementors in the market for aviation fuel but competitors in the market for business air travel.

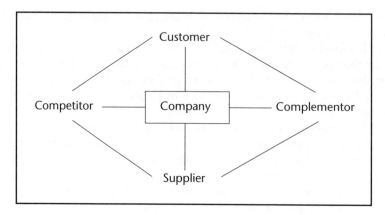

FIGURE 5.5

The value net

The value net thus gives the game structure by identifying the players and the relationships between them.

The game is defined first as a set of relationships between players. The idea behind the value net is that players come together to create value as well as to divide it up. The first of these activities is cooperative and the second is competitive – the players thus have both to cooperate and to compete with each other all the time, and this holds for all dimensions of the game. Excessive competition, as in the prisoners' dilemma, may be destructive for both parties. The purpose of the game is to structure the relationships in such a way as to walk away with the maximum value, even if this means taking away less than the other players. In this type of analysis a firm is as likely to be competitive with its customers as to cooperate with them, and as cooperative with its competitors as it is with its suppliers.

To apply the game, follow the following steps.

1. Draw the value net

Identify each of the players in each of the categories, for example for a university (Figure 5.6).

2. Identify values

The next step is to identify the value of each player in the game in terms of economic value added. This means adding up the total value of all the players. Draw the game without yourself as part of the value net, and add up the payoffs. The difference between the two totals is your value in the game – your value to the other players. If you are actually receiving less value than this, then you are playing too cooperatively and you should restructure the game to achieve a higher payoff for yourself.

One way to use the value net is to decide whether there is enough value in a game before you start to play it. Here again you draw the value net first with and then without your involvement. The difference between the two is

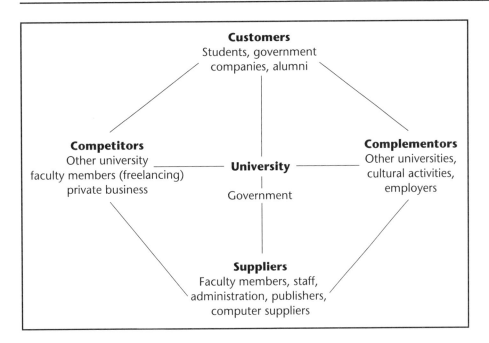

Value for a university **FIGURE 5.6**

the maximum value you can expect from the game – if this is not as high as you would like, you should either not enter the game or attempt to restructure the value net before you enter.

3. Change the game

If you do not like the look of the game you are in, or might soon be in, what can you do to improve the situation? One approach is to use a tool called PARTS, (Players, Added values, Rules, Tactics and Scope). You can reshape the game by changing any of these five constituents.

Players By drawing a value net for Sheffield Readymix we can assess how it might have played the game (Figure 5.7).

Sheffield Readymix can bring in extra players and thus increase its value in the game. The most obvious benefit is to be had by bringing in more customers – this will increase the value of the pie and increase the size of the slice owed to Readymix.[8] The only problem with this is it is difficult to do. However there may be certain things that Sheffield Readymix has overlooked that are outside the game-theoretic approach. Potential new customers have a value in the value net, and one way to induce them to enter is to pay them their full value: in essence, pay them to play.

Added values and rules If Sheffield Readymix wants to attract DIY customers for small amounts of concrete it may find it worthwhile to offer an aggressively low price that reflects their true value to the game. Thus it brings

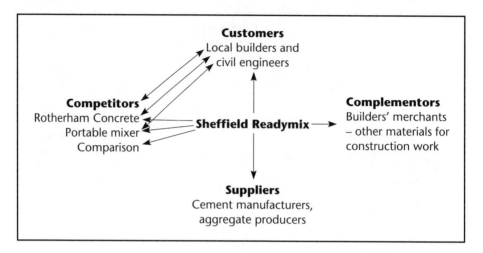

FIGURE 5.7 *Value net for Sheffield ready mix*

into its value net the customers of its own customers, and this increases its own value and reduces the value of its customers. In this way the value net leads to the development of market development strategies, and the usefulness of the game is that it shows the logic of paying someone to play the game by rewarding them with their share of their value to you. One outcome of this could be forward integration for self-reward – effectively this would mean Sheffield Readymix becoming its own customer by setting up a civil engineering and/or building subsidiary to buy its own products at very low prices.

Sheffield Readymix could also bring in more suppliers. One way to do this would be to form a buying club with Rotherham Concrete. Combined purchasing would boost competition for their business amongst their suppliers resulting in lower prices than those offered by less-organized builders' merchants. This might make all the difference when competing for customers against builders.

Bringing in a complementor could also work. For instance Sheffield Readymix might be able to negotiate lower prices for other materials used by builders, and these could be sold to its customers at reduced cost when tied in with the purchase of its own products. This works very well if the complementor can not respond.

Tactics and scope It may even be beneficial to bring in another competitor to change the scope of the game. We have already seen how Sheffield Readymix and Rotherham Concrete could cooperate to bring in more suppliers and complementors. The more competitors who joined the buying club, the better. Tactics involve signalling (for example the desire to be cooperative), and scope involves increasing or reducing the size of the game.

Evaluation of the potential role of game theory in strategy

Strengths: game theory as a potentially unifying language

The idea that game theory has unifying properties, and hence can act as a paradigm for corporate strategy, is supported by the fact that it has unified certain aspects of economics and is still doing so.

Areas that have been generalized and integrated into the game theory paradigm include the following:

- A more unified theory of horizontal mergers, allowing for advances at both the public policy and the business policy level in that it enables both the value and the allocation of value in pre/post-merger scenarios to be determined. Until now this type of prediction has been rather unsystematic.
- Investment in physical capital, which is now modelled as a commitment to compete vigorously as well as being a cost shifter.
- Investment in intangible assets has been analyzed, leading to new theories in the area of patent races, using tournament models. Game theory is able to analyze R & D strategies where there are spillovers, and also to theorize joint ventures in a systematic way.
- Strategic control of information is analyzed via learning models within repeated games.
- Network competition and product standardization now have a more unified theoretical language, as does the theory of contracting as an entry deterrent, which examines the implications of large firms being unambiguously at a disadvantage in declining industries.

Weaknesses

Rasmussen (2001) offers (perhaps with tongue half in cheek) an interesting technique for operationalizing game theoretic concepts in corporate strategy. He describes this as the 'no fat' approach, which involves the following process:

1. Observe and stylize some facts about the industry in question. These stylized facts are empirical regularities that are more or less known or may be discovered by an empirical process, for example by correlating trends.
2. Select a set of premises that are consistent with it.
3. Explain the causality of the process from 2 to 1 (that is, think backwards).

The appeal of game theory is that it can explain almost anything and can therefore be used as part of the no-fat process of modelling. In this sense game theory has the potential to act as an engine of theory, as it has done in economics, where it is not without its critics since its very facility can produce facile theory.

Notes

1. Equilibrium means neither player has an incentive to change their strategies, and thus the game is in a position of stability.
2. Morgenstern was an economist at Princeton. His contribution was to take game theory on the road, attending conferences and loudly proclaiming that all other economists could not do maths. This meant he was not especially popular.
3. One criticism of game theory when applied to business problems is that you have to be a mathematician to be good at it. Clearly this is only true in the sense that you have to be as good at maths as a baboon. Most MBAs are at least this good.
4. $57.60 - (64.80 - 57.60)$.
5. Unfortunately, except when practiced by sovereign governments or explicitly allowed by them, cartels are illegal.
6. Note that this does not mean playing head-tails heads-tails: this eventually means being certain of playing heads in odd numbered plays of the game, which is not truly random.
7. Named after the Stanley Kubrik film about nuclear defence.
8. Here we mean bringing new customers into the game, not attracting existing customers from your competitors. The latter would not add value, merely capture it.

References and further reading

Brandenburger, A. M. and B. J. Nalebuff (1995) 'The Right Game: Use Game Theory to Shape Strategy', *Harvard Business Review*, vol. 73, no. 4, pp. 57–71.

Dixit, A. N. and Nalebuff, B. (1991) *Thinking Strategically: The Competitive Edge in Business and Everyday Life* (New York: Norton).

Nalebuff, B. and A. Brandenburger (1996) *Co-opetition* (London: HarperCollins).

Neumann, J. von and O. Morgenstern (1947) 'The Theory of Games and Economic Behaviour', 2nd edn (Princeton, NJ: Princeton University Press).

Porter, M. E. (1980) *Competitive Strategy* (New York: Free Press).

Porter, M. E. (1985) *Competitive Advantage* (New York: Free Press).

Rasmussen, E. (2001) *Games and Information*, 3rd edn (Oxford: Blackwell).

Rumelt, R., D. Schendel and D. J. Teece (eds) (1991) 'Fundamental Research in Themes in Strategy and Economics', *Strategic Management Journal*, special winter issue.

6 Transaction Costs and the Economics of Institutions

Stephen Regan

Basic principles

The essence of transaction cost economics is that it considers the firm as though it were a market: a firm is a special form of dense market that has evolved for organizing certain types of transaction in the most cost-effective way. Hence the approach of a transaction cost economist is not to take the existence of firms for granted, but to see them as phenomena that exist because the economy has chosen to create them.

Firms are specialized institutions that are ideal for handling certain types of transaction, and their superiority over markets in these transactions explains their existence, and likewise with markets. However markets and firms are only two of many modes of organizing economic activity, which we call 'institutions', and thus our transaction cost theory will include a theory of firms and a theory of markets (and types of market), as well as of institutions in general, such as families, political parties and even spontaneous 'institutions' such as riots. Because of this broad range of phenomena, and because its focus on institutions is constructed for economic reasons, rather than being taken for granted, it is sometimes convenient to talk of institutional economics rather than transaction cost economics. However in this chapter we shall use the term transaction cost economics.

The most simple form of transaction in an economy is the instantaneous exchange of goods or services,[1] but despite its simplicity a great many complex processes make up even this straightforward transaction. For instance there is the search process the parties go through to find each other, and the processes of negotiating a price, setting a delivery date and agreeing future measures if the product fails to perform. These are all *ex ante* transaction costs, incurred before the transaction, but there are also *ex post* transaction costs, such as the cost of monitoring the supplier's performance (if a service is being supplied) and using a third party to arbitrate in the event of dispute. The basic principle of transaction cost economics is that the institutional structure that emerges to organize these transactions will be the one that minimizes the transaction costs.

Case study

The situation

Filtex Ltd is a small family-owned business that produces filters for diesel engines. The company is one of three in a group owned by the Harper family. Filtex turns over £2–3 million per annum and supplies mostly to manufacturers of diesel-powered earthmoving equipment for the construction industry. The other two companies in the group are much smaller. One is a servicing and parts business that Filtex bought because the business was a major debtor and was threatened with liquidation. The other is a trading business that buys and sells for the import and reexport market.

There are two principle decision makers at Filtex. Alan Harper is the founder of the business, and his main skills are as an engineer and designer. His daughter Lola has an MBA and gave up her career in merchant banking to run the business. She now acts as both production director and finance director, and is the principal family member responsible for the day-to-day running of the business. Two non-family members are also very important: Barry Glen and John Moran, who run the sales and distribution elements of the business, respectively.

Filtex's main customers have implemented several changes in recent years, such as statistical process control, ISO 9000 and just-in-time manufacturing. All of these innovations have put added cost pressure on Filtex.

Lola is increasingly concerned that Filtex maybe in need of a major change of direction, and she has decided to discuss the matter with her father (the majority shareholder).

The conversation

> *Lola*: Since I took over the control of production I have become increasingly concerned about our manufacturing capability.
>
> *Alan*: What do you mean, we are very highly thought of for our quality and reliability: we wouldn't keep a demanding customer like [he names their major customer] if we weren't pretty close to world class. I know we are small, but . . .
>
> *Lola*: Yes, we are successful in the sense that we are manufacturing some of the highest-quality diesel filters in the UK and Europe.
>
> *Alan*: So why don't you like our manufacturing capability?
>
> *Lola*: For two reasons. First, we manufacture the best diesel filters in the world, but diesel filters are a tiny portion of the total value of our customers' final product. Second, diesel filters are now bulk commodities – our customers could, if they wanted, go to South-East Asia or Portugal or Poland tomorrow and get a perfectly adequate diesel filter at about 60 per cent of what we charge them.
>
> *Alan*: So we stick at the top end of the market: we are a niche player. We have to focus on those customers who want engineering excellence.
>
> *Lola*: But they don't want engineering excellence: they want manufacturing excellence.

Alan: Sorry, you've lost me there. I don't see the difference.

Lola: We give them a great product, manufactured to the highest speci-fication. That's because we are terrific engineers. Always have been: your filters solved problems for the industry 20 years ago and that really mattered.

Alan: So what are we doing wrong?

Lola: Because now they buy from us because we can deliver the exact amount, in a 24-hour cycle, and at a guaranteed price, regardless of the level of demand. They don't just want a high-quality product, they ex-pect it and know they can get it more cheaply elsewhere. What they want from us is a high-quality logistics operation. Quite frankly, they are paying us a premium not for product quality, but for delivery performance.

Alan: So what's your point? Where is this heading?

Lola: I think we should split what we do into two tasks. First, we have a design and engineering capability. We should sell this expertise in fil-tration systems on a consultancy basis – we should offer to design solutions for them, as we did when we invented your filter 20 years ago.

Alan: What about the factory?

Lola: At the moment we produce up to 3000 filters a day at peak produc-tion. This means we have invested in expensive machinery and two production lines, and have production operatives on good wages and permanent contracts. We own a factory, which takes up about four acres of valuable land. We run a fleet of lorries and vans, and we hold about 30 days of stock of various kinds.

Alan: Yes, because we are a manufacturer of diesel filters.

Lola: But we do this without really thinking about either its value to the customer or its cost to us. We may be able to raise the former *and* re-duce the latter if we focus on what our customers want, rather than on just being a manufacturer.

Alan: Go on, I'm interested.

Lola: In five years' time I'd like us to have developed and patented three new filtration systems – complete packages, not just the filters, but the housing and all the ducting. One for diesel, one for petrol, and one for air conditioning in factories.

Alan: Perfectly possible, we could do that if we focused on it.

Lola: I'd also like us to have sold our factory, but increased our sales of filters.

Alan: How would we pull that one off?

Lola: We give Barry and John control of a new distribution business that handles customer relationship management. They take orders and de-velop new business. When they take the order, it comes into a centralized database. We instantly inform our haulage contractors to visit the ware-house of our intermediary, who manages our inventory for us. This warehouse contains thousands of different products, but has a dedicated loading bay for *our* hauliers' vans and *our* filters. These filters have been made in Poland and/or Malaysia to our specification, for a fraction of the cost at which we can make them, but under our licences, because those filters are patented by us.

Alan: Isn't this all rather risky? What if a supplier lets us down?

Lola: Our skill, in this system, is in ensuring the delivery of our products to our customers by taking the risk over from them. If we aren't prepared

> to do this, then they can bypass us and go direct to the intermediary we are using, who will have to pay us a design royalty anyway.
>
> *Alan*: And the reason we have their business is because we are better, more specialized in this than they are?
>
> *Lola*: Yes, we are better at *organizing* this than they are. We are minimizing their transaction costs because we are specialists in filter technology and they are specialists in assembly. My point is that our current structure is not minimizing our transaction costs.
>
> *Alan*: So, at the moment we are bundling three things into the product price, if what you say is right. We design high-quality filters, we produce these filters, and we deliver them on time. And you are saying we should split these three costs out. We should charge directly for our design, rather than overengineering our products. We should reduce production costs by outsourcing, and we should add a premium to those commodity production costs by managing the costs of transactions for them.
>
> *Lola*: What do you think?
>
> *Alan*: I think I understand what you mean, but it implies major changes to our business. I'm not sure...

The issues

Lola is concerned to identify the real source of profit in a modern manufacturing business. Like many modern manufacturers she has realized that product quality is now a basic requirement of all customers, and something they expect from any supplier. Building in more product quality than the customer wants is not the route to competitive advantage.

Lola has realized that the competitive advantage of Filtex over other suppliers is its ability to deliver superior logistics performance: the exact amount of the product required, with minimal lead times, and that to do this cost effectively is of great value to the customer. It is clearly the case that the ability to retain customers comes from the ability to organize a supply chain for them, and that this may not necessarily mean locating all that supply chain inside the firm. Filtex currently ensures supply continuity by owing large parts of the filter manufacturing process. Lola's concern is that this is an expensive way to guarantee performance in the contract with their customers – outsourcing is one way of reducing such costs. There are obviously risks in this, but handling contracts (transactions) in a cost-effective way is essential for leveraging low-cost global production. Modern, logistics-based manufacturing means being a transaction cost minimizer as much as a production-cost minimizer.

Key contributions

The origin of the perspective

There have been two prime movers in transaction cost economics: Ronald Coase (1937) and Oliver Williamson (1985). We shall start, as the theory did, with Coase.

Coase was born in Middlesex in 1910, and initially taught at the London School of Economics, from which he received his PhD in economics in 1951. His name, however, has been more associated with the 'Chicago School' as he subsequently became emeritus professor of economics and senior fellow at the Chicago Law School. His great contribution to economics was to provide theory of institutions, and particularly an economic theory of law. For this reason he is often credited with founding the hybrid subject of law and economics, which examines how law is used in the economy and how the economy is used to create law. For our present purpose we shall concentrate on one area of this work – the economic theory of a particular legal entity, the firm. What are the economic origins of this legal institution: where do firms come from, and why?

Coase's insight is that most economic theories suggest that resources are allocated by the price mechanism, but that this is not the case within firms, where they are allocated very differently. Why, Coase asks, has the economy decided to set aside the price mechanism and construct a firm, especially given the great theoretical arguments in economics for the efficiency of the price mechanism? Coase refers to firms as 'islands of conscious power in this ocean of unconscious co-operation',[2] and asks, why do we need these islands of conscious power? Coase's answer is that the firm is one of many alternatives to the market as a way of coordinating production, and that each of these alternatives has its own costs of organizing. Moreover the alternative chosen will be the one that incurs the least costs when organizing a given productive activity – these organizing costs are referred to as transaction costs. There is nothing special about the firm, and both the existence and structure of firms will change if economic forces dictate they should.

Oliver Williamson (1985) has developed Coase's insight into a more fully developed theory known as transaction cost economics. Williamson breaks down the costs of organizing (transaction costs) into different types, and identifies the kinds of institution (governance relations, such as laws, norms or contracts) that will emerge appropriately to handle these transaction costs. His conclusion is broadly the same as that of Coase, that the governance structures that emerge will be those with the lowest costs of organizing a given activity. In other words the economy will tend to evolve institutions that are efficient.

Williamson's major contribution to transaction cost economics has been to extend Coase's insights into a unified summary of its implications for business. However there have been other contributions to the field that provide different treatments from that of Williamson, and in particular some adopt a more rigorous mathematical approach. The advantage of this approach is that it allows transaction cost economics to connect with other problems in economics that have not yielded to economic analysis in the absence of transaction costs as a theoretical framework.

One such problem is in the area of supply chain economics, where a great deal of applied work using transaction costs has been conducted recently. Transaction cost economics has been used to analyze the relative efficiencies of Japanese and American supply chains in manufacturing (Macmillan, 1990), in particular the degree to which trust is seen as an important way of minimizing transaction costs, and how 'contracts' (psychological as well as financial) can be an important way of facilitating trust.

Grossman and Hart (1986) apply transaction cost economics to decisions on investment in specific assets in the case of supply chain partners. Their model shows the circumstances in which it will be optimal for (1) the supplier to buy out his or her customer; (2) the customer to buy out his or her supplier and (3) the two to maintain an arms-length relationship short of ownership. As such this model begins to formalize important questions about the nature of alliances and partnering, which are important questions in management.

Further work has applied transaction cost economics to specific cases, often involving interfirm relations. Of particular interest are 'GE vs Westinghouse in Large Turbine Generations, A, B, C' (Harvard Business School Case Studies, nos 9-380-128, 9-380-129, 9-380-130), and 'International Business Machines (E): Negotiating with Electronic Component Suppliers' (Harvard Business School, no. 9-577-158).

Key principles

Transaction costs economics considers the firm as though it were a market, and then asks questions about how this 'market' has evolved the structures it has. These structures range from spot transactions between anonymous sellers (for example on the stock market) to guaranteed employment in a public-sector business. This is a subtly different approach from the one taken by most non-economists, who tend to take for granted the existence of firms and to assume that markets are simply convenient ways of trading firms' products. This is obviously not good enough, since it amounts to a non-theory of the firm: it just assumes they exist. The transaction cost approach sees markets as mechanisms for transacting, and firms as a special type of market for organizing certain types of transaction.

The relevant concept is opportunity cost – perhaps the most important concept in economics and, paradoxically, often the least well understood. The essence of opportunity cost is that the cost of action A is the lost opportunity of action B. For instance if action A is the decision to buy a number of different raw materials and manufacture a component whilst action B is simply to buy the component ready-made from a supplier, then the efficient firm will choose between A and B on the basis of minimizing the opportunity costs. These costs are of two types – production costs and transaction costs.

Opportunity cost suggests that if A is cheaper than B, then A will be chosen. This decision creates as a by-product a choice between using the market (option B) or using the firm (option A). The essence of transaction cost economics is that firms and markets exist because of the need for efficiency. The difference between the two alternative modes of organizing can be thought of as largely based on transaction costs: option A involves making many transactions and making them frequently, which is obviously expensive; while option B allows an outsider to bear all the expense of transacting – however this may mean losing control over product quality or service reliability. The firm balances the costs associated with the two types of transaction and selects the one that minimizes the overall costs.[3]

A particular transaction will be placed within a firm when it is more efficient to do so than to leave it to the market, and *vice versa*. So let us have a look at the nature of transactions and their costs by way of an example. Table 6.1 shows hypothetical production and transaction costs per unit of a typical com-

Filtex's costs: manufacturing in-house versus outsourcing (pounds)   TABLE 6.1

	Option A: manufacture in-house	Option B: outsource
Production cost (per unit)	8.41	5.23
Transaction costs		
Metering costs	1.02	0.50
Hold-up costs*	0.00	0.70
Total	9.43	6.43

* Hold-up costs are often referred to as opportunism – there is a possibility that under option B the other party may use your reliance on him to extract a higher price, known as a hold-up.

ponent in manufactured goods. If it helps to make things concrete, think about it as filters for diesel engines, and the firm making the choice is Filtex.

With option A the production costs are £8.41 per unit, much higher than the production costs of option B (£5.23) – this is because when you outsource you buy from a specialist, and this specialist has economies of scale in producing the product, which you do not have. It is only one component in your production process – it is the specialist's entire production process. The latter may also have other economies (that is, cost savings) not available to you, such as economies of scope (the specialist may make different versions of the product, and this may allow him or her to run the production line closer to capacity than you could). The specialist may also have learning economies (he or she may have invented the product you are trying to copy, so may be able to give you advice and consultancy, along with the product). This and many other things give you potential production cost savings. The basic rule is that outsourcing reduces production costs because of economies of scale.

However with outsourcing your transaction costs could be higher (as in this example). We have listed just two types of transactions cost. The first, 'metering', is the cost of such things as accounting and control – it is governed by the complexity of the transaction structure chosen and in this case there are many more activities to watch over in transaction A than in transaction B, so the firm's cost 'meter' has to be pretty sophisticated and will be heavily used in order to manage this complexity.

So far B seems very much the superior option, giving reduced production and metering costs. However the 'hold-up' problem, or the cost of uncertainty, is a main drawback with option B. The producer will probably have to hold larger stocks of finished goods to offset the risk of being held up by a supplier who fails to deliver as promised. This might involve the supplier looking for a price increase after the contract is signed, since he or she is aware of having supplier power over the customer. One could view hold-up costs as costly measures the buyer engages in to reduce his or her own switching costs, such as holding buffer stocks or using a second supplier.

Note that there is a fairly subtle distinction in practice between transaction costs and production costs – so much so that you may have a problem deciding whether metering should really be seen as a distinct type of cost driver from, say, production overheads, and thus the term transaction costs may seem like theoretical hair-splitting rather than practically relevant. There is some merit in this point of view. Clearly what matters to the managers who make these decisions is the overall costs of decision A versus decision B: the opportunity cost in the aggregate is what drives the management decision, and managers will not waste time categorizing costs into production versus transaction if it is not relevant for decision making.[4]

Strategic management involves making decisions of a different order, based on a quite strong understanding of what is going on in and around the firm. If there is a distinction between transaction costs and production costs, then managers need to be aware of these distinctions. Often, because the operational decision maker makes decisions on the basis of overall costs, the distinction between types of cost is often overlooked. However the strategist should not overlook this, since transaction costs are real costs, and they can be managed. The fact that transaction costs are not always immediately apparent makes the case for understanding them even stronger. The purpose of this chapter is to help you to understand transaction costs, their strategic implications and how to manage them.

The contention of this chapter is that firms constantly balance production costs against transaction costs, and that they will make decisions that minimize the aggregate of these two costs. The strategist needs to understand the basic drivers of business performance in order to manage each of them. The weakness of mainstream economic theory and the strategy derived from it, is not that it completely ignores transaction costs (since the long-run average total cost curve is based on opportunity costs and thus includes the costs of both production and transaction, and in fact, any other cost we care to come up with), but that it fails to specify the nature of the transaction costs. This chapter adds to strategy by making transaction costs explicit.

For example, when undertaking a transaction the parties to the transaction incur costs that depend on the way they choose to conduct the transaction. This might include the time, trouble and legal expense of drawing up a contract, or the negotiations over the terms of the contract (whether written or verbal). Other parties may need to be consulted, and the previous history of similar transactions between the parties might need to be discussed. Personal relationships between the people who are engaged in the transaction (referred to as social capital) may take time to develop, but are an essential investment in the transaction being agreed.

There are also *ex post* transaction costs, incurred by the need to monitor the performance of the other parties or the goods being exchanged. The contract may not have fully specified every possible contingency, and the parties may incur the cost of reinterpreting their agreement in the light of such unforeseen events or the cost of arbitration in the event of dispute, or they may end up in court. Some or all of the value of the contract may disappear for some or all of the transactors as a result of such events, or the contract may be cancelled.

The importance of transaction cost economics to strategy is that it gives the strategist a greater amount of detail. This enables better strategic decision making, in the ways we now turn to.

Links to strategy

Context: the nature of exchange

According to transaction cost economics the main determinant of the type of institutional structure that emerges is the context in which the exchange takes place. For instance if a buyer and a seller come together to trade apples in exchange for cash, the context is very different from one in which a large bank is entering a long-term contract to outsource its information system. Williamson (1975) identifies three main differences between these contexts: asset specificity, uncertainty and frequency.

An exchange has high *asset specificity* if one or more of the parties to it have to invest in assets (tangible or otherwise) that are of limited value outside the transaction in question. Sometimes this is essential for efficiency, for instance car assemblers often require suppliers to relocate within a certain distance of the assembly plant in order to meet just-in-time delivery. Both parties need to agree in advance of the transaction exactly how the benefits of the arrangement will be shared out between them. We would expect a great deal of *ex ante* negotiations over the terms of the contract, and a great deal of *ex post* monitoring of the performance of each side to ensure the contract is working. More importantly, we would expect the nature of the contract to reflect an efficient way of handling the context in which the parties find themselves. It is likely that this will differ from the contract to buy applies from a greengrocer in some very important ways, for instance, by being much more long term and including much more detail about the terms of business.

The second contextual element is the degree of *uncertainty*. Some business relationships are subject to a great deal of uncertainty and an efficient institutional structure would be that which trades the costs of this uncertainty between the parties in the most efficient way. For instance one could view the relationship between a worker and a firm as one in which the worker employs the firm, rather than the reverse. In particular the worker is more concerned than the firm about the possibility of not finding a market for the products of his or her labour and is prepared to accept lower average earnings in return for the firm guaranteeing to pay him or her continuously. The difference between the market value of the skills of the worker and the wage the firm agrees to pay is what the worker pays the firm to find employment for him or her. If this difference is too great, the worker will quit.[5] In a sense there is an implicit insurance contract within the employment contract.

A third contextual variable is the *frequency* of the transaction. If a transaction is frequent there are economies of scale in transaction costs, and thus the transactors may go to the trouble of designing a very specific type of institutional management. These heavy, up-front costs are reduced quite quickly as the transactions continue over time. However if the transaction is just a-one-off then the parties are likely to use a general purpose mechanism, which may not be ideal but is cheaper to use than a unique contract.

Culture: the organizational dimension of transactions

There are two broad types of transaction cost: those associated with the person who makes the transaction (such as hold-up costs, which are higher when the buyer and seller do not trust each other), and those associated with the technical complexity of the transaction itself, regardless of who makes it (such as metering costs).

As far as hold-up costs are concerned, the assumption in transaction cost economics is that human beings are imperfectly rational and imperfectly honest.[6] The imperfectly rational aspect is important since without it the parties to a contract would be unable to incur transaction costs – every contract, from now to eternity, could be written with perfect foresight, including contracts for settling disputes that arose as a result of unforeseen events.

In fact human beings are only boundedly rational at best, and they have to incur the costs of gathering information about each other, and about the nature of the transactions they are undertaking. For instance they might need to employ an independent expert to value the property they are transacting. Many contracts for the construction of property include a clause covering contingent claims should things not turn out as expected (and given bounded rationality, this is precisely what will happen).

In addition to being boundedly rational, human beings are also imperfectly honest in their dealings with each other. By this we do not just mean that people are self-interested and care only for themselves, we also mean that they can be actively dishonest, and the costs of transacting are higher when people cannot be trusted. Building up trust can reduce these costs (for example, via long-term business relationships), but the process of building trust is best seen as an investment: developing trust to facilitate transactions is a cost of those transactions. Trust does not come free.

For instance, because financial advisors cannot always be trusted to sell you the right pension their behaviour is regulated. They have to take exams (which only shows they are honest enough to take exams, but at least it's a start). They also have to comply with a code of conduct and their firms have to employ expensive compliance managers to ensure they do. Because these firms and their compliance departments cannot be trusted (or not completely) there is an independent regulator to whom consumers can complain. All of this institutional architecture costs money, and all of it adds to the cost of the pension or bank loan the consumer receives. And all these costs are transaction costs. The essential point we are making here is that this 'context' (regulation, auditing and so on) is a transaction cost incurred because of the nature of the transaction. Both human nature and the nature of the product generate certain contexts for managing transactions. The strategic goal is obviously to make sure that the context is the lowest-cost one: the context should minimize the transaction costs.

We could classify all organizations according to two dimensions: their rationality, that is, whether they are completely rational, boundedly rational or 'behavioural' – this we would define as the information-processing competence of the organization; and their honesty, whether they are completely altruistic, selfish or self-interested with guile[7] – this we would define as the

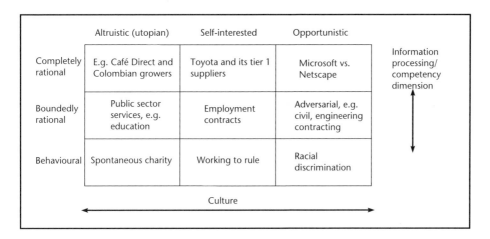

Culture of the organization   FIGURE 6.1

culture of the organization.[8] Figure 6.1 shows nine types of organization that accord with these two dimensions. Each of the nine boxes represents a different organizational response to the transaction cost problem. We shall discuss two of the extremes to give an insight into how concepts affect strategy.

In the top left-hand corner we have an example of a culture of openness and trust, and a very high information-processing competence. Another example might be a long-term supply chain relationship where each partner is fully aware of the other's business and is able instantly to respond to a changing environment with minimal discussion and deliberation. Furthermore the culture is one in which each party genuinely sees the other's interests as identical to its own, and thus they can trust each other to respond in an appropriate way, with a minimum need for costly discussion and monitoring. For instance if raw material costs rise for the supplier, the customer knows the supplier will absorb as much of these costs as it can before attempting to renegotiate the terms of the agreement. Such contracts are often very loosely defined and informal.

Moving on to the middle section of Figure 6.1, Toyota delegates tremendous autonomy to its tier 1 suppliers, up to and including design input for new models. These suppliers are guaranteed immense volumes of business from their relationship with Toyota. Both parties can be trusted to look after their own interests and thus to protect the value of the alliance. The risks each party takes on behalf of the other forms a commitment between self-interest agents, and thus allows them to cooperate.

In the right-hand section of the matrix we have the extremes of both culture and competence and hence a very low level of commitment. Microsoft's battle with Netscape to dominate access to the internet seemed opportunistic. Allegedly, Microsoft was prepared both to deceive its own customers about its ability to run internet search engines within Windows 95/98, and to harm its own suppliers if they helped Netscape as it pursued a systematic campaign to destroy the latter as a potential rival. This strategy was also rather behavioural, in that it was driven by a sort of reflex action by Microsoft to control all potential sources of value in the information technology business by always attacking rivals aggressively.[9]

Occasionally it pays to make a commitment to behave aggressively, and this can be done by repeatedly acting in an aggressive way so that the other agent (firms in this case) are likely to behave in a more accommodating way towards you. (See the Hawk–Dove game referred to in Chapter 5.)

Microsoft's recent problems with the US Department of Justice strongly suggest an organization that has become destructive in this way. In particular it failed to see that its aggression towards other players in the industry would lead to a court case and that the company might be forced to split up. Note that developing a reputation in the market place means making a commitment to act in a certain way, either cooperatively or aggressively, or rationally or behaviourally. The trick is to choose the behaviour that minimizes the transaction costs.

The bottom-right relationships are expensive in terms of transactions costs, as evidenced by the huge legal expenses currently being incurred by firms facing race and sex discrimination suits. However the fact that the top-left culture/rationality architecture did not emerge is *a priori* an indicator that the context (see the previous section) was not appropriate to it. One of the great problems in economics is to work out why people engage in behaviour that is not only immoral, but also very costly.

Competing: using transaction cost economics to outperform competitors

There are two views of competitive advantage in strategic management. The first is that firms do well because they are in a privileged position *vis-à-vis* their industry structure. This view is most strongly associated with the structure–conduct–performance mode (see Chapter 2). The leading strategist in this area is Michael Porter (1980), who suggests that it is the structural characteristics of an industry (the 'five forces') that determine the relative success or failure of a firm. Strategy is reduced to industry selection – if you like the structure, enter the industry; if you don't, get out. This sort of strategy has had a real impact, especially at the top level of corporate strategy, where multidivisional firms choose how to allocate their funds. Firms such as Du Pont, Shell, General Electric and IBM might use this type of analysis. Typically, corporate-level strategists look at the different divisions of the business, often called strategic business units, and decide how much financial capital to allocate to the business concerned. If the business looks as though it is in an industry structure where return on capital employed (ROCE) will decline because of new entrants (as in the case, say, of General Electric facing new entrants into the domestic appliance business), then it may decide to sell off that business. Rough rules of thumb emerge from this, such as General Electric's aim to be number one or number two in each market in which it operates, or the Du Pont formula or Shell's directional policy matrix. The path of acquisitions and R & D capability could also be determined by such thinking – the business's future development will be into areas where the structural variables are favourable.

However this level of strategy is not the only level, and it is not immediately obvious that the structuralist approach is of much use to the manager of a single-sector business, where all corporate choices relate to just one sector. This business-level strategy requires making the best of an existing industry structure in the short to medium term. The second major view of strategic management, the resource-based view (see Chapter 7), is that firms are not merely passive processors of favourable or unfavourable environments, but powerful sources of their own competitive advantage. Competitive advantage resides inside the firm, in a key resource or set of resources, not outside the firm in a given market structure. There is strong evidence to support this view of the firm: the fact is, there is more variability in firm profitability *within* a given industry than there is in the average rate of profits *between* industries. The unique sources of competitive advantage are located inside the firm – say, technology or know-how – and the firm is able to deter entry to these resources. To make a link with Porter's (1980) view of strategy, in the resource-based view superior profit performance is derived from the entry barrier to the firm and to its key resources, rather than the entry barriers to the industry and its customers. Both views have their merits and there is a pleasing symmetry to them – one view considers that profits come from blockading entry to markets, the other from blockading entry to firms.

There are links with the principles of transaction cost economics that are worth making: transaction cost economics sees neither firms (and their resources) nor markets (and their structures) as basic entities, but as two variations of the same theme, simply as two of many ways of arranging economic activity. Thus a transaction cost economist would suggest that it is the ability to create an optimal institutional structure to handle a certain set of transactions that is the key to competitive advantage. Sometimes this institution is a market with a particular structure, sometimes it is a firm with a particular structure. Either way it is the efficient processing of transactions – the lowest-cost means of organizing production – that generates profits. In other words transaction cost economics provides a bridge between structuralist views of strategy and firm-level, resource-based views. It suggests that firms should give considerable attention to the extent to which they use the market, as opposed to their own internal resources. Ultimately the distinction between the market and the firm becomes an artificial one, and firms use a range of contractual and institutional arrangements to maximize efficiency. For instance the development of alliance relationships from joint ventures to strategic alliances immensely enriches the number of ways firms can organize themselves, and is best understood within a transaction cost framework.

One interesting variant of this view is that success may lie neither inside a firm nor outside it (in a market), but somewhere in between. Networks of firms may be more efficient than either a single firm spanning the network, or a set of firms competing in a market. The notion of alliance management, or partnering, as a source of competitive advantage is emerging as a third theory of competitive advantage (see Doz and Hamel, 1989).

If the source of a firm's superior profits is the strength of its relationships, then if it is able to design an institutional architecture that is optimal it may have a transaction-cost-based source of competitive advantage. This may give it the ability to locate itself in an industry with superior profit potential, or to acquire and retain control of an important set of resources by partnering. The key point in transaction cost economics is that it is not the firm or the market that is the appropriate unit of analysis, but a broadly defined class of institutions. When a firm emerges as the appropriate institution for managing a set of transactions, it does so because the institution of the firm itself is the key resource. It is not the ownership of the resource, but the ability to control it better than anyone else, and this is due to the fit between the transactions being conducted and the structures for conducting them.

This transaction cost of the firm suggests that a competitive firm will place contracts in the optimal way (that with the lowest opportunity cost), otherwise it will threatened by another that will. This means sometimes placing contracts in the market, sometimes inside the firm and sometimes in a hybrid form, say with one or more partner firms.

The fact that the sources of a firm's success may lie in its 'architecture' (both internal and external) rather than in limiting competition (as Porter suggests) or owning key resources (as the resource-based view suggests) means that the firm should shape itself in such a way that it is part of an efficient transaction-cost-minimizing structure. The importance of minimizing transaction costs is perhaps indicated by the fact that 55 per cent of the value of the final value produced by the average US manufacturing firm is sourced from a supplier; in Japan the figure is nearer to 70 per cent. A firm that is 10 per cent better at managing its transaction relationships could have a cost advantage over its rivals of between 5.5 per cent (10 per cent × 55 per cent) for the US and 7 per cent (10 per cent × 70 per cent) for Japan. This sort of advantage is very significant.

But transaction cost savings do not just come from outsourcing (to gain a supplier's production cost advantages) and then managing the outsourced relationships very effectively. They can also come from the firm's internal institutional architecture, since the firm is just a 'dense market' as far as transaction cost economics is concerned. For instance using labour effectively means designing the internal institutional structure, such as hierarchies, relationships and 'culture', in such a way as to gain the most from the existing workforce and its skills.

Consider the rise of Japan (or for that matter Germany) as a dominant exporting economy since 1945. Neither the resource-based view of the firm nor the market-structure-based industrial organization theory of competitive advantage can explain why the Japanese economy came to dominate global manufacturing in the 50 years after the Second World War. Japanese firms' resource costs were about 20 per cent higher than those of their American rivals: they had to learn basic technologies such as production engineering and electronics from the West since these were largely Western inventions. This gave them a resource-based disadvantage. The same could be said of the Dutch flower industry, the Swiss food industry, the Finnish electronics industry and the French defence industry. But they were all globally successful.

And this success cannot have been due to highly privileged access to a protected market – the industries in question were export-led (for instance 40 per cent of Toyota's sales are overseas). The Japanese economy needed to export in order to import, and it needed to import because of the absence of natural resources in Japan. Thus there was no option for Japan but to compete in overseas markets, in every industry from semiconductors and cars to cameras. And this meant taking a 20 per cent resource disadvantage into a protected market, competing in the US and Europe. These markets were not open to Japanese competition: in North America and Europe there were strongly protectionist measures, especially non-tariff barriers, to protect domestic business, and these were targeted specifically at the Japanese.

Nonetheless in the 1980s, when these barriers became stronger, the Japanese began to locate inside the European and US markets, producing side by side. If their success had been due to the ownership of a key resource (say low labour costs, or technology) then this would have been eradicated by having to compete using US and European labour and technology. But it was enhanced: the Japanese firms that have weathered recessions best are those which are most globalized and located outside Japan, such as Sony and Toyota.

The answer lies in the institutional structures that emerged inside Japanese businesses in the 1950s and 1960s as a competitive response to the disadvantages they faced. Things such as just-in-time production, lifetime employment, quality circles, total quality management, outsourcing and tacit knowledge management were all needed to squeeze transaction costs to a level that would make 'Japan Inc.' competitive in the US and Europe. Some of those responses existed within firms, some between firms and some at the level of the economy and even the interface with politics, as in the case of MITI. The key point is that referring to them as firm-specific or market structure-based is to focus on one manifestation of a more general phenomenon – the basic source of competitiveness was the ability to design institutional arrangements that lowered transaction costs so much that they overcame production cost disadvantages. Low transaction costs can therefore be seen as powerful engines of competitive advantage.

Corporate strategies: the market as a firm, and external sources of competitive advantage

Imagine a firm that faces a dominant incumbent in a potential market place. The incumbent has huge economies of scale and could engage in predatory pricing. The resource-based view of this is that the firm has a strategic resource (its capacity) that a new entrant will find difficult to imitate. Porters (1980, 1985) view is that this strategic resource is valuable because it creates an entry barrier. Our view is that the distinction is irrelevant: the resource-based view and the market-based view are two sides of the same coin.

The institutional view offers a genuine opportunity to get around this, since it suggests that a potential entrant may be able to enter this market and compete if it selects the correct transaction cost architecture. Ownership of a key resource should not block entry if there are potential transaction cost efficiencies that will enable an entrant to compensate for the resource-based disadvantage.

One way of doing this would be to form an alliance within the industry or between the industry and an outsider in order to gain a competitive advantage over the dominant rival. Thus a firm can obtain competitive advantage by locating its crucial resources in such a way that they span firm boundaries. The competitive advantage may be embedded in a set of relationships between firms, rather than 'belonging' to an individual firm. The phenomenal rate of growth of alliances/networks/joint ventures as a key feature of (particularly global) strategy can be partly explained by the realization that interfirm relationships can be a paradigm-shifting solution to the traditional logic of firm-versus market-based sources of competitive advantage. In short, profits emerge from the construction of relationships across the boundaries between firms. The most successful firms are those which are best able to exploit these potential sources of profit, and this is a new type of management, focused on transactions and relationships to facilitate those transactions. The great paradigm shift is that competitive advantage can best be built by cooperative strategy. This is a new skill set, and transaction cost economics is the starting point for building up these skills. For instance the diversified growth of Virgin has included entry into highly defended markets (airlines) and markets where the resources needed are so different for example financial services and cola) as to make a resource-based strategy untenable.[10] – Virgin's successful entry into trans-Atlantic airline travel must be at least partly explained by its ability to manage alliances with other stakeholders – such as regulators, staff and suppliers.

Essentially we are talking about structuring networks both to create and to share out the optimal value. Excessively competitive behaviour by any member of the network to increase its share always runs the risk of destroying the total amount of value in the network, perhaps by forcing members to leave or to withdraw some of what they have contributed. (See Chapter 5 for examples of how this might be managed.)

Control: transaction costs as a theory of management

If the boundaries between firms are indeed increasingly permeable, and if in reality value is not created within firms, but between subtly cooperative networks of firms, then what does transaction cost economics have to say about the internal workings of the imperfectly bounded entities called firms? Since they clearly still exist, they must have a purpose.

Essentially the same logic applies to the firm as to the market: markets can be seen as efficient institutional responses to the need to manage resources efficiently, and one type of market structure is the network structure, but firms can be seen as networks too. A firm is simply an alternative institutional structure to a market, and it has evolved as a convenient way of handling transactions.

According to this view the owners of the resources (factors of production) that make up the firm have to choose whether to locate those resources inside the firm, inside another firm or outside the firm, and simply offer them in the market. Their criterion will be the efficiency with which those resources are used. Thus labour, finance (debt and equity), raw materials, fixed capital, trademarks and software are all bundled together and controlled in the context of a firm. The firm is a team effort by the resource owners, each performing separate functions that contribute to the success of the overall enterprise.

The important point is that what holds this firm together is no different from what holds an interfirm alliance together: *management*, and particularly the management of transaction costs. This perspective pushes to one side the traditional view that a firm is owned and acts in the interests of these owners (usually thought to be the shareholders). In the transaction cost economics view, shareholders are just one factor of production among many, and they contribute (risk) capital in return for a claim on the residual value of the business. They certainly do not own the physical assets of the business (the debt holders will have legally enforceable covenants over these), nor do they own the labour. In fact to think of a modern corporation as having owners in any meaningful sense is pretty unfeasible. Each factor retains some degree of ownership over the resources it contributes, and the firm is simply an arrangement between them, a set of transactions organized by its managers to use those resources optimally.

The special factor of production in all this is not capital or labour, but management.[11] The role of management is to arrange the contracts between all the other factors. Thus when a manager agrees to purchase new materials from a supplier a contract is being created between the firm and the supplier, but this contract is not bilateral, it is multilateral. The manager contracts on behalf of all the other suppliers, all the other labour, all the shareholders, the banks and so on. Thus the role of management is central in a way that no other resource in the firm even comes close to. Shareholders have an almost trivial involvement in and importance to the firm compared with this.

If managers create the wrong mix of contracts, so that the costs of organization rise, then all the other parties will start to suffer and the firm will begin to underperform. As a result the firm's key resources will start to dissolve back into the market place: staff will leave, shareholders will sell their shares, customers will move to rival firms and eventually the firm will disappear. Thus what the firm is, what distinguishes it from a market, is its management: both its managers and how they manage. The key source of the success of a firm is how its resources are managed, and the central function in a modern firm is not ownership, but control, not shareholders, but managers.

Change

The ability to encourage change is increasingly important to the achievement of long-term competitive advantage. Often for technological reasons, product life cycles are shortening, and time to market is becoming a key factor in corporate success in every industry from retail banking to cars, telecommunications, the media and even business schools. The existence of certain political and economic forces means that firms are facing more competitive threats than ever as markets deregulate and globalize at the same time, and firms respond to this either by dropping prices or by innovating: either way they have to outpace the competition. A once-and-for-all price cut or a once-and-for-all new product launch is not a sustainable source of competitive advantage: the real differentiator is the ability continually to cut prices (and hence reduce costs) and/or continually to innovate. Business is increasingly about managing change.

The ability to manage change can also be thought of as part of the architecture of the firm and some institutional structures are better than others at this task. The ability to manage change is intrinsically related to the ability to manage human resources. In certain types of institutional structure, the transaction costs of getting human resources to change are so high that they use up all the potential benefit the change will deliver, and so the change fails.

One such type of institutional structure is the Type A labour contract. The A refers to American, but it could be applied more generally to European or UK firms that adopt this type of institutional structure. (Many American firms do not conform to this type.) The origin of Type A was the highly successful labour management system put in place to underpin Fordist mass production in the early twentieth century. In Fordist production the labour contract was a financial one: the organization offered pay that was significantly above the required minimum, and thus was able to select the best workers (that is, those least likely to sabotage the production line). The contract between workers and management was primarily a financial one: a worker would leave the firm if he or she received a better offer elsewhere, and workers knew that the organization had the right to shed labour in response to the need to cut costs. There was not a lot of trust. To this day people refer to the Type A labour contract as a 'flexible' labour model (where flexibility means a low degree of trust and commitment). However it tended to attract workers who demanded high pay but offered little commitment, and responded to change by leaving.

An alternative labour model is referred to as Type J. This refers to Japanese employment practice. Here there are two contracts: a financial one and a psychological one. The financial one is less generous than Type A: pay is by seniority, and hence there are flat hierarchies and little opportunity for rapid promotion. However the psychological contract guarantees a high degree of commitment by the firm to the employee, and *vice versa*.

For instance until recently the typical Japanese firm offered guaranteed lifetime employment, and as a result there was no secondary market for labour in Japan. This psychological contract offered long-term commitment to the employee, and the same was expected in return. It has been argued that the revolutionary changes made to production engineering in Japanese manufacturing were only possible because of the high degree of trust established by the Type J model. Japanese employees were highly responsive to change because change was not seen as threatening jobs. Thus Japanese firms were able to bring about quality improvements, new product innovation and cost reductions at the same time, achieved through a labour–management relationship where common interests were well defined.

With the Type A model, labour cost reductions can be achieved massively and quickly, but the remaining workers are left with a survivor syndrome, and are unlikely to embrace further change since they perceive themselves as being identified as part of the problem. Nevertheless the resurgence of the US economy in the 1990s and the relative decline of Japanese manufacturing during the same period challenges the view that Type J labour contracts are the ideal model. At the moment the highly paid, flexible labour force of the Type A model appears to be resurgent, but 10 years ago the clear superiority of Type J was not questioned. The principle conclusion to be drawn from this is not whether Type A is better or worse than Type J, but that competitiveness depends on the type of institutional structure governing the labour contract. The task of management is to find the appropriate structure for the type of change required.

Notes

1. Sometimes referred to as a 'spot transaction'.
2. '[L]ike lumps of butter coagulating in a pail of milk'.
3. This is what Lola effectively does in the case study.
4. One type of transaction cost is the cost of decision making, and efficient firms will not incur the costs of gathering information if the information is irrelevant.
5. Workers whose skills are particularly scarce, for instance valuable IT staff, may be paid above the market wage, and thus receive a type of insurance premium from the firm to ensure loyalty.
6. And that these two failings add greatly to the cost of transactions.
7. Opportunistic is another term, but deceitful is what we mean.
8. The leader will reflect on the reputation of rival firms in his or her own industry – some firms are identified as highly competent and honest, others have less of a reputation for honesty.
9. Rationality involves fitting the behaviour to the ends. Behavioural organizations are not smart enough to do this: they have certain programmed responses, and they always behave in this way. They act first, think later.
10. Describing the Virgin brand as a resource ignores much of what is known about brands – Virgin has many brands and all have to perform well in their respective markets to keep the corporate trademark as valuable as it currently is.
11. Management is obviously a type of labour, but it is a special type in this analysis.

References

Coase, R. (1937) 'The Nature of the Firm', *Economica*, vol. 4, pp. 386–405.

Doz, Y. L. and G. Hamel (1989) *Alliance Advantage: The Act of Creating Value Through Partnering* (Boston, Mass.: Harvard Business School Press).

Macmillan, J. (1990) 'Managing Suppliers: Incentive Systems in Japanese and United States', *California Management Review*, vol. 32, pp. 38–55.

Porter, M. E. (1980) *Competitive Strategy* (New York: Free Press).

Porter, M. E. (1985) *Competitive Advantage* (New York: Free Press).

Simon, H. (1983) *A Reason in Human Affairs* (Stanford, CA: Stanford University Press).

Williamson, O. (1975) *Markets and Hierarchies* (New York: Free Press).

Resource-Based View of the Firm

Véronique Ambrosini

Basic principles

The resource-based view of the firm examines the link between the internal characteristics of a firm and firm performance (Barney, 1991). Broadly speaking, this means that the resource-based view is concerned with the relationship between a firm's resources and competitive advantage. It suggests that an organization can be regarded as a bundle of resources, and that resources that are simultaneously *valuable, rare, imperfectly imitable* and *imperfectly substitutable* (ibid.) are a firm's main source of sustainable competitive advantage.

The underlying assumptions upon which the resource-based view of the firm is based are that:

- Resources are heterogeneous across organizations – that is, firms differ with respect to their resources; there is asymmetry in firms' resource endowment.
- This heterogeneity can remain stable over time, which means that resource transferability is limited. The resource-based view of the firm assumes that resources are not perfectly mobile across firms.

Before we embark on a more detailed elaboration of the approach, the following case study provides a practical context within which to explore this perspective.

Case study

The situation

The situation is a meeting of senior partners in Hart, Watchus and Massingham, a management consultancy that specializes in project management, strategy and managing change. The partnership employs 80 consultants and operates mainly in the UK, but some assignments are undertaken abroad.

David Watchus is the managing partner (CEO), Tony is the partner with responsibility for marketing the consultancy, Steve specializes in strategy projects and Kay specializes in 'change' projects. The partnership was founded 15 years ago by David and two other ex-McKinsey consultants (Hart and Massingham), who have since retired from the partnership. The conversation that follows comes from a regular monthly meeting.

The conversation

David: So if we stick to this agenda the next item is 'New Business'. Tony, can you kick us off?

Tony: If you look at these [hands around copies of a spreadsheet] . . . this summarizes the current status of all our major projects. The ones with a single asterisk are projects that are already up and running or nearing completion. The ones with two asterisks are ones that we are in the process of, hopefully, securing. I suggest we focus on those. The first is the Insurance strategy project. As I understand it – and Steve, maybe you can bring us right up to date on this – we are still on the shortlist, right?

Steve: Yes, that's right. If you remember this thing started out as a training programme for their branch managers. We were up against Wyatts, Andersons and we think Nicholls, and we were in with a reasonable chance of getting it. But then they shifted the 'spec' and now they say that they are looking for someone who can do the training, *and* help them with a much bigger change project. Unfortunately we didn't have much time to prepare for the presentation, and no-one from Kay's group was available on the day, so Trevor [one of the strategy consultants in Steve's group] had to wing it.

David: So what happened?

Steve: Well we got a call from Fiona Hall [from the insurance company] who seems to be batting for us, saying that the executives were not impressed, but if we can convince them on Friday that we're capable of handling the whole job, we're still in with a shout.

David: Why would she be wanting us to get it?

Kay: Well, I used to work with her at Coopers. We did a major change project for DHL in Frankfurt together. From what I gather from Trevor she expected to see me at the presentation.

David: And you couldn't make it?

Kay: No. I was in Singapore.

David: Well given that you have this connection is there any reason why you couldn't get involved at this stage? Can you make the presentation on Friday?

Kay: Well I'd obviously have to cancel some meetings, but if it's important, I'll be there.

David: That OK with you, Steve?

[Later in the same meeting]:

David: Right, now Steve you wanted to discuss USN. What's the problem?

Steve: As you know we've had work from USN for over five years now. It started out as a small project management training job, helping them learn how to use a software package, which seemed to go well. Then we managed to get involved in their reorganization programme, when they moved to product-based divisions, and now we're working with the top team on integrating the two most recent acquisitions. Remember the takeover of the insurance brokers? The problem is I feel we're being stretched too far. Glen Whittle is leading the team. He's been in there from the start and seems to have a good relationship with the executive in charge of Info Systems. So far we haven't screwed up, but I feel that in some of the areas we're getting involved in, we're skating on some very thin ice.

David: Well, I'm sure that's sounds a familiar situation to all of us! Half the fun is flying by the seat of your pants and we've always come good in the end.

Steve: Yes, I agree but frankly David, that was OK a decade ago, but now the clients are far more sophisticated. Half of the people who call us in are either ex-consultants or have worked for one of the big six [accounting firms]. You *could* get by in the past by thinking fast on your feet, but now there seem to be hundreds of consultancies all pitching for business that we would have expected to get a few years ago.

David: Well it's not all doom and gloom. We do manage to still win business? I think you're being overdramatic, Steve.

Tony [cutting in]: Yes, we do win some contracts, David. But I'm inclined to go along with Steve on this. Where we win business it's usually because we've already got some sort of relationship with the organization. We're not so good at getting completely new clients.

David: What about [names a recently secured project]?

Tony: Well, that's an example of new business, I agree. But let's be honest, part of the reason we got it was because Brian Lawrence, the human resources director [of the client organization] had worked with us when he was at BT.

Kay: Look, can I come in here? I agree with David that its not as gloomy as maybe Steve makes out. But we are increasingly becoming dependent on a few larger clients. Although in the change area we have been trying to build new business, particularly in the public sector, so far we have had no real successes. The closest we've come is with the restructuring project with the CAA. We think we were down to the last two, but they gave it to Ernst and Young in the end.

David: Did you talk to them afterwards? the CAA?

Kay: Yes, they said we were very close, and the guy who spoke to us said he'd actually preferred our approach, but the rest of the panel went for Ernst and Young. They said that Ernst and Young had more experience of this sort of project, which is of course true. I'm mean they've got a track record they can point to, whereas all our examples we could give them were from the private sector.

Issues

This executive meeting raises issues about how a firm gets business, keeps business and loses business to rival firms. The resource-based theory of the firm provides a rich perspective for exploring these fundamental business issues. At the end of the chapter we shall return to this conversation, but as you grapple with the material in the chapter, try to keep these four questions at the back of your mind:

- How does Hart, Watchus and Massingham win business?
- How does it hold on to clients?

- Why do you think it loses out to rival consultancies such as Ernst and Young?
- How could it improve its chance of winning really new business, such as the public sector work Kay refers to?

Key contributions

The origin of the perspective

Before embarking on the study of the resource-based view of the firm it may be worth recalling that strategic management is concerned with how some organizations outperform others, that is, how sustained advantage, expressed in the form of above-average profit levels or supernormal profits, is achieved.

Until the early 1980s strategic management was dominated by neoclassical economics, and notably the structure–conduct–performance paradigm of industrial organization economics (IO – see Chapter 2) (Caves and Porter, 1977; Caves, 1980; Porter, 1980). Briefly, IO's main thesis is that competitive advantage derives from a privileged market position. It argues that the prime determinant of an organization's performance is its external environment, the structure of the industry it belongs to. In other words, according to the IO perspective the sources of organizational profits are market positions – protected by barriers to entry into the market.

The resource-based theory of the firm takes a different approach. As mentioned at the start of this chapter, it claims that an organization can be regarded as a bundle of resources (Rumelt, 1984; Amit and Shoemaker, 1993), and it is some of these resources that enable a firm to obtain sustainable competitive advantage. In other words the resource-based view rests on the belief that competitive advantage does not depend on market and industry structures but on internal resources. This means that the resource-based view locates the source of superior profitability inside the firm. Superprofits are called 'rents', and they accrue to the specific assets and resources controlled by the firm.

The resource-based view of the firm is based on Selznicks' (1957) seminal work on 'distinctive competences', and on Penrose's (1959) argument that a firm is a collection of resources and that a firm's performance depends on its ability to use them. The resource-based view as such started with Wernerfelt's 1984 article and was developed by Barney (1986) and Dierickx and Cool (1989). However the resource-based view of the firm really took off in the 1990s (Barney, 1991; Conner, 1991; Mahoney and Pandian, 1992; Peteraf, 1993) and is now receiving the full attention of the strategic management community.

Although this wide exposure of the resource-based view is a recent phenomenon, it is worth noting that the perspective is highly consistent with the strategic management tradition as in essence it focuses on the strengths and weaknesses elements of the widely used SWOT analysis. This suggests that it would be misleading to argue that the resource-based view is in full opposition to IO or other economics-based perspectives. It may be more appropriate to consider this perspective as a complement to other theories. Finally, although the last decade has seen an explosion of conceptual work in this area, empirical studies have not followed the same pattern. There are still very few studies (Collis, 1991; Henderson and Cockburn, 1994; Miller and Shamsie, 1996) and there is little doubt that even if theoretical work is still needed, the future of the resource-based view lies very much in the search for empirical evidence.

Elaboration of the key principles of the resource-based view of the firm

Barney's (1991) work on the principles of the resource-based view is key to the perspective. His main contribution has been to characterize what allows a resource to be a source of competitive advantage, and in doing so to highlight the importance of the intangible, hard-to-define elements that can be found in organizations. We have structured what follows on Barney's work, complementing it where necessary.

What is a resource?

Before considering in more depth what the resource-based view is about, let us define what a 'resource' is. There is little argument about what it is, as actually it can be anything. For instance it has been defined as 'anything which could be thought of as a strength or weakness of a given firm' (Wernerfelt, 1984: 172), or as 'those (tangible and intangible) assets which are tied semi-permanently to the firm' (ibid.: 172). Resources can be categorized as physical resources (for example machinery, buildings), human resources (for example knowledge, experience, workers' insights), organizational resources (for example organizational culture, organizational structure, informal processes) and financial resources (for example debt, equity) (Barney, 1991).

Sometimes a distinction is made between resources and capabilities. 'Resource' is understood as resource possession and 'capability' as resource utilization (Brumagin, 1994). This means that when such a distinction is made, resources are usually seen as consisting of inputs into the production process, and capabilities as the processes by which the resources are utilized. Very often though, the general meaning of 'resources' is used, that is, the term encompasses both resources and capabilities.

Another distinction that is frequently made is that between tangible and intangible (or invisible) resources. Tangible resources are physical resources and include, for instance, equipment and finance, whereas intangible resources include resources such as brand, reputation, knowledge and organizational culture. Intangible resources have no physical features. As we shall see, intangible resources are the resources that are most often argued to be a source of competitive advantage, a source of performance difference among organizations, primarily because they are usually the most difficult resources to imitate.

Basic principles

The resource-based view does not propose that just any resource can be a source of competitive advantage. It must possess a number of characteristics and these characteristics must be held simultaneously:

- Resources must be *valuable*. A resource is said to be valuable if 'it exploits opportunities and/or neutralizes threats in a firm's environment' (Barney, 1991: 105), or expressed differently, if it 'enable[s] a firm to conceive of or implement strategies that improve its efficiency and effectiveness' (ibid.: 106). Note that although a resource may have added value in the past or is adding value now, changes in the environment such as new technology, changes in customers' needs or new competitors may render this resource less valuable in the future (Barney, 1995). A resource may even become dysfunctional. Resources may become 'competency traps' (Levitt and March, 1988) or 'core rigidities' (Leonard-Barton, 1992). Thus embedded resources that have worked in the past can cause dysfunctionality – they may block adaptation to changes in the environment, hinder innovation and lead to the continuation of inferior work practices. Generally speaking authors do not mention this feature separately because they consider it to be part of the definition of the term resource. When they employ the term it is assumed that the resource is valuable.
- Resources must be *rare*, that is, they must not be possessed by a large number of firms. A resource that is possessed by a large number of firms cannot be a source of sustainable competitive advantage; resources that are all the same cannot have a 'differential ability' (Conner, 1994). Resources that are valuable but not scarce can only be sources of competitive parity (Barney, 1995). Some resources may be essential but they are only pre-requisites, they are order-qualifying, not order-winning criteria. This does not imply that these resources do not matter, they do – they are needed by a firm if it is to be a player in the industry, they enable the firm to compete, to survive. This means that only resources that can make a positive difference can be a source of competitive advantage.
- Resources must be *imperfectly mobile*, that is, not easily traded. If resources can be easily bought and exchanged they cannot be a source of difference and therefore cannot be a source of sustainable competitive advantage.
- Resources must be *imperfectly imitable*, that is, other firms cannot obtain them by copying them. Once again, an organization's resource does not have a 'differential ability' (Conner, 1994) if its competitors can copy it, because if they can the organization's advantage will be nullified.
- There cannot be any strategically *equivalent substitutes* for them. If a resource can be easily substituted by another resource with the same strategic implications it cannot be a source of competitive advantage.

Rarity, imperfect immobility and imperfect imitability

As we have just seen, in order to be a source of sustainable competitive advantage a resource, must be simultaneously unique (rare), difficult to trade and difficult to duplicate and substitute. This raises the following questions. What makes a resource rare? What restricts a resource's mobility? What hinders the imitation of a resource? It is difficult to separate these questions from each other as each element affects the others and they can be fairly dependent on each other: a resource that is easy to imitate is unlikely to be unique, a difficult to trade resource is unlikely to be very common and so on. Hence we shall deal with the three questions together.

Resources can be difficult to imitate for various reasons, but the main one is that organizations have 'isolating mechanisms' (Rumelt, 1984). These mechanisms protect the organization's resources from imitation and preserve the stream of profits accruing to them. 'Causal ambiguity' is one such mechanism (Lippman and Rumelt, 1982). It relates to the uncertainty that 'stems from a basic ambiguity concerning the nature of the causal connections between actions and results, the factors responsible for performance differentials will resist precise identification' (ibid.: 418). Lippman and Rumelt argue that causal ambiguity 'acts as a powerful block on both imitation and factor mobility' (ibid.: 420). This is because competitors do not know the source of a rival firm's effectiveness, therefore they do not know what they should be imitating (Rumelt, 1987). Moreover it is often the case that a firm is as unaware as its competitors of the reasons for its competitive advantage, and therefore this advantage is likely to be sustained because imitation cannot take place (Barney, 1991) – the resources remain within the firm.

Barney (ibid.) implies that causal ambiguity can only be a real source of competitive advantage if firms themselves ignore the link between their resources and their advantage, because if they can understand this link, then so can others. Other firms can just go through the process of purchasing the resources they need and reproduce the same policies, and thus acquire the same advantage as the other organization. As a result the first organization loses its competitive advantage through the imitation of its resources. Thus it appears that a competitive advantage can only be sustained if a firm ignores its origin, which makes replication almost impossible. Lippman and Rumelt (1982: 420) acknowledge that immobility can frequently be explained by uniqueness, but they affirm that uncertainty and uniqueness are independent because, 'in the absence of uncertainty, the creation of a unique resource could be repeated and its uniqueness destroyed'. They state that factors are immobile not because they are unique but because they cannot be replicated due to their causal ambiguity.

Causal ambiguity is certainly one of the main reasons for a resource's inimitability and immobility, but it is not the only one. Other factors that can cause a resource to remain immobile (and rare) include:

- *Time compression diseconomies* (Dierickx and Cool, 1989). This is essentially linked to the 'path dependency' of certain resources. These resources are firm-specific and imperfectly imitable because they are history-dependent (Barney, 1991). Factors such as routines, organizational culture, past investments and so on strongly affect the development of resources. This is at the root of the suggestion that inimitability can stem from the difficulty of discovering and repeating the development processes responsible for a resource's existence. In other words, 'this idiosyncrasy makes them difficult to imitate and their development time cannot be easily be compressed' (Amit and Shoemaker, 1993: 39).
- *Asset mass efficiencies and interconnectedness of asset stocks* (Dierickx and Cool, 1989). Resources can remain immobile and cannot be replicated or transferred because the initial level of an asset influences the pace of further accumulation, and because the accumulation of a particular stock does not depend just on the level of that stock but also on the levels of other

stocks. More precisely, asset mass efficiencies relate to the fact that some assets can be more difficult and perhaps more costly to accumulate when the organization's current stock of that particular asset is small (Verdin and Williamson, 1994). Interconnectedness of asset stocks refers to the situation where a 'lack of complementary assets can often impede a firm from accumulating an asset which it needs to serve its market successfully' (Verdin and Williamson, 1994: 87). For these reasons, replicating a resource can be extremely difficult, if not impossible.

More simply, we could say that time-compression diseconomies, asset-mass efficiencies and the interconnectedness of asset stocks are about the fact that history matters. As organizations develop they acquire resources and develop traditions, ways of doing things, and hence develop a unique personality or culture: they develop reputation and knowledge and these resources are extremely difficult to imitate because their existence is due to the firm's unique history, the unique paths the firm has travelled (founder, employees, events, industry and so on). The firm has resources it can only have because of the situations it has faced. Resource accumulation cannot be reproduced overnight, and it might be impossible to reproduce at all because the same historical circumstances are not likely to be repeated.

- *Complexity and social complexity*. Reed and DeFillippi (1990) suggest that resources that are complex can generate ambiguity. This argument is very close to the ones above. It states that resources can emerge from a large number of technologies, experiences and routines, and that this combination of elements renders replication almost impossible (Reed and DeFillippi, 1990; Kogut and Zander, 1992). Barney (1991) emphasizes the importance of social complexity. He argues that some resources can be difficult to replicate because they are socially complex; they are 'beyond the ability of firms to systematically manage and influence' (ibid.: 110). Examples of socially complex phenomena include interpersonal relations among managers in a firm, organizational culture and a firm's reputation among suppliers and customers.

- *Specificity*. Some resources 'are specialized to a particular usage or firm' (Castanias and Helfat, 1991: 162), and due to the transaction-specificity to a firm of these resources they cannot be fully copied. This can be easily understood with Nonaka's (1991: 103) explanation that 'what makes sense in one context can change or even lose its meaning when communicated to people in a different context'. This means that some resources could perhaps be transferred from one organization to another, however their efficiency or effectiveness would not be as great as it was before because the environment, the context as a whole would be different.

- *Codifiability*. This could be seen as almost a summarizing idea. If resources are tangible, or if their structure is defined by a set of identifiable rules (Kogut and Zander, 1992) – that is, if they can be articulated (Winter, 1987) – then resources are likely to be easily imitated and consequently they cannot be a source of competitive advantage. Hence in the resource-based view they are not resources at all. The fact that resources that are difficult to codify are potential sources of sustainable competitive advantage has led strategy researchers to argue that tacit knowledge plays a central part in the development of sustainable competitive advantage. They propose that because of the ability of competitors quickly to acquire resources, 'sustainability of competitive advantage . . . requires resources which are idiosyncratic . . . and not so easily transferable or replicable. The criteria point to knowledge (tacit knowledge in particular) as the most strategically-important resource of the firm' (Grant, 1993: 2).

What is tacit knowledge and why can it be a source of sustainable competitive advantage?

Most definitions of tacit knowledge begin with Polanyi's (1966: 4) assertion that 'we can know more than we can tell'. Based on this assertion, it has been argued that tacit knowledge has three main characteristics:

- It cannot be verbalized. Tacit knowledge is hard to formalize. Because of that, tacit knowledge is said to be attached to the knower. It is personal knowledge.
- It is practical. Tacit knowledge is a knowledge about how to do things. It is purposive, it is not about 'knowing about'.
- It is context-specific. Tacit knowledge is organization-specific, it depends on particular relationships, settings, tools, tasks and so on.

These characteristics explain why tacit knowledge is seen as critical in the resource-based view: it possesses the features that define a resource. Because tacit knowledge is deeply ingrained in people or organizations it is taken for granted and 'it becomes difficult for outsiders to imitate or copy' (Sobol and Lei, 1994: 171). Indeed tacit knowledge cannot quickly migrate – that is, it cannot be transposed to other firms – because it depends on specific relationships (between colleagues, customers, systems and so on) and because, 'unlike knowledge of a computer code or a chemical formula, it cannot be clearly and completely communicated to someone else through words or other symbols' (Badaracco, 1991: 82). Tacitness also generates ambiguity because the organization is unaware that such resources and some of the actions it takes are sources of its competitive advantage. In other words the relation between actions and results is causally ambiguous (Reed and DeFillippi, 1990).

Thus all the characteristics of tacit knowledge described in the resource-based view show that it is heterogeneous across firms, inimitable, not transferable and rare because it is firm- and job-specific, and hence it is likely to play a central part in the development of competitive advantage.

Links to strategy

The major contribution of the resource-based view of the firm is that it encourages managers to look inside for competitive advantage. The resource-based view directs attention to vital sources of advantage that have hitherto been avoided, misunderstood or unrecognized by other strategic management perspectives such as industrial organization (IO) economics. By focusing attention on resources that are rare, imperfectly imitable and imperfectly mobile, the resource-based view recognizes that since tangible resources are easily traded (equipment, software and so on can be bought off the shelf), competitive advantage is likely to derive from intangible/idiosyncratic resources. What is also likely to create a difference between firms is how these resources are utilized. One consequence of the recognition that intangible resources are the most likely source of competitive advantage is the acknowledgement that people matter. However this does not signify that physical resources are irrelevant to organizational success, they are important but they are not likely to be a source of sustained advantage.

In the following discussion we shall concentrate on how the resource-based view of the firm addresses our central strategy topics: the 7 Cs of strategic management: (context, competences, culture, control, competing, change and corporate strategies).

Context

In the resource-based view of the firm the external environment receives little attention. This perspective is only interested in the external environment insofar as it allow firms to make profits, to realize value. As mentioned previously, Barney (1991) argues that a resource must be valuable, and he defines valuable in the following terms: 'it exploits opportunities and/or neutralizes threats in a firm's environment' (ibid.: 105). Other proponents of the perspective have also looked at the environment as a source of value. For instance some have defined a resource as valuable if it enables customers' needs to be better satisfied (Verdin and Williamson, 1994).

The general lack of attention to the external environment by resource-based theorist may be because they have not had time to develop the theory as the field is fairly new, or they may be satisfied by the IO analysis (provided notably by Porter's five forces framework). If the latter is right then we can argue that the resource-based view of the firm and IO are not in direct opposition and may complement each other.

Another reason why the external environment has received little attention from resource-based theorists is that it is not believed to be generator of competitive advantage. Most organizations have access to the same environmental information. Even if a firms is the first to gain access to information other firms soon follow suit, and therefore the advantage gained will be short-lived.

Before tackling the issue of core competences it is worth considering one of the parallels between IO economics and the resource-based view. One similarity has to do with the IO concepts of 'barriers to entry' (barriers that protect industry participants from potential entrants) and 'mobility barriers' (barriers that serve to isolate groups of similar firms in a heterogeneous industry) – 'barriers to imitability' and 'isolating mechanisms' are the resource-based terms for these concepts. While all these concepts are fairly similar (Mahoney and Pandian, 1992) there are differences in the level of analysis involved. Entry barriers are at the industry level, mobility barriers at the strategic group level and isolating mechanisms at the firm level. However all these barriers are a theoretical explanation for the existence of sustained advantage and sustained rents. They are all means of protecting rent-generating resources.

Competences

As pointed out earlier, because of the dynamic conditions of the market place there are very few resources that can be argued to be a long-term source of advantage. Most tangible resources can be purchased or replicated. Hence it has been argued that intangible assets are now the most strategically important resource of the firm. There are numerous terms for these intangible assets. In the strategic management literature they are described as resources, capabilities, strategic assets, organizational competences, competencies and core competences, among others.

The use of so many expressions means that the resource-based literature is not always easy to comprehend. There is no one unique definition, but they all share some characteristics. Competences (or intangible resources and so on) are:

- Intangible.
- Similar to know-how.
- Embedded in the organization.
- Reside in people (not in machines).

This means that they respect the basic principles of the resource-based view of the firm, they possess the criteria considered as a *sine qua non* for a resource to be a source of advantage (see the first section of this chapter).

The term 'core competences' comes from Prahalad and Hamel (1990; Hamel and Prahalad, 1994), whose work made resource-based arguments more widely known among the business community. They define a core competence as a bundle of skills and technologies rather than a single discrete skill or technology. It represents the sum of learning across individual skill sets and individual organizational units, and it is unlikely to reside in its entirety in a single individual or small team. Hamel and Prahalad emphasize that (and this is similar to the resource-based view of the firm criteria) for a competence to be core it must meet three criteria:

- *Customer value.* A core competence must make a disproportionate contribution to perceived value. That does not imply that the core competence will be visible to or understood by the customer. There is an exception to the 'customer value' rule. Any bundle of skills that yields a significant cost advantage in the delivery of a particular customer benefit may also be termed a core competence.
- *Competitor differentiation.* To qualify as a core competence a capability must also be competitively unique. This does not mean that to qualify as a core competence a competence must be uniquely held by a single firm, but it does mean that any capability that is ubiquitous across an industry should not be defined as core. It makes little sense to define a competence

as core if it is omnipresent or easily imitated by competitors. Benchmarking an organization's competences against those of competitors helps guard against a natural tendency to overstate the uniqueness of one's own capabilities.

- *Extendibility*. In defining core competence managers must abstract the core competence from the particular product configuration in which the core competence is currently embedded and imagine how it might be applied in new product arenas. A core competence is truly core when it forms the basis for entry into new product markets.

Hamel and Prahalad (1994) make clear what a core competence is *not*. In doing so they emphasize the difference between tangible and intangible resources. They highlight that core competences are not assets in the accounting sense – they do not appear on balance sheets. Factories, distribution channels, brands or patents are not core competences, but an aptitude to manage them may be one. Thus if we were to discriminate between resource and capability, as explained previously, it would be appropriate to use the term capability rather than resource when referring to core competences. Finally, Hamel and Prahalad argue that all core competences are sources of competitive advantage, but not all competitive advantages are core competences. For instance an advantage based on a physical asset or on luck does not derive from a core competence.

Culture

As discussed earlier, intangible resources are more likely to be sources of sustained advantage than are tangible assets. When we discussed the reasons for rarity, imperfect immobility and imperfect imitability we explained that path dependency and social complexity are source of inimitability and we gave organizational culture as an example of a socially complex phenomenon. Barney (1986: 657) defines culture as 'a complex set of values, beliefs, assumptions and symbols that define the way in which a firm conducts its business'. He argues that culture can be valuable because it can enable things to happen in the organization that can positively affect its performance (culture can encourage innovation, customer focus, flexibility and so on, which help a firm's efficiency).

He explains that cultures are unique to individual organizations because they develop over time. Organizational culture is embedded in a firm's history and heritage – it reflects the unique circumstances of the firm's birth and growth, the experiences of its employees and so on. This mix is idiosyncratic to each organization – no two organizations ever follow identical patterns of development. Barney also argues that culture is very difficult to imitate. This is because culture is socially complex, path dependent and difficult for outsiders to observe. It is even difficult for insiders to describe, and this problem with articulating and codifying their organizational culture means that it is difficult or impossible for competitors to emitate that culture. Barney (1992: 48) adds that 'because of the subtle multidimensional character of socially complex organizational resources [such as culture], they are not likely to have close strategic substitutes'.

Competing

The resource-based view of the firm focuses almost entirely on how firms can achieve competitive advantage through internal resources that enable them to exploit opportunities in their environment or conceive or implement strategies to improve their efficiency and effectiveness.

The main implications of this perspective in terms of competitive strategy are that in order to compete firms need to manage their resources. This requires three kinds of effort: they must protect their current resources, they must continually improve their resources and they must build new resources. Firms cannot depend on their current resources as these may cease to be valuable. Changes in the environment may render them obsolete.

A firm must be able to identify its resources, in particular it must try to identify those 'which are durable, difficult to identify and understand, imperfectly transferable, nor easily replicated, and in which the firm possesses clear ownership and control' (Grant, 1991: 129), that is, it must identify those which conform to the basic principles of the resource-based view of the firm (see the section on key principles above).

Once it has done so the firm can start to design its strategy. From the resource-based standpoint, strategic choice is limited by what the firm's resources are. If firms adopt strategies that are not based on their core competences they will only be able to realize short-term returns, at best. Their advantage will not be sustainable as it is likely to be quickly competed away by imitators.

This raises the question of what 'sustainable' advantage means. A firm has a sustainable competitive advantage when it is implementing a value-creating strategy that is not simultaneously being implemented by current or potential competitors and when these other firms are unable to duplicate the benefits of this strategy. This means that sustained advantage is not linked to the period in which the advantage is sustained. The resource-based view recognizes that *competitive* advantage may sometimes not derive from rare, non-imitable and immobile resources, but that *sustained* advantage does derive from these resource qualities.

The most favourable way to boost long-term prospects is for firms to design strategies that build on their current resources. Resources are not product-specific and therefore organizations can attempt to leverage their resources. Can the resources be used in different markets? Can they be used in order better to serve the same market? However, when considering strategies that build on current resources the firm should not ignore questions such as the following. Do we need new resources to exploit our current market? Are there any new market opportunities and do we need new resources to exploit them?

Competitive strategy is conceptually easy to grasp in that it incorporates mainstream strategic ideas and is fully consistent with the core principles of the resource-based view of the firm: organizations should build on what they are good at, and they should establish where resource gaps lie and try to fill these gaps. There are not, as we shall see, many tools in the resource-based tool kit to help develop competitive strategies. However it might be worth mentioning Porter's approach. He asserts that organizations can examine what they are currently doing and identify what makes them unique by answering the following questions (Porter, 1996: 76):

- Which of our product or service varieties are the most distinctive?
- Which of our product or service varieties are the most profitable?
- Which of our customers are most satisfied?
- Which customers, channels or purchase occasions are the most profitable?
- Which of the activities in our value chain are the most different and effective?

He also argues that companies must examine what they did in the past and determine whether this is still appropriate.

Corporate strategy

The resource-based view of the firm can have serious implications for corporate strategy, notably in terms of diversification. Proponents of the resource-based view argue that diversification is most likely to be successful if it is based on the firm's specific resources. In other words diversification is recommended to exploit resources that have uses in markets that are not currently exploited by the firm. This means that the resource-based view supports related diversification. It argues that 'the rationale for multibusiness organizations ultimately lies in sharing strategic capabilities among businesses' (Robins and Wiersema, 1995, p. 279). It suggests that related diversification can increase firm value by sharing specific assets such as production capacity, know-how and so on, and that because unrelated diversification is not based on shared resources it will not increase the firm's cost or differentiation advantage (Wiersema and Liebeskind, 1995). It could be noted that this argument is not only theoretical, there is also empirical evidence to show that there is a correlation between the relatedness of the businesses in a portfolio and corporate performance: the economic performance of organizations with unrelated, diversified businesses is lower than that of those with related businesses (Rumelt, 1974; Robins and Wiersema, 1995). This position is very much in the tradition of strategic management. Diversification is seen as a way of matching a firm's resources with market opportunities. The crux of the resource-based prescription for corporate strategy is that firms should adopt strategies that their resources can support (Peteraf, 1993).

More precisely Collis (1996) argues that corporate strategy should be about relatedness, that what he calls the three elements of corporate strategy – resources, portfolio of businesses, and organizational structure, processes and systems – must be aligned. Resource relatedness is the match between the organization's resources and what is needed to generate competitive advantage. Business relatedness is about the extent to which the 'activities of the businesses are mutually reinforcing and exploit economies of scope' (ibid.: 134), and each of the businesses should contribute to the development of the corporation's resources. Finally, organizational relatedness is about how the structure, processes and systems 'used to control and co-ordinate the corporation fit with the resources it is leveraging across markets' (ibid.: 127), and about the relevance to the business of the 'dominant logic' (personality, ways of thinking, experience and so on) of the managers in the corporation. In short Collis argues that 'when businesses fit the alignment of the elements of corporate strategy, they are related and deserve to be in the corporate portfolio, regardless of how disparate they appear in product market terms. When businesses do not fit this alignment, they do not belong inside the corporation, regardless of how similar the products may be. He concludes that 'the best corporate strategies are indeed related – just not related in the traditional way of thinking' (ibid.: 139).

This issue of relatedness implies that outsourcing is a corporate decision, and this lies within the framework of the resource-based view of the firm. Corporations should not try to do what they cannot do well enough to achieve competitive advantage. The outsourcing of activities that are not core to the business is thus a corollary of the focus on valuable resources.

An obstacle that corporations might face when searching for novel ways of using their resources is the problem of specificity of resources. As we saw earlier, specificity is a great isolating mechanism: it hinders resource transfer. What works in one part of the corporation may not work as well (or not at all) in other parts, and what works in one environment may not work in another. Resource specificity can have important ramifications for corporations: if the cause of success is based on specific, idiosyncratic resources, this suggests that one cannot transfer strategy 'recipes' from one business unit to another, or even from one part of a business unit to another. Generic strategies just become the equivalent of tangible resources that are available to any organization and therefore may not be sources of advantage. Organizations have to be able to tailor their strategies to each specific situation they are facing.

Change

If intangible resources are a source of competitive advantage it is of prime importance for organizations to be aware of them and to deploy them in an effective and efficient manner. Yet because intangible resources generate causal ambiguity (organizations are not aware of the links between their actions and results), managers may not know exactly how competitive advantage is generated in their organization. Causal ambiguity is an important issue for any organization and it can be seen as both a positive and a negative element. On the positive side, if managers do not know the source of the organization's success they cannot explain to anybody else why the organization is successful, and hence this source of advantage cannot be imitated. However, because of their lack of awareness managers may destroy the source of success, for instance when embarking on an organizational change programme. If managers are not aware of what generates success they may inadvertently change something that is vital to it, for example by delayering or business process re-engineering.

Control

Control versus possessing

Control is a crucial issue in the resource-based view of the firm. We have seen that it is resources that are rare and so on that enable a firm to achieve competitive advantage. This perspective argues that causal ambiguity is one of the best isolating mechanisms, that is, if a resource displays causal ambiguity then it is unlikely to be imitated and is therefore likely to remain a source of sustainable competitive advantage. In other words the resource-based view implies that it may best for a firm not to understand its resources or how they generate competitive advantage because this will prevent imitation. This is a real dilemma – what should organizations do?

Should they try to identify their sources of competitive advantage and strive to nurture and develop them? Or should they leave things as they are and hence limit the risk of imitation by their competitors? Either way they are vulnerable: if they do not identify and manage the resources that render them successful they may inadvertently destroy them and lose their competitive advantage; but if they do, those resources may be imitated. In short the question is: should organizations try to control their resources or adopt a more laissez-faire strategic approach?

Value capture

The resource-based view of the firm pays attention to the control of value-generating resources. If the original owners of a resource recognize its true value, and if they are in a position to bargain with the firm, they may be able to capture all the rents from the resource. For example if a top-class footballer can negotiate a huge wage when signing with a new club, the 'rent' from the skills he deploys in the team may accrue to him and not the club owners.

When organizations downsize the focus shifts to the core activities of the firm. This may well lead to the identification of groups or individuals who are vital resources, that is, those who do most to help the firm win business (for example a salesperson, a creative designer or a consultant). Because the resource-based view starts with the premise that resources are heterogeneous across firms, this can help us understand some factors in the capture of value, as well as its creation.

Organizational structure

The resource-based view has no one prescription for organizational structure. We might assume that the structure advocated is the structure that will allow the best exploitation of the firm's resources. Thus the resource-based view would lead us to consider structuring the organization in a way that best develops, nurtures and exploits competences. This may be seen as an argument for reorganizing staff into competence-based groupings, rather than grouping by function, product or project; or for divisions being defined by their competences, rather than geographically or by product scope. As Prahalad and Hamel (1990) comment, corporations used to be structured into strategic business units (SBUs) – that is, into a portfolio of businesses related in product market terms – and the autonomy of SBUs used to be sacrosanct. Now, with the resource-based view of the firm, corporations are encouraged to base their structure on their core competences.

Finally, new specialisms are emerging that reflect a resource-based perspective. 'Competence champions', 'knowledge management consultants', staff that address linkages across the organization and specialists that focus on knowledge creation, or the development of a 'learning organization', synergy and so on could all be linked to this perspective.

Tools and techniques

So far there are no techniques that are specific to the resource-based view of the firm. Traditional research methods (surveys, interviews, desk research) have been used in the few empirical studies conducted from this perspective. It has not yet spawned a set of tools and techniques that can be easily used by managers or help elicit a firm's core competences (and not a generalized notion of resources). However causal mapping techniques can be adapted to reveal some of the cultural and tacit elements of the organization (Ambrosini and Bowman, 1997) and generate useful insights into these aspects, which are typically not easy to express or amenable to analysis. Causal maps are in many respects similar to Porter's (1996) activity-system maps, but they are much more detailed. Activity-system maps are akin the first step of a causal map – they describe the activities in which the organization is engaged. A causal map goes beyond this: it allows the exploration of 'how', the detail of how things are done in the organization, the 'nitty gritty' of the organization.

Case study revisited

In light of the discussion in the preceding sections, what issues can be raised from the conversation in the case study, and how can the four questions asked subsequently be addressed?

The resource-based view of the firm encourages us to look at what is happening inside Hart, Watchus and Massingham and how that is affecting its performance.

How do Hart, Watchus and Massingham win business?

The partnership has competences in certain areas of consulting that make it a credible contender for this kind of work. However winning business for which it is short-listed depends on particular resources that give it an advantage, such as a track record or reputation in the field. This resource is actually in the minds of potential customers rather than under the direct control of the partnership. Another order-winning resource it possesses has to do with the personal relationships that individuals have with particular clients.

How does Hart, Watchus and Massingham hold on to clients?

Again, the partnership relies on personal relationships with clients to sustain its current business, but unless it has competences that are specific to its consultancy assignments, even strong personal ties will be insufficient to retain its clients. These competences may lie in the past development of certain approaches that are effective and valued by clients, for instance training people in project management. The resource-based view of the firm alerts us to some of the dangers here. First if these ways of doing things are implicit and operate at a tacit or an intuitive level, they may be difficult to instil into new staff. Second, if senior managers are not aware of these sources of advantage they may inadvertently destroy them, for example by placing stronger emphasis on cost efficiency or by reorganizing into different, more 'logical' groupings. Third, if the partnership does succeed in understanding and specifying its sources of advantage, by making these explicit and inculcating them into new staff it runs the risk of other consultancies imitating what it does.

Why does Hart, Watchus and Massingham lose out to rival consultancies?

Relationships with consultants usually operate at the individual level. Rival consultancies will have their own relationships with their clients, leading to some inertia and making it difficult to persuade these clients to shift to Hart, Watchus and Massingham.

However the partnership may be losing business because it does not fully understand what particular clients are looking for, and how they make their judgements. Although the partnership may have excellent technical competences in conducting consultancy assignments, it may lack the insights required to win over new clients.

What can the resource-based view of the firm prescribe for Hart, Watchus and Massingham?

The partnership should try to identify its current sources of advantage. It should establish the nature of its core competences and where they reside. By doing so it may reveal that some people (and others whom they know) are key to the organization. It may also more fully appreciate that the relationships it has with present clients are vital to its business. It might discover what it is that keeps clients loyal. Does it have a special competence in customer relations?

The partnership should then reassess the contracts it is trying to win. Does it have the competences needed not only to win these contracts but also to fulfil them? Up to now the partnership has been doing business predominantly in the private sector, but now it wants to target the public sector. Do it have the resources to do so? Are its private sector competences transferable to the public sector? Does its organizational culture allow it to understand the public sector, or is it trying to apply a private sector mind set to the public sector? If it does have the competences to serve the public sector, does it have enough people to battle on so many fronts?

Further reading

Barney, J. R. (1991) 'Firm resources and sustained competitive advantage', *Journal of Management*, vol. 17, no. 1, pp. 99–120.

Conner, K. R. (1991) 'A historical comparison of resources-based theory and five schools of thought within industrial organisation economics: do we have a new theory of the firm?', *Journal of Management*, vol. 17, no. 1, pp. 121–54.

Dierickx, I. and K. Cool (1989) 'Asset stock accumulation and sustainability of competitive advantage', *Management Science*, vol. 35, no. 12, pp. 1504–11.

Grant, R. M. (1991) 'The resource-based theory of competitive advantage: implications for strategy formulation', *California Management Review*, vol. 33, no. 3, pp. 114–35.

Wernerfelt, B. (1984) 'A resource-based view of the firm', *Strategic Management Journal*, vol. 5, pp. 171–80.

References

Ambrosini, V. and C. Bowman (1997) 'An empirical exploration of tacit knowledge', paper presented at the Strategic Management Society annual conference, Barcelona.

Amit, R. and P. J. H. Shoemaker (1993) 'Strategic assets and organizational rents', *Strategic Management Journal*, vol. 14, pp. 33–46.

Badaracco, J. L. (1991) *The knowledge link* (Boston, Mass.: Harvard Business School Press).

Barney, J. B. (1986) 'Organizational culture: can it be a source of sustained competitive advantage?', *Academy of Management Review*, vol. 11, no. 3, pp. 656–65.

Barney, J. B. (1991) 'Firm resources and sustained competitive advantage', *Journal of Management*, vol. 17, no. 1, pp. 99–120.

Barney, J. B. (1992) 'Integrating organizational behavior and strategy formulation research: a resource-based analysis', *Advances in Strategic Management*, vol. 8, pp. 39–61.

Barney, J. B. (1995) 'Looking inside for competitive advantage', *Academy of Management Executive*, vol. 9, no. 4, pp. 49–61.

Brumagin, A. L. (1994) 'A hierarchy of corporate resources', *Advances in Strategic Management*, vol. 10, pp. 81–112.

Castanias, R. P. and C. E. Helfat (1991) 'Managerial resources and rents', *Journal of Management*, vol. 17, no. 1, pp. 155–71.

Caves, R. E. (1980) 'Industrial organization, corporate strategy and structure', *Journal of Economic Literature*, vol. 18, pp. 64–92.

Caves, R. E. and M. Porter (1977) 'From entry barriers to mobility barriers: conjectural decisions and contrived deterrence to new competition', *Quarterly Journal of Economics*, vol. 91, pp. 241–62.

Collis, D. (1991) 'A resource-based analysis of global competition: the case of the bearings industry', *Strategic Management Journal*, vol. 12, pp. 49–68.

Collis, D. (1996) 'Related corporate portfolio', in M. Goold and K. Sommers Luchs (eds), *Managing the multibusiness company: strategic issues for diversified groups* (London: Routledge), pp. 122–42.

Conner, K. R. (1991) 'A historical comparison of resources-based theory and five schools of thought within industrial organisation economics: do we have a new theory of the firm?', *Journal of Management*, vol. 17, no. 1, pp. 121–54.

Conner, K. R. (1994) 'The resource-based challenge to the industry-structure perspective', Best Paper Proceedings, annual meeting of the Academy of Management, Dallas.

Dierickx, I. and K. Cool (1989) 'Asset stock accumulation and sustainability of competitive advantage', *Management Science*, vol. 35, no. 12, pp. 1504–11.

Grant, R. M. (1991) 'The resource-based theory of competitive advantage: implications for strategy formulation', *California Management Review*, vol. 33, no. 3, pp. 114–35.

Grant, R. M. (1993) 'Organisational capabilities within a knowledge-based view of the firm', paper presented at the annual meeting of the Academy of Management, Atlanta, Georgia.

Hamel, G. and C. K. Prahalad (1994) *Competing for the Future* (Boston, Mass.: Harvard Business School Press).

Henderson, R. and I. Cockburn (1994) 'Measuring competence? Exploring firm effects in pharmaceutical research', *Strategic Management Journal*, vol. 15, pp. 63–84.

Kogut, B. and U. Zander (1992) 'Knowledge of the firm, combinative capabilities, and the replication of technology', *Organisation science*, vol. 3, pp. 383–96.

Leonard-Barton, B. D. (1992) 'Core capabilities and core rigidities: a paradox in managing new product development', *Strategic Management Journal*, vol. 13, pp. 111–26.

Levitt, B. and J. G. March (1988) 'Organizational learning', *Annual Review of Sociology*, vol. 14, pp. 319–40.

Lippman, S. A. and R. P. Rumelt (1982) 'Uncertain imitability: an analysis of interfirm differences in efficiency under competition', *Bell Journal of Economics*, vol. 13, no. 2, pp. 418–38.

Mahoney, J. T. and J. R. Pandian (1992) 'The resource-based view within the conversation of strategic management', *Strategic Management Journal*, vol. 13, pp. 363–80.

Miller, D. and J. Shamsie (1996) 'The resource-based view of the firm in two environments: the Hollywood film studios from 1936 to 1965', *Academy of Management Journal*, vol. 39, no. 3, pp. 519–43.

Nonaka, I. (1991) 'The knowledge-creating company', *Harvard Business Review*, vol. 69, no. 6, pp. 96–104.

Penrose, E. T. (1959) *The theory of growth of the firm* (New York: Wiley).

Peteraf, M. A. (1993) 'The cornerstone of competitive advantage: a resource-based view', *Strategic Management Journal*, vol. 14, pp. 179–91.

Polanyi, M. (1966) *The tacit dimension* (New York: Doubleday).

Porter, M. E. (1980) *Competitive Strategy: techniques for analysing industries and competitors* (New York: Free Press).

Porter, M. E. (1996) 'What is strategy?', *Harvard Business Review*, vol. 74, no. 6, pp. 61–78.

Prahalad, C. K. and G. Hamel (1990) 'The core competence of the corporation', *Harvard Business Review*, vol. 68, no. 3, pp. 79–91.

Reed, R. and R. J. DeFillipi (1990) 'Causal ambiguity, barriers to imitation and sustainable competitive advantage', *Academy of Management Review*, vol. 15, no. 1, pp. 88–102.

Robins, J. and M. F. Wiersema (1995) 'A resource-based approach to the multibusiness firm: empirical analysis of portfolio interrelationships and corporate financial performance', *Strategic Management Journal*, vol. 16, pp. 277–99.

Rumelt, R. P. (1974) *Strategy, Structure, and Economic Performance* (Cambridge, Mass.: Harvard University Press).

Rumelt, R. (1984) 'Toward a strategic theory of the firm', in R. Lamb (ed.), *Competitive strategic management* (Englewood Cliffs, NJ: Prentice-Hall), pp. 556–70.

Rumelt, R. (1987) 'Theory, strategy and entrepreneurship', in D. J. Teece (ed.), *The competitive challenge* (Cambridge, Mass.: Ballinger), pp. 137–58.

Selznick, P. (1957) *Leadership in administration: a sociological interpretation* (New York: Harper and Row).

Sobol, M. G. and D. Lei (1994) 'Environment, manufacturing technology and embedded knowledge', *International Journal of Human Factors in Manufacturing*, vol. 4, no. 2, pp. 167–89.

Verdin, P. J. and P. J. Williamson (1994) 'Core competences, competitive advantage and market analysis: forging the links', in G. Hamel and A. Heene (eds), *Competence-based competition*, (Chichester: John Wiley and Sons), pp. 77–110.

Wernerfelt, B. (1984) 'A resource-based view of the firm', *Strategic Management Journal*, vol. 5, pp. 171–80.

Wiersema, M. F. and J. P. Liebeskind (1995) 'The effects of leveraged buyout on corporate growth and diversification in large firms', *Strategic Management Journal*, vol. 16, pp. 447–60.

Winter, S. G. (1987) 'Knowledge and competence as strategic assets', in D. J. Teece (ed.), *The Competitive Challenge* (Cambridge, Mass.: Ballinger), pp. 159–84.

8 Military Strategy
Philip Davies

Basic principles

Carl von Clausewitz's seminal work *On War*, published in 1832, was based on 20 years operational experience in the Napoleonic Wars, followed by 12 years of teaching military tactics and strategy at the Berlin Military Academy. He therefore had a unique perspective on military strategy as a practitioner and as a teacher. He believed that theory must be based on observation and should avoid spurious claims. Above all 'it must stick to the point and never part company with those who have to manage things in battle by the light of their native wit' (Clauswitz, 1982:231). What he had to say about warfare can, I believe, also be applied to business. If we were to substitute 'business' for 'Strategy' in the following quotation, how much support would there be among strategic management scholars and executives for the views expressed? 'In Strategy, everything is simple but not on that account very easy . . . to carry out the plan without being obliged to deviate from it a thousand times by a thousand varying influences' (ibid.: 243).

Similar statements are often made about strategic management. Some of the early Harvard strategists described general or strategic management as 'fuzzy, complicated and imprecise' (Uyterhoeven *et al.*, 1973: 4). More recently Hill and Jones (1998: 17) have almost paraphrased Clausewitz in support of the case for the process of strategy being messy and emergent: 'The principles, rules, or even systems of strategy must always fall short, undermined by the world's endless complexities. . . . In strategy most things are uncertain and variable.'

Echoes of military theory can be heard throughout the strategic management field. This chapter seeks to demonstrate the relevance of military strategy for strategic management theory and practice.

What is military strategy about? It is concerned with the development, deployment and use of, or threat to use, armed forces in support of national or multinational strategy. 'War is not merely an act of policy, but a true political instrument . . . the political object is the goal, war is merely the means, and means can never be considered in isolation from their purpose' (Clausewitz, 1982: 87). Military strategists seek to gain a better understanding of war in order to develop methodologies, doctrines, principles and theories that will enable better use of military forces. These principles are for guidance only: each situation must be judged on its merits. Military strategy is an evolving conversation on the nature and practice of warfare, and is used to inform and shape national defence policy, war fighting, war planning and the choice of technology and force structures.

153

While the strategy processes in armies, navies and airforces display all the characteristics that can be seen in civilian organizations – institutionalism, political games and inertia – what always stops the study of war from becoming sterile is the high cost of failure and the reality of casualties in combat. Military commanders are normally chosen from among those who have had experience of combat – whether at sea, on land or in the air.

This chapter has two objectives:

- To position military strategy within the broad sweep of management thinking.
- To show how an understanding of this field is both interesting in itself and of value to strategic management scholars.

Why is military strategy relevant?

An understanding of military strategy is relevant for strategic management scholars and business management students because of their common history and language. Practitioners commonly use military metaphors, and business and military leaders have a common problem set: how to decide what to do under conditions of uncertainty and stress when the consequences of failure will be very unpleasant.

Strategy as a military concept dates back to sixth-century BC Athens, where the *strategos* was a person elected to fight a campaign and control all the forces – an early example of the principle of unity of command. Much of what is now commonplace in strategic thinking, such as positioning, capabilities, strategic intent and focus, is evident in the campaigns of Alexander the Great (356–323 BC).

Business management scholars frequently misunderstand the language of military theorists – and *vice versa*. This has led some to question the value of military experience for business. Yet the arguments used by opponents are often fallacious. The conduct of campaigns commonly regarded as disasters, such as the battle of the Somme (1916) in World War One and US counter-insurgency operations in Vietnam in the 1960s and early 1970s, are cited as reasons to discount the value of all military thinking by association. Military organizations of a certain type developed for a certain purpose – such as Frederick the Great's eighteenth-century Prussian Infantry, who were drilled to perform exact manoeuvres under fire – are also condemned as too inflexible a structure for modern society (which is also true for modern warfare). Military organization *per se* is thus questioned. Such criticism misunderstands the social nature of military organization and culture, which is a reflection of the society they come from. Military organizations are in fact very flexible and include structures as different as the Prussian regiment, the raiding party, guerrilla bands and aircrew.

An alternative approach is to state that business is not war because competitors do not seek to destroy each other but will act in cooperative as well as competitive ways for the common good. There are two counterarguments to this assertion. First, some competitors do seek to destroy an opponent, either by aggressive price competition or by acquisition: this has certainly been Wal-

Mart's strategy when entering small towns in the US where there is only room for one store. Caterpillar also famously declared that its strategy was to destroy Komatsu. Second, as British Prime Minister Palmerston, declared in the nineteenth century, countries have no friends or enemies – merely vital interests. So in grand strategy enemies become friends and *vice versa*. Thus the US was a friend of Germany until 1914, its enemy twice between 1914 and 1945, and a NATO partner from 1955. In the commercial sector there are similar trends. BAE Systems both competes and cooperates with aerospace partners as it seeks to create a new structure for the European defence and aerospace sector. Their network of alliances appears very similar to the network of relationships among European states in the eighteenth century. Of course competition is not decided by battle, but there are winners and losers.

Military strategy is not predominantly concerned with war fighting – it is more concerned with how to use military force to achieve the goals of state policy. This may include an element of war fighting, but for a great deal of recorded history war fighting has not been the main activity of military forces. Indeed the best victories are those achieved without fighting (Sun Tzu, 1981). The most serious conflict of modern times – the Cold War (1947–90), upon whose outcome depended the future of global civilization – was won not by direct combat but by military deterrence.

Warfare was a global phenomenon well before multinational corporations went global. Most countries of the world have had recent experience of warfare or compulsory military service. In the twentieth century large numbers of citizens were trained for warfare, and the organizational principles they learnt were sometimes applied to their civilian roles. Some of the first strategy consultants, for example, were former military personnel who had taken part in the planning of large-scale operations such as the invasion of Normandy in 1944. In some emerging economies the military are directly involved in business, and ex-military personnel are a source of trained manpower for such departments as sales or administration. Military culture is a pervasive global phenomenon and it leaks into the business world by means of media reports of conflict, employees who once served in the military, and contact with defence industries or governments. Military and business organizations often compete for the same types of executive, and their personnel are increasingly trained in similar ways. Business schools are modelled on the Berlin War Academy, and case studies are simply campaign studies in a different form. Management development, logistics and strategic planning all draw heavily on military concepts.

Military strategy has always involved business strategy. Historically, grand strategy – which concerns how and why nations fight wars – has been dominated by commercial and economic considerations, and hence implicitly by business strategy. Military means are simply the instrument by which economic and political objectives are reached. The British Empire grew on the back of trade expansion and declined mainly because there was insufficient economic power to maintain the military forces stationed in the colonies (Kennedy, 1988). Likewise military power without economic power is of limited value. Thus when Reagan decided to challenge the Soviet Union in the 1980s he identified its poor industrial and technological base as a target and launched Star

Wars – the Strategic Defence Initiative. The inability of the Soviet Union to match the West's initiative because of its economic weakness was a significant factor in its collapse in 1991. Another factor was its military defeat in Afghanistan.

As already stated, military and business strategy are both concerned with building and sustaining competitive advantage and organizational effectiveness under conditions of danger and uncertainty where an unsuccessful outcome will have adverse consequences. The first organizations – hunting bands – were small groups who carried out organized violence to achieve economic ends, that is, to obtain food. They also fought with rival hunting bands for access to resources and territory. Competitive advantage came from their capacity to cooperate and their level of military technology. The first large permanent organizations were the armies of Sumeria, Persia, Greece, Rome and China. More than 2000 years before Ford and General Motors, these armies practised division of labour, routines, span of command and planning. More recently the early model of US management originated from the first professional managers – West Point engineering graduates who managed the early railways and had studied the military organization of Rome from Caesar's *De Bello Gallico* (1982). West Point text books (Greiss, 1985) share or may even predate the Harvard view of strategy process. Early consultants often had a military background or were employed on military and governmental tasks.

Military and business organizations may have different purposes, but they share many common requirements such as the need for cohesion, clear direction and division of labour. This commonality of purpose means that practitioners have an instinctive interest in learning from military examples and find military metaphors useful when considering their own issues (Ramsey, 1987; Boar, 1995).

In summary, there are three reasons why it is valid to utilize military strategy concepts in strategic management:

- They share a common history and language.
- Practitioners are comfortable with military examples and routinely use military metaphors to help make sense of their experiences (Ramsay, 1987). Some strategic management scholars also use military metaphors.
- Both deal with a common problem set: deciding what to do next under conditions of great stress when the outcome is both important and unpredictable (Clausewitz, 1982: Hamel and Prahalad, 1994). Therefore one field may be able to learn from the other.

This chapter seeks to demonstrate the utility of military strategic thinking by means of a case study – that of International Wines and Spirits and its market entry into China.

Case study

The situation

International Wines and Spirits plc (IWS) is a medium-sized conglomerate based in London. It has a number of successful global brands, notably Salmon whisky,

Coventry low tar cigarettes and Tsarina – a cherry flavoured vodka. It also bottles and distributes a number of leading soft drinks. It now wants to develop its own distribution network in the developing Chinese market, having relied on agents to date. The global market is becoming more competitive and margins are declining in Europe and North America, so the corporate view is that IWS needs to boost its profits in China, South America and North Africa.

A meeting is called to discuss the strategy for China. Present are Fa Su Win (IWS's corporate affairs country representative and former Chinese ministry employee), Ross Behm (the newly appointed Far East marketing manager), James Buchanan (whose advertising agency is supporting the campaign) and three of IWS's brand managers, including Jane Neumann, brand manager for Coventry cigarettes.

The conversation

Fa Su Win: The most important factor in building brands in China is getting a presence in Beijing. Without top government support there is no way that we can win. We also need to be careful how we treat former agents in case they are snapped up by competitors. However we don't know exactly how things will work out so we need to keep balanced to deal with unforeseen events.

Ross Behm: [Behm thanks Fa and then reminds the brand managers of the corporate perspective.] As you know from the briefing papers you have seven key objectives: (1) establish a presence in the market in two years; (2) build effective distribution networks that can support all the brands; (3) achieve profits after two years; (4) maintain excellent government relationships; (5) beat the competition; (6) cooperate with colleagues; (7) contribute to global brands. Any questions?

[James Buchanan chips in and assures everyone of his agency's full support within any budgetary limitations. The brand managers then begin to debate what needs to be put in place to make it happen. There is considerable difficulty in achieving clarity of objectives.]

Jane Neumann: I'm feeling a little uneasy here. Which objective is more important? What do we do if there is a clash?

Ross Behm [with growing impatience]: Look! We pay you to solve problems not to complain. You've all been on management courses and you are experienced. Just fix it. I've got a load of other stuff to sort out and this one is your problem.

Issues

The firm is expanding into new markets and needs to develop an appropriate strategy. The brand managers have been given the task of implementing the strategy but are clearly uncomfortable about what this means in practice. The key issues seem to be:

- How to turn a general set of corporate objectives into a clear mission.
- How to launch the brand.
- How to motivate IWS employees while the implementation process is under-way and before any successes appear.
- What to do when competitors react.

Hence the case study is essentially about developing a competitive business strategy under conditions of uncertainty in a new market.

Key contributions

The origin of the perspective

Military strategists analyze actual campaigns, deducing from practice the essential principles of war and then constructing a clear doctrine on the basis of which commanders can plan and fight battles. It is a highly pragmatic, theory-building process. When new technologies emerge that have not been tested in combat, then simulations and exercises are undertaken to test their impact. Military strategy is developed both theoretically and as a consequence of experience, so past campaigns are studied in detail and potential campaigns, as happened before the Gulf War in 1991, are simulated on computers so that the actual operations can proceed as effectively as possible.

Defeat is a great teacher and most of the innovations in military strategy, such as the tank (1916), arose out of military failures. Military strategists assert that there is a set of universal principles to guide commanders – the principles of war.

Warfare and military strategy have been studied for a considerable time and much has been written about the nature of war, and when it is right to use force, by writers as diverse as Sun Tzu (fourth-century BC China), St Thomas Aquinas (twelfth-century Europe), Machiavelli (early sixteenth-century Italy), Clausewitz (early nineteenth-century Germany), Mahan (nineteenth-century America) and MaoTse Tung (twentieth-century China). There is still considerable intellectual investment in military strategy and technology in academic departments and specialist professional journals as well as in large military training and development organizations such as staff colleges. While the prospect of a general nuclear war that will destroy the planet now seems less likely, states and groups are still engaging in various forms of conflict. Reports of the end of warfare are greatly exaggerated – as demonstrated by the conflicts in the Balkans, Iraq, India, Pakistan, Central Asia, Columbia, Sri Lanka, Northern Ireland, Sudan and Sierra Leone. Wars now seem to last longer, remain unresolved and result in great human suffering. They are like bushfires that die down only to start again in unexpected places.

How to counter assymetric warfare in which weak states or terrorist groups attack strong states is the current global challenge as the horrendous attack by suicide pilots on Manhattan and the Pentagon on 11 September 2001 have demonstrated. And while the situation is unfamiliar the process of military strategic thinking is still recognisably Claustwitzian.

Military strategy is the process by which the overall direction of the campaign takes place at every level, from grand strategy to the fighting of battles. In peacetime, military strategy informs the political process through which significant decisions are taken, such as those the British took between 1947 and 1960 to help contain Russia, remain a close ally of the US, help rearm Germany, withdraw from most colonies, develop a nuclear capability and end conscription. However the line between peace and war is now extremely blurred, and in practice nations maintain a warfighting capability that can be used for other purposes, such as peacekeeping or peacemaking.

A conundrum faced by military strategists is that while capability – such as the capacity to exert force overseas – can take a considerable time to build up, the necessity to carry out such an operation can arise at very short notice. Politicians who take decisions on military advice often fail sufficiently to appreciate this factor. Even more intangible is the fighting spirit of troops, which is built up over decades. Once fighting spirit is lost it can be difficult to recover. Fighting spirit is built on the confidence and cohesion that is essential for effective military activity. This confidence and cohesion is weakened when commanders cease to be believed, if the strategy being pursued is obviously not working, if there is no popular support at home, or if weapons systems fail in combat. After its defeat in Vietnam the US Army took some time to recover its former prestige.

Contemporary military strategists discuss every aspect of conflict, from general nuclear warfare to low-level terrorist and insurgency campaigns. They have looked at how wars start and end, peacekeeping, conflict management, the impact of new technologies (particularly the battle for control of the electromagnetic spectrum), leadership and whether in fact war has been abolished. The consensus is that as long as there are independent states, disagreements over territories and resources, and minorities whose political and religious aspirations are being denied, then there will be conflicts. And while general nuclear war is unlikely, less intensive conflicts are now more likely. It is less certain how long the US will be able or willing to continue as the world's policeman. Experience suggests that domination by a single superpower is not sustainable (Kennedy, 1988). This raises serious concerns for countries such as the UK and Australia that rely heavily on US nuclear forces and intelligence-gathering capabilities.

There have been many attempts to elaborate the key principles of war. The process can be dangerous if principles are applied without taking all circumstances but especially new technology into account, as all changes in military practice are a consequence of the successful application of new technology (Archer Jones, 1987). Taken to extremes, over-reliance on theory can have disastrous consequences. Late-nineteenth-century military theorists believed that as offensive spirit was the most important thing in combat, nothing could stop a bayonet attack by infantry. The theorists of the time, who drew their ideas from the Napoleonic Wars, did not study more recent campaigns such as the US Civil War, which clearly showed the dreadful result of massed rifle fire on an infantry assault. The consequences of the failure of European military establishments properly to study modern war was that all general staff in 1914 thought that the impending war would be open, involve cavalry, end quickly, and be decided by offensive action. They were dreadfully wrong. The lessons of the First World War have now been learnt and the principles of war remain just that – a series of factors that need to be taken into account when considering military action.

Elaboration of the key principles

This section first defines strategy and the levels at which it is applied, and then elaborates on the principles of war. It then discusses the role and importance of doctrine.

Strategy is 'the art of creating a desired pattern to events, where the ends and means of achieving them may be brought into balance, within the prevailing environment despite the efforts of the enemy to create an entirely different pattern' (*BDD*, 1996: 4.2). It takes place at a number of levels. Grand strategy concerns the application of national resources, including military forces, to achieve national objectives. The operational level of military strategy concerns planning for and fighting campaigns. The lowest level is the tactical, which is about actual engagements. How military and business strategy relate to each other is shown in Table 8.1.

TABLE 8.1   *The link between military and business strategy*

Military strategy	Business strategy
Grand strategy: • Alliance strategy • National strategy	International and national strategy: • economic policy
Military/strategic: • How military forces contribute to grand strategy: deployments, force structures, technologies, strategic plans	Corporate strategy: • Strategic intent • Positioning • Building competences • Alliances and acquisitions • Technologies
Operational art: • Campaigns	Competitive strategy: • Sustainable competitive advantage • Business-level strategies
Tactical: • Fighting battles	Functional strategies: • Implementation

Military strategy needs to be developed in an orderly manner, with clear objectives and missions for the component elements. The first stage of developing a strategy is deciding on the policy objectives (*BDD*, 1996: 1.10). At this point political views dominate, with the military giving advice on what is feasible. During the Gulf War the agreed objective was recovery of the territories seized by Iraq, not the destruction of Saddam Hussein or the invasion of Iraq. The subsequent difficulties over Allied military strategy after Saddam's defeat have stemmed from a lack of consensus among those concerned about what the policy objectives in the region should be.

The present disagreement over the best strategy to pursue in the Balkans reflects strategic uncertainty and a poor strategy process in NATO. What is the end state: a greater Albania; a UN-protected Kosovar micro-state within Greater Serbia; a Kosovar microstate defended by an armed Kosovar Liberation Army; Milošović on trial for war crimes in the Hague; the destruction of the Serbian war machine? The lack of a defined end state has led to a lack of agreement over military strategy, and hence to mismanagement of the campaign. The initial inability of NATO to define the end state led to events acquiring a momentum of their own, and hence strategy was at first reactive, with NATO losing the information war. While arguments at the start of campaigns are not unusual but subsequent success normally allows them to be forgotten, the current situation – in which NATO military dominance led to a Serbian climb-down but problems still remain – is a good example of military success with no clear political resolution, stemming from disagreement about the end state. The continuing problems in Kosovo bear witness to the poor strategic thinking behind the intervention.

Principles of war

There are ten principles of war in British defence doctrine (*BDD*, 1996: Annex A). These are very similar to those of NATO and the US Army.

Selection and maintenance of the aim

Before planning any military operation it is essential to select a single, unambiguous military purpose. Once the aim has been established it must be maintained. This aim is normally encapsulated in a mission, which should be a clear, concise statement of the task of the commander and the purpose of the action. Usually the mission will be broken down into a series of objectives.

Maintenance of morale

Good morale is primarily a mental state and depends above all on trust in the leadership at all levels. Good morale fosters the will to win and to withstand provocation and adversity, and it sustains offensive spirit and group cohesion. Morale is created through high standards in training, an ethically based code of conduct and a determination to succeed. Individuals identify strongly with the group under conditions of danger, and this group cohesion gives individuals the courage to endure extreme danger.

Security

Security is the protection of bases, platforms, weapons systems, men, matériel and information to preserve a commander's freedom of action and minimize the effects of enemy action. Without security it is impossible to achieve surprise.

Surprise

Surprise is a potent psychological weapon. It causes confusion and paralysis in the enemy's chain of command and can destroy the cohesion and morale of its military units. The elements of surprise are secrecy, intelligence about the enemy, deception, concealment, audacity and speed. Time is a key factor.

Offensive action

Offensive action gives the initiative to the attacker. It forces the enemy to react to the attacker's movements and improves the morale of its forces. Most campaigns involve a judicious mix of offensive and defensive action. Offensive action involves risk.

Concentration of force

Military success goes to the side that is able to concentrate superior forces at the decisive time and place. The underlying principle is to concentrate force at the point of main effort, whilst economizing elsewhere.

Economy of effort

The corollary of concentration of force is economy of effort. The application of this principle in practice can be summed up as a balanced deployment combined with a prudent allocation of resources strictly related to the aim.

Flexibility

Flexibility is vital so that the commander can take advantage of changes in circumstances to alter plans. Outside conflict the necessity to adjust military operations to suit the prevailing political situation makes flexibility an important quality.

Cooperation

All military operations, including war fighting, require cooperation in order to be successful. This is especially important when working with allies. Cooperation is based on team spirit and training, and entails the coordination of all activities to achieve the optimum effect. Three elements are essential to cooperation: goodwill, a common aim, and a clear division of responsibilities, including an understanding of and respect for the capabilities and limitations of others.

Sustainability

This is the ability of a force to maintain the necessary level of combat power for the time required to achieve its objectives. Without sustainability a significant proportion of the means to fight and the will to win will be lost. Here logistical factors are vital and no operation can succeed without logistic support that is commensurate with the aim of the operation.

The above principles of war have to be adapted to context. Their relative importance varies according to circumstance and there is no firm hierarchy. National views of what is most important are a result of historical experience. For example Australia, whose troops fought in Vietnam in the 1960s, is very conscious of mission creep – the situation in which a small initial commitment becomes a major involvement. Consequently Australia will only deploy ground forces if there is a clear mission and a defined time frame for the deployment. The US, again following the Vietnam War, is very conscious of the need to maintain morale, especially civilian morale, and the need to minimize casualties. So during the Gulf War there was an intense and successful management of the media. The UK, because of what happened in the Second World War, is very focused on seeking allies and cooperation.

Other insights

There have been many others who have provided insights into military strategy. Three whose influence will be briefly discussed are Sun Tzu, T. E Lawrence and Mao Tse Tung. These writers put more emphasis on the human and psychological factors in combat than do most Western writers. They also saw war not in Hegelian terms as an absolute state, but as a continuum. According to Sun Tzu (1981), the best general wins without fighting and this concept of bloodless victory has influenced the nuclear deterrence debate, where the intention of nuclear force is not to fight but to deter others. T. E. Lawrence (1962) wrote in almost mystical terms about how the will of a people can be used to defeat a stronger enemy. Mao had a similar concept of people's war, with a move from the countryside to the towns and an emphasis on winning the hearts and minds of the people. Their ideas still inform the strategies of national resistance movements and terrorist groups.

Doctrine

Armed forces have to be trained to operate under conditions of extreme confusion, danger and stress. Doctrine – defined as 'that which is learnt' – is therefore very important. At the tactical level these doctrines are highly prescriptive and become drills. This is due to the nature of the activity and the speed with which it needs to be carried out – that is, how to carry out a platoon attack. At higher levels commanders are selected according to their ability to develop imaginative and effective solutions, guided by rather than ruled by doctrine.

Links to strategy

How can these principles be applied to business strategy? Essentially the military strategy approach fits well into the classic business strategy framework of analysis, choice and implementation. Greater emphasis, however, is placed on what to do once an operation is under way, as military experience shows that the situation will rapidly change in unforeseen ways. The military mindset implicitly recognizes that strategy is emergent but uses the strategic planning process to inform the decision-making process.

The framework used here is the 7 Cs model: context, competences, culture, competing, corporate, change and control. Most links are to building competences and to competing, that is, fighting. Corporate strategy is concerned with alliance formation and grand strategy. How then does military strategy improve our understanding of these frameworks?

Context

Context is the environment in which the potential or actual campaign will take place. Military analysts break down context into a set of factors that need to be taken into account – very similar to the PEST analysis (Greiss, 1985). All soldiers are trained to carry out an assessment of the enemy forces, their own forces and the terrain on which the battle will take place. At a higher level the concept of terrain includes social, psychological, economic, historical and political factors as well as the key features of the terrain. The conclusions of an assessment of context are used for battle planning. For example if the enemy is stronger, we defend. If the enemy is defending a place that has no value, we bypass. Context is not a static concept. On operations the context is continually checked to see what has changed and whether the assumptions made are still valid. The product of this assessment is intelligence, which is information that has been processed and made available to those who need it.

Assessments of context take place at all levels, from the national level down to units on operations. The national assessment of a threat is used to target intelligence resources, initiate weapons programmes and seek allies. The process resembles a series of Chinese boxes. There are dangers in this top-down approach. During the Cold War there was a strong institutional tendency – on both sides – to overestimate the threat. The process is also ponderous and can fail to notice major changes. Greater use of outsiders in the process is useful, as is scenario planning. Context is now more complex and less predictable, so assessments are faster and more specific about the assumptions – especially political assumptions.

Finally, an assessment of context needs to have a purpose – a defined end state and mission. Analysis without any purpose is a waste of resources. Defining an end state can be quite easy or very complex, but unless there are reasons and assumptions behind the analysis the process will not yield value. The analysis process also needs to include a clear understanding of what your own organization can achieve – its competences.

Competences

Competences are termed capabilities by the military: the capability to achieve a defined military purpose at various levels – tactical, operational or strategic – no matter what the enemy might do to prevent that action. An example of a strategic capability is a cruise missile that can travel considerable distances to destroy the enemy's strategic assets, while tactical capabilities influence only the actual battlefield as they have a shorter range. Capabilities can be delivered by a variety of means. For example a maritime capability to prevent enemy forces from using a sea area can be delivered by a combination of space-based surveillance and aircraft, and need not involve actual naval units at all. Capabilities are constructed from the building blocks of force structures and are defined in time and space. In the Cold War a British armoured division in West Germany was expected to defend an area for a given period against Soviet attack. Forces and weapon systems have a number of capabilities, for instance an infantry battalion can be deployed for general war, peacekeeping or counterinsurgency duties. Technology is a decisive element in capability. In the nineteenth century Europeans with firearms always defeated larger numbers of Africans with spears – with the exception of the Zulus at Isandhlwana.

Force components are designed to deliver capabilities in line with the assessment of threats. Some capabilities are permanent, for example space surveillance, while others take time to build up, for instance the capability to send a large force overseas. But while force structures are multitasked, they self-evidently cannot achieve more than one capability at a time – deploying a force overseas means it cannot be used elsewhere. One of the biggest problems in military deployment is maintaining a capability and avoiding degrading the morale of units by overstretching them. The increasing complexity and turbulence of the post Cold War world has made planning more difficult. There is also the danger that ceasing to practice a capability will lead to its loss. In 1984 some 131 000 British and Allied troops carried out a field training exercise in what was then West Germany – Exercise Lionheart. That could never happen again even if the German government requested it. The divisions have left and, more significantly, the operational capability would be difficult to rebuild. The tacit knowledge has been lost.

The military and business perspectives on competences are very similar. Force planners in defence policy implicitly use resource-based theory to argue for capabilities, while business strategists have applied resource-based theory to help explain Britain's defeat of the Franco-Spanish fleet at Trafalgar in 1805 (Pringle and Kroll, 1997) in terms of the superior resources that the British had in respect of tactical ability. They argue that the Royal Navy had developed superior competences in terms of skill with weapons, acceptance of casualties and a more aggressive tactical doctrine. These competences were non-imitable because the Royal Navy had, by means of its naval blockade, prevented French and Spanish naval units from acquiring the necessary experience.

Culture

Culture is the glue holding military forces together and each service, regiment, ship or air squadron has its own carefully managed traditions, mythologies and rituals. Military sociology explicitly studies the role of culture. Culture is important because, as research has shown (Marshall, 1978), people ultimately do not fight and die for their country or for an ideology but for their friends – the members of their team. Indeed soldiers are very cynical about nationalism, as shown in the First World War by Wilfred Owen, the poet and infantry company commander. Owen hated the war but chose to return to the battlefield, after recuperating from concussion and trench fever, to be with his troops. He died in action in 1918.

What is significant in military culture is that it creates a separate world from that of the civilian. This world is entered by rites of passage and once in that world the warrior is marked out as different by virtue of clothing, life style, rank and what is expected of him – to kill or be killed. The military world provides everything and in return asks everything of its members. This is a very powerful message for some, especially young men who want to belong – indeed those who have been soldiers never entirely lose their sense of separate identity. This separate military life is being changed in the UK by the entry of women, the cost of maintaining a separate lifestyle and the withdrawal of forces from overseas, but it remains a very powerful force.

The military techniques of building and sustaining culture and hence morale are transferable to a non-military context. The techniques involve a tough selection process, the replacement of one set of values with another and inculcating a sense of belonging to an elite. The techniques work best on younger people. Physical discomfort and sleep deprivation helps the process of indoctrination. Finally there is a rite of passage into the organization, to which, no matter what happens, you will belong even after you leave or die. The management consultants McKinsey's use some of these techniques. Potential entrants have to pass a series of tough of interviews. The new consultant is made to feel that she or he belongs to something different and special. When consultants leave they are still part of the alumni and their achievements are celebrated. Those who enter professions also join strong cultures. A strong culture gives a sense of identity and hence loyalty to the organization. It changes an employee into a partner.

The military culture is value-based and demands certain behaviours from leaders and subordinates. Those whose behaviour does not match the standard are punished and dishonoured, while those whose behaviour is exceptional are rewarded with medals – also called honours. The names of those who have died are preserved and publicly remembered. A value-based system that relies on self-discipline may be more suited to complex global operations than a bureaucracy.

There is an inherent tension in the military between the warrior and the technocrat: those who fight and those who manage them. This tension is creative but can become dysfunctional if one or other dominates. To the outsider the military seems to be a top-down bureaucracy, but in fact it is a collection of tribes with a veneer of bureaucracy superimposed.

Large multinationals can display some of these characteristics and there is sometimes an expressed desire to have a common culture. However the military experience leads to the conclusion that a common culture is only needed to the extent that it facilitates effective cooperation. Culture is best understood as a small group phenomenon, and requires colocation, common tasks and common leadership. Under such circumstances a common culture grows naturally. The military does not have a common culture although its members can and do cooperate at all levels. What is important for defence policy and grand strategy is for the senior executive to be able to cooperate on a personal level.

The military tribes cooperate but retain their own sense of identity. For example the Australian military describes its separate service cultures as the Three Ds: dumb (army), devious (air force) and defiant (navy). The fact that this terminology is actually approved of by the services themselves is perhaps indicative of their self-confidence.

Competing

How, when and where do you choose to compete and for what purpose? How do you decide what to do? These questions are fundamental to strategic choice. The military approach is to start by defining the end state – normally given out at the political level. Once the end state has been established it is possible, following an assessment, to devise a suitable mission with a set of objectives. This mission frequently needs to be broken down into individual missions for each component of the force. For example if a brigade has to destroy a bridge over a large river, part of the force, say the combat engineers, will have a specific mission – to prepare the bridge for demolition. Turning a general mission into a set of activities for each part of the force is called mission analysis. An important part of mission analysis is keeping in mind the reason for the operation, so that if circumstances alter, changes can be made to the plan. Mission analysis also allows individual commanders to decide what is vital and what is not in any proposed action.

Another contribution made by military strategy to our understanding of competitive strategy is the principle of offensive action. In a fluid, open campaign with widely dispersed forces, offensive and hence risky action is usually more successful than remaining locked into a defensive enclave. T. E. Lawrence (1962) describes how the Arab forces in the Middle East gained the initiative over the Turks by means of such tactics. Offensive action is important in new markets where as yet there are no established competitors or when developing new technologies. However an offensive risk-taking spirit may not suit other contexts.

Corporate

The corporate level in military strategy is concerned with grand strategy. This mainly involves gaining the consensus of the stakeholders as to the desired end state of the operation. So the Allies in the Second World War put the defeat of Germany before that of Japan. Grand strategy is often about maintaining relationships with allies in order to ensure access to resources such as intelligence in peace and joint action in war. Sometimes forces will commit themselves to help an ally for no reason other than to ensure that the relationship remains strong. The national interest is the key determinant when choosing a relationship.

In peacetime policy makers have to choose how to allocate scarce resources among competing projects and services. Ideally such decisions should be rational, but in practice they are not. A defence policy organization may seem similar to a large multinational, but in practice it has less freedom to act and is often difficult to manage. The corporate decision-making process at the national level is now being reformed in the US, the UK and Australia.

Change

The military manages change within its existing paradigm extremely well. Infantry battalions undergo fundamental change in respect of the people who serve in them – soldiers are replaced every three to four years in peacetime, and sadly much more frequently in combat. It also manages change in physical locations, the technology it uses and the type of terrain it fights in. The culture in fact supports and facilitates change. When regiments merge the traditions of the constituent parts meld into the new entity fairly quickly.

However there are problems with dealing with changes that lie outside the paradigm. Here the process of reflecting on experience is valuable. When troops first encounter a new situation they try to deal with it in the old way. When that does not work, new ways are tried and developed until one becomes doctrine. It is interesting to see how quickly a new idea becomes 'the way we have always done it'. An example is the introduction of the tank in 1916 – this was fiercely resisted by the cavalry. The same section of the British Army is now resisting the replacement of the tank by the helicopter and portable antitank missile launcher.

Change is therefore welcomed – provided it is within a known context and is well led. The military puts enormous emphasis on the power of leadership in a crisis. The culture is full of stories about how a single act of leadership saved the day. Leadership outside combat is more difficult to exercise but is helped by the rapid turnover of officers. Individual careers are dependent on filling the right jobs as quickly as possible. Getting noticed is important, and finding a new concept or idea and then promoting it is a good way to be noticed in peacetime. The competition among individual officers acts as a catalyst for change as they challenge accepted military wisdom.

A lesson for businesses from the military experience is the value of investing in culture building before, during and after change. One benefit of the military approach is that once a decision is taken, open opposition is not allowed. The certainty of the outcome helps deal with dissent.

Control

Loss of control over military forces is called mutiny and is feared. Control is therefore extremely important. Control is exercised via orders, culture and norms of behaviour. Military police and a separate legal system ruthlessly enforce control. During operations, control is exercised by extreme measures, which in the past included the summary execution of deserters. In 1942 when the German Army was advancing on Moscow, Stalin issued a no retreat order and enforced that order by deploying squads of secret police to execute those who did not obey it. His action saved the Red Army.

Control during peacetime is exercised by means of deadlines for the production of reports and through personal relationships. Commanders, for example, always give orders to subordinates face to face. The voice is a powerful instrument with which to exercise the will. Officer cadets are taught how to give commands. Those who do not meet deadlines or behave in ways that are inappropriate are dealt with as quickly as possible.

Control over strategy in war is operationalized by means of a map, which shows the extent to which forces have succeeded in reaching their objectives and the enemy's reactions. The measurement of success is clear because it can be seen by everyone involved – including the enemy. Specialists at headquarters are responsible for monitoring what is happening in their sectors and there is a centralized planning, operations and intelligence function. Control in low-intensity operations or in guerrilla warfare is more difficult. Poor measurements such as counting the number of enemy dead or the tonnage of bombs dropped, which the US Army did in Vietnam, degrades operational effectiveness and can lead to strategic failure.

Tools and techniques

There are many potentially useful military techniques. This section will cover just three concerned with competitive strategy: the military assessment, the sequence of orders for a campaign and the process of managing operations in the field. Business examples will be used to illustrate the arguments.

Military assessment

The military assessment – also known as a staff paper – is a short essay that is used to decide strategy. The process includes answering the following questions:

- What is the corporate strategy or desired end state to which this operation is seeking to contribute?
- What assumptions do I make about the situation; that is, how much time do I have and what forces are available?
- What key factors do I need to take into account? (These include the nature of the ground, the enemy forces present, what forces are available, political factors and so on.)
- What courses of action could the enemy take, and which is most likely?
- What courses of action can I take, and which of these is most likely to succeed?
- On the basis of the evidence, what course of action do I propose?

The staff assessment is made by the commander with the assistance of their staff. It can be presented either as a written document or more usually as a series of graphic displays. Sometimes the process is entirely mental with an element of intuition. Wellington was especially competent at this – for example he chose Waterloo as the site for battle several days before the battle was fought. The important point in this process is to make any assumptions clear so that if they change the plan can be reviewed.

Orders sequence

The orders sequence is a process that allows for the speedy implementation of plans and the clear transmission to subordinates of what they need to know, and no more. The purpose is to achieve a common understanding and then to initiate action. The orders sequence is taught as a drill and every commander follows a similar sequence: situation, mission, execution, administration, and command and control.

- *Situation*: what is the enemy doing? What are the activities and intentions of our forces, including our allies?
- *Mission*: what purpose will this activity achieve and why is it important?
- *Execution*: how the mission will be carried out in general terms, and then with reference to specific elements of the force, for example C Company will advance to the riverline and secure the far bank by 0600 hours.
- *Administration*: matters concerned with all aspects of logistics, including medical.
- *Command and control*: how will the operation be controlled, for example will radios be used, and where will the commander be? Who will take over if the commander is killed?
- Are there any questions? (People must be allowed to clarify issues about which they are not clear.)

Subordinate commanders then brief their own people, down to the lowest level, which in a rifle company of three platoons of 35 is the rifle section of eight commanded by a corporal. All orders are given face to face if possible. The value of this process is that it ensures that everyone understands and is committed to the operation, and that questions are dealt with at the right level. A good orders sequence improves morale and in combat is vital to success. Finally, before giving orders the commander should seek advice from subordinates.

Operational processes in the field

Once involved in operations there must be a capacity to ensure, via a sense-making process, that the commander and his staff know what is happening, whether the operation is proceeding as planned and if not what needs to change. Headquarters maintain a staff dedicated to tracking the current situation and also have a smaller planning team looking at future options. Briefings take place at set times or as needed and follow a set sequence. First the intelligence officer gives a briefing on what the enemy has done and is likely to do, then the operations officer describes the events since the last briefing and highlights concerns. Commanders of the various specialist forces, such as air forces or artillery, then give their briefings and the logistics advisor describes the situation and outlines his concerns. The commander then initiates any necessary changes. Headquarters in the field are colocated and understand each other's concerns and problems. Planning is initiated on the basis of what has been described. This seems to be a rather formal process but on actual operations it is fast and fluid. The important point is that the process is aimed at reducing the fog of war and the consequent friction to a minimum.

Case study revisited

What help can the brand managers of IWS gain from an understanding of military strategy? They have identified four areas of concern: corporate strategy, product launch, staff morale, and competitive reactions. The following sections propose various tools and techniques that might help.

How to turn a general set of corporate objectives into a clear mission

IWS has outlined why it wants a successful launch in China but there is some confusion about who is to do what, where and when. There is a great danger that uncoordinated activities by the brand managers could jeopardize key relationships with government and allow competitors to counter IWS's activities. Therefore the firm should carry out a more detailed analysis involving the brand managers and the corporate advisor. They need to generate some options together, especially as there is no need to have a different distribution system for each of the three brands. What will emerge from this analysis is a better understanding of the roles of the corporate advisor and the brand leaders and how they can be coordinated. For example the corporate advisor ought to keep control of political liaison as well as advertising.

Once the plan is clear, then each brand manager needs to develop his or her own plan, in consultation with colleagues, on how they intend to begin the campaign. This plan needs to be clearly communicated to their key staff while maintaining security.

How to launch the brand?

Establishing brands in China is difficult because of its size and the nature of the market. Taking Mao Tse Tung's strategy of starting at the periphery and then working inwards it would be useful to start the brand launch not in Beijing but in some other large city, say Shanghai or Guangzhou. It would also be possible to use China's size as an opportunity to carry out price testing in, say, the north and the south without consumers being aware of the difference. Locating in Beijing would also signal to competitors that some major activity was planned. Some concealment of IWS's intention might be useful.

The actual brand launch needs to be coordinated like a military operation. All three brands should be launched at the same time to maximize the impact. Tight security will be necessary to prevent competitors launching a spoiler bid. The campaign needs to have a clear and simple message, and this should be maintained. An orders sequence might be a useful way of achieving this outcome.

How to motivate IWS employees while the implementation process is underway and before any successes appear?

When the outcome is unclear, leadership is always a problem, and when the organization is new this is especially difficult. The managers should involve new staff in some part of the planning of the brand launch, and use their local knowledge to improve the plan. Some activities designed to improve the cohesion of the team would be useful, such as visits by high-ranking IWS executives to raise the profile of the activity. If this prelaunch activity is effective the inevitable post-launch depression that occurs when things do not work out as planned will be fixable. The culture needs to be developed and managed and the trust and respect of staff earned.

How to deal with the reaction of competitors and other unforeseeable events?

All military commanders expect operational plans to change once the campaign starts. The important thing is that they keep in mind what they are trying to achieve overall, and make adjustments that allow that end to remain a possibility. Strategic positioning allows rapid concentration against an enemy who is unable to predict where your attack is coming from. It is normally better to attack even when defending, otherwise the opponent will retain the initiative. A battle is ultimately between the will of the commanders, but it is decided by the separate actions of innumerable tactical battles.

In this situation IWS should expect a competitive reaction in China and be as well prepared as possible to counter quickly whatever occurs. It is vital to preserve secrecy for as long as possible beforehand and then to launch quickly so as to overwhelm as much of the desired territory as possible. IWS needs to establish a reporting system to update everyone on what is happening and to provide fighting reserves to respond to countermoves by competitors. These reserves could be financial, or they could take the form of people brought in from other parts of the global firm to help if necessary. Another strategy would be to draw the attention of competitors to another market – this could be a real market testing activity, but its main purpose would be to deflect interest from what IWS is doing in China.

Another military approach would be to try to game plan what a competitor might do to prevent the launch or disrupt it once the brands are being sold. A useful exercise would be to set up teams to play the various competitors. This could prove a very creative activity, and in the process of the teams trying to beat their own firm a number of operational weaknesses could come to light.

Armies train hard and fight easy. They should not be surprised by what an opponent does, and once the initial shock of combat is over and they see that their tactics are working, their feeling of confidence grows. In a business environment confidence is vital because talented executives will leave if they see a more attractive opportunity with a different firm.

Summary

The principles of war do not offer a panacea but are an aid to thinking. In this analysis a picture of a resource-based approach to strategy has emerged. Resources are the most important factor for commanders. They do not adjust military operations to what the stakeholders want but to their competences – to what they are capable of achieving. Protecting and sustaining these competences, which include culture, is the main task of commanders in peacetime, because these are vital for successful operations. Competences fluctuate over time and degrade or increase according to the performance of the troops. The attitude of senior commanders in peacetime towards budget allocations demonstrates the focus on retaining and building competence. The challenge to military commanders and their political masters is building the capability to deal with new situations. Their tendency is to be conservative and to stick with familiar technologies and structures. This is currently causing major tensions as resources are cut. It could also lead to serious shortfalls in capability in some areas, such as the rapid deployment of light forces to carry out peacemaking, and the maintenance of unnecessary strength in other areas, such as heavy armour.

Business is not and never will be war. We do not actually kill competitors – indeed we may actually cooperate with them. But we can learn from the practices and wisdom of other contexts. The main lesson to be learnt from this reflection on military practice is the importance of human factors in the strategy process. The general – as Clausewitz, who took part in the Napoleonic War, reminds us – lives in a realm of emotion, fear and intellectual turmoil. He has to take decisions based on inadequate data while physically tired and afraid. His mistakes could result in national defeat. Even victory is painful. Wellington, as he inspected the battlefield of Waterloo in 1815 after the French had been defeated, said that there was only one thing worse than a battle won – and that was a battle lost. Under such conditions of extreme fear the individual strategist cannot rely merely on a sound analytical technique. Strategists need to understand and deal with emotions.

Finally, can the military learn from business practice? This chapter was written while I was researching executive behaviours in a defence organization. The military in peacetime are essentially industrial age organizations run largely as bureaucracies. Hidden within them are the frustrated warriors of the clans and tribes of the preindustrial past. Perhaps the new information age and its postmodern management practices of devolution and decentralization will allow the warriors more freedom? I believe that the military can learn from business practice – indeed it must.

Further reading

Clausewitz, Carl von (1982) *On War* (London: Penguin).
Keegan, John (1988) *The Mask of Command* (London: Unwin).
Kennedy, Paul (1988) *The Rise and Fall of the Great Powers* (London: Unwin).
Sun Tzu (1981) *The Art of War* (London: Hodder and Stoughton).

References

Boar, Bernard (1995) 'Sun Tzu and Machiavelli on Strategy', *Journal of Business Strategy*, vol. XXVI, no. 1, pp. 16–18.

British Defence Doctrine (BBD) (1996) Joint Warfare Publication 0–01.

Caeser, Julius (1982) *De Bello Gallico – The Conquest of Gaul* (London: Penguin).

Clausewitz, Carl von (1982) *On War* (London: Penguin).

Greiss, T. E. (1985) *Definitions and Doctrine of the Military Art* (Wayne, NJ: Avery).

Hamel, G. and C. K. Prahalad (1994) *Competing for the Future* (Boston, Mass.: Harvard University Press).

Hill, C. W. L. and G. R. Jones (1998) *Strategic Management* (Boston, Mass.: Houghton Mifflin).

Jones, A. (1987) *The Art of War in the Western World* (New York: Barnes and Noble).

Kennedy, P. (1988) *The Rise and Fall of the Great Powers* (London: Unwin).

Lawrence, T. E. (1962) *The Seven Pillars of Wisdom* (London: Penguin).

Machiavelli, N. (1962) *The Prince* (London: Penguin).

Marshall, S. L. A. (1978) *Men against Fire* (Gloucester, Mass: Peter Smith).

Pringle, C. D. and M. J. Kroll (1997) 'Why Trafalgar was won: Lessons from resource-based theory', *Academy of Management Executive*, vol. 11, no. 4, pp. 73–89.

Ramsey, D. (1987) *The Corporate Warriors* (London: Grafton).

Sun Tzu (1981) *The Art of War* (London: Hodder and Stoughton).

Uyterhoven, H. E. R., R. W. Ackermann and J. W. Rosenblum (1973) *Strategy and Organization: Texts and Cases in General Management* (Homewood, Ill.: Richard D. Irwin).

Part 3
The Individual

9 Managerial and Organizational Cognition

Gerard P. Hodgkinson and Mark Jenkins

Basic principles

Managerial and organizational cognition draws on concepts, theories and methods from cognitive science (especially cognitive psychology, cognitive anthropology and social cognition) to create a perspective that focuses on the subjectivity and limitations of human information processing. As we shall see, this rapidly developing and highly exciting line of inquiry has raised a number of fundamental questions and led to new insights that challenge the very foundations of the strategy field.

The basic principles of the managerial and organizational cognition perspective can be summarized as follows:

- Individuals are limited in their ability to process the rich variety of stimuli contained in the external world. (In Simon's, 1947, terms they are constrained by 'bounded rationality'.)
- Consequently they employ a variety of strategies in order to reduce the burden of information processing that would otherwise ensue.
- This culminates in the development of a simplified representation of reality that is encoded in the mind of the individual.
- Once formulated, these 'mental representations' act as filters through which incoming information is subsequently processed, which in turn may lead to biased and inappropriate decisions, but under certain circumstances may also form the basis of creative ideas and new insights.

Introductory background: some key concepts

The foundations of the managerial and organizational cognition perspective were laid with the development of cognitive psychology as a major subfield of study within psychology. Cognitive psychology evolved in part as reaction against behaviourism, the approach advocated by Skinner and his followers (for example Skinner, 1938; Mowrer, 1947). Behaviourists believe that since all human behaviour is essentially generated in response to stimuli, it should be possible to develop satisfactory accounts of behaviour in stimulus–response (S → R) terms, without recourse to concepts relating to 'under-the-skin phenomena', such as 'perception', 'attention' and 'memory'. In order to render psychology a truly scientific endeavour, behaviourists argued that such concepts should be eschewed in favour of much simpler concepts, concepts that could be readily subjected to direct observation and measurement.

In practice S → R theories are unable to account for all but the most simple of behaviours, and for this reason behaviourism was subsequently displaced by cognitive psychology, although by no means entirely. In the field of marketing, for example, there are still researchers who argue that behaviouristic theories of learning can better account for consumer purchasing behaviour than cognitive theories (see for example Foxall, 1997).

Human information processing

Rejecting the central theoretical tenets of behaviourism, cognitive psychologists (and cognitive scientists in general) focus on the analysis of the various intervening mental processes that mediate responses to the environment. In order to aid understanding of the complex mental processes performed by the brain in response to environmental stimuli, researchers have found it useful to conceptualize these operations as a sequence of activities (see for example Broadbent, 1958; Welford, 1976). Figure 9.1 presents a human information-processing model taken from Wickens (1984). Although highly simplified, this general model, or framework, captures the essential processes associated with virtually all tasks involving human cognition.

This model suggests that the way in which individuals act is ultimately driven by the way in which they interpret their worlds (perception), this in turn being shaped in part by their past experiences and learning. Often, in an effort to reduce the amount of cognitive activity required, past experience, stored in long-term memory, is influential in determining an individual's responses to current situations or stimuli; actions that worked in the past are routinely applied to the present, so as to free up mental capacity. Cognitive psychologists employ the term 'top-down processing' to denote this type of processing activity.

A second type of processing activity, known as 'bottom-up processing', occurs when incoming environmental stimuli influence actors' cognitions and actions directly, without reference to past memories. In practice, at a given point in time information processing may be affected by what an individual brings to the task at hand (for example prior expectations, influenced by previous experience and contexts) and/or key features of the stimuli present in the current task environment. Clearly the balance between bottom-up (stimulus driven) and top-down (conceptually driven) information processing strategies is likely to vary across tasks and situations; in the contexts in which senior managers operate, however, it is the latter that is likely to predominate (see Walsh, 1995, for a detailed explanation as to why this is the case).

Mental representations: schemata, cognitive maps and mental models

Precisely how knowledge is represented in the mind and what types of computation can be carried out on these representations in order to bring about such activities as remembering, perceiving, reasoning, problem solving and

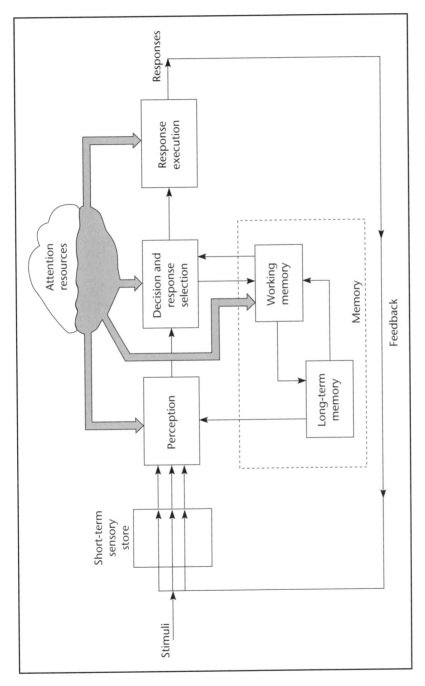

FIGURE 9.1 A basic information-processing framework for the analysis of human cognition. (Wickens/Holland, Engineering Psychology and Human Performance, 3/E, © 2000, p. 11. Reprinted by permission of Pearson Education, Inc., Upper Saddle River, New Jersey)

decision making are the fundamental questions to which basic and applied research in the field of cognitive science is ultimately addressed (see for example Anderson, 1990; Johnson-Laird, 1993). Not surprisingly, therefore, much of the scholarly activity of managerial and organizational cognition researchers has been devoted to operationalizing the notion of mental representations in such a way as to shed light on issues of primary concern to strategy scholars and organization theorists more generally.

It is useful at this point to introduce three further preliminary concepts: the related notions of 'schemata' (Bartlett, 1932), 'cognitive maps' (Tolman, 1932) and 'mental models' (Johnson-Laird, 1983). Schemata may be broadly defined as follows:

> Schemata contain collections of knowledge derived from past experience which serve the function of directing perceptual exploration towards relevant environmental stimuli. Such exploration often leads the perceiver to sample some of the available stimulus information. If the information obtained from the environment fails to match information in the relevant schema, then the information in the schema is modified appropriately (Eysenck and Keane, 1995: 81).

The notion of 'cognitive maps,' which originated from work on the ways in which animals and humans navigate the physical world, is similarly intended to capture the idea that knowledge is internally represented in a form that both simplifies reality and provides a basis for subsequent action. Likewise Johnson-Laird's theory of mental models, and the pioneering work of Kenneth Craik upon which it is based (for example Craik, 1943), assert that:

> The psychological core of understanding . . . consists in your having a 'working model' of the phenomenon in your mind. If you understand inflation, a mathematical proof, the way a computer works, DNA or divorce, then you have a mental representation that serves as a model of an entity in much the same way as, say, a clock functions as a model of the earth's rotation. . . . Many of the models in people's minds are little more than high-grade simulations, but they are none the less useful provided that the picture is accurate (Johnson-Laird, 1983: 2–4).

Managerial and organizational cognition scholars have tended to use these notions interchangeably to convey the general idea that actors develop internal representations of their worlds, which in turn are linked to organizational action (see for example Huff, 1990; Walsh, 1995; Reger and Palmer, 1996). Arguably, these notions are sufficiently similar in meaning to justify this general usage, and for present purposes it is convenient to follow this trend. In the remainder of this chapter, therefore, we use the terms 'schemata', 'cognitive maps' and 'mental models' synonymously to capture the overarching idea that individuals internalize their knowledge and understanding of organizational life in the form of a simplified representation of reality. When doing so, however, we must also be mindful of the fact that scholars pursuing a variety of research problems in cognitive psychology, albeit centred on the general notion of mental representations, originally developed these terms for differing purposes.

Case study

The situation

The box below contains extracts from a conversation held with the owner of a small jewellery shop to explore the owner's views on how he sees his business growing. His comments provide us with some useful material for gaining insights into his mental model of the business and its longer-term strategy. Using a variety of cognitive mapping techniques – such as those reviewed in Huff (1990), Fiol and Huff (1992), Hodgkinson (1997a, 2001a) and Hodgkinson and Sparrow (2002), we can gain a clearer idea not only of the way in which the jeweller defines his business and the bases on which he sees it competing with rival firms, but also the way in which he plans to develop the strategy of his business over the longer term. The comments below relate to the jeweller's views on the need for growth in a very specific niche of the market.

The conversation

Jeweller: Fortunately in the UK it's just about possible to be independent; jewellery is the most independent of any retail operation in the high street. This is because people are often buying gifts, so they often want something that is unique, and they're prepared to pay a bit more for that. We decided that there would be no point in trying to sell, as Ratner does, a pair of earrings for ninety pence. Our products aren't particularly price sensitive, because there isn't the direct competition. That's not to say that you don't have to be competitive because, as with any high street shop as we've got, you have to carry a range of goods that are the bread and butter of the market and if we put a chain in the window that's twenty pounds more than the price charged by a chap down the road, the customers will go down the road.

We get most of our enjoyment out of the special pieces and the commissioned pieces, because that's where we get the real positive feedback from customers and pick up most of our profit. Obviously we do a lot of handmade wedding rings, which are very important; it's nice to know when you look in the paper that half the people who got married have your wedding rings on. They know they're unique because we make them specially for them, and that's good advertising for us because if they're happy they'll go and tell four or five people; if they're not happy, they'll tell nine or ten; so it's an important part of our advertising, it's an internal advertisement.

Managerial and organizational cognition starts from the basic premise that it is the jeweller's mental representations of his business and its strategy that will drive his actions towards the longer-term development of the business. We shall return to his comments later in the chapter. In the meantime, consider the following interrelated questions while reviewing the substance of the cognitive perspective:

- What are the key elements (variables and concepts) that inform the jeweller's view of his business strategy, and how are these interconnected in his reasoning?
- Which organizations would the jeweller regard as the major competitors to his business, and for what reasons?
- Are there any significant threats and/or opportunities that may go unnoticed but which might have a major bearing on the longer-term well-being of his business?
- What fundamental assumptions underpin his responses to the above questions, and to what extent are these assumptions reasonable?

Key contributors

Although the application of cognitive theory and research to managers and organizations is a relatively recent phenomenon, it can be argued that the need for a cognitive approach to managerial and organizational analysis was implicitly acknowledged in a number of the early classic works on strategy and organization theory. Hence Stubbart (1989) contends that research on managerial and organizational cognition provides a vital missing link between environmental conditions and strategic action, a link that was implied strongly in the work of early strategy scholars such as Andrews (1971), Hofer and Schendel (1978), while Weick (1995) notes that Chester Barnard's (1938) seminal text on the functions of the executive introduced the notion that organizations could be viewed as systems of action, consciously coordinated by controlled information processing and communication.

We began this chapter with a brief reference to Herbert Simon's (1947) notion of 'bounded rationality'. This concept captures the idea that actors are unable to take decisions in a completely rational manner because they are constrained by fundamental information processing limitations (of the type depicted in the model outlined in Figure 9.1). Nevertheless they strive for rationality within their cognitive limits. Undoubtedly *Administrative Behavior* (Simon, 1947), the book in which this notion was introduced, made a seminal contribution that has shaped much of recent theory and research on managerial and organizational cognition. March and Simon's *Organizations* (1958) has also profoundly influenced the development of the managerial and organizational cognition perspective by drawing attention to the ways in which organizational routines free up attention that can be used to concentrate on non-routine events (see also Cyert and March, 1963). While the origins of the cognitive perspective in strategic management, and organization studies more generally, can be traced back to these earlier works, only during the past 15–20 years has the study of managerial and organizational cognition come of age.

Drawing on Simon's notion of bounded rationality, Hambrick and Mason (1984) developed a theoretical model of strategic choice, known as 'the upper echelons perspective'. According to Hambrick and Mason it is the psychological and demographic characteristics of the 'dominant coalition', the group of powerful actors at the very top of the organization, that ultimately determine its direction and outcomes. Hambrick and Mason posit a three-stage filtration process, comprising: (1) a limited field of vision, (2) selective perception and (3) interpretation, which they argue underpins the tendency for executives to perceive only a limited portion of all potentially relevant information in the internal and external environment, often deriving idiosyncratic interpretations of reality and assigning differential weights to the various potential outcomes. A diagrammatic representation of this model is presented in Figure 9.2.

The first stage of this filtration process – limited field of vision – arises from the fact that decision makers are exposed to a limited subset of the available stimuli; while the second stage – selective perception – occurs because only a portion of the stimulus information in their limited field of vision is actually attended to. The third stage – interpretation – entails the attachment of meaning to stimuli. Starbuck and Milliken (1988) employ the term 'sensemaking' to describe this stage.

As noted by Finkelstein and Hambrick (1996), much of the empirical work on executive perception has focused on this third stage. For example, as part of a wider programme of research into strategic issue diagnosis, Jane Dutton and Susan Jackson (Dutton and Jackson, 1987; Jackson and Dutton, 1988) have analyzed the processes by which managers categorize particular strategic issues as opportunities or threats (see also Dutton et al., 1989). This work shows that managers are more sensitive to the issues they believe to be threatening than those perceived as opportunities. Another example of the work on sensemaking processes in organizations is Lant et al.'s (1992) study of the way in which managers explain poor performance records. This work demonstrates that within turbulent environments, organizational actors are more likely to attribute poor performance records to external factors, whereas in stable environments no such tendency is observed. On the basis of these findings, Lant et al. conclude that such biased sensemaking leads ultimately to poor adaptation, not least because managers fail to learn from their experience, that is, attributional biases prevent managers from learning about the effect of their behaviour on organizational outcomes.

Karl Weick (1969, 1979) has provided another seminal contribution to the development of the managerial and organizational cognition perspective with his notions of 'enactment' and 'the enacted environment'. Many of the sequential information processing models advanced by cognitive psychologists (such as the one presented in Figure 9.1) imply that the environment is an objective entity, and that the reason why subjective differences in perception occur is that the objective environment can only be partially comprehended due to limited processing capacity (i.e. 'bounded rationality'). Weick challenges this limited view of the environment (which he terms 'the perceived environment'), arguing that theories that stress the notion that reality is selectively perceived over-emphasize the object–subject relationship, at the expense of the idea that the subject often exerts considerable influence on the object:

> managers construct, rearrange, single out, and demolish many 'objective' features of their surroundings. When people act they un-randomise variables, insert vestiges of orderliness, and literally create their own constraints . . .

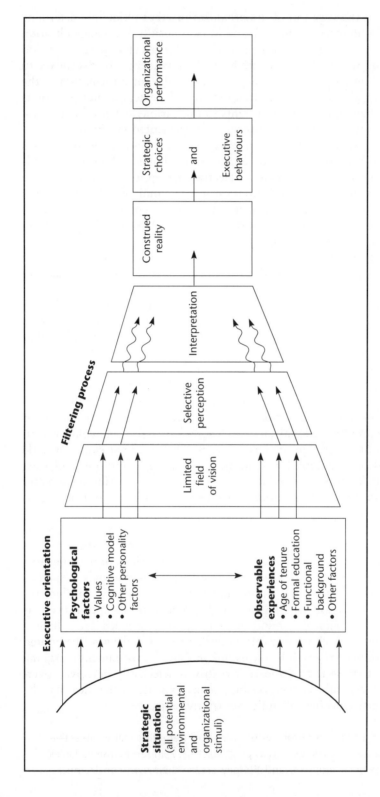

FIGURE 9.2 Strategic choice under bounded rationality: the executive's constructed reality (adapted from Humbrick and Mason, 1984, by Finkelstein and Hambrick, 1996: 42, © Thomson Learning. Reproduced with permission)

> There is a reciprocal influence between subjects and objects, not a one-sided influence such as implied by the idea that a stimulus triggers a response. This reciprocal influence is captured in the organizing model by the two-way influence between enactment and ecological change (Weick, 1979: 164, 166).

By drawing attention to the fact that the environmental constraints and opportunities faced by organizations are actively constructed by the actions of particular individuals and groups, the notions of 'enactment' and 'the enacted environment' have laid an important conceptual foundation for better understanding of the processes of sensemaking in organizations (see Weick, 1995).

Having outlined the historical background to the development of the managerial and organizational cognition perspective, and briefly introduced some of its key principles, concepts and frameworks, we shall now consider the ways in which this approach is beginning to shed light on specific issues and problems in the wider strategy field.

Linking managerial and organizational cognition to strategy

In many ways the analysis of managerial and organizational cognition is still in its infancy. Nevertheless, the rate and pace of its development over the past 10–15 years precludes a detailed treatment of the many and varied topics in the strategy field that are now being addressed from a cognitive perspective. In order to illustrate some of the potential insights to be gained from the adoption of this approach, we shall use the 6C framework to provide a selective overview of several issues and themes in strategic management that are currently capturing the attention of managerial and organizational cognition researchers.

Context (external environment)

The notion that businesses should analyze their environments if they are to compete effectively is a fundamental and familiar prescription in many of the standard texts on strategic management and marketing strategy (for example Abell, 1980; Porter, 1980, 1985; Luffman et al., 1987; Greenley, 1989; Oster, 1990; Piercy, 1992; Hitt et al., 1996; Grant, 1998; Johnson and Scholes, 2001). The various frameworks and techniques that have been put forward to assist this endeavour are predicated on the implicit assumption that business environments are objective entities waiting to be discovered through formal analysis. However the notions of selective perception and the enacted environment challenge this basic premise. Perhaps this is best illustrated with reference to the enduring SWOT framework (Andrews, 1971).

As we saw earlier, the way in which managers classify strategic issues into 'threats' and 'opportunities' entails a considerable degree of interpretation; this is essentially a sensemaking process in which meaning is actively assigned to ambiguous and uncertain stimuli, rather than an 'objective' analysis based on the facts of the situation (Dutton and Jackson, 1987; Jackson and Dutton, 1988;

Dutton *et al.*, 1989). If we are to take the notions of selective perception, enactment and sensemaking seriously, the fundamental question that needs to be addressed when considering the results of any form of environmental analysis is: 'from whose perspective has the analysis been undertaken?' Different findings are likely to emerge depending on where particular actors are located in the wider social arena. For example it is highly likely that a SWOT analysis undertaken by a CEO will yield rather different findings from a similar analysis undertaken by a maintenance engineer in the same firm. Similarly, an analysis of the competitive environment undertaken by a group of senior managers located at the headquarters of a firm is likely to yield different insights from those obtained from a group of managers located in the sales field.

Culture (internal environment)

Whilst a wide range of studies have explored actors' mental models of external environments, there has been relatively little work on cognitive constructions of the intraorganizational environment. A notable exception is the insightful paper by Harris (1996), in which schema theory from the social cognition literature is employed to advance a theory of organizational culture and sensemaking at the individual level of analysis. According to Harris, culturally embedded aspects of the organization – 'the way we do things around here' – manifest themselves in individuals' cognitive structures and sensemaking processes:

> Schema theory applied to organizational culture is not a cure for all that currently ails culture theory and research. However, the perspective on culture offered by schema theory is significant because it highlights and challenges the neglect of the individual level dynamics of organizational culture (ibid.: 303).

From this perspective culture can be represented as a set of common mental models or schemata that allow individuals to understand how things work in a particular organization.

Competences (resources/capabilities/skills/knowledge)

Eden and Ackermann (1998, 2000) use a cognitive mapping approach to help managers elicit the distinctive competences of their organizations. Their work focuses on enhancing strategic thinking through the use of cognitive mapping techniques:

> Our experience suggests that a necessary part of the journey of strategy making is for any management team in any type of organization to jointly reflect upon the organization's competencies which are distinctive. However, the crucial activity is to go on and discover the *patterns* of distinctive competencies so that *core* competencies can be identified (Eden and Ackermann, 1998: 102)

Bowman and Ambrosini (2002) employ cognitive mapping techniques to explore organizational-level tacit knowledge. The role of tacit knowledge in creating non-imitable competences is discussed more fully in Chapter 7. Core competences are context-dependent, and therefore need to be understood within a specific organizational situation. One of the advantages of using cognitive mapping as a basis for exploring the nature of core competences is that they 'impose structure on vague situations' (Weick and Bougon, 1986: 107). Another important dimension of the cognitive perspective and the mapping tools it has encouraged (see 'Tools and techniques' below) is that it has permitted the explicit linking of higher-level competences to organizational action. In turn this has allowed managers to bring greater clarity to bear on the way in which they identify and influence the crucial competences of the organization.

Competing (ways of outperforming competitors)

Much of the conventional literature on business competition has been dominated by attempts to refine techniques for the analysis of competitive structures in industries and markets, based on the notion of strategic groups (for a review see McGee and Thomas, 1986). The commonly accepted definition of the strategic group concept is that provided by Porter (1980: 129):

> A strategic group is the group of firms in an industry following the same or a similar strategy along the strategic dimensions. An industry could have only one strategic group if all the firms followed essentially the same strategy. At the other extreme, each firm could be a different strategic group. Usually, however, there are a small number of strategic groups which capture the essential strategic differences among firms in the industry.

In recent years there has been growing recognition that this predominantly economic approach is fundamentally limited in terms of its ability to explain how or why competitive structures in industries and markets come to develop, and on what basis particular strategies are chosen (see for example Barney and Hoskisson, 1990; Pettigrew and Whipp, 1991). In response to these criticisms a growing number of theorists have developed 'social constructionist' accounts of the formation of strategic groups, centring on the notion of 'competitive enactment' (for recent reviews see Hodgkinson 1997a, 2001a, 2001b; Hodgkinson and Sparrow, 2002).

Drawing on the work of Berger and Luckmann (1967) and Weick (1979), Porac and his colleagues (for example Porac et al., 1989; Porac and Thomas, 1990) argue that, over time and within a given industry, individuals' beliefs about the identity of competitors, suppliers and customers become highly unified through mutual enactment processes, in which subjective interpretations of externally situated information are objectified via behaviour. Thus in keeping with out earlier discussion of enactment in general, this notion depicts a continual objective–subjective–objective cycle that underpins the development of competitive structures. Viewed from this perspective, 'industries' and 'strategic groups' are sociocognitive constructions – created through a shared interpretation of reality among business rivals – that come to define both the boundaries of the competitive arena and the bases on which the battles for competitive success are to be fought.

Porac *et al.* (1989) have empirically demonstrated the basic features of competitive enactment in a study of the Scottish knitwear industry (see also Porac *et al.*, 1995). In this study the senior executives of a number of firms were interviewed to ascertain the structure and content of their mental models of the competitive arena. While the combined output of Scottish knitwear producers accounts for a mere 3 per cent of the total amount of knitted outerwear manufactured world-wide, when asked to define their competitors the participants in this study tended to focus exclusively on other Scottish firms. Despite the fact that producers from Italy, the Far East, the US and other parts of the UK far outstripped the Scots in total output, firms from these other geographical areas were not typically regarded as serious competitors.

Porac *et al.* contend that the reason why the Scottish firms have come to regard one another as major competitors is that there exists a strongly held collective mental model that has directed the managers' attention inward, towards firms that are highly similar to their own, that is, other Scottish producers of high-quality, expensive cashmere sweaters in classic designs. In the words of Huff (1982) and Spender (1989), an 'industry recipe' has developed, informing rivals as to the bases on which they should compete with one another. This group-level mental model has come to define the boundaries of the competitive arena and has led individual firms to consider a relatively narrow range of strategic options and competitors. Only firms in the immediate locality of Scotland that produce a similar range of goods to one another, using similar technological processes of production and common channels of distribution, are regarded as serious competitors. Porac and his associates employ the term 'cognitive oligopoly' to describe this state of affairs. The fact that the participants in this study only considered a subset of the total number of competitors that could pose a serious threat to their businesses is entirely in keeping with the notions of 'bounded rationality', 'limited field of vision' and 'selective perception' introduced earlier in this chapter, and this is borne out by a number of other studies that have investigated managers' mental models of competitive industry structures (for example Gripsrud and Grønhaug, 1985; de Chernatony, *et al.*, 1993; Johnson *et al.*, 1998).

In keeping with our earlier discussion of environmental analysis more generally, in recent years a growing number of studies have found striking differences between cognitive maps of competition elicited from multiple informants within and between organizations in the same industrial sector (for example Daniels *et al.*, 1994; Hodgkinson and Johnson, 1994; Johnson *et al.*, 1998) and this has led some researchers (most notably Daniels *et al.*, 1994) to challenge the cognitive foundations of strategic groups theory, as advanced by Porac and his colleagues. However, as noted by Porac and Rosa (1996), the notion that competitive fields are socially constructed entities does not necessarily imply that actors' mental representations of competition are identical in all respects. Moreover, as observed by Hodgkinson (1997a, 2001a, 2001b) and Hodgkinson and Sparrow (2002), there are several methodological weaknesses associated with these studies that render premature such an interpretation at this stage.

Change (types of organizational change/change processes)

Business history is littered with the names of organizations that ceased to exist because they were unable to adapt successfully to major environmental shifts. Population ecology theorists such as Hannan and Freeman (1977, 1988) contend that inertial forces often prevent organizations from achieving such adaptation. In recent years a number of managerial and organizational cognition researchers have argued that one possible source of inflexibility is the 'cognitive inertia' often found among key individuals and groups in situations where there is clearly an urgent need for them to alter radically their thinking and behaviour.

Earlier we drew attention to the fact that – in an effort to reduce the amount of cognitive activity required – experience, captured in long-term memory, can be influential in determining an individual's response to current situations or stimuli. Actions that worked in the past are routinely applied to the present, so as to free up mental capacity. While such top-down processing is ordinarily functional, there is a danger that actors may become overly dependent on their extant mental models of their situations, to the extent that they fail to notice the need for change until the key environmental stimuli signalling this need have become so widespread, or significant in other ways, that their organization's capacity for successful adaptation has been seriously undermined (see, for example, Senge, 1990; Baden-Fuller and Stopford, 1992; Morecroft, 1994). A growing number of empirical studies lend support to this notion (see for example Reger and Palmer, 1996; Barr and Huff, 1997; Hodgkinson, 1997b).

An investigation into the impact of environmental change on organizational performance by Barr et al. (1992) illustrates the importance of this stream of research. This study suggests that it is not the degree of attention to environmental changes per se that delineates the extent to which a firm is able to harness its adaptive capabilities and thereby survive the rigours of a turbulent environment. Drawing on documentary sources of evidence, these researchers examined the views of the top managers of two US railway companies (C & NW and Rock Island), both of which were facing deregulation over an extended time period. It was found that the executives of both companies recognized the threat that deregulation posed to their businesses (as evidenced by changes in their mental models), but only one of the companies understood that it had to realign its business strategy in order to respond effectively to the environmental changes. Not surprisingly it was this company that ultimately survived in the longer term. Barr et al. contend that although the mental models of the executives of both companies changed over time, only C & NW exhibited a true learning process, in marked contrast to Rock Island. While the former remains viable to this day, the latter sought bankruptcy protection in the mid 1970s and was wound up accordingly.

Control (how do managers control what is happening in the organization/structure?)

The recent upsurge of interest in managerial and organizational cognition arose from a fundamental conviction shared by a growing number of scholars that the field of strategic management has placed too much emphasis on the largely unquestioned assumption (although for notable exceptions see Chaffee, 1985; Johnson, 1987; Mintzberg, 1994; Mintzberg *et al.*, 1998) that managers control and define a strategy process that is inherently rational, that is, that managers make the best possible decisions on the basis of all available information, informed by dispassionate, objective analysis. Research conducted from a managerial and organizational cognition perspective has directly challenged this fundamental assumption of rationality, upon which many of the dominant theoretical perspectives in the strategy field – such as the design school (for example Christensen *et al.*, 1982), the planning school (for example Ansoff, 1965; Steiner, 1969; Ackoff, 1983) and the positioning school (for example Porter, 1980, 1985) – are to varying extents, implicitly or explicitly based. Backed by an impressive body of theory and research evidence from the cognitive psychology and behavioural decision-making literatures (for example Tversky and Kahnemen, 1974; Fischhoff, 1975; Fischhoff *et al.*, 1977; Kahneman *et al.*, 1982), a number of cognitively-oriented strategic management researchers (for example Bukszar and Connolly, 1988; Lant *et al.*, 1992; Schwenk, 1995; Das and Teng, 1999; Maule and Hodgkinson, 2002) have highlighted several key deficiencies in the way in which individuals process strategic information (and information in general) that render such a viewpoint untenable. These researchers argue that strategic decision makers employ various heuristics, or 'rules of thumb,' that enable them to cope with a complex and uncertain business world by making a series of simplifying assumptions that reduce the burden of information processing that would otherwise ensue. While heuristics render the world manageable (by reducing the information-processing requirements of the decision maker), unfortunately there are several deleterious consequences that may result from the adoption of these procedures. A number of laboratory experiments and field studies (reviewed in Schwenk, 1995; Das and Teng, 1999; Hodgkinson, 2001b; Maule and Hodgkinson, 2002) have demonstrated that actors' cognitions and judgements may become biased as a result of adopting these heuristics, which in turn may lead to suboptimal decision choices. Table 9.1 presents a selective summary of the some of the commonly identified heuristics and biases that Schwenk (1988) argues have a significant effect on strategic decision making.

Tools and techniques

How, then, can we facilitate individual and collective learning so as to minimize the potentially catastrophic impact of cognitive bias and inertia? What is ultimately required is the development of intervention techniques that will enable individuals and groups to explore their largely taken-for-granted assumptions that drive their day-to-day behaviour, so that they can change or reframe their mental representations in such a way that they not only register the nature and significance of new events or situations, but are also able to ensure that the strategic capabilities of the organization are realigned accordingly. In this respect, the various mapping techniques that have been employed to shed light on the nature and significance of cognition in the strategy process may have an invaluable role to play. The application of these procedures as a practical means of facilitating strategic conversations may enable those charged with

An evaluation of selected heuristics and biases in terms of their TABLE 9.1
effects on strategic decision making (adapted from Schwenk, 1988
© Blackwell Publishers Ltd. Reproduced with permission)

Heuristic/Bias	Effects
1. Availability	Judgements of the probability of easily recalled events are distorted
2. Selective perception	Expectations may bias observations of variables relevant to strategy
3. Illusory correlation	Encourages the belief that unrelated variables are correlated
4. Conservatism	Failure to sufficiently revise forecasts based on new information
5. Law of small numbers	Overestimation of the degree to which small samples are representative of populations
6. Regression bias	Failure to allow for regression to the mean
7. Wishful thinking	Probability of desired outcomes judged to be inappropriately high
8. Illusion of control	Overestimation of personal control over outcomes
9. Logical reconstruction	'Logical' reconstruction of events that cannot be accurately recalled
10. Hindsight bias	Overestimation of predictability of past events

the responsibility for strategy making and implementation to overcome their blind spots and ensure that they question the appropriateness of their organization's *modus operandi* on a continuous basis.

In recent years a large number of cognitive mapping techniques and related procedures have been developed and used to further the theory and practice of strategic management. A detailed review of the available alternatives is beyond the scope of this chapter. Here we can only provide a brief illustration of three of the more popular techniques available for use as research tools and bases of intervention, namely causal mapping, repertory grids and scenarios. Comprehensive overviews of these and the many other techniques currently available for mapping strategic thought are provided by Huff (1990), Fiol and Huff (1992), Walsh (1995), Eden and Spender (1998), Hodgkinson (2001a), Hodgkinson and Sparrow (2002), and Huff and Jenkins (2002).

Causal mapping techniques

Ranked among the most popular of cognitive mapping procedures, causal mapping techniques are designed to capture actors' causal belief systems. In their most basic form, cause maps are depicted graphically, using the medium of influence diagrams (Diffenbach, 1982), the pathways interconnecting the concepts contained in the diagram denoting patterns of causality in the reasoning of the participant(s) concerned. Causal mapping procedures have been employed fruitfully not only to investigate individual thinking (Cosette and

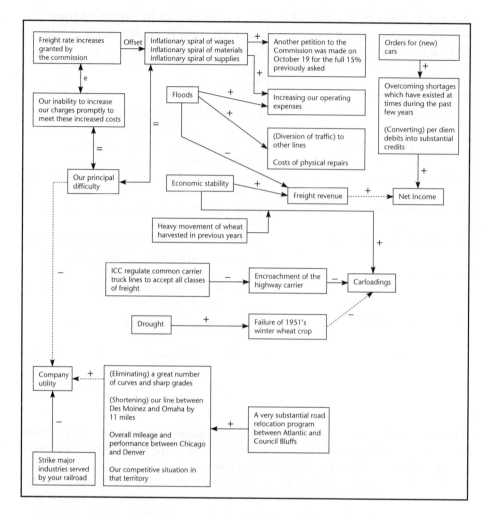

FIGURE 9.3 Cause map of the Rock Island Railroad Company in 1951 (Cognitive change, strategic action and organizational renewal, Barr, Stimpert and Huff, 1992. © John Wiley & Sons. Reproduced with permission)

Audet, 1992) but also to represent the collective logics of organizations and wider communities as a whole (Roberts, 1976).

Figure 9.3 provides an example of a cause map, taken from a study by Barr *et al.* (1992) of US railway companies outlined above. In this diagram, variables that are thought to be causally related to one another, directly or indirectly, are connected by means of a series of lines that emanate from the independent variables and terminate on the dependent variables, the arrowheads depicting the directions of causality. Perceived positive causal relationships, in which increases in one variable are thought to cause an increase in one or more other variables, are depicted by means of plus signs, which accompany the arrow-headed pathways linking the variables in question. Conversely, perceived negative causal relationships, in which increases in one variable are thought to cause decreases in one or more other variables, are depicted by means of arrow-headed pathways accompanied by minus signs.

Cause maps can be far more complex than that illustrated in Figure 9.3. Increasingly sophisticated variants of causal mapping procedures are available in which a range of different relationships between variables are evaluated, in addition to basic positive and negative causality. While relatively simple cause maps can be represented in diagrammatic form, when the number of variables and relationships contained in a map increases this greatly complicates our ability to capture adequately the information contained in a map. Fortunately, however, such maps are amenable to a variety of quantitative analyses, based on the mathematics of graph theory, and researchers are increasingly developing software to facilitate such analyses (see for example Eden *et al.*, 1992; Laukkanen, 1994; Markoczy and Goldberg, 1995). For further illustrations and a discussion of some of the methodological issues associated with the wider application of causal mapping techniques see Jenkins and Johnson (1997a, 1997b), Jenkins (1998), Hodgkinson (2001a) and Hodgkinson and Sparrow (2002).

Causal mapping procedures are increasingly being used as a basis for intervening in the strategy process. For example, as noted earlier Eden and Ackermann (1998, 2000) have used this form of mapping to identify organizational competences, and Bowman and Ambrosini (2002) have used it to reveal tacit knowledge within organizations. Despite the growing popularity of these techniques in these and other practitioner contexts, there is vitually no evidence (other than basic anecdotal evidence) that such applications actually improve the quality of strategic decision making (for a notable exception in this regard see Hodgkinson *et al.*, 1999; Hodgkinson and Maule, 2002).

Repertory grid techniques

Another set of techniques that have proven highly popular in the analysis of strategic thought are 'repertory grid' techniques. These techniques originated in the field of clinical psychology and are based on the notion of 'personal construct theory' (Kelly, 1955).

This theory asserts that individuals navigate their intra- and interpersonal worlds using a series of bipolar dimensions (termed 'personal constructs'), which they employ to make sense of the stimuli (known as 'elements') they encounter. According to personal construct theory, individuals by and large construe their worlds differently from one another, hence the term 'personal construct theory'. The theory is based on the fundamental premise that individuals behave in a manner akin to natural scientists as they go about their everyday business, formulating hypotheses about their worlds, which they then seek to verify through observation. If their hypotheses are confirmed their personal construct systems are said to be validated. If their hypotheses are falsified, however, ordinarily individuals will set about revising their construct systems.

The primary strength of repertory grid techniques lies in their inherent flexibility, from the point of view of both data collection and analysis (see for example Slater, 1976, 1977; Fransella and Bannister, 1977; Smith and Stewart, 1977; Dunn and Ginsberg, 1986; Ginsberg, 1989; Reger, 1990a, 1990b), and in recent years these approaches have enjoyed considerable success in applied studies of social cognition in a wide variety of domains that lie well beyond their clinical roots and ideographic origins (see for example Forgas, 1976, 1978; Forgas *et al.*, 1980; Stewart *et al.*, 1981; Smith and Gibson, 1988). In its original form, each participant is required to draw up a list of elements (for example various competing firms in a market domain), which are then used to elicit the constructs (for example the attributes that differentiate competing firms). The elements are randomized by the researcher and presented to the participant in triads. The participant is required to explain the ways in which any two of the three elements presented are similar to one another but different from the third. This exercise is continued until it becomes evident that all possible constructs have been elicited. The constructs elicited in this way are used as a basis for forming a series of bipolar rating scales, which the participant is required to use to evaluate each of the elements in turn. The end result is an n × m matrix (or 'grid'), one grid per participant, containing his or her complete set of evaluative judgements. These matrices form the basis of subsequent statistical analyses (usually involving the application of one or more multivariate techniques) to reveal the participants' cognitive maps of the phenomenon under investigation.

Repertory grid techniques have been successfully employed in several cognitive studies of competitive industry structures. Reger (1990a), for example, employed a repertory grid approach to elicit the construct systems of the participants in her study of the US banking industry (see also Walton, 1986; Reger and Huff, 1993; Reger and Palmer, 1996), while Daniels *et al.* (1994, 1995) adopted a variant of the technique in their study of firms that supply pumps to the North Sea off-shore oil industry, as did Hodgkinson (1997b) in an investigation of cognitive inertia among UK estate agents.

Scenarios

One method that has been popularized in the practitioner-oriented literature as a means of overcoming the potentially deleterious consequences of cognitive bias and cognitive inertia is scenario planning (see, for example, Wack, 1985a, 1985b; Mobasheri *et al.*, 1989; Schoemaker, 1995). In contrast to traditional strategic planning techniques, which seek to forecast the future in probabilistic terms in an attempt to plan for a predetermined future, scenario planning techniques seek to develop a series of stylized portraits of the future that capture what may or may not happen, thereby providing a basis for the development of a strategy to deal with the various contingencies identified, thus directly incorporating uncertainty in the analysis (van der Heijden, 1994). According to van der Heijden (1996: 41) the benefits that stem from the application of a scenario planning approach are twofold:

- In the longer term, the development of a more robust organizational system that will be better able to withstand the unexpected shocks that come its way.
- In the shorter term, increased adaptability by virtue of more skilful observation of the business environment.

Eden and his colleagues (for example Eden and Radford, 1990; van der Heijden, 1996; Eden and Ackermann, 1998) have developed a variety of cognitive mapping approaches which can be readily incorporated in the scenario planning process. Building on the technique of causal mapping, outlined above, Eden and his colleagues have devised a range of procedures for eliciting, in systematic and structured ways, managers' views of the future, which can then be turned into graphical representations using specialist support software. The object of this exercise is to help individuals and teams to share and reconcile a multiplicity of ideas about the future environment. While scenario planning appears to have high face validity as a basis for overcoming cognitive bias and cognitive inertia, as with the related causal mapping procedures – which are increasingly being used as a key element in the scenario process – thus far there is very little evidence for its efficacy, other than basic anecdotal evidence (though for a notable exception in this respect see Schoemaker, 1993).

One of the main drawbacks of cognitive mapping and scenario planning procedures in general is that they rely on what individuals or groups are prepared to say. The assumption that these tools and techniques capture the cognition and 'deep' thinking of individuals is questionable, and this needs to be remembered when using them. (For an analysis of the limitations of scenario planning procedures, in the context of a failed intervention in the strategy process of a commercial organization, see Hodgkinson and Wright, in press.)

Case study revisited

Before concluding this chapter we shall return briefly to the series of questions posed earlier in respect of the conversation with the owner–manager of the small jewellery business. One way of approaching these questions is to analyze the jeweller's comments with the help of one or more cognitive mapping procedures. Figure 9.4 shows our representation of his comments, based on the technique of causal mapping.

- Question 1: what are the key elements (variables and concepts) that inform the jeweller's view of his business strategy, and how are these interconnected in his reasoning?

It can be seen from Figure 9.4 that the jeweller's business strategy is based on the manufacture of bespoke jewellery. Hence this business is vertically integrated, and the fact that all the pieces it makes are both designed and manufactured by it means it has adapted a niche strategy that focuses on offering differentiated products for significant occasions such as weddings: 'It's really on the special pieces and the commissioned pieces that we can actually get most of our enjoyment, because that's where you get the real positive feedback from customers and that's where we pick up most of our profit.' From a cognitive point of view, in this statement there is a set of causal connections that seem to summarize the basis of the business. The concept 'commissioned jewellery' is central to the jeweller's strategic vision because it is central to the identity of his business (as a niche player) and ultimately creates the marginal revenue

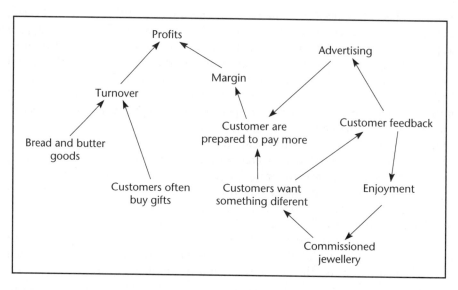

FIGURE 9.4 Cause map representing the comments of the owner–manager of a jewellery shop

from which the business derives its profits. This will become clearer if we edit the causal map to remove the less central elements (Figure 9.5).

• Question 2: which organizations would the jeweller regard as the major competitors to his business, and for what reasons?

While at one level the jeweller is acknowledging competition in terms of the jeweller 'down the road', the implication seems to be that because his business makes its own jewellery there is no direct competition for this part of its operations. Although no competitors are named as such, it is evident that other niche players specializing in the design and manufacture of commissioned jewellery present the greatest competitive threat. This can be inferred from the fact that 'commissioned jewellery' is the key source of revenue and central to the market identity of the business, as viewed from the perspective of the owner–manager.

• Question 3: are there any significant threats and/or opportunities that may go unnoticed but which might have a major bearing on the longer-term well-being of his business?

The most likely threat to this firm's strategy will come in the form of competition or substitution. For example the jeweller does not seem to consider the fact that other jewellers also offer a bespoke service. Presumably he employs skilled staff who could either move to other jewellers or set up on their own. Another possibility is that jewellery craftsmen may offer a similar service to a range of retail outlets, both large and small. The threat of substitution

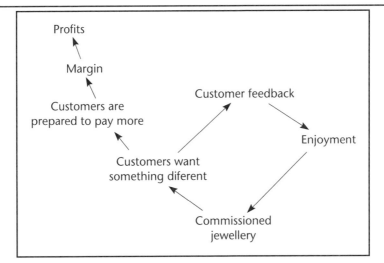

Section of cause map revealing the fundamental   FIGURE 9.5
elements of the owner–manager's business strategy

will vary according to the buying situation; for weddings this is probably low, but in the case of gifts, new technologies and social trends may move the emphasis away from the value of jewellery.

- Question 4: what fundamental assumptions underpin his responses to the above questions, and to what extent are these assumptions reasonable?

An examination of the jeweller's comments reveals that inherent in his strategy are a number of assumptions that may or may not be explicitly recognized by him. One of the strengths of the managerial and organizational cognition perspective on strategy is that it helps both to reveal such assumptions and to address the implications they raise for strategy development. Some of the main assumptions underpinning the jeweller's strategy relate to the nature and characteristics of buyers: 'This is because people are often buying gifts, so they often want something that is unique, and they're prepared to pay a bit more for that. . . . Our products aren't particularly price sensitive, because there isn't the direct competition.' These statements reveal several highly questionable assumptions about: (1) regular demand, (2) the desirability of being 'different', (3) the price insensitivity of buyers and (4) the lack of competition.

It is clear from this brief illustration that the cognitive perspective in general, and the technique of causal mapping in particular, offer a potentially effective way of identifying the core assumptions that underpin the jeweller's strategy for his business. Our analysis has revealed a number of limitations in his thinking, which if left unchecked would surely threaten the long-term viability of his venture.

Concluding remarks

The managerial and organizational cognition perspective highlights a number of potential weaknesses in the way in which individuals and groups handle information, weaknesses which can and frequently do undermine the strategy process. In drawing attention to these potential dangers, we do not wish to imply that selective attention and limited information search are invariably dysfunctional. In the absence of such filtering strategies we would be greatly overwhelmed by the sheer complexity of the world. Indeed, there is evidence to suggest that strategies that are simple, coherent and easily understood may lead to better performance than those which are sophisticated and highly complex (Pettigrew and Whipp, 1991). A simplified view of the world may help unite an organization's members, which is undoubtedly a key factor in successful strategy implementation. This discussion highlights a fundamental tension in the strategy process: it is increasingly the case that actors must be open-minded enough to consider new and innovative ideas and approaches, but also single-minded enough to offer the commitment and focus needed to implement such ideas.

The cognitive perspective on strategic management shifts the focus of analysis away from the objective characteristics of firms, industries and markets and towards the subjective and intersubjective worlds of individuals and groups. In so doing it challenges two core assumptions of neoclassical economics: that all firms have equal access to information about the marketplace, and that they will invariably respond to such information in similar ways. It is clear that the assumption that business environments are objective entities waiting to be discovered through the application of analytical procedures and techniques, which is implicit in much of the mainstream literature on competitive strategy and strategic planning, does not stand up to theoretical and empirical scrutiny.

Further reading

Eden, C. and J.-C. Spender (eds) (1998) *Managerial and Organizational Cognition: Theory, Methods and Research* (London: Sage).

Finkelstein, S. and D. C. Hambrick (1996) *Strategic Leadership: Top Executives and Their Effects on Organizations* (St Paul, Minn.: West).

Hodgkinson, G. P. (2001a) 'The psychology of strategic management: Diversity and cognition revisited', in C. L. Cooper and I. T. Robertson (eds), *International Review of Industrial and Organizational Psychology*, vol. 16 (Chichester: Wiley), pp. 65–119.

Hodgkinson, G. P. (2001b) 'Cognitive processes in strategic management: some emerging trends and future directions', in N. Anderson, D. S. Ones, H. K. Sinangil and C. Viswesvaran (eds), *Handbook of Industrial, Work and Organizational Psychology: Volume 2 – Organizational Psychology* (London: Sage), pp. 416–40.

Hodgkinson, G. P. and P. R. Sparrow (in press) *The Competent Organization: A Psychological Analysis of the Strategic Management Process* (Buckingham: Open University Press).

Huff, A. S. (ed.) (1990) *Mapping Strategic Thought* (Chichester: Wiley).

Huff, A. S. and M. Jenkins (eds) (2002), *Mapping Strategic Knowledge* (London, Sage).

Meindl, J. R., C. Stubbart, and J. F. Porac (eds) (1996) *Cognition Within and Between Organizations* (Thousand Oaks, CA: Sage).

Walsh, J. P. (1995) 'Managerial and organizational cognition: Notes from a trip down memory lane', *Organization Science*, vol. 6, pp. 280–321.

Weick, K. E. (1995) *Sensemaking in Organizations* (Thousand Oaks, CA: Sage).

Like many of the perspectives that underpin the field of strategic management, there are a number of distinct interpretations of the managerial and organizational cognition literature. Unfortunately, there are relatively few overviews of the literature as a whole. One notable exception is an article by J. P. Walsh, 'Managerial and organizational cognition: Notes from a trip down memory lane' (*Organization Science*, vol. 6, 1995, pp. 280–321). One of the most comprehensive and up to date surveys that relates specifically to strategic management is G. P. Hodgkinson and P. R. Sparrow's *The Competent Organization: A Psychological Analysis of the Strategic Management Process* (Buckingham: Open University, 2002). Another useful, though rapidly dating overview of this literature, specifically relating to the strategy field, is provided by A. S. Huff in *Mapping Strategic Thought* (Chichester: Wiley, 1990). This book, an edited collection of specially commissioned chapters with accompanying commentaries, provides a basis for considering some of the empirical research that has been undertaken in the strategy field from a cognitive perspective. It is also an invaluable guide to management researchers as it provides useful step-by-step introductions to a wide range of alternative cognitive mapping procedures. The themes in this book have been taken up and combined with a more specific focus on mapping approaches and their use in strategy in *Mapping Strategic Knowledge* edited by A. S. Huff and M. Jenkins (London: Sage, 2002). A book edited by Colin Eden and J.-C. Spender, *Managerial and Organizational Cognition: Theory, Methods and Research* (London: Sage, 1998), in many ways serves as another useful update to the earlier book by Huff (1990). J. R. Meindl, J. C. Stubbart and J. F. Porac (1996) provide yet another useful collection of up-to-date readings in *Cognition Within and Between Organizations* (Thousand Oaks, CA: Sage, 1996). K. E. Weick's *Sensemaking in Organizations* (Thousand Oaks, CA: Sage, 1995) and S. Finkelstein and D. C. Hambrick's *Strategic Leadership: Top Executives and their Effects on Organizations* (St Paul, Min.: West) provide highly scholarly reviews of the literature on these two key topics. Finally, the edited book chapters by Hodgkinson (2001a, 2001b) comprise critical state of the art reviews, which comprehensively survey the very latest theory, methods and empirical research findings relating to a number of themes introduced in the present chapter.

References

Abell, D. F. (1980) *Defining the Business: The Starting Point of Strategic Planing* (Englewood Cliffs, NJ: Prentice-Hall).

Ackoff, R. L. (1983) 'Beyond prediction and preparation', *Journal of Management Studies*, vol. 20, pp. 59–69.

Anderson, J. R. (1990) *Cognitive Psychology and its Implications*, 3rd edn (New York: Freeman).

Andrews, K. R. (1971) *The Concept of Corporate Strategy* (Homewood, Ill.: Irwin).

Ansoff, H. I. (1965) *Corporate Strategy* (New York: McGraw-Hill).

Baden-Fuller, C. and J. M. Stopford (1992) *Rejuvenating the Mature Business* (London: Routledge).

Barnard, C. I. (1938) *The Functions of the Executive* (Cambridge, Mass.: Harvard University Press).

Barney J. B. and R. E. Hoskisson (1990) 'Strategic groups: Untested assertions and research proposals', *Managerial and Decision Economics*, vol. 11, pp. 187–98.

Barr, P. S. and A. S. Huff (1997) 'Seeing isn't believing: understanding diversity in the timing of strategic response', *Journal of Management Studies*, vol. 34, pp. 337–70.

Barr, P. S., J. L. Stimpert and A. S. Huff (1992) 'Cognitive change, strategic action, and organizational renewal', *Strategic Management Journal*, vol. 13, Summer Special Issue, pp. 15–36.

Bartlett, F. C. (1932) *Remembering: A Study in Experimental and Social Psychology* (Cambridge: Cambridge University Press).

Berger, P. L. and T. Luckmann (1967) *The Social Construction of Reality* (Harmondsworth: Penguin).

Bowman, C. and V. Ambrosini (2002) 'Mapping Successful Organizational Routines', in A. S. Huff and M. Jenkins (eds) *Mapping Strategic Knowledge* (London: Sage).

Broadbent, D. E. (1958) *Perception and Communication* (London: Pergamon Press).

Bukszar, E. and T. Connolly (1988) 'Hindsight bias and strategic choice: Some problems in learning from experience', *Academy of Management Journal,* vol. 31, pp. 628–41.

Chaffee, E. E. (1985) 'Three models of strategy'. *Academy of Management Review,* vol. 10, pp. 89–98.

Chernatony, L. de, K. Daniels and G. Johnson (1993) 'A cognitive perspective on managers' perceptions of competitors', *Journal of Marketing Management,* vol. 9, pp. 373–81.

Christensen, C. R., K. R. Andrews, J. L. Bower, G. Hamermesh and M. E. Porter (1982) *Business Policy: Text and Cases,* 5th edn (Homewood, Ill.: Irwin).

Cosette, P. and M. Audet (1992) 'Mapping of an idiosyncratic schema', *Journal of Management Studies,* vol. 29, pp. 309–48.

Craik, K. *The Nature of Explanation* (Cambridge: Cambridge University Press).

Cyert, R. M. and J. G. March (1963) *A Behavioral Theory of the Firm* (Englewood Cliffs, NJ: Prentice-Hall).

Daniels, K., L. de Chernatony and G. Johnson (1995) 'Validating a method for mapping managers' mental models of competitive industry structures', *Human Relations,* vol. 48, pp. 975–91.

Daniels, K., G. Johnson and L. de Chernatony (1994) 'Differences in managerial cognitions of competition', *British Journal of Management,* vol. 5, Special Issue, pp. S21–9.

Das, T. K. and B.-S. Teng (1999) 'Cognitive biases and strategic decision processes', *Journal of Management Studies,* vol. 36, pp. 757–78.

Diffenbach, J. (1982) 'Influence diagrams for complex strategic issues', *Strategic Management Journal,* vol. 3, pp. 133–46.

Dunn, W. N. and A. Ginsberg (1986) 'A sociocognitive network approach to organizational analysis', *Human Relations,* vol. 40, pp. 955–76.

Dutton, J. and S. Jackson (1987). 'Categorizing strategic issues: links to organizational action', *Academy of Management Review,* vol. 12, pp. 76–90.

Dutton, J., E. J. Walton and E. Abrahamson (1989) 'Important dimensions of strategic issues: Separating the wheat from the chaff', *Journal of Management Studies,* vol. 26, pp. 379–96.

Eden, C. and F. Ackermann (1998) *Making Strategy: The Journey of Strategic Management* (London: Sage).

Eden, C. and F. Ackermann (2000) 'Mapping distinctive competencies: A systematic approach', *Journal of the Operational Research Society,* vol. 51, pp. 12–20.

Eden, C., F. Ackermann and S. Cropper (1992) 'The analysis of cause maps', *Journal of Management Studies,* vol. 29, pp. 309–24.

Eden, C. and J. Radford (eds) (1990) *Tackling Strategic Problems: The Role of Group Decision Support* (London: Sage).

Eden, C. and J.-C. Spender (eds) (1998) *Managerial and Organizational Cognition: Theory, Methods and Research* (London: Sage).

Eysenck, M. W. and M. T. Keane (1995) *Cognitive Psychology: A Student's Handbook,* 3rd edn (Hove: Psychology Press).

Finkelstein, S. and D. C. Hambrick (1996) *Strategic Leadership: Top Executives and their Effects on Organizations* (St Paul, Min.: West).

Fiol, C. M. and A. S. Huff (1992) 'Maps for managers. Where are we? Where do we go from Here?', *Journal of Management Studies,* vol. 29, pp. 267–85.

Fischhoff, B. (1975) 'Hindsight and foresight: The effect of outcome knowledge on judgment under uncertainty', *Journal of Experimental Psychology: Human Perception and Performance,* vol. 1, pp. 288–99.

Fischhoff, B., P. Slovic and S. Lichtenstein (1977) 'Knowing with certainty: The appropriateness of extreme confidence', *Journal of Experimental Psychology: Human Perception and Performance,* vol. 3, pp. 552–64.

Forgas, J. P. (1976) 'The perception of social episodes: Categorical and dimensional representation in two subcultural millieus', *Journal of Personality and Social Psychology*, vol. 34, pp. 199–209.

Forgas, J. P. (1978) 'Social episodes and social structure in an academic setting: The social environment of an intact group', *Journal of Experimental Social Psychology*, vol. 14, pp. 434–48.

Forgas, J. P., L. B. Brown and J. Menyhart (1980) 'Dimensions of aggression: The perception of aggressive episodes', *British Journal of Social and Clinical Psychology*, vol. 19, pp. 215–27.

Foxall, G. (1997) 'The explanation of consumer behaviour: From social cognition to environmental control', in C. L. Cooper and I. T. Robertson (eds), *International Review of Industrial and Organizational Psychology*, vol. 12, (Chichester: Wiley) pp. 229–87.

Fransella, F. and D. Bannister (1977) *A Manual for Repertory Grid Technique* (New York: Academic Press).

Ginsberg, A. (1989) 'Construing the business portfolio: A cognitive model of diversification', *Journal of Management Studies*, vol. 26, pp. 417–38.

Grant, R. M. (1998) *Contemporary Strategy Analysis*, 3rd edn (Oxford: Blackwell).

Greenley, G. (1989) *Strategic Management* (London: Prentice-Hall).

Gripsrud, G. and K. Grønhaug (1985) 'Structure and strategy in grocery retailing: A sociometric approach', *Journal of Industrial Economics*, vol. XXXIII, pp. 339–47.

Hambrick, D. C. and P. A. Mason (1984) 'Upper echelons: The organization as a reflection of its top managers', *Academy of Management Review*, vol. 9, pp. 193–206.

Hannan, M. and J. Freeman (1977) 'The population ecology of organizations', *American Journal of Sociology*, vol. 82, pp. 929–64.

Hannan, M. and J. Freeman (1988) *Organizational Ecology* (Cambridge, Mass.: Harvard University Press).

Harris, S. G. F. (1996) 'Organizational Culture and Individual Culture: A Schema-Based Perspective', in J. R. Meindl, C. Stubbart and J. Porac (eds) *Cognition Within and Between Organizations* (Thousand Oaks, CA: Sage), pp. 283–306.

Heijden, K. van der (1994) 'Probabilistic planning and scenario planning', in G. Wright and P. Ayton (eds) *Subjective Probability* (Chichester: Wiley).

Heijden, K. van der (1996) *Scenarios: The Art of Strategic Conversation* (Chichester: Wiley).

Hitt, M. A., R. D. Ireland and R. E. Hoskisson (1996) *Strategic Management: Competitiveness and Globalization*, 2nd edn (St Paul, Min.: West).

Hodgkinson, G. P. (1997a) 'The cognitive analysis of competitive structures: A review and critique', *Human Relations*, vol. 50, pp. 625–54.

Hodgkinson, G. P. (1997b) 'Cognitive inertia in a turbulent market: The case of UK residential estate agents', *Journal of Management Studies*, vol. 34, pp. 921–45.

Hodgkinson, G. P. (2001a) 'The psychology of strategic management: Diversity and cognition revisited', in C. L. Cooper and I. T. Robertson (eds), *International Review of Industrial and Organizational Psychology*, vol. 16, (Chichester: Wiley), pp. 65–119.

Hodgkinson, G. P. (2001b) 'Cognitive processes in strategic management: some emerging trends and future directions', in N. Anderson, D. S. Ones, H. K. Sinangil and C. Viswesvaran (eds), *Handbook of Industrial, Work, and Organizational Psychology: Volume 2 – Organizational Psychology* (London: Sage), pp. 416–40.

Hodgkinson, G. P., N. J. Bown, A. J. Maule, K. W. Glaister and A. D. Pearman (1999) 'Breaking the frame: An analysis of strategic cognition and decision making under uncertainty', *Strategic Management Journal*, vol. 20, pp. 977–85.

Hodgkinson, G. P. and G. Johnson (1994) 'Exploring the mental models of competitive strategists: the case for a processual approach', *Journal of Management Studies*, vol. 31, pp. 525–51.

Hodgkinson, G. P. and A. J. Maule (2002) 'The individual in the strategy process: Insights from behavioural decision research and cognitive mapping', in A. S. Huff and M. Jenkins (eds), *Mapping Strategic Knowledge* (London: Sage), pp. 196–236.

Hodgkinson, G. P. and P. R. Sparrow (2002) *The Competent Organization: A Psychological Analysis of the Strategic Management Process* (Buckingham: Open University Press).

Hodgkinson, G. P. and G. Wright (in press) 'Confronting strategic inertia in a top management team: Learning from failure', *Organization Studies*.

Hofer, C. and Schendel, D. (1978) *Strategy Formulation: Analytical Concepts* (St Paul, Min.: West).

Huff, A. S. (1982) 'Industry influences on strategy formation', *Strategic Management Journal*, vol. 3, pp. 119–31.

Huff, A. S. (ed.) (1990) *Mapping Strategic Thought* (Chichester: John Wiley).

Huff, A. S. and M. Jenkins (eds) (2002) *Mapping Strategic Knowledge* (London: Sage).

Jackson, S. E. and J. E. Dutton (1988) 'Discerning Threats and Opportunities', *Administrative Science Quarterly*, vol. 33, pp. 370–87.

Jenkins, M. (1998) 'The theory and practice of comparing causal Maps', in C. Eden and J. C. Spender (eds.), *Managerial and Organizational Cognition* (London: Sage) pp. 231–49.

Jenkins, M. and G. Johnson (1997a) 'Linking managerial cognition and organizational performance: A preliminary investigation using causal maps', *British Journal of Management*, vol. 8, Special Issue, pp. S77–90.

Jenkins, M. and G. Johnson (1997b) 'Entrepreneurial intentions and outcomes: A comparative causal mapping study', *Journal of Management Studies*, vol. 34, Special Issue, pp. 895–920.

Johnson, G. (1987) *Strategic Change and the Management Process* (Oxford: Blackwell).

Johnson, G. and K. Scholes (2001) *Exploring Corporate Strategy: Text and Cases*, 6th edn (London: Prentice-Hall).

Johnson, P., K. Daniels and R. Asch (1998) 'Mental Models of Competition', in C. Eden and J.-C. Spender (eds), *Managerial and Organizational Cognition* (London: Sage), pp. 130–46.

Johnson-Laird, P. N. (1983) *Mental Models* (Cambridge: Cambridge University Press).

Johnson-Laird, P. N. (1993) *The Computer and the Mind*, 2nd edn (London: Fontana).

Kahneman, D., P. Slovic and A. Tversky (eds) (1982) *Judgment Under Uncertainty: Heuristics and Biases* (Cambridge: Cambridge University Press).

Kelly, G. A. (1955) *The Psychology of Personal Constructs*, 2 vols (New York: W. W. Norton).

Lant, T. K., F. J. Milliken and B. Batra (1992) 'The role of managerial learning and interpretation in strategic persistence and reorientation: An empirical exploration', *Strategic Management Journal*, vol. 13, pp. 585–608.

Laukkanen, M. (1994) 'Comparative cause mapping of organizational cognitions', *Organization Science*, vol. 5, pp. 322–43.

Luffman, G., S. Sanderson, E. Lea and B. Kenney (1987) *Business Policy: An Analytical Introduction.* (Oxford: Blackwell).

March, J. G. and H. A. Simon (1958) *Organizations* (New York: Wiley).

Markoczy, L. and J. Goldberg (1995), 'A method for eliciting and comparing causal maps', *Journal of Management*, vol. 21, pp. 305–33.

Maule, A. J. and G. P. Hodgkinson (2002) 'Heuristics, biases and strategic decision making', *The Psychologist* vol. 15(2), pp. 68–71.

McGee, J. and H. Thomas (1986) 'Strategic groups: Theory, research and taxonomy', *Strategic Management Journal*, vol. 7, pp. 141–60.

Meindl, J. R., C. Stubbart and J. F. Porac (eds) (1996) *Cognition Within and Between Organizations* (Thousand Oaks, CA: Sage).

Mintzberg, H. (1994) *The Rise and Fall of Strategic Planning* (London: Prentice-Hall).

Mintzberg, H., B. Ahlstrand and J. Lampel (1998) *Strategy Safari: A Guided Tour Through the Wilds of Strategic Management* (London: Prentice-Hall).

Mobasheri, F., L. H. Orren and F. P. Sioshansi (1989) 'Scenario planning at Southern California Edison', *Interfaces*, vol. 19 (5), pp. 31–44.

Morecroft, J. D. W. (1994) 'Executive knowledge, models and learning', in J. D. W.

Morecroft and John D. Sterman (eds), *Modelling for Learning Organizations* (Portland, Or.: Productivity Press).

Mowrer, O. H. (1947) 'On the dual nature of learning: A reinterpretation of "conditioning" and "problem solving" ', *Harvard Educational Review*, vol. 17, pp. 102–48.

Oster, S. (1990) *Modern Competitive Analysis* (Oxford: Oxford University Press).

Pettigrew, A. M. and R. Whipp (1991) *Managing Change for Competitive Success* (Oxford: Blackwell).

Piercy, N. (1992) *Market-Led Strategic Change* (Oxford: Butterworth-Heinemann).

Porac, J. and A. Rosa (1996) 'Rivalry, industry models, and the cognitive embeddedness of the comparable firm', *Advances in Strategic Management*, vol. 13, pp. 363–88.

Porac, J. F. and H. Thomas (1990) 'Taxonomic mental models in competitor definition', *Academy of Management Review*, vol. 15, pp. 224–40.

Porac, J. F., H. Thomas and C. Baden-Fuller (1989) 'Competitive groups as cognitive communities: The case of Scottish knitwear manufacturers', *Journal of Management Studies*, vol. 26, pp. 397–416.

Porac, J. F., H. Thomas, F. Wilson, D. Paton and A. Kanfer (1995) 'Rivalry and the industry model of Scottish knitwear producers', *Administrative Science Quarterly*, vol. 40, pp. 203–27.

Porter, M. E. (1980) *Competitive Strategy: Techniques for Analyzing Industries and Competitors* (New York: Free Press).

Porter, M. E. (1985) *Competitive Advantage: Creating and Sustaining Superior Performance* (New York: Free Press).

Reger, R. K. (1990a) 'Managerial thought structures and competitive positioning', in A. S. Huff (ed.), *Mapping Strategic Thought* (Chichester: Wiley), pp. 71–88.

Reger, R. K. (1990b) 'The repertory grid for eliciting the content and structure of cognitive constructive systems', in A. S. Huff (ed.), *Mapping Strategic Thought* (Chichester: Wiley), pp. 301–9.

Reger, R. K. and A. S. Huff (1993) 'Strategic Groups: A Cognitive Perspective'. *Strategic Management Journal*, vol. 14, pp. 103–24.

Reger, R. K. and T. B. Palmer (1996), 'Managerial categorization of competitors: using old maps to navigate new environments', *Organization Science*, vol. 7, pp. 22–39.

Roberts, F. S. (1976) 'Strategy for the energy crisis: The case of commuter transport policy', in R. Axelrod (ed.), *The Structure of Decision: Cognitive Maps of Political Elites* (Princeton, NJ: Princeton University Press), pp. 142–79.

Schoemaker, P. J. H. (1993) 'Multiple scenario development: Its conceptual and behavioral foundation', *Strategic Management Journal*, vol. 14, pp. 193–213.

Schoemaker, P. J. H. (1995) 'Scenario planning: A tool for strategic thinking', *Sloan Management Review*, Winter, pp. 25–40.

Schwenk, C. R. (1988) 'The cognitive perspective on strategic decision making', *Journal of Management Studies*, vol. 25, pp. 41–55.

Schwenk, C. R. (1995) 'Strategic decision making', *Journal of Management*, vol. 21, pp. 471–93.

Senge, P. (1990) *The Fifth Discipline: The Art and Practice of the Learning Organization* (London: Century).

Simon, H. A. (1947) *Administrative Behavior* (New York: Macmillan).

Skinner, B. F. (1938) *The Behavior of Organisms* (New York: Appleton-Century-Crofts).

Slater, P. (ed.) (1976) *The Measurement of Intrapersonal Space by Grid Technique: Vol. I – Explorations of Intrapersonal Space* (Chichester: Wiley).

Slater, P. (ed.) (1977) *The Measurement of Intrapersonal Space by Grid Technique: Vol. II – Dimensions of Intrapersonal Space* (Chichester: Wiley).

Smith, M. and J. Gibson (1988) 'Using repertory grids to investigate racial prejudice', *Applied Psychology: An International Review*, vol. 37, pp. 311–26.

Smith, M. and B. J. M. Stewart (1977) 'Repertory grids: A flexible tool for establishing the contents and structure of a manager's thoughts', in D. Ashton (ed.), *Management Bibliographies and Reviews*, vol. 3 (Bradford: MCB Publications) pp. 209–29.

Spender, J.-C. (1989) *Industry Recipes: The Nature and Sources of Managerial Judgement* (Oxford: Blackwell).

Starbuck, W. H. and F. J. Milliken (1988) 'Executives' perceptual filters: What they notice and how they make sense', in D. C. Hambrick (ed.), *The Executive Effect: Concepts and Methods for Studying Top Managers* (Greenwich, Conn.: JAI), pp. 35–65.

Steiner, G. A. (1969) *Top Management Planning* (New York: Macmillan).

Stewart, V., A. Stewart and N. Fonda (1981) *The Business Application of Repertory Grids* (London: McGraw-Hill).

Stubbart, C. I. (1989) 'Managerial cognition: A missing link in strategic management research', *Journal of Management Studies*, vol. 26, pp. 325–47.

Tolman, E. C. (1932) *Purposive Behavior in Animals and Men* (New York: Century).

Tversky, A. and D. Kahneman (1974) 'Judgment under uncertainty: Heuristics and biases', *Science*, vol. 198, pp. 1124–31.

Wack, P. (1985a) 'Scenarios: Uncharted waters ahead', *Harvard Business Review*, Sept.–Oct., pp. 73–90.

Wack, P. (1985b) 'Scenarios: Shooting the rapids', *Harvard Business Review*, Nov.–Dec., pp. 131–42.

Walsh, J. P. (1995) 'Managerial and organizational cognition: Notes from a trip down memory lane', *Organization Science*, vol. 6, pp. 280–321.

Walton, E. J. (1986) 'Managers' prototypes of financial firms', *Journal of Management Studies*, vol. 23, pp. 679–98.

Weick, K. E. (1969) *The Social Psychology of Organizing* (Reading, Mass.: Addison-Wesley).

Weick, K. E. (1979) *The Social Psychology of Organizing*, 2nd edn (Reading, Mass.: Addison-Wesley).

Weick, K. E. (1995) *Sensemaking in Organizations* (Thousand Oaks, Cal.: Sage).

Weick, K. E. and M. G. Bougon (1986) 'Organizations as Cognitive Maps: Charting Ways to Success and Failure', in H. P. Sims and D. A. Gioia (eds), *The Thinking Organization: Dynamics of Organizational Social Cognition* (San Francisco, CA: Jossey-Bass) pp. 102–35.

Welford, A. T. (1976) *Skilled Performance* (Glenview, Ill.: Scott Foresman).

Wickens, C. D. (1984) *Engineering Psychology and Human Perfomance* (Columbus, Ohio: Merrill).

10 Role Theory
Pauline Weight

Introduction

Why a role perspective on strategy?

Research and anecdotal evidence abound on the influence that the individual's psychological and sociological characteristics have on organizational strategies and their effectiveness (Hambrick and Mason, 1984).

Understanding the complexity that is tied up in the word 'influence' continues to occupy researchers in many fields. One example of this is the influence of careers. Studies that link managers' careers and the strategic behaviour of the organizations they manage are contradictory and confusing (Gunz and Jalland, 1996). The challenge is to understand what is different and confusing rather than to look for similarities and leap to generalizations.

We do know that for strategies to be effective, organizations rely on significant and powerful actors to develop a set of shared expectations among the workforce (Gabbarro, 1988; Kotter, 1990; Bennis, 1994). How individuals interpret strategic issues in order to create a set of shared expectations is important to the understanding of strategic action, organizational change and learning (see Chapters 2 and 3). In support of the need for understanding the individual in a strategic role, some researches are now arguing that the emphasis in the study of strategic management should shift towards micro-level aspects of managing and organizational behaviour (Johnson and Bowman, 1999). It is the processing and interpretation of information by the individual that leads to a 'workable version of reality' (Weick, 1979).

Understanding the combination of psychological and sociological characteristics of an individual that come together in a specific context at a particular time is of interest to role theorists. This chapter considers one set of individuals in similar roles and contexts to illustrate the influences of role on strategic behaviour.

Basic principles

What is role theory? This question provokes as much debate as the subject itself. Role theory can be defined as a science concerned with the study of behaviours that are characteristic of persons within contexts and with various processes that produce, explain or are affected by these behaviours (Biddle, 1979). A role orientation has gradually evolved from related interests in several of the social sciences. Some advocate seeing role theory as a vehicle for amalgamating the three core social sciences of anthropology, sociology and psychology into a single discipline whose concern is the study of human behaviour (ibid.). Others see role theory as partitioned into two contrasting fields, one stemming from symbolic interactionism and the other representing structured psychology (Heiss, 1968). Other social sciences, for example economics, political science and demography, view human behaviour more as an independent variable than as a dependant variable. Role theory can contribute by informing these disciplines of behaviours that operate in various contexts.

Role theory continues to lack a propositional structure that ties the field together. However there are several underlying propositions about which there appears to be general, if informal, agreement (Biddle, 1979):

- Role theorists assert that some behaviours are patterned and are characteristic of persons particular in contexts (that is, they form *roles*).
- Roles are often associated with sets of persons who share a common identity (that is, they constitute *social positions*).
- People are often aware of roles, and to some extent roles are governed by this awareness (that is, by people's *expectations*).
- Roles persist in part because of their consequences (*functions*), and because they are often embedded in larger social systems.
- People must be taught roles (that is, they must be *socialized*), and they may find either joy or sorrow in the performance thereof.

It has to be said that there is not likely to be agreement about these propositions in the wider community of social scientists.

Role theory lies at the intersection of individual and organizational behaviour. This makes it useful for considering both the influence of expectations on managerial behaviour, and the effect of individual actions and preferences on behaviour (Hales, 1986). Looking at the development and implementation of strategy through the lens of role theory offers an insight into how strategic roles are constructed and enacted in organizations. The term 'enacted' is defined here as what the individual actually does in the role. In the literature this is also referred to as role behaviour and role interpretation.

Whilst not underestimating the importance of strategy processes such as analysis and planning, plans mean little until the strategy is implemented. How well the strategy is delivered depends on the competence and performance of the individuals who implement it. Answering the question 'why do individuals enact roles in the way they do?' is extremely complicated as it can be explored from a number of perspectives. Two approaches are discussed in this chapter, the first being to assess the career history and experience of individuals and how this affects their performance in a role. The second is understanding how individuals form a view of what is expected of them in a role, where that expectation comes from, and if and how individuals assess changes to meet the expectation.

Some role theorists (for example Graen *et al.*, 1975; Graen and Scandura, 1987) see the process in which individuals interpret and construct their role as a phenomenon that exists only in the early weeks of job occupancy, and only under special circumstances. However others argue that role making occurs continually as a by-product of the job holder's interaction with members of the role set, that is, those who have an interest in the performance of the individual in her or his job (Fondas and Stewart, 1992).

Role making can be described as a type of negotiation process that operates consciously and subconsciously. Researchers view the process of negotiation from different perspectives. There is the economic term 'satisficing', alongside other descriptions, which give a sense of interaction and exploration through the use of words such as social moulding, reciprocal determinism, reciprocal influence process and mutual adjustment. The attraction of role theory is that it allows us to explore and consider the nature of the interaction between individuals in different contexts and with different backgrounds and experiences. Whatever label we give this interaction, we know that managers spend a large percentage of their time engaged with others (Mintzberg, 1973). This only heightens the relevance of role theory in the study of managerial behaviour and its link with strategic management.

Case study

The situation

The situation is the change experienced by senior clinicians (consultants) in the UK National Health Service (NHS). The NHS is the largest employer in the Western world and since 1985 successive governments have encouraged consultants to take on a strategic role as part of their responsibilities. This move from a functional to a general management philosophy has attracted much interest from both practitioners and the academic community, and it has been argued that it will enhance this enormous organization's strategic management capability (Harrison and Miller, 1999). In the US there has also been a movement of physicians into formal management roles in a variety of health care settings. American researchers have identified a need for greater knowledge about the way individual doctors in medical management see their roles and themselves in it (Hoff, 1998).

These individuals are powerful actors in one of the two 'acknowledged professions' – law and medicine (Carr-Saunders and Wilson, 1933). These professions share a complex set of characteristics that have been identified by researchers across the decades (Parsons, 1954; Millerson, 1964; Burrage *et al.*, 1990). In essence these characteristics fall into four groups: knowledge and skills; service ideal; independence; and professional community.

The biggest group of professional characteristics fall into the *knowledge and skill* category: skills based on theoretical knowledge; practice modified by general knowledge; the application of principles to concrete professional practice; foresight based on theory; theory based on understanding; and the application of skills to the affairs of others (Millerson, 1964).

The second largest group is based loosely on the ethical beliefs and behaviours associated with the *service ideal*: putting clients' interests before one's own (altruism); adherence to a professional code of conduct; loyalty to colleagues; a preparedness to contribute to professional development; best impartial service given; fiduciary client relationships.

Thirdly, to the characteristics of knowledge base and service ideal was added autonomy on the basis of public trust (Ovretveit, 1992), which introduced an *independence* and power perspective to the discussion.

The final group comprise the 'institutional elements of professions' (Torstendahl, 1990): the provision of training and education supervised by professional organizations; recognized status; definite compensation (that is, fee or fixed charge); profits not dependent on capital; guaranteed service raises the association's prestige, thus securing employment and improving income. This cluster is referred to as the *professional community*.

It is argued that these career characteristics influence how individuals enact their a strategic role.

Other professions and vocations often exhibit some of these characteristics. For example, although the role of clinical director relates to a specific context, many business executives face similar situations. Other professionals, such as engineers and accountants, move to occupy managerial positions that require them to take up strategic responsibilities for which they have received little or no preparation. This case study may lead others to consider the part their professional development plays in the way they carry out new roles.

The conversations

The conversations took place in England with senior clinicians (known in many NHS hospitals as clinical directors). The following brief extracts from the conversations demonstrate how some aspects of the strategic role and the professional clinical role are enacted, and reveal factors that require consideration and understanding when individuals move into strategic roles. The statements in the extracts are representative of the general responses of the clinicians.

> ### The professional role
>
> 'I am a consultant . . . I like the fact that it really matters, what I do . . . what we do is never trivial. It's at the core of being useful [and] I actually enjoy it and see the necessity of it.'
>
> 'In a way it's more difficult to describe [than the strategic role], because you have been doing it for much longer. It's become a way of life, I come to work . . . we make people better you know [said with wry laughter].'
>
> 'The clinical role is much more clear cut, it's much less nebulous than the strategic role. I think there is no argument about the expectations that people have. There's not really any debate.'
>
> 'I am still the consultant that sees the most patients, I can see patients very quickly and sort them out when I get to them.'
>
> 'As soon as the patients come through the door, they are my responsibility. My job description reads that you will look after all the patients that come through the door.'
>
> 'I always start with the patient. The patient really does have an expectation, and justly so, that you will look after them to the best of your ability, that you will be competently trained and keep your skills up to date and you will guide them safely through whatever medical care they need . . . The nurses expect you to be available for patients when they need medical

input. I am not sure what nurses expect [for themselves] from consultants. I'm not sure I've even thought about it.'

'During your training you are pointed to the next hill based on interviews and people feeling you are ready for the next step, it's a long process, it's an apprenticeship.'

The strategic role

'I think communication is a big area . . . to get feedback as to where the problems are. . . . I stretch the rotas so we can meet in the operating theatre.'

'I am quite determined about what I want to get done and I have made it quite clear, never verbally, but by my actions, that if I want it done it will be done. That's how doctors work, doctors think that way, it's the medical mindset.'

' . . . one thing you don't say is what you are going to do . . . just do what matters.'

'I think you can either be a manager or not. I think you can learn the skills to be a better manager. One is not better than the other because of their skills, but because of their approach, and that is something you learn from when you are a baby.'

'I think people can do the strategic role naturally, but I think some management training is important, throughout your clinical role you are training all the time, so I think that is a major difference.'

'A lack of information holds me back.'

'[One is] constrained by having to work with everybody else.'

'It is very stressful . . . you get aggressive letters and representations. It involves sleepless nights sometimes, which I find irritating. . . . [The] stress is the aggression that goes with being the person who is seen to be introducing change.'

'Some of the stress is a personal wish to do things to a very high level and worrying that you are going to let someone down.'

'In my consultant role I ask myself, am I getting this right? In my director role I ask myself, how the hell am I going to do this?'

'As a personal choice you can do it in as much depth as you have the energy to do.'

'We have quite a few choices. It would be a sterile job if there were no choices, what would be the point of doing it.'

'So much of the budget is already committed and the things we have choices in are relatively small.'

'How well I do is difficult to judge, there is no role model for my position.'

'I would hope that if there was something I should be doing as a director someone would tell me.'

'I don't get the impression the Chief Executive wants to get rid of me . . . so I assume I am doing a reasonable job.'

Issues

When we take up a new role our perceptions about the role and what we actually do in that role are influenced in part by our past experience. The above extracts illustrate the influence of past experience, as articulated by individuals who have spent many years developing a professional career. Their statements on their strategic role reveal perceptions that may be partly informed by their career history. Without doubt the roles are viewed very differently. Many of the clinicians were unprepared for a strategic role and appear to be struggling through uncertainty.

The descriptions of the professional role demonstrate a sense of personal identity with the role. The clinicians display a sense of confidence in their ability to perform their professional role, which allows them to work quickly. Long service in the role has brought a familiarity that for some makes the role difficult to describe in broad terms. Confidence in the role emanates from long professional training, which is referred to as an apprenticeship that goes up in steps. Status is acquired with this training.

There is clarity about the professional role, in that the boundaries are readily and easily articulated, with a great sense of the priorities. In parallel with this is a feeling of independence, of autonomy in the decision-making process. The expectations others have of them in the clinical role centre on the patient, but they are treated as self-evident. The expectations of other clinicians who work with them are known and are therefore not discussed.

The clearest relationship for these individuals is with 'the patient', in this case meaning the collective body of people who come under the care of the clinician, usually involving a short number of time-limited contacts. Here the clinician is very clearly in a professional leadership role, where service to the patient is central to the role.

The strategic leadership role is described in quite different terms. Communication is seen by many clinicians as a fundamental part of the role. It is often described as a task, but there is little clarity about why and how the task has to be done. However a few feel that verbal communication is not important, that it is actions rather than words that count. Some think that the skills for the strategic role are almost innate, others feel the need for a degree of training. There is certainly no sense that the strategic role is a professional role or that long training is required for it.

The big challenge of this role appears to be separating the clinical work from the strategic work. Here emotions run higher – it is more than just an issue of time management, most talk about the stress of the role and speak of a very different type of stress from that experienced in their clinical work. Furthermore the boundaries are not clear. There is little consensus about what actually has to be done or how much choice there is in the role. Also, assessing and measuring performance is not easy. The taken-for-granted assumptions exercised with confidence in the professional role are not present in the strategic role and an attitude of 'no news is good news' prevails.

Table 10.1 summarizes these views and seeks to promote thought on how the career history and past experiences of individuals might shape the way new roles are enacted. Little in the professional role seems to equate with the ambiguous and 'messy' strategic role.

Examples of differences between the roles and conflicting   TABLE 10.1
views on the strategic role

Professional role	Strategic role
• Strong personal identity	• Little consensus about the role
• Individualism, autonomy in decision making	• Strongly held, differing views about communication
• Long training, progression with approval	• Little or no training required.
• Confident in the role	• Concerns about performance
• Codes of conduct, standards	• Measurement is difficult
• Clear boundaries and priorities, role clarity	• Not a profession
• Strong professional networks	• Approach is important
• Contribution understood and visible	• Stressful – uncertainty about the role
• The patient is a centre of the role	• Opposing views on the degree of choice in the role
• Little understanding of the expectations of those with whom they work	
• Action-oriented mindset	

As pointed out earlier, the challenge of advancing a professional career by taking on a more strategic role is faced by other professionals. Many progress to very senior positions in their profession with little or no prior management experience. While many will have taught, supervised and managed juniors, these relationships will normally have been based on clear structural lines, where formal authority and power was understood and acknowledged (they will also have experienced being a junior themselves). The general management role – with partial responsibility for setting and implementing the strategy of the organization – is quite different. On the surface, much of what is learned in the professional role does not appear to facilitate successful performance of the strategic role.

Learning that has been reinforced and practised over a long period of time may have to be unpacked and rearticulated. In the clinical role, complex decision-making processes are often performed quickly and routinely with little communication. The skill of analyzing complex problems is valuable in a strategic role, but may have to be performed differently, by sharing the process with others to gain commitment and develop a set of shared expectations. There is a need to build on what can be helpfully transferred from one role to another and 'unlearn' other things that could block the development of the new role.

What can a role theory perspective do to help our understanding of the performance of strategic roles? We shall first look at the history of the perspective and then consider its links with the key components of strategy by means of parts of the 7 Cs framework.

Key contributions

The origin of the perspective

> All the world's a stage,
> And all the men and women merely players.
> They have their exits and their entrances;
> And one man in his time plays many parts,
> His acts being seven ages.
> (W. Shakespeare, *As You Like It*, Act II, Scene 7)

This well known quotation from Shakespeare leads us to an analogy of role theory with the theatre (adapted from Biddle and Thomas, 1966).

When actors portray a character in a play their performance is determined by the script, the director's instructions, the performance of fellow actors and the reactions of the audience, as well as by the acting talents of the players. Apart from differences between actors in the interpretation of their parts, the performance is programmed by all these factors; consequently there are significant similarities in the performance of actors who play the same part.

Taking this analogy into real life and using some of the terms of role theory, individuals in society occupy positions, and their performance in these positions is determined by:

- Social norms.
- Demands and rules.
- The performance of others in their respective roles; by those who observe and react to the performance.
- The individual's particular capabilities and personality.

The 'social script' may be as constraining as that of a play, but it frequently allows more options. In organizational life there is usually a manager, who has parallels with a theatre director, and there is an audience who watch us. How well we play our organizational role is linked to how well we know our 'part', our personal history, our personality and the 'script', which others define for us in so many ways.

While the word role has been part of the English language for centuries it does not appear to have been used to refer to a technical concept until the 1930s. The term derives from the French *rôle*, an actors' script. We use the language of the theatre in organizational life, with work being 'front of house' or 'on stage' when employees are 'performing' in front of customers, or when those in leadership positions act as role models for those working with them. Also, we frequently use role-play to practise and learn behavioural management skills, such as negotiating and giving and receiving feedback.

Contributions to the perspective

Hales (1986), in his review of the role literature, suggests that role concepts could provide a suitable theoretical framework for research. He provides a general statement on the utility of role theory, arguing that its location at the intersection of individual and organizational behaviour makes it useful for analyzing both the influence of expectations on managerial behaviour and the effect of individual actions and preferences on behaviour. The attractiveness of role theory is further enhanced by the fact that a high percentage of managers' time is spent in interpersonal contact with others.

Findings from their own study and research by others have led Martinko and Gardner (1990) to support earlier conclusions on the brief, varied, fragmented and interpersonal nature of managerial work. Their results also point to the important relationship between the environment and managerial behaviour.

Many early studies were given renewed attention by the academic community following the much quoted Mintzberg (1973) report on the behaviour and work activities of five chief executive officers. He describes ten roles divided into three categories: interpersonal roles, informational roles and decisional roles. Stewart (1982) and Kotter (1982) describe similar roles to those identified by Mintzberg. Both Mintzberg and his critics, however, have pointed out that more research is needed to clarify the link between management roles on the one hand and types of jobs, hierarchical positions, organizational effectiveness, industry characteristics, national features and so on on the other (Tsoukas, 1994).

Despite the apparent attractiveness of role theory for investigating managerial jobs and behaviour, a review by Hales (1986) found little use of the frameworks for such analysis by researchers. Hales argues that role concepts facilitate comparisons between managers by, for example, considering who conforms to expectations and why. Within this understanding of enactment lies overt and covert activity where power and influence lies in relationships.

Frameworks have been developed that consider role behaviour as a set of interdependent behaviours that comprise a social system or subsystem, a collective pattern in which people play their parts (Katz and Kahn, 1966). The framework developed by Graen (Figure 10.1) captures the process of role making as a dynamic, iterative process between individuals. This process is explained below.

In the performance of a role (role making) there are other people around the individual role holder who are referred to as the role set (Merton, 1957). The role set consists of various people with whom the individual (role holder) has contact. These people have expectations of the individual and a stake in their performance in the role. They are also referred to as role senders, and in our context these will be the people with whom the clinical director works, who communicate their expectations during their interactions with the him or her as the role holder. The role senders develop beliefs about what the role holder should or should not do and how they expect him or her to behave and treat them. What happens between role sender and role holder is a psychological process consisting the role holder's perceptions and cognitions of what was sent. Figure 10.1 shows the interaction between a role sender and a role holder. A role expectation is sent by the role sender to the role holder, whereupon the role holder becomes the role receiver and interprets the role and behaves in a certain way. This behaviour is monitored by the role sender, who interprets the behaviour and reacts by adjusting any perceived discrepancy. This model demonstrates the flow of role making for one role holder, for example the clinical director, and one role sender, for example the chief executive. It highlights the complex set of interpretations that individuals are required to make if they want to influence their entire role set towards a specific outcome.

The concept of the role set provides a different way of looking at an

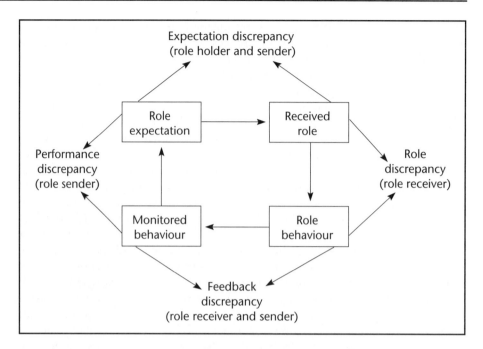

FIGURE 10.1   Role making: model for one role receiver and one role sender from Graen, 1976

individual's contacts from that of a network (Kotter, 1982), which is more commonly used in research on managerial jobs and behaviour. A network is described from the manager's perspective, with emphasis on the manager's purpose and actions in relating to the network. By contrast, with the role set the emphasis is more on communication episodes and attempted influence by others with whom the manager interacts.

The Graen (1976) model does not draw attention to the complexities that surround and underpin the interaction between role holder and role sender. These are more clearly shown Katz and Kahn's (1978) model (Figure 10.2). Here the role holder is referred to as the focal manager, but the principles of the interaction are the same. However, surrounding the interaction are other factors that influence the process of role making. These are the attributes and interpersonal features of the individuals, and organizational factors such as the culture and climate.

The complexity and ambiguity of strategic roles invites role conflict. Often there are many individuals giving the role holder – that is, the focal manager – different and conflicting objectives. Role conflict is defined as the simultaneous occurrence of two or more role expectations, where compliance with one will make compliance with the other more difficult (Katz and Kahn, 1966).

The creation of roles is an ongoing, indeterminate process that does not reach a quick conclusion. Differences and ambiguities in the demands of role senders lead role holders to make social comparisons with relevant people and enact their roles in a manner that reflects what they want as well as what others want (Smith, 1973; Weick, 1976). One reason for paying attention to

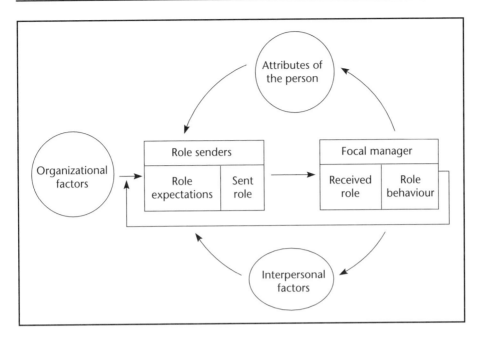

The Katz and Kahn (1978) model　　　　　*FIGURE 10.2*

the interaction between the role set and the role holder is that when a manager fulfils the role set's expectations, he or she is judged by them to be effective, which leads to better performance appraisals, more frequent promotions and other indicators of success (Tsui, 1984).

To further the general understanding of the role making framework (Figure 10.1), Fondas and Stewart (1994) integrated research from the fields of managerial behaviour, leadership dyads, symbolic interactionism and idiosyncratic jobs. From this they produced a model that posits characteristics of the role senders (role set), the role holder (focal manager), the relationship between the role senders and the role holder, and the organizational determinants of managerial impact on the role senders' expectations. This is an example of using role theory to link fields of research in order to provide a theoretical perspective for further work.

What other uses are these for role theory? What is the contribution of this perspective? At its most basic level it provides a vocabulary for discussing human affairs and the way in which people think about those affairs. The word 'affairs' is used to show the broad appeal of role theory, which has been applied to many institutions, events and problems in contemporary life. Concepts such as role, social position and status, and expectations are easy to operationalize. Data and research in these areas is of interest to researchers and practitioners. From role research, knowledge has accrued in areas such as conformity, role conflict resolution and organizational morale. Role theory has also contributed to social planning, and it is used by many professions, for example psychiatry and social work, to understand behaviour. More recently the importance of understanding human behaviour in organizational life has been acknowledged, and as a result role theory has been used to examine managerial behaviour.

Links to strategy, or how the perspective addresses major strategy topics

Context

The external environment is always changing. We can argue about the rate and pace of change, but there is consensus about the need to avoid strategic drift (Johnson and Scholes, 1998) and not lose sight of changes in the environment. In different contexts the degree to which individuals can shape their environment and are shaped by it will vary. Many individuals move from operational roles to strategic roles. This often means shifting the balance from a predominantly internal to an external focus, which is not an easy transition. Seeking intelligence from those around you and developing an understanding of others' expectations of you in your role may improve organizational effectiveness and avoid misunderstandings in key relationships.

Competences

Successful strategic management is often considered to rely on the competences of those in strategic roles in the organization. The reality is that many more people are involved in the success of an organization than those with a strategic label. Harnessing and developing the competences of those who deliver the strategy is an important part of strategic management.

The idea of enacting a role in a way that brings success through satisfying the expectations of the role set leads to consideration of the relationship of role to two sociological concepts. These concepts are analytically distinct but they often empirically overlap in their meaning. The first concept is status, the second is the meaning of the label associated with the role. Labels, of themselves, often suggest a competence in a role. They send out messages to others about a perceived role. Many individuals have a professional or a functional role, for example as an engineer, an accountant or a personnel specialist. From these titles we construct in our minds what these people do, what skills, knowledge and training and qualifications they might have.

Roles with a label associated with strategy are usually senior roles and are perceived as having high status in the organization. It is claimed that high-status roles 'validate our personal sense of self-esteem and gain us personal recognition from others, even when we know much of that esteem is based not on our personal qualities, but on our public position' (Bensman and Lilienfeld, 1979). Many professionals, especially doctors and lawyers, view their profession as having a higher status than managers in a strategic role.

For functional specialists and professionals, taking on a role associated with strategic management is often the only career path open to them. Many have a status associated with a profession or function and are puzzled by the seemingly mixed bag of competences associated with the status afforded to those in a strategic role. There is little agreement about what preparation and training is needed for this role – it appears that anyone is able to enter the strategic world. Those who talk of complexity and ambiguity in a manner that suggests they understand it often veil this world with a mystique.

It is argued that competence accumulation by individuals, through boundaryless careers can make a vital contribution to the growing competences of firms and their host industries (Delfillippi and Arthur, 1994). This approach identifies three types of competence: know-why, which relates to beliefs and identities; know-how, which relates to knowledge and skills; and know-whom, which relates to networks of relationships and contacts. The approach is derived from a line of strategic inquiry based on a competency view of the firm and has some links with the career literature.

As careers progress, many leave behind the tangible functional and professional competences associated with their chosen careers and move increasingly into roles where the most important skills are less tangible, for example leadership, influencing and motivational skills. In these roles negotiating a role with those around you is exceedingly important. Negotiation involves being able to explore sensitive issues, to stray into the zone of uncomfortable debate (Bowman, 1998) where real problems often lie hidden and unresolved. An understanding of the expectations that others have of you and those with whom they interact has to be purposefully sought. A full understanding can rarely be developed without a mature and trusting relationship.

Culture

> Not only the possession of skills but [also] the creation or maintenance of overall mood and affect are intrinsic parts of successful role performance (Bensman and Lilienfield, 1979).

As the above quotation suggests, role performance has a subtlety that can differentiate success from mediocrity or failure. The way in which the 'social script' is written and played out by individuals and groups in an organization can you tell you much about the culture that exists in the organization, and yet the magic combination of words, actions and 'mood' that makes leaders successful and aligns with the strategic direction of the organization eludes many.

Schein's (1996) view is that inattention to social systems in organizations has led researchers to underestimate the role of culture (shared norms, values and assumptions) in how organizations function. In his view, concepts for understanding culture in organizations have value only when they derive from observations of real behaviour in organizations, reinforcing the need for context-specific knowledge and understanding.

Change

Some models of change stress the need for a three-stage process to achieve change. The first stage is concerned with understanding the current situation in an organization and creating the motivation to change. Understanding what will drive the change and what will hold it back is an essential prerequisite of any change initiative. The second stage involves the development of new ways of working, thinking and behaving. There is a growing belief that the secret to transformation is the organization's ability to change its employees' behaviour (Ghoshal, 1995). The third stage is about creating a period of stability to reinforce and realize the benefits of the change. Kurt Lewin (1951) refers to this stage as 'refreezing'. With the ever quickening pace of change many feel that organizations never have the time to 'refreeze', instead managers now have to create a culture where continuous change is considered the norm.

In all three stages there is a clear need to provide motivation for and promote ownership of the change. With the emphasis placed on individual behaviour, a role perspective can be a valuable part of the change process. Understanding how new roles are made and the interactions between role holders and role senders before and during the change is essential to success.

In senior roles there is generally, a high degree of individual discretion about how the role should be performed. Those moving into senior strategic roles during a process of change often feel they should automatically know what to do as they are senior people in the organization. It may also be that there is little in their previous role to help them understand the new role. Ascertaining the expectations that others have of them, particularly when there is a lot of uncertainty and ambiguity, would help individuals move forward with confidence in themselves and those around them. Unfortunately such questions are often never asked, because this might be seen as a weakness, or because the thought never occurs. The role theory perspective offers an opportunity to understand the complexities underlying the behaviour of individuals, and the interactions amongst individuals and groups during periods of change. It is certainly the case that universal solutions cannot be applied to managerial behaviour. The context of the change will influence behaviour, and understanding how much the individual shapes the environment and how much the environment is shaped by the individual continues to occupy researchers.

The view that successful change is context-dependent has been reinforced by many researchers, and change is seen as far too complex to be modelled on prescriptive guidelines. The key is to educate individuals so that they will be better able to make informed judgements about the approach to change (Balogun and Hope Hailey, 1999).

Control

Role clarity can be viewed as a control process. It can be achieved by means of formal mechanisms such as job descriptions, with clear lines of accountability. Performance can be measured with the help of frameworks such as managing by objectives, the balanced scorecard and the business excellence model. Individuals can be developed and monitored through appraisal systems, 360° feedback and a range of reward systems. The problem with most of these processes is that they concentrate on data that inevitably measures the past. The news of the day, conjecture and rumours about the future are usually a significant part of managers' lives – social interaction, talking to people. This takes us back to the importance of role playing and role making in controlling everyday activities in organizational life.

The case study revisited

The statements highlighted in the case study are specific to the individuals in question, all of whom have their own personality and history but have a profession in common, and function in broadly similar roles and contexts. These individuals are, in the main, highly competent and are respected by those around them for their professional skills. They are in a profession that many would view as stressful enough, but they talk about strategic management as being even more stressful than their professional role. In the list of differences between the roles (Table 10.1) confidence is clearly expressed about their professional role, derived from a long history of training and experience. However there is little consensus about what the strategic role actually is, how it should be performed and how they can tell if they are doing it well. This bears out the view that strategy making is an ongoing, messy and incomplete process (Huff, 1998).

The 'script' for the clinicians' professional role is clear, and has been performed and perfected over many years. Furthermore there seems to be no uncertainty about the (assumed) expectations of others. In contrast, if there is a 'script' for the strategic role it is written in invisible ink and the nebulousness of the role is considered stressful, especially given the certainty felt about the professional role. And yet the expectations that others have of the clinicians in this role have not been sought out, and they rely on a 'no news is good news' approach. This is likely to continue as only a brave, or perhaps foolish, person would tackle such a sensitive matter with these powerful senior individuals. Few people other than a chief executive would feel they have the right to have their expectations met. The power of the chief executive is legitimized through his or her formal role, which carries responsibility and authority. He or she has the right to set performance criteria for all employees in the organization. However a chief executive is vulnerable when medical consultants unite against his or her actions.

Acquiring the competences to perform the strategic role seems to be a tortuous process. These individuals have the label of clinical director, but their status emanates more from their professional role than their strategic role. The skills of consultants are usually vested in very tangible and visible acts and outcomes, and it is easy to see and measure many aspects of their work. They motivate many around them because of their mutual clinical interest, and they manage others through power relationships. Some are not known for their interpersonal skills and most are not rewarded for their 'soft' skills. The competences required for the strategic role, where less tangible skills are important, seem to be viewed as either innate or acquired with a minimal degree of training.

Clinical directors are well used to changes in their professional role as advances in research and technology constantly change the nature of their work. They also experienced change when the Thatcher government tried to enforce competition in the NHS in the 1980s and early 1990s, coupled with a move for patients to be seen and treated as customers. The latter changes have been difficult for many clinicians to embrace, and some changes have challenged values they hold dear about the NHS. Other changes have required shifts in behaviour that have been resisted by some and implemented only slowly by others. One example is the resistance by some to rearrange appointment times and processes in clinics so that they are convenient to the patient as well as the clinicians.

In the strategic role the clinical director has to have a real understanding of the current state of the organization and the degree of motivation required for change to take place. Although most have been in the same institution for many years, they do not necessarily see the situation as others see it, especially if the right questions are not being asked. Clinicians do not usually change hospitals when take on a clinical directorship, so their past behaviour has an important bearing on how others see them in that role. An awareness of the impact they have on others would help them understand the change process as they and others experience it.

This brief discussion of the attitudes and comments of clinical directors and the links to concepts relating to strategy shows the necessity of thoroughly understanding the context, history and experience of individuals. A role perspective that recognizes patterns and differences in the 'social scripts' of individuals by considering research in different fields would add value to our understanding of the interpretation of strategic roles.

References

Balogun, J. and V. Hope Hailey (1999) *Exploring Strategic Change* (London: Prentice-Hall).

Bennis, W. (1994) *An Invented Life: Reflections on Leadership and Change* (London: Century).

Bensman, J. and R. Lilienfield (1979) *Between public and private* (New York: Free Press).

Biddle, B. J. (1979) *Role Theory: Expectations, Identities and Behaviours* (London: Academic Press).

Biddle, B. J. and E. J. Thomas (1966) *Role Theory: Concepts and Research* (New York: Wiley).

Bowman, C. (1998) *Strategy in Practice* (New York: Prentice-Hall).

Burrage, M., J. Jarausch and H. Seigrist (1990) 'Introduction: the professions sociology and history', in M. Burrage and J. Torstendahl, in *Professions in Theory and History – Re-thinking the Study of Professions* (London: Sage).

Carr-Saunders, A. M. and P. A. Wilson (1933) *The Professions* (Oxford: Clarendon Press).

Delfillippi, R. J. and M. B. Arthur (1994) 'The boundaryless career: a competency-based perspective', *Journal of Organizational Behaviour*, vol. 15, pp. 307–24.

Fondas, N. and R. Stewart (1992) 'Enactment in Managerial Jobs: A Role Analysis', *Management Research Papers*, 92/16 (Oxford: Templeton College).

Fondas, N. and R. Stewart (1994) 'Enactment in Managerial Jobs: A Role Analysis', *Journal of Management Studies*, vol. 31, no. 1, pp. 83–103.

Gabbarro, J. B. (1988) 'Executive Leadership and Succession' in D. Hambrick (ed.), *The Executive Effect; Concepts and Methods for Studying Top Managers* (Greenwich, CT: JAI Press).

Ghoshal, S. (1995) 'Using people as a force for change', *Personnel Management*, 19 October, pp. 35–7.

Graen, G. (1976) 'Role-making processes within complex organizations', in M. D. Dunnette (ed.), *Handbook of Industrial and Organizational Psychology* (Chicago: Rand McNally), pp. 1201–45.

Graen, G. and J. F. Cashman (1975) 'A Role-Making Model of Leadership in Formal Organizations: A Developmental Approach', in J. G. Hunt and Larson (eds), *Leadership Frontiers* (Kent, Ohio: Kent State University Press), pp. 143–65.

Graen, G. B. and T. A. Scandura (1987) 'Toward a Psychology of Dyadic Career Reality', *Research in Personnel and Human Resource Management*, vol. 4, pp. 147–81.

Gunz, H. P. and R. M. Jalland (1996) 'Managerial Careers and Business Strategies', *Academy of Management Review*, vol. 21, no. 3, pp. 718–56.

Hales, C. P. (1986) 'What Do Managers Do? A Critical Review of the Evidence', *Journal of Management Studies*, vol. 23, no. 1, pp. 88–115.

Hambrick, D. C. and P. A. Mason (1984) 'Upper Echelons: The Organization as a Reflection of Its Top Managers', *Academy of Management Review*, vol. 9, no. 2, pp. 193–206.

Harrison, R. and S. Miller (1999) 'The Contribution of Clinical Directors to the Strategic Capability of the Organization', *British Journal of Management*, vol. 10, pp. 23–39.

Heiss, J. (1968) *Family roles and interaction: An anthology* (Chicago, Ill.: Rand McNally).

Hoff, T. J. (1998) 'Physician Executives in Managed Care: Characteristics and Job Involvement Across Two Career Stages', *Academy of Management Proceedings*.

Huff, A. (1998) 'Preface', in C. Eden and F. Ackermann, *Making Strategy: The Journey of Strategic Management* (London: Sage).

Johnson, G. and C. Bowman (1999) 'Strategy and Everyday Reality: The Case for the Study of "Micro-Strategy"', paper presented at the *EGOS Conference*, Warwick University, 4–6 July.

Johnson, G. and K. Scholes (1998) *Exploring Corporate Strategy*, 5th edn (Englewood Cliffs, NJ: Prentice-Hall).

Katz, D. and R. L. Kahn (1966) *The Social Psychology of Organizations* (New York: Wiley).

Katz, D. and R. L. Kahn (1978) *The Social Psychology of Organizations*, 2nd edn (New York: Wiley).

Kotter, J. P. (1982) *The general managers* (New York: Free Press).

Kotter, J. P. (1990) *A force for change. How leadership differs from management* (New York: Free Press).

Lewin, K. (1951) *Field Theory in Social Science* (New York: Harper and Row).

Martinko, M. J. and W. L. Gardner (1990) 'Structured Observation of Managerial Work: A Replication and Synthesis', *Journal of Management Studies*, vol. 27, no. 3, pp. 331–57.

Merton, R. K. (1957) *Social theory and social structure*, rev. edn (New York: Free Press).

Millerson, G. (1964) *The Qualifying Associations* (New York: Routledge and Kegan Paul).

Mintzberg, H. (1973) *The Nature of Managerial Work* (New York: Harper and Row).

Moreno, J. L. (ed.) (1960) *The Sociometry Reader*, reprinted from *Who Shall Survive?*, 2nd edn (Glencoe, Ill.: Free Press).

Overtveit, J. (1992) *Therapy Services – Organization, Management and Autonomy* (Reading: Harwood).

Parsons, T. (1954) *The Professions and Social Structure, Essays in Sociological Theory*, revd edn (Glencoe, Ill.: Free Press).

Schein, E. H. (1996) 'Culture: The Missing Concept in Organisation Studies', *Administrative Science Quarterly*, vol. 41, pp. 229–40.

Smith, P. B. (1973) *Groups Within Organizations* (London: Harper and Row).

Stewart, R. (1982) *Choices for the Manager: A Guide to Understanding Managerial Work and Behaviour* (Englewood Cliffs, NJ: Prentice-Hall).

Tallman, S. and K. Fladmoe-Lindquist (1999) 'Internationalisation, Globalisation and Capability-Based Strategy', paper presented at the AIM Conference. Charleston, South Carolina, November.

Thomas, J. B. (1990) 'Interpreting Strategic Issues: Effects of Strategy and the Information-processing Structure of Top Management Teams', *Academy of Management Journal*, vol. 33, no. 2, pp. 288–306.

Torstendahl, R. (1990) 'Introduction: promotions and strategies of knowledge based groups'. in R. Torstendahl and M. Burrage, *The Formation of Professions–Knowledge, State and Strategy* (London: Sage).

Tsoukas, H. (1996) 'What is Management? An Outline of a Metatheory', *British Journal of Management*, vol. 5, pp. 289–301.

Tsui, A. S. (1984) 'A Role Set Analysis of Managerial Reputation', *Organizational Behaviour and Human Performance*, vol. 34, pp. 34–96.

Weick, K. E. (1976) 'Educational Organisations as Loosely-Coupled Systems', *Administrative Science Quarterly*, vol. 21, pp. 1–19.

Weick, K. E. (1979) *The social psychology of organizing* (Reading, Mass.: Addison-Wesley).

Willcocks, S. (1994) 'The Clinical Director in the NHS: Utilizing a Role-Theory Perspective', *Journal of Management in Medicine*, vol. 8, no. 5, pp. 68–76.

11 Leadership Perspective
Steven Sonsino

Basic principles

The literature on great leaders deserves attention because it offers insights into generic leadership competences and strategic leaders. The case study in the second section of this chapter roots the debate on the usefulness of this canon in practical concerns of managerial succession, and the rest of the chapter traces the historical development of leadership theories in the general management literature. The 7 Cs section remaps themes from the great leader literature by defining leadership competences in the current language and concepts of strategic management. This remapping rejects the stereotypical view of heroic, top-down leaders as dysfunctional. It also suggests that strategic leadership models derived from complexity theory will become increasingly relevant and useful. From the perspective of complexity theory, the competences of a strategic leader are more likely to be those of an organizational coach and facilitator than a 'take-charge' or command-and-control autocrat.

Before exploring the issues raised in the case study it is worth reflecting on the popular business literature of the past 50 years, in which successful CEOs have published their recipes for business success, recipes that today are worth millions of dollars in book advances and on the conference circuit. This populist literature of the great leader has been memorably described by Mintzberg (1973) as 'rich in specific anecdotes, poor in general theory'. Many of the biographies and autobiographies that constitute this genre focus on leadership in times of crisis or change, which gives them a racy and readable journalistic style. There is almost certainly a degree of post-rationalization in the writings and not all will stand the test of time as accurate reflections of business history.

Leadership raises complex issues and has long been the subject of vigorous debate in the academic literature (Table 11.1). For instance as many as 65 definitions of leadership have been recorded (Fleischman *et al.*, 1991). Many academics might therefore ask what value there can be in reviewing a populist literature that develops few if any theories and lauds the cult of the individual – a homogeneous group of individuals at that. When reviewing this literature it becomes obvious that the CEO literature is based largely on the experiences of middle-aged, white American males.

Judging by sales volume, however, the general public loves the great leader literature, especially if the authors have something new to say. This perhaps is the rub. Leadership is a complex and subjective matter involving complex individuals involved in a complex web of relationships within complex

Key twentieth-century leadership theories   TABLE 11.1

• *Trait theory.*	The study of leadership traits, from the beginning of the twentieth century, was aimed at determining what made people great leaders. Essentially the philosophy suggests that leaders are born and not made – their innate qualities marking them out as leaders.
• *Style theory.*	In the 1940s style theories were developed, focusing on how leaders behaved. This canon sought to describe how leaders managed both task and relationship behaviours.
• *Situational theory.*	From the 1960s the widely recognized situational leadership approach developed, for the first time placing leaders in particular contexts or situations. The core concept is that different situations demand different leadership behaviours.
• *Contingency theory.*	Building on the ideas of style theory and situational theory, the contingency branch of leadership theory suggests that the effectiveness of a leader depends on how well his or her style fits the prevailing context.
• *Transformational theory.*	Much research since the 1980s has been devoted to defining and exploring transformational leadership in respect of values and beliefs, ethics and strategic long-term goals. Elements of this family of theories include visionary leadership theory and the theories of charismatic leadership, a return almost to the born-and-not-made school of trait theory.

organizations. The chance of ever encapsulating a new, single, overarching theoretical perspective on leadership is slim indeed. In this sense, if the literature can offer *any* new insight into the competences of leadership, or what to look for in the search for tomorrow's leaders, it will have done a good job.

This chapter sets out to explore what insights the great leader literature can offer in the search for leadership competences. After the case study, which establishes the debate, the section on key contributions traces the historical development of the search for leadership competences, rooted as it has been in the psychology literature. The 7 Cs section attempts to update or remap the great leader literature by defining leadership competences in the current language and concepts of strategic management. After a short section summarizing the key tool of leadership research – the questionnaire – the case study is revisited to explore one possible outcome of the search for great leaders.

Case study

The situation

A working lunch begins for three board directors at Jonas Industries Inc., a struggling US-based engineering firm that operates in 17 countries and has over

15 000 employees. Patricia Meyer, the human resources director, turns the conversation to the urgent search for the next CEO, following the surprise announcement the previous week of the early retirement of the present incumbent, Peter Herbert. He's leaving on the grounds of ill-health after only 18 months in the job. With her are Mike Nesbitt (finance director) and Steve Snaith (director of operations). Both are deputy CEOs, but both are close to retirement and have ruled themselves out of the race for the CEO's post.

The conversation

Patricia: Thanks for coming, guys. I've been inundated with calls from the media asking for news of the next CEO and we haven't even started looking. [Patricia turns to Mike Nesbitt.]
What do you think we should do?

Mike [shrugging and sitting back in his chair]: Isn't that rather your problem? You're personnel after all. Why not place an advertisement for the ideal CEO in the papers?

Patricia [after a pause]: Of course, advertising the post may well be part of the recruitment strategy, Mike, but I wondered more what your thoughts were on who or even what kind of CEO we should be looking for. Who would be the ideal CEO for us now? You two have been here longer than anyone and I wanted to know what you thought.

Mike [irritably]: Look, I can't imagine we'll have any trouble finding someone – we're a company with vast potential – there's bound to be some glory-hungry second in command somewhere waiting to snap it up. So just draft an advert and trot it out. I can't believe we didn't do that last time instead of just promoting the longest serving board director. You know, I might have been interested back then, but I won't touch it now it's been fouled up. Me, I'm ready to retire.

Steve: I don't think you've been listening, Mike. Patricia is trying to step back and ask about the kind of person we want as CEO. Who are we looking for exactly? What particular skills or experience do they have that would suit us right now? This seems a good opportunity to ask the question. But it's a tough world out there, we're not in good shape resources-wise and we do have some prima donnas on the board, too. Who do you think could lead this outfit?

Mike [taking stock and beginning to think]: Well, OK. But Peter Herbert isn't exactly Mr Charisma, is he, so all we need to do is find a charismatic guy that will get us the attention we need. We need another Lee Iacocca. All leaders are born to the job, right? You can spot 'em a mile away. And we don't have any on the current board. So what about poaching Mike Bramer from Smithson Inc, he's exactly the right kind of front man we need, he's got charisma. And he's got a track record in this industry.

Patricia: I think there's more to being a CEO than being a front man, Mike. For instance I'm concerned that we have someone who can support the people development programmes I'm putting in place. From what our latest recruits from Smithson have been telling me, Bramer's focus on cost cutting means people are the last thing on his agenda. [She turns to Steve Snaith.] What are you looking for, Steve?

> *Steve*: I can understand your concern about the people round here, and development, but I must say I am worried about the downturn in business. If we don't win some big contracts soon – and I mean soon – most operations will be mothballed and soon enough we'll *all* be out of work. I guess we need someone who can give us a clear idea of where the whole business is headed and how the hell we're going to get there. That's the job as I see it. [There is a pause in the conversation while Mike pours coffee.]
>
> *Patricia*: What about the issue of internal candidates – as soon as the news was announced I had an email from Jake West expressing interest. He's really well regarded by his staff – and by customers.
>
> *Mike*: Jake West? No way. That woolly no-hoper has no chance if I have any say. He doesn't have a degree in engineering or anything remotely technical and his staff have absolutely no respect for him. Not one of them calls him Mr West.
>
> *Patricia*: So, we're looking for someone who can manage the people strategy *and* win business *and* straighten out the board *and* . . . [she slumps back in her chair].
>
> *Steve* [after a brief pause]: Why don't we sleep on it and meet again tomorrow. [He suddenly grins]. Maybe we should each read Iacocca's autobiography tonight and see what he has to say about the situation and whether we can pull it back. [He throws his coffee cup expertly across the room and into the waste bin].

The issues

This informal lunch meeting raises key issues about the competences of those who should lead firms and how new leaders are selected and recruited. The leadership theories developed over the past century suggest a range of perspectives for addressing the issue of leadership competences. They include the following:

- Can leadership be nurtured and developed, or are leaders born not made, as Mike suggests?
- To what extent can leadership behaviour be predicted from someone's previous experience? In other words, what relevance has previous business success – for example Bramer's – for future leadership potential?
- How much does personality matter? Should Jonas industries simply find another Iacocca?
- Given the breadth of the problems facing Jonas Industries, can a single individual turn round the situation?

Key contributions

Origins of the perspective

It was the philosophers of the ancient civilizations who first tackled the question of what constitutes the competences of leaders. The Greek philosopher Plato, for instance, writing in the fourth century BC, believed leadership and especially the development of leaders to be essential. He went as far as to set up an academy to create statesmen who could both manage the pressures of office and resist the powers of the dark side of leadership. His ideas on inspiring trust and confidence and providing psychological support, as recorded in his *Republic* (Lee, 1987), still have meaning for managers today.

Much of the simple, homespun wisdom of Lao Tzu's *Tao Te Ching* ('The way of life' or 'How things happen') also has special meaning for aspiring leaders. It is one of China's best-loved books of wisdom, originally addressed to the sage and to the wise political rulers of the fifth century BC. Perhaps its most famous aphorism is 'The journey of a thousand miles begins with a single step'. Now the text has been specifically adapted for teaching leadership (Heider, 1985), concentrating on the inner, psychological aspects of behaviour. 'Imagine that [the leader is] a midwife,' writes Heider. 'You are assisting at someone else's birth. . . . If you must take the lead, lead so that the mother is helped, yet still free and in charge. When the baby is born, the mother will rightly say: "We did it ourselves!"'

In stark contrast to this facilitative leadership philosophy are the tenets of the 'born to lead' school, typified by Nietzsche's nineteenth-century *Ubermensch* or superman (Kaufmann and Hollingdale, 1967). In essence, Nietzsche's *Ubermensch* had a unique ability to lead and transform, but only as a result of his exceptional human nature. He was – literally – born to lead.

Until the mid twentieth century it was not the born-to-lead philosophy but the developmental philosophy of leadership – teaching the importance of values and self-discovery, for instance – that was clearly most popular, or at least in terms of book sales. This being so, Kakabadse and Kakabadse (1999) rightly ask: 'How is it then that the great leader school of leadership has emerged with such popularity?' Kakabadse and Kakabadse offer as one explanation the profound impact that biographers and historians have had in promoting this theme, glorifying the cult of the personality of individual leaders.

Can it be largely through promotion and publicity, then, that the philosophy of the charismatic leader (Conger and Kanungo, 1998) has remained strangely attractive, weaving in and out of fashion for more than 2000 years? Or is there something more to it? The next section briefly traces the elements of key leadership theories to contextualize the competences outlined in the great leader literature.

Elaboration of the principles of the perspective

Perhaps the core of the great leader school is trait theory, the idea that there is an elite officer corps of leaders who inherited or somehow acquired the requisite capabilities for leadership. While leadership theory in the twentieth century underwent broad development (Table 11.1), current transformational theories of leadership and the so-called 'new leadership' theories – often based on 'charisma' – could almost be said to be echoes of pure trait theory.

Trait theory

Trait theory is simple and seductive. It takes as its starting point one individual – the leader – and asks what is it about this person that marks him or her out as different? All the research focuses exclusively on leaders, not on their followers or on the situations in which they find themselves. Furthermore the theory suggests that the search for effective leadership stops when you have found someone with an accepted set of leadership characteristics or competences. In addition the theory suggests that the personality of the leader is the key to organizational success and that this personality is largely immutable. Hence the reason why so many companies use personality assessment devices in recruitment may be to ensure that enough diversity is brought into the corporate gene pool.

There are many inherent strengths to trait theory, which is appealing in its simplicity. Not least is the fact that it has almost a century of research data to support its main thesis: that personality traits have some impact on the effectiveness of leaders. This affords some credibility in the area of leadership theory, an area many find weak in research terms.

A by-product of the large body of research is that by elucidating the capabilities of leaders from all walks of life, some believe we now have an effective tool for assessing leadership skills and competences. This, theoretically at least, allows organizations to recruit effective leaders and, some believe, to develop leadership skills in managers. There is a weakness here in that if, as is supposed, personality traits and characteristics are immutable, how can individuals be taught and learn them?

Perhaps trait theory's key weakness, though, lies in the fact that there is no one universally agreed set of innate leadership competences. Many studies were conducted in the twentieth century and even in the selected handful in Table 11.2 the variety of traits identified is alarmingly wide.

Another problem for trait theory is that it tends to take traits out of context. An early study by Stogdill (1948) highlights the fact that it is difficult to isolate leadership characteristics without considering the situation that leaders find themselves in. The context for leadership is all important, Stogdill suggests.

According to Northouse (1997), Stogdill's studies (which as shown in Table 11.2 were 25 years apart) are a useful microcosm of trait studies as a whole.

Studies of leadership traits and characteristics   TABLE 11.2

Stogdill (1948)	Mann (1956)	Stogdill (1974)	Lord, et al. (1986)	Kirkpatrick and Locke (1991)
Intelligence	Intelligence	Achievement	Intelligence	Drive
Alertness	Masculinity	Persistence	Masculinity	Motivation
Insight	Adjustment	Insight	Dominance	Integrity
Responsibility	Dominance	Initiative		Confidence
Initiative	Extroversion	Self-confidence		Cognitive ability
Persistence	Conservatism	Responsibility		Task knowledge
Self-confidence		Cooperativeness		
Sociability		Tolerance		
		Influence		
		Sociability		

Source: Northouse (1997)

In the first survey Stogdill (1948) analyzed 124 trait studies conducted between 1904 and 1947 and the results suggested that who took on the role of leader or functioned most effectively as leader depended largely on the situation, not on the particular traits of the leader in question. The results of Stogdill's second survey (1974), an analysis of a further 163 trait studies conducted between 1948 and 1970, suggest a more balanced view. In other words, Stogdill concludes that both personality traits and context are equally significant in defining the success of a leader's actions.

Style theory

Style theory focuses not on the personality traits of the leader, but on what the leader does and, explicitly, the way the leader behaves. Emanating from this are the two key strands of style theory: leaders must demonstrate both task behaviours (how to get the job done) and relationship behaviours (how to support subordinates through the task). Not all leaders are necessarily good at both.

Simplistically, the style theories can be reduced to one leadership continuum, with autocratic (or structuring) and participative (or supporting) behaviour at the two extremes (Table 11.3). Some studies, notably the Ohio State research (Hemphill and Coons, 1957) that grew out of Stogdill's work, view these as two separate continua, allowing an individual leader's behaviour to be gauged as high or low in both behaviours rather than as one or the other.

Perhaps the best known model of managerial behaviour is Blake and Mouton's managerial grid, renamed the leadership grid in 1991 (Blake and McCanse, 1991). This also uses twin dimensions: concern for results and concern for people.

The strength of the style theories, again apart from the large body of research work underpinning them, is the simple but striking fact that leadership

TABLE 11.3   *Studies of leadership styles*

	Autocratic	<==>		Democratic
Harbison/Myers (1966)	Autocratic	Paternalistic	Consultative	Participative
Likert (1961)	System 1	System 2	System 3	System 4
Tannenbaum/ Schmidt (1958)	Leader control	Shared control	Shared control	Group control
Vroom (1973)	Leader decides	Consults	Shares	Delegates
Ohio State studies (1957)	Initiating structure			Consideration
Hersey/Blanchard (1969)	Telling	Selling	Participating	Delegating

Source: Handy (1993).

depends not so much on who you are, but on a combination of what you do and how you do it. If the trait theories predicate leadership as something you are born to, then the style theories at least pose an alternative. There are different things you can do in different situations, and different ways of managing people to achieve the task.

Although some findings (for example Misumi, 1985) have highlighted the value of leaders being effective in both autocratic and participative dimensions (Table 11.3), much of the research on leadership style is inconclusive (Yukl, 1994). For instance, although supportive styles of leadership tend to be associated with higher-producing work groups, Handy (1993) reports that the average productivity differential over a number of studies is 'only 15 per cent – a figure well below what some theorists would lead one to expect'. So style alone is not enough.

Situational leadership theory

The development of situational leadership, the idea that the leadership style you adopt depends entirely on the context or situation you face, is a logical extension of the style theories. It builds on the ideas of the twin continua of task and relationship by establishing that each must be applied appropriately in a given situation. Furthermore leaders must constantly evaluate or diagnose the context in which they operate before taking appropriate action. Another corollory is that because situations change constantly, leaders must also adapt their behaviour. Staff, for instance, may no longer need such close task control.

Perhaps the most significant strength of the situational leadership approach is its practicality. It has been used widely, in the form outlined by Blanchard *et al.* (1985), to teach leaders and managers in organizations around the world. In addition it is simple and easy to use because of its prescriptive nature. If subordinates are not competent to do their job, for example, the model suggests a directive leadership style. This flexibility is a strikingly different view of leader behaviour in comparison with the inflexible idea of trait theory that you are what you are.

If this theory has a weakness it is that it is not grounded in extensive research. The theoretical basis for the approach must therefore be called into question. Does the approach work with all subordinates, for instance the experienced as well as the inexperienced, and how does the approach work when leading teams or organizations?

Contingency theory

Contingency theory, or what Charles Handy (1993) calls the best-fit approach, offers a different view on leadership, where the situational variables have been mapped against different leadership styles. In work conducted largely with the military, Fiedler (1964, 1967; Fiedler and Garcia, 1987) has found that leaders' effectiveness hinges mainly on how well their style matches the context of their organization.

Fiedler identifies two key leadership styles – task-motivated and relationship-motivated – and three key situational variables:

- Leader–member relations (the relationship the leader has with members of the workgroup).
- Task structure (the higher the better).
- The leader's formal positional power (the leader's ability to reward/punish).

In general Fiedler finds that task-oriented leaders are likely to achieve better results in group situations that are either favourable or unfavourable to the leader, while relationship-oriented leaders tend to achieve better results in situations that are neither favourable nor unfavourable. Significantly, leaders should not expect to be able to lead in all situations – they are simply not effective in all situations. If your preferred leadership style matches the situation or context you will be good at the job. Conversely, if your style does not match the situation you are likely to fail in the task. The implication for top management teams (and indeed for recruitment) is to place leaders only in situations they can handle. If this is not possible and it becomes obvious that a leader is performing poorly, the theory suggests that the work variables should be changed or the leader moved to another context.

The strengths of the contingency theory are its history of empirical research, which has been tested and found reliable, and the fact that it directly links leadership style and organizational context. In addition the theory is predictive in that it can gauge how successful leaders are likely to be in certain situations. The downsides to the theory include the following:

- It fails to explain why certain leaders are effective in certain situations.
- It is cumbersome to use in practice (analyzing leadership style and three situational variables is time consuming).
- It suggests that leaders cannot be developed, that the situation should be engineered to suit their skills.

Transformational leadership theory

Situational and contingency theory emphasize the transactional nature of leadership – how individuals negotiate on a deal-by-deal basis to achieve their objectives. In comparison transformational leadership, or what Bryman (1992) calls the 'new leadership' paradigm, has higher aims. Transformational leadership is a broad-brush process intended to address and inspire individual and organizational motivation. However, although transformational leaders play a crucial role in initiating change they too are affected by the change, not just their followers. Classic examples of transformational leaders from the political world include Mahatma Gandhi and Nelson Mandela, both of whom led their people through difficult times and were themselves changed in the process.

The key strength of transformational leadership theory is that it is research based, based on qualitative interviews with CEOs and high-flying managers. The theory is also wide ranging, covering the concepts of visioning, communication and change management. Some critics suggest the theory is *too* wide ranging. In addition it is complex and difficult to teach in a practical way. Its proponents often dip heavily into issues of morality and, occasionally, religion, which undermines its credibility for some academics (Northouse, 1997).

Another criticism is that the data has been drawn from high-ranking officers in organizations. Who knows whether the theories apply at section-leader level? More research is needed. Furthermore there is a strong argument that transformational leaders are simply charismatic leaders (Conger and Kanungo, 1998), as defined by Weber (1947) and House (1976) in a subset of transformational leadership theory. If leaders are leaders simply because they have charisma, a set of innate personality traits, then surely – the argument has it – this is nothing more than trait theory revisited. If this is the case, then transformational leadership is on shaky ground.

Born or taught?

Twentieth-century leadership studies began and appear to have ended with the cult of the individual, the born leader, having the upper hand. The key question, then, in respect of whether leadership really is governed by trait or whether it is transformational, seems to be 'can it be taught?' A range of leadership commentators think it can (McCall, 1998; Conger and Benjamin, 1999; Kakabadse and Kakabadse, 1999).

The quandary over whether leadership can or cannot be taught is a fundamental issue in the great leader debate. If we assume we are carved out for leadership by our genes then, no, the rest of us cannot be taught to lead. At least not without a definite idea of the behavioural traits that make up effective leaders. This highlights an even more fundamental question: what is leadership anyway? Is it a set of personality traits, or a relationship between leader and group members. Is it a way of behaving to achieve personal, group and corporate objectives, a set of strategic behaviours (Grundy, 1998)? In other words, is leadership simply what leaders do? And does this – if they do it effectively – enable the organization, through its employees, to achieve its strategic objectives?

Links to strategy

Although leadership research has long taxed management researchers (Bryman, 1996; Northouse, 1997), we can see that the leadership theories that have developed often revolve round the personality characteristics of the leader. Furthermore, many of the leadership studies underpinning these theories involve a description of leadership personality in terms of a number of two-factor models (Yukl, 1999). Often-cited examples include transactional versus transformational leadership (see the previous subsection, and Tichy and Devanna, 1986) and charismatic versus non-charismatic leadership (synthesized in Conger and Kanungo, 1998, as leadership behaviours intended to motivate and mobilize followers).

While these dichotomies provide many insights, they oversimplify a complex phenomenon and contribute to stereotyping (Yukl, 1999), reinforcing the tired view of leader as superhero (Mintzberg, 1973; Huczynski, 1996) or as born not made (Kakabadse and Kakabadse, 1999). In parallel with what might be called the 'traditional' or 'old' leadership literature (Northouse, 1997), which is often rooted in psychology (Kets de Vries, 1991), a distinct strategic leadership literature has developed (Finkelstein and Hambrick, 1996). This defines leadership mainly in terms of top executives and their role, offering the view that it is a combination of positional power and functional experience that drives individual leadership behaviour. In the psychological literature this might be termed a combination of style and transformational theory.

However a number of significant leadership commentators (Bennis, 1999; Ireland and Hitt, 1999; Shamir, 1999) are now beginning to conclude that these heroic, top-down views of leadership are dysfunctional and unsatisfactory. Instead of dictating the development of tomorrow's top-down strategy, they suggest, top managers should contemplate the position of the boundaryless organization (Shamir, 1999) in the new competitive landscape (Ireland and Hitt, 1999). As a result, today's leadership competences should be based on the development of diverse or cross-functional teams in which strategic leadership takes place among a range of people with different talents (ibid.) This develops what Bryman (1996) calls the new leadership paradigm, and shifts the locus of responsibility for the formation of adaptive solutions from the organization's leaders to the employees in the wider organization (Heifetz and Laurie, 1997).

Although this appears to be an argument for empowerment and the participation of the workforce in the management of the organization, it is not a recipe for the abdication of responsibility, as suggested by Nohria and Berkley (1994). Even though the details of how effective strategic leadership will be operationalized may be unknown or tacit (Petric et al., 1999), the global economy will undoubtedly continue to evolve (Ohmae, 1997), and the task of steering the firm through the complexity rests squarely on the CEO's shoulders (Ireland and Hitt, 1999). In addition the top management team will continue to remain accountable for the entire firm's performance (ibid.)

This next section, therefore, develops the idea of leadership competences, derived initially from the great leader literature, and shows how a series of related themes intertwine with current perspectives – the 7 Cs – from strategic management (Figure 11.1). The section starts by looking at the historical context of the great leader literature, and suggests that the recent exploration of elements of complexity theory within the organization sciences (Anderson, 1999), notably the ideas on complex adaptive systems and self-organization, may offer new insights for business leaders. The section concludes with an explanation of why the impact of complexity theory on the study of leadership competences might be worth exploring.

Context

In his exploration of management gurus, Huczynski (1996) provides a broad historical background to explain the significance of the literature of the great leaders, who he describes as hero-managers. 'Managers running organizations in capitalist economies', he says, 'face recurring problems such as maintaining control, increasing productivity and motivating staff. The particular management idea favoured as a solution to these problems, at a given point in time, will be greatly influenced by the social, economic and political factors of the period' (ibid.: 116). In traditional leadership theory terms it would appear that contingency theory applies here – how well does a leader's style

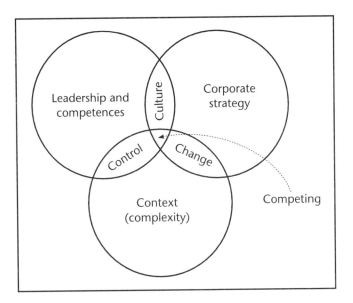

The 7C framework, from the leadership perspective   *FIGURE 11.1*

or experience suit the time? Situational leadership theories take a different line: that a leader may change his or her style to suit the times. Both of these theories, however, at least address context as a significant part of the equation.

Huczynski traces four broad historical periods from the leadership literature, encompassing both academic heroes and hero-managers (Table 11.4). He goes on to describe why successful CEOs, or hero-managers, are so successful in print. 'The rise in popularity of the hero-managers might be explained by the needs of the reading managers for gossip or their optimistic belief that they too could do well if they learned the tricks' (ibid.: 50). However, hero-managers' experience is not grounded in rigorous research, long years of study or consulting experience. Their authority comes directly from success. Huczynski adds: 'By distilling the essence of what successful managers do (irrespective of context)

Broad historical periods encompassing the great leader literature   *TABLE 11.4*

Period	Representatives (examples)	Period of original development
Rational-economic	Taylor (1911), Fayol (1940), Weber (1947)	1890–1930s
Social	Mayo (1933)	1920s–1950s
Psychological	Maslow (1954), McGregor (1960)	1940s–1950s
	Bennis (1985)	1960s–1970s
Entrepreneurial	Peters (1982), Kanter (1985), Iacocca (1985)	1980–1990

Source: Huczynski (1996).

it is believed that the secrets of success can be revealed. . . . [The secrets] tend to be of the "treat people well and they will work hard" variety' (ibid.: 50). While this may be a valid, common-sense message, the lack of academic rigour is a problem. A conclusive test of the ideas is unavailable and some ideas appear trite and unverifiable.

Competences

There appear to be two broad views on the competences of leaders:

- They cannot be identified and isolated. The argument here is that there are no clear competences because even after so many years of study they have not been identified.
- They can be identified. – This might explain why, after so many years, organizations are still trying to discern the key capabilities of leadership. This describes well the efforts of trait theorists who attempt to capture the characteristics of effective leaders.

That leadership competences cannot be identified perhaps explains why the necessary competences of leadership are still being explored around the globe, long after Fayol's (1949) planning, organizing, coordinating, commanding and controlling checklist was first published in 1916. For instance the International Consortium for Executive Education Research (Davids, 1995) asked 1450 executives in 12 global corporations to name the competences that would emerge as essential for leadership effectiveness in the next three years. The top three were as follows:

- Possession of tangible vision, values and strategy.
- The ability to empower others to do their best.
- The ability to be a catalyst/manager of strategic change.

Based on a comprehensive survey for the UK Industrial Society, Turner (1998) highlights the characteristics of leaders that are 'liberating', suggesting that enthusiasm, support for others and recognition of individuals' efforts are the most desirable characteristics. These could be described as the key attributes of transformational leaders. The least desirable characteristics, the survey found, were 'inspiring fear', 'making sure things are done their way' and 'telling us what to do'. The autocratic style of leadership from style theory still has widespread support, especially among command-and-control organizations such as the armed forces.

Another survey, the ongoing GLOBE survey in the US, uses a multifactor leadership questionnaire to assess the competences of transformational leadership (House *et al.*, 1998). The survey has been conducted for about two decades and is now being applied around the world through a network of 170 academic scholars. Perhaps conscious of critical charges about the difficulty of measuring leadership behaviours, Bass (1999) has explored empirical data derived from work with the multifactor leadership questionnaire. He found that applied research has been abundant, usually correlating transformational factors with outcomes in effectiveness and satisfaction of colleagues, but that basic research and theory have been in short supply.

One appealing explanation for researchers' inability to define the competences of leadership is the fact that the competences are tacit and intangible. In other words, leadership consists of individual and collective competences in style and substance to envision, formulate and implement strategies (Petric *et al.*, 1999). This explanation is supported by the resource-based view of the firm, which can be used to argue that top management may be one of those rare and difficult to imitate internal resources of the firm that brings increased rents for the firm (Castanias and Helfat, 1991). This is just one angle on the increasingly persuasive argument that the intellectual and social capital of firms – the firms' people and their interrelationships – are perhaps their most valuable asset. Taken as a whole, those competences may be said to define the overarching culture of the firm, which in turn can be said to offer competitive advantage (Barney, 1986; see also Chapter 7 of this volume).

Culture

Looking at the link between corporate strategy and leadership competences, Barney (1986) argues that culture may be a source of sustainable competitive advantage. Building on this, Castanias and Helfat (1991) suggest that the potential for generating rents by leveraging the organization's culture cannot be realized without effective leadership by the top management team. The ability to manage effectively may require an in-depth understanding of an organization's culture. According to William Steere, chairman and CEO of Pfizer, leaders 'often underestimate the role that culture plays in the business performance of a company and fail to realise that a critical part of the leader's job is cultural definition and development' (Hesselbein *et al.*, 1996: 266).

This relationship between culture and an organization's top management is what Hampden-Turner (1994: 17) describes as a 'most vital connection': 'Successful leaders . . . exert their most direct influence upon their companies by using the corporate culture. The leaders help to shape the culture. The culture helps to shape its members.' John Harvey-Jones (1988: 247), former chairman of ICI, has an even more extreme view: 'Eventually, large business enterprises consist only of people and their collective values.' These values are usually traceable to individuals much further back in the history of the company, he suggests. The implication for business leaders is that the values and examples they set 'will be handed on in turn to another generation for the future' (1988: 248).

This whole question of leadership and culture is explored at length by Schein (1985) in terms of leadership style theory – perhaps even of contingency theory – and the stage that organizations have reached in their life cycle. Schein summarizes this link with strategy theory as a continuum of leader involvement in culture management:

> A dynamic analysis of organizational culture makes it clear that leadership is intertwined with culture formation, evolution, transformation and destruction. Culture is created in the first instance by the actions of leaders; culture also is embedded and strengthened by leaders. When culture becomes dysfunctional,

leadership is needed to help the group unlearn some of its cultural assumptions and learn new assumptions. Such transformations require what amounts
to conscious and deliberate destruction of cultural elements, and it is this
aspect of cultural dynamics that makes leadership important and difficult to
define. (1985:316)

Taking a similar angle, Kotter and Hesketh (1992: 5) describe the impact of
culture on corporate performance as a brake on change: 'The beliefs and practices called for in a strategy may be compatible with a firm's culture or they
may not. When they are not a company usually finds it difficult to implement
the strategy successfully.' The competence of the leader, then, is crucial: 'The
single most visible factor that distinguishes major cultural changes that succeed from those that fail is competent leadership at the top' (ibid.: 84).

There is, however, much evidence to suggest that managing culture is
difficult if not impossible. Sadtler *et al.* (1998) suggest that far from merging organizations and cultures to create value, breaking them up is the key
means of creating value today. Managers and leaders often fail to recognize
that the time has come to break up an organization because of their strong
belief in 'unity: one company, one enterprise, one culture, one oneness'. They
quote one manager in the aftermath of corporate break up:

> We were schizoid. It was not until we separated that we realised how much
> effort was going into creating a common culture. We were forever com-
> promising and trying to be alike. Now we are two companies, the cultures
> have finally leapt apart and are accelerating away from one another. It would
> be impossible to put it back together again without a bloodbath (1988: 92).

More research is needed if there is to be a clear understanding of whether
leaders can meaningfully influence culture, either as a means of helping the
corporation to survive or to develop a competitive and sustainable corporate
strategy.

Corporate strategy

> My biggest challenge will be to put enough money on the right gambles
> and to put no money on the wrong ones. But I don't want to sprinkle money
> over everything (Jack Welch, quoted in Lowe, 1998: 109).

Since the early 1980s corporate strategy has been a pendulum swinging
between consolidation and globalization as a basis for competing. Perhaps the
most astute business leaders have been able to combine both of these in their
growth strategies.

When Jack Welch became CEO of General Electric (GE) in 1981 he inherited
350 strategic businesses. Of each of these he asked one simple question: could
this business become number one or number two in the markets it serves? He
subsequently reduced 350 to 15, then 14, then 11 core businesses. In Tom Peters'
terms he wanted to 'stick to the knitting' (Peters and Waterman, 1982: 292).

Welch drew three large circles around the businesses. In the first circle was core manufacturing, such as lighting and locomotives; in the second circle were technology-intensive businesses; and in the third circle were services. 'Anything outside the circles we will fix, close or sell', he said. He took offence at the suggestion that he was afraid to compete outside his first- and second-ranked businesses. 'I think one of the jobs of the businessperson is to get away from the slugfests and into niches where you can prevail. There's no virtue in looking for a fight. If you're in a fight your job is to win. But if you can't win, you've got to find a way out' (quoted in Lowe, 1998:119).

Following the emphasis on consolidation Welch turned his attention to internationalization, focusing strongly on Japanese competitors. 'As we stand on the threshold of the 1990s we face not only an even more powerful Japan, but [also] a revitalized, confident Europe moving closer together and led by bold, aggressive entrepreneurs of the kind we simply didn't encounter in the 1970s and 1980s' (1998:118). He highlighted the fact that winning an order for a power turbine would, in 1980, have been a straight head-to-head between GE's gas turbine business and Westinghouse. 'To win it in 1989 we had to go to the mat with Asea/Brown Boveri, a Swedish/Swiss combination, Siemens of Germany and a Westinghouse/Mitsubishi consortium' (1998:118).

Writing of the same period (the end of the 1980s), ICI's Sir John Harvey-Jones (1988: 128) said 'I do not believe the true international company yet exists, although some of the oil companies and perhaps IBM are closer to such a picture than most others.' In his time with ICI Sir John sought to internationalize the board with high-quality, non-executive directors of different nationalities. 'We have gained immeasurably by this, but the day of the true international company will dawn when instead of the majority of a board being of one nation, with perhaps, non-executive advice from other countries, we will be operating in a truly international way.'

Sanders and Carpenter (1998) report that globalization was still a major issue a decade later. According to these authors the question of what attributes large firms need in order to cope with the complexity arising from the internationalization of their operations remains one of the most important in the fields of international and strategic management. They stress that 'a critical determinant of a firm's ability to successfully deal with such complexity is its governance structure. In particular the ways in which top management teams are rewarded, the composition of the top team and board structure have weighed heavily in the dialogue on firm governance' (1998:158).

This issue of governance by the corporate centre perhaps outranks consolidation and globalization as the essential issue for corporations to address. Campbell *et al.* (1995b) ask critically, what value does the centre add? If it adds none, then by default surely the centre destroys value? Campbell and Goold's key contribution here is to distinguish between different styles of corporate 'parenting' – from financial control through to assembling a logical portfolio of businesses.

The question of how a global firm should be assembled should increasingly be the focus of today's business leaders, according to Lewin and Koza (2000: 116). 'In the old multinational corporation,' they suggest, 'the focus was on the allocation of capital across the various business units ... Managing the global multibusiness, however, involves the need continuously to animate self-renewal of the total enterprise.' In other words, 'leaders must infuse the organization as a whole with the life-force necessary for institutionalising change.'

Change

Andrew Grove (1996), CEO of Intel Corporation, has a prosaic perspective on change and competitive success. 'When a change in some element of how one's business is conducted becomes an order of magnitude larger than what that business is accustomed to, then all bets are off. There's wind and then there's a typhoon. There are waves and then there's a tsunami' (1996: 30). In the face of what Grove calls a '10x' change you can lose control of your destiny.

Of all the competitive forces at work on and in an organization, potentially the most deadly – says Groves – is the force described by Porter (1980) as substitution. 'New techniques, new approaches, new technologies can upset the old order, mandate a new set of rules and create an entirely new climate in which to do business' (1996: 28). In the view of Sir John Harvey-Jones (1988: 95), such a revolution engenders major change, which brings its own problems for leaders. 'Change management, like all aspects of management and leadership, requires understanding and attention, and a great degree of sensitivity to the needs and fears of the people who are affected by it.'

The problem (and perhaps the opportunity) for leaders is that there are no worldwide prescriptions for change – indeed there is no unified theory of change that can be drawn upon to evolve such a thing. 'The theories [that have evolved] have been strongly affected by their socio-historical context', says Dunphy (1996:541). 'Many have represented managerial fads', he adds, 'while other approaches have proved to be more enduring and gone on to form core theoretical approaches in the field.'

Key elements of the strategic change literature that are relevant for leaders are the agents of change (Buchanan and Boddy, 1994) and organizational politics (Buchanan and Badham, 1999). Striking, too, are the links with the literature on the learning organization (Edmondson, 1996; Hendry, 1996; Senge, 1990; de Geus, 1997).

Perhaps the most significant issue for leaders of change and change management today, according to Dunphy (1996), is how to ensure a continuously adaptive organization. Few theoretical approaches cover change initiatives that extend from the executive level to the general workforce. In addition most commentators are still exploring whether change can be directed strategically or whether it is emergent, brought about by the interplay of competing interest groups, rather than being planned and logically executed. All of this suggests a role for leaders that is far from that of the general in the command-and-control organization.

Control

> We had constructed over the years a management apparatus that was right for its times, the toast of the business schools. Divisions, strategic business

units, groups, sectors, all were designed to make meticulous, calculated decisions and move them smoothly forward and upward. This system produced highly polished work. It was right for the 1970s . . . a growing handicap in the early 1980s . . . and would have been a ticket to the boneyard in the 1990s. So we got rid of it . . . along with a lot of reports, meetings, and the endless paper that flowed like lava from the upper levels of the company (Jack Welch, speech to shareholders' AGM in 1989, quoted in Lowe, 1998).

It has been a thesis of this book that good management rests on a reconciliation of centralisation and decentralisation, or 'decentralisation with co-ordinated control' (Sloan, 1963).

Most business leaders are aware of the immensity of their roles. 'A leader is a not appointed because he knows everything and can make every decision' (Carlzon, 1987: 32). Leaders are appointed to bring together the knowledge that is available and then create the prerequisites for the work to be done. They create the systems that enable them to delegate responsibility for day-to-day operations.

Alfred Sloan's concept of decentralization with coordinated control is also relevant here. 'From decentralisation we get initiative, responsibility, development of personnel, decisions close to the facts, flexibility – in short all the qualities necessary for an organisation to adapt to new conditions. From coordination we get efficiencies and economies.' And he shows tremendous insight when he says 'It must be apparent that coordinated decentralisation is not an easy concept to apply' (Sloan, 1963:429).

Despite the essential need for control systems, Sloan is convinced that senior business executives have a role to play in the management of an organization's strategy. 'An organization does not make decisions', he says. 'Its function is to provide a framework, based upon established criteria, within which decisions can be made in an orderly manner. Individuals make the decisions and take the responsibility for them' (1963:443). He is also scathing of the formulaic, prescriptive approach to management: 'The task of management is not to apply a formula, but to decide issues on a case by case basis. No fixed inflexible rule can ever be substituted for the exercise of sound business judgement in the decision-making process' (1963:443).

One of the founding fathers of managerial control is Henri Fayol (1949), whose composite functions of planning, organizing, coordinating, commanding and controlling established the agenda for leadership for decades to follow. However, against the trend in the popular literature almost 80 years later, Nohria and Berkley (1994) were forced to ask in the title of their 1994 paper 'Whatever happened to the take-charge manager?' By the 1980s managers had 'abdicated their responsibility to a burgeoning industry of management professionals. . . . Although some companies are starting to question this reliance on quick fixes, the adoption of off-the-shelf innovations continues at a disturbing rate.' Their inevitable conclusion was that sustainable competitive strategy only comes from a leader's pragmatic resistance to innovation for innovation's sake.

Competing

Jack Welch of GE, often described as the business leader of the twentieth century, has stated categorically (Tichy and Sherman, 1993) that if a company does not have a competitive advantage it simply should not compete. In the 1970s and 1980s, when the competitive invasion by Japanese companies hit many US industries, GE chose its market battlegrounds very carefully, staying only in businesses where it held a powerful competitive position and a technological edge, and exiting businesses where it did not, such as consumer electronics. This decision on where and when to compete had fundamental implications for GE's corporate strategy and played to the well-known views expressed by Michael Porter in his seminal book *Competitive Strategy* (1980). To compete effectively in industrial markets, says Porter, one must seek first-mover advantage (the benefits of being first into a new market), or at least be a fast second.

Being competitive, though, is not simply a question of how fast or responsive your business is. Alfred Sloan of General Motors, writing four decades ago, said 'General Motors has become what it is because of its people and the way they work together. The field was open to all; technical knowledge flows from a common storehouse of scientific progress; the techniques of production are an open book, and the related instruments of production are available to all' (Sloan, 1963:449). In other words, 'It ain't what you do, it's the way that you do it'. It seems that tacit knowledge, an element of the resource-based view of the firm, is something that business leaders have understood – albeit intuitively – for some time.

So while the traditional competitive strategy literature has focused impersonally on profitable markets for the last twenty years or so (Porter, 1980), or on profitable competences (Prahalad and Hamel, 1990), the great leaders described in the populist literature have long known that the real answer lies in managing people. Pfeffer (1995) sums it up well: the only guaranteed way of generating sustainable competitive advantage is through the effective management and leadership of people.

Conclusions

What is tomorrow's role for business leaders and what can the strategic management literature offer that the great leader literature does not or cannot? Another look at the increasing complexity of the modern business context may offer an insight. Using complexity in its scientific sense, and not just in an abstract sense, offers new insights for leaders because research exploring the processes of strategy formation (Bailey and Avery, 1998), especially of the more formal planning processes, tends not to be able to explain the emergence within organizations of radically new products or services. A different mechanism is required to explain – in a strategic sense – radical process or product innovation within the organization.

Many commentators believe that one such mechanism is complexity theory, which defines the operation of non-linear systems with positive feedback loops. These systems are guided by simple order-generating rules and operate far from equilibrium (Stacey, 1993, 1996; Anderson, 1999). In these environments, Anderson (1999) suggests, strategic adaptation and organizational change must evolve and cannot be planned by organizations or – significantly – by individuals, whether leaders or not. He suggests that successful strategic adaptation is 'the passage of an organization through an endless series of microstates that emerge from local interactions among agents trying to improve their local payoffs' (1999: 228).

Perhaps the most significant elements of complexity theory for leaders – in terms of explaining unanticipated yet significant organizational innovation – are the related concepts of self-organization and emergence. What is described as self-organizing behaviour arises in complex systems where, from some random state, they usually evolve towards order instead of disorder (Kauffmann, 1993). This significant and observable phenomenon is a defining feature of complexity (Anderson, 1999). Building on these ideas, Brown and Eisenhardt (1998) suggest that the most effective organizations, functioning as 'complex adaptive systems', evolve strategies that lie neither in a zone of complete stability nor in a complete state of flux – instead they lie 'at the edge of chaos'.

Considering these twin issues of self-organization and emergence, that crucial question for the complexity perspective re-emerges: where in all this is the role for business leaders? Supporters of complexity theory suggest that it has enormous implications for managers. If complexity holds for organizations, and if it is not simply being used as an analogy or a metaphor, then according to various commentators (Stacey, 1993, 1995; Morgan, 1997; Lewin and Koza, 1999) it is important for leaders to:

- Rethink what they mean by organization, especially the concepts of hierarchy and control.
- Learn the art of managing and changing contexts.
- Learn how to use small changes to create large effects.
- Live with continuous transformation and emergent order as natural states of affairs.
- Be open to new processes that can facilitate the processes of self-organization.

In short, highly responsive, innovative, self-organizing firms do emerge as a result of complexity-perspective leadership (McKelvey, 1999), and if this holds true, then complexity theory offers a strong business case for empowerment and a facilitative, participative management style. The key leadership question now becomes, how do leaders facilitate or influence self-organization in complex organizations?

Of course this in its turn raises many other questions, such as how much are these facilitative processes context dependent? To what extent can the competences of facilitation be described and taught to other managers or leaders? Can the facilitation of change processes (among others) be routinized, systematized and perhaps copied by other organizations, thus destroying their value according to the resource-based perspective?

In conclusion it seems appropriate to consider the context of complexity theory as offering a paradox of control for business leaders, where less is more. Richard Pascale (1999) brings this brief exploration of complexity leadership theory full circle. He suggests that a complexity model of leadership is significant in that 'the primary task of leadership [is] to create a context that calls forth and taps . . . emergent potential'. It is also significant, he suggests, not because it rejects previous leadership theories, but because it builds on them, specifically on the situational and contingency theories of leadership. Clearly the application of complexity theory to leadership and management is an active research stream that has the potential to offer many new insights. It therefore needs further exploration (Anderson, 1999; McKelvey, 1999).

Tools and techniques

The most widely used tool for exploring leadership – both from a trait and a behavioural perspective – is the leadership questionnaire. Many different questionnaires have been devised, supporting the different leadership theories.

Trait questionnaires

The leadership trait questionnaire (Northouse, 1997) measures an individual's traits and highlights areas of strength and potential weakness. It quantifies the perceptions of individual leaders and selected observers, such as subordinates or peers, in a type of 360° assessment. As in all the questionnaires described in this section, there is no right or wrong answer. The purpose of the instrument is to give individuals who undertake the exercise a means of assessing their strengths and weaknesses, to evaluate areas where observers agree with that assessment and to explore other areas where there are discrepancies.

Style questionnaires

The Leadership Behaviour Description Questionnaire (LBDQ) (Stogdill, 1963) and the leadership grid (Blake and McCanse, 1991) are leadership style questionnaires that assess the degree to which leaders are task-directed as opposed to people-directed. They both assess what leaders actually do rather than who leaders are, and they show how leaders combine the task- and people-oriented behaviours to influence others.

The LBDQ originated at Ohio State University and has been used in style research since the 1960s. It defines task behaviours under the heading 'initiation of structure' and people-oriented behaviours as 'consideration'. Similar studies at the University of Michigan use the terms 'production orientation' and 'employee orientation'.

The leadership grid, which arose from Blake and Mouton's widely used managerial grid, tends to be used by practitioners in a training and development setting. It describes leadership behaviours along two axes: 'concern for production' and 'concern for people'. Overall the style approach is not a refined theory with a tested set of prescriptions for effective leadership. Rather it provides a valuable set of practical frameworks for managers, reminding them that they are assessed by others on how they manage both tasks and people.

Situational leadership

Various questionnaires have been devised to explore situational leadership. The main approach is to present case descriptions for the individual to assess. The respondent identifies the development level of an employee in a particular situation and then selects an appropriate response that represents the style of leadership they would most likely use in that situation.

The most widely used questionnaires are undoubtedly based on the situational approach described by Hersey and Blanchard (1969) and enshrined in their successful *One Minute Manager* series of books. Hersey and Blanchard's situational approach is itself based on Reddin's (1979) 3-D management style theory.

The inherent value of the approach for practitioners is the placing of leadership in different contexts. In other words, being an effective leader involves engaging in different kinds of leadership behaviour at different times, depending on the situation. Most of the other leadership theories suggest that leadership behaviour cannot be greatly altered, no matter what the situation.

Contingency theory

The 'least preferred coworker' (LPC) scale (Fiedler and Chemers, 1984) is used in contingency theory to measure an individual's style by having her or him describe a relationship with a coworker. This coworker must be someone with whom the respondent has had difficulty completing a task and the questionnaire explores this working relationship in 18 sets of paired adjectives. A low response suggests the respondent is task motivated, while a mid-range response suggests the individual is socio-independent and not overly concerned with the task or how others see him or her. A high response identifies individuals who are motivated by relationships and derive most workplace satisfaction from interpersonal relationships.

Because the LPC is a personality measure it tends to remain stable over time, and research shows (Fiedler and Garcia, 1987) that the reliability of the questionnaire upon retesting is very strong.

Transformational leadership

The most widely used instrument to measure transformational leadership is the multifactor leadership questionnaire, which has gone through a number of revisions (Avolio *et al.*, 1999). It is used to measure followers' perceptions of a leader's behaviour in eight areas under three headings.

1. *Transformational leadership (the four Is)*:
- Idealized influence (or charisma).
- Inspirational motivation.
- Intellectual stimulation.
- Individualized consideration.

2. *Transactional leadership*:
- Contingent reward or constructive transactions.
- Management by exception (both active and passive).

3. *Non-leadership*:
- Laissez-faire leadership.
- Non-transactional.

Perhaps the earliest version of the MLQ was developed by Bass (1985), based on interviews with 70 executives in South Africa. He constructed the questions after exploring the behaviour of leaders the executives had worked with and admired. A range of short and long versions of the questionnaire, all regularly tested for reliability and validity, exists for use in a variety of situations.

Case study revisited

The situation

Patricia Meyer, the human resources director of Jonas Industries, is again meeting Mike Nesbitt (finance director) and Steve Snaith (director of operations), to discuss the search for a new CEO after their abortive lunch meeting three days ago.

The conversation

Mike: Well I'm no better off, really. The stuff I've been reading hasn't given me any clear ideas about who we should look to recruit.
Patricia: What's your main conclusion?
Mike: The feeling I get is that if there's no evidence for a set series of characteristics that makes a good leader we're lost aren't we? We can't specify who we want or the sort of experience they might have.
Patricia: What do you think, Steve?
Steve: I don't see it quite so black as that. My thinking is that there are leaders out there who have experienced the issues and difficulties that face us now. Maybe we need to look for someone who's gone through what we're going through now. I think that would work.
Patricia [after a moment's silence]: I think you're both right. And I think there's also more to it. It seems to me that we can't predict whether anyone will be successful as a leader. But we can tell – albeit subjectively – whether someone has a good grasp of the current issues facing us, the context. We can also tell whether they have an understanding of the current culture of Jonas and what it is we do well, what our competences are. We, for our part, might be able to help them understand the control systems that exist in the organization. It seems to me that perhaps the biggest plus point in someone's favour might be whether or not they have managed a change programme in a similar organization.
Mike and Steve [in unison]: Jake West!

Revisiting the key questions posed earlier:

- To what extent can leadership be nurtured and developed, or are leaders born rather than made?
- Can leadership behaviour be predicted from someone's previous experience? In other words, of what relevance is previous business success?
- To what extent does personality matter?
- Given the breadth of the problems facing Jonas Industries, can a single individual turn round the situation?

Considering the trait and contingency theories of leadership it is easy to see why people such as Mike Nesbitt think that leaders are born and not made. The many books written by men and women without formal education and training reinforces this view.

Kakabadse and Kakabadse (1999) and McCall (1998), however, believe that leadership can be learned and prescribe a mix of on-the-job experience and off-the-job education for those involved in management development. ICI's Sir John Harvey-Jones (1988) calls it the problem of stretch. 'The reality is that we are conservative in our appreciation of others' abilities and we are reticent and uncertain about our own. Not only is it necessary organizationally to stretch others, but it is also necessary that we should stretch ourselves. . . . The art of "growing people" lies to a great degree in this stretching process' (ibid.: 62).

The idea of providing on-the-job experience is less significant if you accept the pure contingency theories that suggest that leaders do best in situations that suit them. For Jonas Industries therefore, all that might be necessary is to find someone with experience of turning round a similar organization. This would be a logical recruitment policy.

This supports a good deal of the succession planning strategy literature (Finkelstein and Hambrick, 1996) and it is more likely that Jonas Industries will be able to find someone with appropriate experience than someone with the 'right' personality, whatever 'right' might be. And as Patricia Meyer now believes, it should be feasible for one individual with enough understanding of the context within which the company works and enough understanding of what it does well to be able to manage a programme to bring about the changes necessary to deliver sustainable competitive advantage.

In conclusion, then, the stereotypical view of heroic, top-down leaders is dysfunctional and unsatisfactory given the current turbulence caused by hypercompetition and globalization. This complexity and the speed of developments in the current business environment is likely to accelerate still further, suggesting that models of organizational change derived from complexity theory will become increasingly relevant and useful. In this scenario the competences of leadership are more likely to be those of an organizational coach, facilitator and teacher than an autocratic general. The search for strategic leaders will continue – only the forum for and the theories in the debate will change.

Further Reading

Balogun, J. and V. Hope Hailey (1999) *Exploring strategic change* (Englewood Cliffs, NJ: Prentice-Hall). (A thorough and modern approach to managing strategic change).

Finkelstein, S. and D. Hambrick (1996) *Strategic leadership: top executives and their effects on organizations* (St Paul, Min.: West). (A broadbrush approach to the strategic leadership literature. A look at senior executives and their impact on corporate performance.)

Iacocca, L. (1985) *Iacocca: an autobiography* (London: Sidgwick and Jackson). (The classic CEO autobiography that has outsold Peters and Waterman's *In search of excellence*, 1982).

Mintzberg, H., B. Ahlstrand and J. Lampel (1998) *Strategy safari* (Englewood Cliffs, NJ: Prentice-Hall). (The chapter on entrepreneurs offers an idiosyncratic account of leadership and strategy.)

Northouse, P. (1997) *Leadership: theory and practice* (London: Sage). (A useful summary of the key mainstream twentieth-century leadership theories.)

Stacey, R. (1998) *Complexity and creativity in organizations* (San Francisco, CA: Jossey-Bass). (A fascinating account of the overlap between the strategy, complexity and psychology literatures.)

References

Anderson, P. (1999) 'Complexity theory and organization science', *Organization Science*, vol. 10, no. 3, pp. 216–32.

Avolio, B., B. M. Bass and D. I. Jung (1999) 'Re-examining the components of transformational and transactional leadership using the Multifactor Leadership Questionnaire', *Journal of Organizational and Occupational Psychology*, vol. 72, no. 4, pp. 441–62.

Bailey, A. and C. Avery (1998) 'Discovering and defining the process of strategy development', in V. Ambrosini (ed.) with G. Johnson and K. Scholes, *Techniques of analysis in strategic management* (London: Prentice-Hall), pp. 181–204.

Barney, J. (1986) 'Organizational culture: can it be a source of sustained competitive advantage?', *Academy of Management Review*, vol. 11, pp. 791–800.

Bass, B. M. (1985) *Leadership and performance beyond expectations* (New York: Free Press).

Bass, B. M. (1999) 'Two decades of research and development in transformational leadership', *European Journal of Work and Organizational Psychology*, vol. 8, no. 1, pp. 9–25.

Bennis, W. (1999) 'The end of leadership: exemplary leadership is impossible without the inclusion initiatives and co-operation of followers', *Organizational Dynamics*, vol. 28, no. 1, pp. 71–80.

Bennis, W. and A. Nanus (1985) *Leaders: The Strategies for Taking Charge* (New York: Harper & Row).

Blake, R. R. and A. A. McCanse (1991) *Leadership dilemmas – grid solutions* (Houston, Tex.: Gulf).

Blanchard, K., P. Zigarmi and D. Zigarmi (1985) *Leadership and the One Minute Manager: increasing effectiveness through situational leadership* (London: Collins Willow).

Brown, S., and K. Eisenhardt (1998) *Competing on the edge* (Boston, Mass.: HBS Press).

Bryman, A. (1992) *Charisma and leadership in organizations* (London: Sage).

Bryman, A. (1996) 'Leadership in organizations', in S. R. Clegg, C. Hardy and W. R. Nord (eds), *Managing organizations* (London: Sage).

Buchanan, D., and D. Boddy (1994) *The expertise of the change agent* (Englewood Cliffs, NJ: Prentice-Hall).

Buchanan, D. and D. Boddy (1999) *Power and politics of change* (London: Sage).

Campbell, A., M. Goold and M. Alexander (1995a) 'Corporate strategy: the quest for parenting advantage', *Harvard Business Review*, vol. 73, no. 2, pp. 120–32.

Campbell, A., M. Goold and M. Alexander (1995b) 'The value of the parent company', *California Management Review*, vol. 38, no. 1, pp. 79–98.

Carlzon, J. (1987) *Moments of truth* (Cambridge, Mass.: Ballinger).

Castanias, R. P. and C.E. Helfat (1991) 'Managerial Resources and Rents', *Journal of Management*, vol. 17, no. 1, pp. 155–71.

Conger, J. A. and B. Benjamin, (1999) *Building leaders* (San Francisco, CA: Jossey-Bass).

Conger, J. A. and R. N. Kanungo, (1998) *Charismatic leadership in organizations* (London: Sage).

Davids, M. (1995) 'Leadership competences', *Journal of Business Strategy*, vol. 16, no. 1, pp. 49–60.

De Geus, A. (1997) *The living company* (London: Nicholas Brealey).

Dunphy, D. (1996) 'Organizational change in corporate settings', *Human Relations*, vol. 49, no. 5, pp. 541–52.

Edmondson, A. (1996) 'Three faces of eden: the persistence of competing theories and multiple diagnoses in organizational intervention research', *Human Relations*, vol. 49, no. 5, pp. 571–95.

Fayol, H. (1949) *General and industrial management*, trans. P. Straws (London: Pitman).

Fiedler, F. E. (1964a) 'A Contingency Model of Leadership Effectiveness', in L. Berkowitz (ed.), *Advances in Experimental Social Psychology*, vol. 1, pp. 149–90 (New York: Academic Press).

Fiedler, F. E. (1964b) 'A contingency model of leadership effectiveness', in L. Berkowitz (ed.), *Advances in Experimental and Social Psychology*, vol. 1, pp. 149–90. (New York: Academic Press).

Fiedler, F. E. (1967) *A theory of leadership effectiveness* (New York: McGraw Hill).

Fiedler, F. E. and N. M. Chemers (1984) *Improving leadership effectiveness: the leader-match concept*, 2nd edn (New York: John Wiley).

Fiedler, F. E. and J. E. Garcia (1987) *New approaches to leadership: cognitive resources and organizational performance* (New York: John Wiley).

Finkelstein, S. and D. C. Hambrick, (1996) *Strategic leadership: top executives and their effects on organizations* (St Paul, Min.: West).

Fleischman, E. A., M. D. Mumford, S. J. Zaccaro, K. Y. Levin, A. L. Korotkin and M. B. Hein (1991) 'Taxonomic efforts in the description of leader behaviour: a synthesis and functional interpretation', *Leadership Quarterly*, vol. 2, no. 4, pp. 245–87.

Grove, A. (1996) *Only the paranoid survive* (London: HarperCollins).

Grundy, T. (1998) *Harnessing strategic behaviour* (London: FT Pitman).

Hampden-Turner, C. (1994) *Corporate culture: from vicious to virtuous circle* (London: Piatkus).

Handy, C. (1993) *Understanding the organization* (London: Penguin).

Harvey-Jones, J. (1988) *Making it happen: reflections on leadership* (London: HarperCollins).

Heider, J. (1985) *The Tao of Leadership* (Aldershot: Gower).

Heifetz, R. and D. Laurie, (1997) 'The work of leadership', *Harvard Business Review*, vol. 75, no. 1, pp. 124–35.

Hemphill, J. K. and A. E. Coons (1957) 'Development of the Leader Behaviour Description Questionnaire', in R. M. Stogdill and A. E. Coons (eds.), *Leader Behavior: Its Description and Measurement*. Columbus: Ohio State University, Bureau of Business Research.

Hendry, C. (1996) 'Understanding and creating whole organizational change through learning theory', *Human Relations*, vol. 49, no. 5, pp. 621–41.

Hersey, P. and K. H. Blanchard (1969) 'Lifecycle theory of leadership', *Training and Development Journal*, vol. 23, pp. 26–34.

Hesselbein, F., M. Goldsmith and R. Beckhard, (eds) (1996) *The leader of the future* (San Francisco: Jossey-Bass).

House, R. J. (1976) 'A 1976 theory of charismatic leadership', in J. G. Hunt and

L. L. Larson (eds), *Leadership: the cutting edge* (Southern Illinois University Press), pp. 189–207.

House, R. J., P. Hanges, A. Ruiz-Quintanilla, P. Dorfman, M. Javidan and M. Dickson (1998) 'Cultural influences on leadership and organizations: Project GLOBE', in W. Mobley (ed.), *Advances in Global Leadership* (Amsterdam: JAI Press).

Huczynski, A. (1996) *Management gurus: what makes them and how to become one* (London: ITBP).

Ireland, R. and M. Hitt (1999) 'Achieving and maintaining competitiveness in the 21st century: the role of strategic leadership', *The Academy of Management Executive*, vol. 13, no. 1, pp. 43–57.

Kakabadse, A. and N. Kakabadse (1999) *Essence of Leadership* (London: Thomson).

Kanter, R. M. (1985) *The Change Master: Corporate Entrepreneurs at Work* (London: Allen & Unwin).

Kauffmann, S. (1993) *The origins of order* (Oxford University Press).

Kaufmann, W. and R. J. Hollingdale (trans. and eds) (1967) *Friedrich Nietzsche: The Will to Power* (New York: Vintage).

Kets de Vries, M. and Associates (1991) *Organizations on the couch* (San Francisco: Jossey-Bass).

Kotter, J. and J. Hesketh (1992) *Corporate culture and performance* (New York: Free Press).

Lee, D. (trans.) (1987) *Plato: The Republic*, 2nd edn (Harmondsworth: Penguin).

Lewin, A. and M. Koza, (1999) 'Managing in times of disorder', *Financial Times*, (22 November).

Lewin, A. and M. Koza (2000) 'How to manage in times of disorder', in T. Dickson (ed.), *Mastering Strategy* (London: Prentice-Hall).

Likert, R. (1961) *New Patterns of Management* (New York: McGraw Hill).

Lowe, J. (1998) *Jack Welch speaks* (New York: Wiley).

McCall, M. W. (1998) *High Flyers: developing the next generation of leaders* (Boston, Mass.: HBS Press).

McGregor, D. (1960) *The Human Side of Enterprise* (New York: McGraw Hill).

McKelvey, B. (1999) 'The dynamics of new science leadership', unpublished manuscript, Anderson School at UCLA, Los Angeles, CA).

Maslow, A. (1954) *Motivation and Personality* (New York: Harper).

Mayo, E. (1933) *The Human Problems of an Industrial Civilization* (London: Macmillan).

Mintzberg, H. (1973) *The nature of managerial work*, (London: HarperCollins).

Misumi, J. (1985) *The behavioural science of leadership. An interdisciplinary Japanese research programme* (Ann Arbor, Mich.: University of Michigan Press).

Morgan, G. (1997) *Images of organization* (Thousand Oaks, CA: Sage).

Myers, M. S. (1966) 'Condition for Manager Motivation', *Harvard Business Review*, January–February.

Nohria, N. and J. Berkley (1994) 'Whatever happened to the take-charge manager?', *Harvard Business Review*, vol. 72, no. 1, pp. 128–38.

Northouse, P. (1997) *Leadership: theory and practice* (London: Sage).

Ohmae, K. (1995) *The evolving global economy* (Boston, Mass.: HBS Press).

Pascale, R. (1999) 'Leading from a different place: applying complexity theory to tap potential', in (eds), J. Conger, G. Spreitzer and E. Lawlor *The leaders' change handbook* (San Francisco, CA: Jossey-Bass).

Peters, T. and R. Waterman (1982) *In search of excellence* (London: HarperCollins).

Petric, J., R. Scherer, J. Brodzinski, J. Quinn and M. Ainina (1999) 'Global leadership skills and reputational capital: intangible resources for sustainable competitive advantage', *Academy of Management Executive*, vol. 13, no. 1, pp. 58–69.

Pfeffer, J. (1995) *The human equation* (Boston, Mass.: HBS Press).

Porter, M. (1980) *Competitive Strategy* (New York: Free Press).

Prahalad, C. K. and G. Hamel, (1990) *Competing for the future* (Boston, Mass.: HBS Press).

Reddin, W. J. (1979) 'The 3–D management style theory', *Training and Development Journal*, vol. 33, no. 6 pp. 63–72.

Sadtler, D., A. Campbell and R. Koch (1998) *Break up: when large companies are worth more dead than alive* (London: Capstone).

Sanders, W. G. and M. A. Carpenter (1998) 'Internationalisation and firm governance: the roles of CEO compensation, top team composition and board structure', *Academy of Management Journal*, vol. 41, no. 2, pp. 158–78.

Schein, E. (1985) *Organisational culture and leadership*, (San Francisco: Jossey-Bass).

Senge, P. (1990) *The fifth discipline* (New York: Random House).

Shamir, B. (1999) 'Leadership in boundaryless organizations: disposable or indispensable?', *European Journal of Work and Organisational Psychology*, vol. 8, no. 1, pp. 49–71.

Sloan, A. (1963) *My life with General Motors* (New York: Doubleday).

Stacey, R. (1993) *Strategic management and organisational dynamics* (London: Pitman).

Stacey, R. (1995) 'The science of complexity: an alternative perspective for strategic change processes', *Strategic Management Journal*, vol. 16, pp. 477–95.

Stacey, R. (1996) *Complexity and creativity in organizations* (San Francisco, CA: Berrett Koehler).

Steere, W. C. Jr (1996) 'Key leadership challenges for present and future executives', in F. Hesselbein, M. Goldsmith and R. Beckhard (eds), *The leader of the future* (San Francisco, CA: Jossey-Bass).

Stogdill, R. M. (1948) 'Personal factors associated with leadership: a survey of the literature', *Journal of psychology*, vol. 25, pp. 35–71.

Stogdill, R. M. (1963) *Manual for the Leader Behavior Description Questionnaire – Form XII* (Columbus: Ohio State University, Bureau of Business Research).

Stogdill, R. M. (1974) *Handbook of leadership: a survey of the theory and research* (New York: Free Press).

Tannenbaum, R. and W. Schmidt (1958) 'How to choose a leadership pattern', *Harvard Business Review*, March–April.

Taylor, F. W. (1911) *The Principles of Scientific Management* (New York: Harper).

Tichy, N. and M. Devanna, (1986) *The transformational leader* (New York: Wiley).

Tichy, N. and S. Sherman, (1993) *Control your destiny or somebody else will* (New York: Doubleday).

Turner, D. (1998) *Liberating leadership* (London: The Industrial Society).

Vroom, V. H. and P. Yetton (1973) *Leadership and Decision Making* (Pittsburg, PA: University of Pittsburg Press).

Weber, M. (1947) *The theory of social and economic organizations* (trans. T. Parsons) (New York: Free Press).

Yukl, G. (1994) *Leadership in organisations*, 3rd edn (Englewood Cliffs, NJ: Prentice-Hall).

Yukl, G. (1999) 'Effective leadership', *European Journal of Work and Organizational Psychology*, vol. 8, no. 1, pp. 33–48.

12 Entrepreneurship

Mark Jenkins and Steve Floyd

Basic principles

When reviewing the field of entrepreneurship it becomes clear that the term is subject to a multitude of interpretations. Determining the basic principles of such an eclectic group of academic research, practitioner books and business anecdotes is, at best, problematic. In order to help resolve this problem William Gartner (1990) attempted to draw together some of the disparate definitions of entrepreneurship. He used a Delphi technique to elicit the opinions of academics, business leaders and politicians. The Delphi study process involves the development of some level of consensus, or at least convergence, among a panel of experts on a particular issue, theme or event. Gartner's study produced 90 attributes of entrepreneurship, which were then factor analyzed into a series of themes. We shall use these themes as guiding concepts for the basic principles of entrepreneurship:

- Entrepreneurship involves individuals with unique personality characteristics and abilities. These characteristics include risk taking, an internal locus of control (the belief that they can influence their situation), autonomy, perseverance, commitment, vision and creativity.
- Entrepreneurship is concerned with innovation. The creation of something new, such as an idea, product, service, market or technology in a new or established organization.
- Entrepreneurship is concerned with creating organizations. This involves creating a new venture by identifying opportunities and mobilizing resources to meet these opportunities.
- Entrepreneurship is concerned with the creation of value, for example by transforming a business, creating a new business, expanding a business, creating wealth or destroying the *status quo*.
- Entrepreneurship is concerned with growth, the creation of a new venture that is intent on significant growth – growth in sales and growth in profits.
- Entrepreneurship involves uniqueness. This is characterized by a special way of thinking, a vision of accomplishment, the ability to see opportunities in everyday situations.
- Entrepreneurship involves the ownership and management of an ongoing business.

These seven themes are just some of the many aspects that are covered under the name of entrepreneurship. There are perhaps two overarching observations

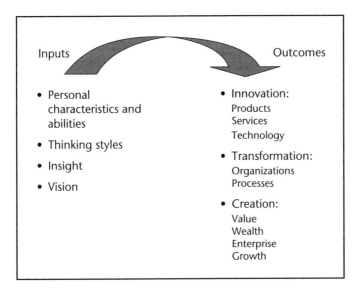

Meta-level characteristics of entrepreneurship   FIGURE 12.1

that can be made about them. The first is that they are all involved in some form of change from the *status quo*, such as the creation of a new business, the transformation of an existing business, some form of new product or service offering or the discovery of a new market segment. The second is that we can consider entrepreneurship either from the perspective of inputs (for example, the particular characteristics an individual needs to possess in order to be classified as an entrepreneur) or from the perspective of outputs (the events or indicators that would lead us to surmise that some form of entrepreneurial activity has taken place, such as the creation of a new venture or new levels of growth in an existing business). These meta-level characteristics of entrepreneurship are summarized in Figure 12.1.

In contrast to some of the other perspectives outlined in this book, the entrepreneurial perspective is not delineated through a series of well-defined concepts or relationships, that is, there is no underpinning theory of entrepreneurship in the way that exists in perspectives such as IO economics and cognition. It is a broad area of interest concerning the concept of change driven by individual activity and endeavour.

Case study

All of the following statements refer to one individual: Anthony Colin Bruce Chapman, founder of Lotus Engineering.

> 'He was very capable, very good at getting other people to help him, and he inspired people to do that, they enjoyed doing it.'

'He managed to instil enthusiasm and respect and people would work 25 hours a day if they had to.'

'He was an innovator, he was also a maverick.'

'He oozed charisma and confidence and he was a brilliant designer. He had a real passion for technology and things new.'

'He was a superb motivator and he taught me how to get the best from the people around me.'

'He inspired people in so many ways because his mind was so clear. He could come into a room full of people arguing about the solution to a particular problem, he'd cut through the bullshit and go straight to the nub of it, but then very often his solutions would be very exciting as well.'

'He was always ahead of his time, always looking for an edge over his rivals.'

'[H]e just loved innovation, he loved new ideas, he had a good feel for them and he was very good at driving them through.'

'He was always willing to just go beyond what was known and sooner or later he was going to be on to something that had a specific advantage.'

'I have always admired him and remember him as a subtle visionary, a wise interpreter of technical regulations, and so talented because of his ability to produce ideas ahead of their time.'

'I think he was the only team owner to possess the three most important elements for success. He could find the money; he could design the cars; and he could run the team. Those three qualities in one man are quite exceptional, even today.'

The Lotus Engineering Company formally started operating in 1952 with £25 Chapman had borrowed from his future wife, Hazel. Chapman's first premises, in Hornsea, North London, were located in a stable block behind his father's public house. The growth and success of Lotus cars was rapid, and soon the company was manufacturing some of the most successful racing cars of the 1950s and 1960s. In order to support its racing car business, Lotus started to make road-going cars in 1957. In 1966 it moved to a purpose-built factory in Norfolk, where it is still based today. In 1968 the company was floated on the stock exchange and capitalized at a value of £9 million – with their 52 per cent shareholding in Lotus, Colin and Hazel Chapman became millionaires. Chapman developed Lotus into a specialist performance car manufacturer with the aim of dominating the pinnacle of motor sport – Formula One. What was particularly unusual about Chapman was that he almost single-handedly created a series of revolutionary technological innovations that radically changed the basis for competition in Formula One. Since his premature death in 1982, no one has come close to his blend of commercial and technological acumen, for which he has been dubbed by many as a true genius. Some of the key developments he introduced are summarized below, and many still form the basis of Formula One car design today:

- 1962: the Lotus 25 was the first car with a monocoque chassis (a concept borrowed from aircraft design). Here the car body was the load-bearing structure, rather than a conventional chassis or tubular frame.
- 1967: the Lotus 49 was the first car to have the engine as part of the structure of the car. The engine, a Ford DFV, was funded by Ford, designed and built by Cosworth Engineering (founded by two ex-Lotus employees) and jointly developed with Lotus.
- 1968: Lotus was the first racecar contructor to introduce sponsor's livery (Gold Leaf cigarettes).
- 1968: the Lotus 49B was the first Formula One car with 'wings' – aerodynamic devices to keep the car on the ground, improving grip and handling.
- 1971: the Lotus 56 was the first gas-turbine Formula One car.
- 1972: the Lotus 72 used a wedge shape, with the water radiators mounted on the sides of the car at the rear in order to keep the front of the car low for aerodynamic downforce.
- 1977: Lotus 78 was the first 'ground-effect' car using underbody aerodynamics to force the car onto the surface of the track, thereby radically increasing cornering speeds.

It was often said that the Lotus engineers and mechanics would work twice as hard as others, continually trying out new ideas on the cars. On a number of occasions Lotus seemed to be to be ahead of itself, with a new racing car being launched, but then having to be replaced by the previous model whilst it was further developed into a reliable performer. Chapman's radical innovations often brought him into conflict with the sport's regulatory bodies. At the start of the 1981 season the new Lotus 88 – which had two bodies: one to carry the suspension, driver and engine and the other to provide the aerodynamic effect – was banned by the governing body after protests by all the major teams. For Chapman such regulation was anathema, his view was that Formula One racing was about building better and better cars, rather than trying to 'level the playing field'; Chapman's objective was continually to tilt the field in his favour.

Chapman had clear views about how to run his organization. He regarded drivers (with one or two exceptions) as simply there to drive the car – they were not qualified to make design changes and incurred his anger if they attempted to do so. He also resented the accumulation of what he saw as unnecessary costs – he once observed that if the staff car park was full the company must be employing too many people.

In addition to his brilliant career as a car designer and innovator, Chapman also became involved in the development of luxury boats and microlight aircraft. In 1972 he purchased the Moonraker boat company and introduced a number of revolutionary ideas, such as a vacuum moulding process for boat hulls, which he later applied to the manufacture of Lotus cars.

Lotus's road-going sports cars were not always as successful as Chapman would have liked and often suffered from the fact that new models, whilst always radical and innovative, were not always sufficiently developed to make them reliable from the outset. In 1982 Lotus was operating at a significant trading loss and had large loan repayments to make to its major funder, American Express. The position of the company looked more precarious than at any time in its 30-year history, but Chapman continued to seek out new alliances with manufacturers for the supply of engines. He also became involved in the notorious De Lorean project, in which Lotus provided the design concepts for the ill-fated De Lorean car.

Tragically Colin Chapman died of a heart attack in October 1982 at the age of 54. Lotus was acquired by General Motors in 1986 and was later sold to Proton cars, for whom it still makes high-performance sports cars. The Formula One team managed to continue until 1994, when it withdrew from the sport. Chapman is best summarized by Gerard Crombac (1986: 363), a close friend who wrote Chapman's biography after his death: 'The motto, now engraved on Colin's tombstone, provides a most apt description of this very remarkable man. It reads "*Crescit sub pondere Virtus*" which, translated, means "In adversity we thrive".'

The case study will be returned to later in this chapter. In the meantime the following questions provide a guide to how we might consider this example from the entrepreneurial perspective:

- What evidence is there to suggest that Colin Chapman was an entrepreneur?
- What suggests that he was not an entrepreneur?
- What were the strengths and weaknesses of Chapman's approach?

Key contributors

The origins of the entrepreneur can be found in work of eighteenth-century French economists such as Richard Cantillon (1931). Cantillon describes an early market economy by distinguishing between the roles of landowner, entrepreneur and hirelings. In this classification the entrepreneur engages in exchanges for profit, using business judgement in the face of uncertainty. Here the roles of capitalist and entrepreneur are distinct and the role of the entrepreneur is to anticipate the processes of demand and supply. After Cantillon other economists introduced the concept of innovation to the entrepreneurial process.

In parallel to the ideas developing in French economics were those of the British school, led by Adam Smith and his seminal book *The Wealth of Nations* (1976). In this book Smith integrated the notions of capitalist and entrepreneur – the individual risking his or her capital in order to generate profits by meeting a demand. His ideas were developed further by focusing on the individual attributes needed to be an entrepreneur, including energy, skill, knowledge, intelligence and trustworthiness (Mill, 1965).

Much of this earlier work focused on opportunism and the notion that the entrepreneur was simply satisfying an existing demand by engaging a series of factors of production in order to supply a particular product or service. Joseph Schumpeter (1934) introduced a distinctive perspective on entrepreneurship, in which the role of the entrepreneur is to create a dynamic, proactive force that disturbs the economic equilibrium through innovation. In Schumpeter's view an entrepreneur is anyone who creates new combinations of factors of production. These combinations can be in the form of new products, new processes of production, the opening of new markets, the capture of new sources of supply or a new organization of industry. In Schumpeter's definition, innovation is the central element of the entrepreneurial process.

One of the outcomes of categorizing the entrepreneur in terms of economic performance has been a focus on the characteristics of the individual entrepreneur. Various traits or characteristics have been applied to entrepreneurs, and while the results of many studies have been highly equivocal, they have played a part in highlighting individual characteristics such as the need for achievement (McClelland, 1987), an internal locus of control (Rotter, 1966), (which relates to how individuals view their ability to influence events around them), the propensity to take risks (Brockhaus, 1980) and tolerance of ambiguity (Schere, 1982; Sexton and Bowman, 1985).

The focus on entrepreneurial characteristics has led to more complex profiles where a wide variety of traits are used to understand the nature of entrepreneurs. For example Timmons *et al.* (1985) list 15 behaviours that they consider to be desirable and learnable, including commitment, a drive to achieve, a focus on goals, and the ability to seek and use feedback. They also identify four behaviours that they consider to be less learnable: energeticness and emotional stability, creativity and innovativeness, being 'streetwise', vision and capacity to inspire. Similar typologies have been offered by a range of researchers (for example Stanworth and Curran, 1976; Webster, 1977; Vesper, 1983; Chell *et al.*, 1991).

To broaden the definition beyond individual characteristics, other studies have considered the social context of entrepreneurship (Glade, 1967; Vesper, 1983), or more specifically, how entrepreneurship operates within formal and informal networks (Birley, 1985; Cooper, 1986; Aldrich and Zimmer, 1986).

In addition to social networks outside the new venture, researchers have studied entrepreneurial behaviour in the context of internal organizational structures – otherwise known as 'intrapreneurship' or 'corporate entrepreneurship'. On the face of it the notion of entrepreneurship within a large organization may seem an oxymoron. However, to survive in the face of rapidly changing markets or technologies, large established corporations rely on entrepreneurial processes to stimulate growth, create new products, develop new competences and even start up entirely new businesses. Thus Venkataraman, *et al.* (1992: 488) define corporate entrepreneurship as a process 'by which members of an existing firm bring into existence products and markets which do not currently exist within the repertoire of the firm'.

Corporate entrepreneurs face a unique set of challenges. On the one hand, any initiative an entrepreneur pursues should take advantage of the organization's existing capabilities. Otherwise the initiative is likely to stretch the organization beyond the boundaries of its core competence and result in poor organizational performance (Hoskisson *et al.*, 1991). On the other hand, the purpose of corporate entrepreneurship is to pursue new business ventures and renew the organizational strategy (Guth and Ginsberg, 1990; Covin and Slevin, 1991; Zahra, 1991). Initiatives that are too close to the *status quo* may not be sufficiently innovative to stimulate real organizational growth. Put succinctly, the task is to overcome the forces of organizational inertia without breaking the link to existing competences (Hannan and Freeman, 1984, 1989).

Leonard-Barton (1992) expresses this challenge more broadly as an organizational paradox. While existing capabilities provide the basis for a firm's current competitive position, without renewal these same capabilities will become rigidities that will constrain the firm's ability to compete.

For example, the United Technologies Corporation recently created dozens of teams of middle-level and operational managers to develop initiatives for the corporation's transformational agenda. This ambitious effort brought together managers from all over the world, plus university faculty members to provide intellectual stimulation. The programme proved useful in defining necessary courses of action, and it successfully energized the participants. Serious problems arose, however, when the team members attempted to implement the initiatives. Divisional executives 'back home' complained that the plans were out of sync with their own intentions and that the teams had failed to consider the organization's ability to respond.

As with independent entrepreneurship, therefore, purposeful behaviour by individuals – those who are willing and able to work outside 'normal' organizational channels – is very important to successful corporate entrepreneurship (Stevenson et al., 1989; Sykes and Block, 1989). This raises a number of important questions. How are corporate entrepreneurs able to identify opportunities that are not obvious to others in the organization? How do entrepreneurs achieve credibility for new ideas within an established social system? How are the entrepreneurs' new ways of thinking translated into tangible outcomes and organizational skills? How are entrepreneurial initiatives ultimately incorporated into the established set of organizational capabilities?

As shown in Figure 12.2, there appear to be three critical mechanisms in corporate entrepreneurship (Bower, 1970; Burgelman, 1983; Kanter, 1985; Floyd and Wooldridge, 1999): the identification of entrepreneurial opportunity, the emergence of entrepreneurial initiative and the renewal of organizational capability. Describing entrepreneurship in this way connects learning at the individual, group and organizational levels. Beginning at the individual level, opportunities are identified as individual intrapreneurs formulate ideas that integrate existing knowledge with information gathered from outside the mainstream organizational structure. At this stage 'weak ties' – casual acquaintances in the intrapreneur's social network – are important for creating a varied set of competing ideas within the organization. In the second stage, group learning occurs when the organization begins to pursue the opportunity in the form of an entrepreneurial initiative. At this point the influence exerted by an organizational champion becomes vital for stimulating the developmental effort. Importantly this individual is not necessarily the same individual who formulated the idea. In the third stage, large-scale innovation occurs as the organization integrates the efforts of individual entrepreneurs into an organizational capability. At this stage the social relationships that emerged among the coalition supporting the initiative's developmental process are formalized as part of the new organizational structure.

Like entrepreneurship outside the established firm, this approach suggests that opportunities are identified within organizations because individuals have access to unique information and are willing to accept ideas based on completely idiosyncratic criteria (Glade, 1967). Either these individuals or others

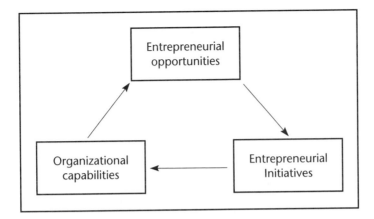

*Corporate entrepreneurship as a
capability-developing process*

FIGURE 12.2

then become associated with an idea, and as they successfully articulate and demonstrate it to others, the idea becomes the focus of an initiative. The shared experience within the group supporting the initiative then becomes the basis for further development (trials, prototypes and so on), and this leads to increased acceptance and skill-building across the larger organization. The final step in the process is to link the initiative to the official goals and integrate it with organization's strategy.

Linking entrepreneurship to strategy

Entrepreneurship has moved from being a peripheral aspect of the strategic agenda to being at the core of strategy, competitive strategy in particular. Referring back to Figure 12.1, the notion of entrepreneurial inputs and outcomes are central to the strategic thinking of today's successful organizations. The scarce and sought after inputs are more likely to be people, specifically those individuals who have the insight, commitment and personal abilities to create entrepreneurial dynamics in the firm, as these are the individuals who can identify opportunities and respond to them rapidly. In the words of Grant (1995: 152). 'The ability to identify these [profit-generating] opportunities and to respond to them are central components of the management activity we refer to as entrepreneurship. To the extent that external opportunities are fleeting or subject to first mover advantage, speed of response is critical to exploiting business opportunity.'

The outcomes that most organizations strive for are undoubtedly value creation and wealth, and increasingly these goals can only be achieved by the entrepreneurial processes of innovation, transformation and creation. In a business context where companies are being created and sold for millions in a matter of months the notion of entrepreneurship moves centre stage on the strategic agenda. In a context where there is a high degree of uncertainty and rapid change, responsiveness is the required core competence for any organization.

To consider the impact of entrepreneurship on the field of strategic management we shall apply the 7 Cs.

Context (external environment)

The entrepreneurial perspective presents the external environment as the arena in which the entrepreneur identifies future opportunities. It is not positioned as a constraining factor, but as the basis on which the entrepreneur identifies a new opportunity to create value. In the case of the traditional entrepreneur, this context relates to factors that are outside the firm. For the intrapreneur these relate to social networks external to the intrapreneur or intrapreneurial group. The context of entrepreneurship is frequently described as one of complexity, uncertainly and risk, a context that is becoming increasing prevalent due to the impact of new technologies and business approaches.

Entrepreneurs are frequently described as having an internal locus of control. This implies that they believe their destiny is in their own hands and they are able, through their own actions, to shape their own future. Works on the network and social context of entrepreneurship (Stanworth and Curran, 1976; Birley, 1985) put the entrepreneurial process in the context of a broader environment that either supports or inhibits the entrepreneurial process. Questions are often raised at the policy level about how governments can generate employment through the new venture creation (Birch, 1979).

Culture (internal environment)

The entrepreneurial perspective sees organizational culture in terms of evidence of entrepreneurial behaviour and the degree to which the culture supports and encourages such behaviour. In this context culture either supports or undermines the entrepreneurial process. This relates particularly to corporate entrepreneurship in which large organizations are trying to recreate the culture of smaller, more nimble organizations where entrepreneurial activity is more likely to be in evidence.

In the case of the small business, it is implicit in the entrepreneurial perspective that the firm's culture is a function of its entrepreneurial character and that it is driven by entrepreneurial objectives.

Competences (resources/capabilities/skills/knowledge)

Competences relate to entrepreneurial capacity. The ability to see opportunities and marshal the resources needed to exploit these opportunities is central to the entrepreneurial perspective. Knowledge is therefore about being able not only to recognize opportunities, but also to gather the resources needed for their exploitation. One of the limiting factors often referred to when entrepreneurs are considered in the context of growth is inadequate managerial competence. Penrose (1959) refers to managerial limitations impeding the development of the entrepreneurial firm beyond a certain size.

Competing (ways of outperforming competitors)

The entrepreneurial route to competitive advantage is concerned with identifying and exploiting more opportunities than competitors are able to do, and being able continually to innovate and take more risks in order to outperform competitors. Examples of this are often cited in the folklore of business, where individuals such as Fred Smith (Federal Express), James Dyson (Dyson) and Richard Branson (Virgin) are portrayed as having changed the rules of the game through radical innovation. Smith's 'hub and spoke' approach to next-day mail delivery revolutionized the mail service in the US; Dyson's idea that vacuum cleaners could only be truly efficient if they had no bag challenged the technical paradigms of big players such as Hoover; and Virgin's concept that financial services could be sold direct to consumers without the added complication of often untrustworthy intermediaries shook up the world of financial services.

Change (types of organizational change/change processes)

At the start of this chapter we characterized entrepreneurship as being concerned with change. Entrepreneurial organizations are therefore in a continual state of flux. They are constantly reconfiguring themselves in order to respond to new opportunities and develop and refine their products and services. This produces particular challenges and raises questions about how entrepreneurial firms should be 'managed', and indeed whether the concept of management is appropriate in this case.

Control (how managers control what is happening in the organization/structure)

The entrepreneurial leader is one portrayed as having the ability to inspire and bring along others with him or her. Bureaucratic control is the antithesis of entrepreneurial spirit, which is concerned with leading from the front and inspiring by example. However entrepreneurship is also associated with an autocratic rather than a consensual style, where the ideas and wishes of particular individuals drive the priorities of the organization. Many of these factors overlap with the concept of leadership discussed in Chapter 11.

Tools and techniques

The entrepreneurial perspective draws on tools and techniques from other areas and applies them to the entrepreneurial situation. These tools and techniques tend to fall into two groups tools and techniques for identifying entrepreneurs, and those for understanding the entrepreneurial process.

One of the most prolific range of tools consists of psychologically derived instruments for identifying entrepreneurial traits. Most of the authors who advocate a trait approach – where entrepreneurs are classified according to a series of identifiable characteristics – tend to have their own instruments for doing so. These include McClelland's (1987) approach to evaluating the need for achievement, Rotter's (1966) measures for the locus of control, and the instruments developed by Timmons (Timmons *et al.*, 1985) and Vesper (1983).

To understand the entrepreneurial process, exploratory techniques such as cognitive mapping have been used to attempt to uncover the entrepreneurial ideas that drive the business (Cossette and Audet, 1992; Jenkins and Johnson, 1997). Techniques such as social networks have also been applied to this area (Birley, 1985).

Case study revisited

The case study provided an account of the achievements of Colin Chapman, founder and CEO of Lotus. Three guiding questions will be used to relate this account to the concept of entrepreneurship.

What evidence is there to suggest that Colin Chapman was an entrepreneur?

At one level Chapman had the profile of the archetypal entrepreneur: an individual who creates an organization and takes it to extraordinary levels by inspiring others, continually seeking new ways of doing things and constantly finding new opportunities to exploit.

Chapman is described by many as possessing unique characteristics that allowed him to bridge the technological and commercial worlds of Formula One racing and the production of sports cars. He is frequently described as being very decisive, knowing his own mind, and able clearly to communicate this to others.

Chapman was also an example of the Schumpterian entrepreneur: an individual who is able, through radical innovation, to transform the basis of competition. Chapman did so by developing concepts such as ground-effect, whereby he adapted and exploited a range of technologies relating to aerodynamics. This not only revolutionized the racing car industry, but was also extended to the design of passenger cars. Part of this process involved fostering a climate of continual change. He seemed to become bored with ideas quickly, particularly once everyone else had adopted them, and was always keen to move on to the next big idea, rather than fully develop existing ones.

What suggests he was not an entrepreneur?

Chapman undoubtedly fits many of the principles outlined earlier. However, whilst he innovated radically within the company, he was not concerned with starting new forms of organization – Lotus was his only 'start-up' company, and whilst this became a highly successful and innovative business, this aspect of Chapman's approach is not consistent with the view that entrepreneurship is concerned with the continual creation of new ventures. Hence Chapman was certainly not a 'serial entrepreneur', rather he confined himself to making Lotus an entrepreneurial organization in terms of focus on change and the continual search for new ways of doing things.

Similarly it could be argued that whilst Lotus created a great deal of value in the early days, this diminished as the organization grew larger. During this time Chapman seemed to distance himself from the car business and focused more on the Formula One team, thereby spending less energy on change and increased value for the car business.

What were the strengths and weaknesses of Chapman's approach?

Chapman's strengths were connected with innovative and creative processes characterized by continual change and technologies and ideas that never stood still. This made it very difficult for competitors to keep up and for governing bodies to regulate against ideas that had yet to be developed fully.

This strength, however, also characterizes the fundamental problem of viewing the entrepreneurial process in isolation. Chapman's ideas were often ahead of their application, and this meant that the company continually needed to back-track or improvise as it went along. In the meantime competitors could wait to see which ideas worked in the long run, and this allowed them to take a more considered approach. This is why Lotus's competitors were often more successful at using Lotus's ideas than Lotus itself (Jenkins and Floyd, 1999). One example of this is the ground-effect concept, which was pioneered by Lotus but ultimately provided most benefit to the Williams team, who developed a simple and robust interpretation of the concept while Chapman was moving to the more complex and ultimately unsuccessful twin-body concept of the Lotus 88.

One of the weaknesses of the entrepreneurial perspective, therefore, is that it focuses on one end of a continuum, the end concerned with being radical, innovative and creating change. At the other end of the continuum is the professional manager or administrator, who is concerned with stability and a systematic approach characterized by low risk and conservatism. In reality organizations need the traits both found at ends of the continuum. It could be argued that Colin Chapman provides an unusual example of the entrepreneurial spirit at its purest extreme. What is certain is that he was a dynamic force for change in Formula One racing, the like of whom has not been seen since his death in 1982.

Further reading

Chell, E., J. M. Haworth and S. A. Brearly (1991) *The Entrepreneurial Personality: Concepts, Cases and Categories* (London and New York: Routledge).
Sexton, D. L. and R. W. Smilor (1986) *The Art and Science of Entrepreneurship* (Cambridge, Mass.: Ballinger).
Timmons, J. A., L. E. Smollen and A. L. M. Dingee (1985) *New Venture Creation*, 2nd edn (Homewood, Ill.: Irwin).

References

Aldrich, H. and C. Zimmer (1986) 'Entrepreneurship through social networks', in D. L. Sexton and R. W. Smilor (eds), *The art and science of entrepreneurship* (Cambridge, Mass.: Ballinger), pp. 2–23.
Birch, D. L. (1979) *The Job Generation Process, MIT Program on Neighbourhood and Regional Change* (Cambridge, Mass.: MIT Press).

Birley, S. (1985) 'The role of networks in the entrepreneurial process', *Journal of Business Venturing*, vol. 1, no. 1, pp. 107–17.

Bower, J. L. (1970) *Managing the Resource Allocation Process* (Boston, Mass.: Harvard Business School).

Brockhaus, R. H. (1980) 'Risk Taking Propensity of Entrepreneurs', *Academy of Management Journal*, vol. 23, no. 3, pp. 509–20.

Burgelman, R. A. (1983) 'A process model of internal corporate venturing in the diversified major firm', *Administrative Science Quarterly*, vol. 28, pp. 223–44.

Cantillon, R. (1931) *Essai sur la nature du commerce en general* (1755), ed. by H. Higgs (London: Macmillan).

Chell, E., J. M. Haworth, and S. A. Brearly (1991) *The Entrepreneurial Personality: Concepts, Cases and Categories* (London and New York: Routledge).

Cooper, A. C. (1986) 'Entrepreneurship and High Technology', in D. L. Sexton and R. W. Smilor (eds), *The Art and Science of Entrepreneurship* (Cambridge, Mass.: Ballinger).

Cosette, P. and M. Audet (1992) 'Mapping of an Idiosyncratic Schema', *Journal of Management Studies*, vol. 29, no. 3, pp. 309–48.

Covin, J. G. and D. P. Slevin (1991) 'A conceptual model of entrepreneurship as firm behavior', *Entrepreneurship Theory and Practice*, vol. 16, pp. 7–25.

Crombac, G. (1986) *Colin Chapman: the man and his cars* (Wellingborough: Patrick Stephens).

Floyd, S. W. and B. Wooldridge (1999) 'Knowledge creation and social networks in corporate entrepreneurship: The renewal of organizational capability', *Entrepreneurship: Theory and Practice*, vol. 23, no. 3, pp. 123–43.

Gartner, W. B. (1990) 'What are we talking about when we talk about entrepreneurship?', *Journal of Business Venturing*, vol. 5, pp. 15–28.

Glade, W. P. (1967) 'Approaches to a theory of entrepreneurial formation', *Explorations in Entrepreneurial History*, vol. 4, no. 3, pp. 245–59.

Grant, R. M. (1995) *Contemporary Strategy Analysis*, 2nd edn (Cambridge, Mass.: Blackwell).

Guth, W. D. and A. Ginsberg (1990) 'Guest editors' introduction: Corporate entrepreneurship', *Strategic Management Journal*, vol. 11, pp. 5–15.

Hannan, M. T. and J. Freeman (1984) 'Structural inertia and organizational change', *American Sociological Review*, vol. 49, pp. 149–64.

Hannan, M. T. and J. Freeman (1989) *Organizational Ecology* (Cambridge, Mass.: Harvard University Press).

Hoskisson, R. W., M. A. Hitt, and C. W. L. Hill (1991) 'Managerial risk taking in diversified firms: An evolutionary perspective', *Organization Science*, vol. 2, pp. 296–313.

Jenkins, M. and S. Floyd (1999) 'The Dynamics of Industry and Firm Level Knowledge: A Case Analysis of the Ground-Effect Revolution in Formula One Racing', paper presented at the First International and Tenth Annual Conference of the MESO Organization Studies Group, Fuqua School of Business, Duke University.

Jenkins, M. and G. Johnson (1997) 'Entrepreneurial Intentions and Outcomes: A Comparative Causal Mapping Study', *Journal of Management Studies*, vol. 34, no. 6, pp. 895–920.

Kanter, R. M. (1985) 'Supporting innovation and venture development in established companies', *Journal of Business Venturing*, vol. 1, pp. 47–60.

Leonard-Barton, D. (1992) 'Core capabilities and core rigidities: A paradox in managing new product development', *Strategic Management Journal*, vol. 13, pp. 111–25.

McClelland, D. C. (1987) 'Characteristics of Successful Entrepreneurs', *Journal of Creative Behavior*, vol. 21, no. 3, pp. 219–33.

Mill, J. S. (1965) *Principles of Political Economy* books 1–5 (London: Routledge and Kegan Paul).

Penrose, E. T. (1959) *The Theory of the Growth of the Firm* (Oxford: Basil Blackwell).

Rotter, J. B. (1966) 'Generalised Expectancies for Internal Versus External Control of Reinforcement', *Psychological Monographs*, vol. 80, no. 609.

Schere, J. (1982) 'Tolerance of ambiguity as a discriminating variable between entrepreneurs and managers', *Proceedings of the American Academy of Management Conference* (New York: Academy of Management), pp. 404–8.

Schumpeter, J. A. (1934) *The Theory of Economic Development* (Cambridge, Mass.: Harvard University Press).

Sexton, D. L. and N. Bowman (1985) 'The entrepreneur: A capable executive and more', *Journal of Business Venturing*, vol. 1, no. 1, pp. 13–28.

Smith, A. (1976) *The Wealth of Nations*, vol. 1, Everyman's Library 412 (London: Dent).

Stanworth, M. J. K. and J. Curran (1976) 'Growth and the Small Firm – An Alternative View', *Journal of Management Studies*, vol. 13, pp. 95–110.

Stevenson. H. H., M. J. Roberts and H. I. Grousbeck (1989) *New Business Ventures and the Entrepreneur* (Homewood, Ill.: Irwin).

Sykes, H. G. and Z. Block (1989) 'Corporate venturing obstacles: Sources and solutions', *Journal of Business Venturing*, vol. 4, pp. 159–67.

Timmons, J. A., L. E. Smollen and A. L. M. Dingee (1985) *New Venture Creation*, 2nd edn (Homewood, Ill.: Irwin).

Venkataraman, S., I. C. MacMillan and R. C. McGrath (1992) 'Progress in research on corporate venturing', in D. L. Sexton and J. D. Kasarda (eds), *The State of the Art of Entrepreneurship* (Boston, Mass.: PWS Kent).

Vesper, K. H. (1983) *Entrepreneurship and National Policy* (Pittsburgh, PA: Carnegie Mellon University).

Webster, F. A. (1977) 'Entrepreneurs and ventures: An attempt at classification and clarification', *Academy of Management Review*, vol. 2, no. 1, pp. 54–61.

Zahra, S. (1991) 'Predictors and financial outcomes of corporate entrepreneurship: An exploratory study', *Journal of Business Venturing*, vol. 6, pp. 259–85.

13 Can Multiple Perspectives on Strategic Management Inform Practice?

Véronique Ambrosini and Mark Jenkins

Each perspective covered in Strategic Management: a Multi-Perspective Approach focuses on certain aspects of strategy, while none of them captures the entirety of the strategy field, despite all their limitations, they all contribute to our understanding of the field. However, there is one question worth raising at the end of such a review of theoretical perspectives. This concerns the relevance of multiple perspectives to the practice of strategic management: can the perspectives contribute both to the understanding and to the practical application of strategic management?

Each chapter in this volume concentrates on a particular academic perspective on strategy. Most of the contributions are discipline-based and research-centred, where the focus is on knowledge – knowing what – rather than direct practical application, or knowing how. The perspectives in question provide an understanding of organizations and how they operate. They do not usually deal with the direct, immediate problems faced by managers. This does not mean, however, that they are not crucial to managerial practice. Without informed research, actions may be taken without solid evidence; they may be taken on the basis of anecdotes or out of context.

One characteristic of the field of strategy is that it is normative. Strategy is characterized by its prescriptions, advice on what managers should do in order for their organization to outperform its competitors. As just mentioned, most of the perspectives covered in this book are more about 'knowing about' than 'knowing how'. However they provide useful insights that can guide decision making within organizations. Lewin's (1945) statement that 'There is nothing so practical as a good theory' is widely used for good reason. However this does not mean that theory should or can indeed be followed to the letter by practitioners. However, well-developed theories are practical because of their rigorous coverage of specific aspects of strategic management. They state clearly what they examine, plus the elements and variables which are of concern to the theory. They also explain the relationships between the constructs under examination. Theories also deal with the 'why'; that is, the assumptions necessary for the theory to work. Finally, theories indicate when and where they can be applied and to whom they can be applied (Whetten, 1989). This means that theories do not live in a vacuum, they specify when and where they can be used and, as a corollary, when they cannot. This implies that theories need to be well understood if they are to be applied properly, that is, in the right context and the right circumstances.

Do theories suggest particular strategies? Do they provide managers with prescriptions? If you were a manager or a strategy consultant, would you have a more insightful understanding of how to act if you were using theories rather than remaining theory free?

Some perspectives offer practical models and tools. For example 'five forces' analysis helps us to understand the competitive environment in which organizations operate (see Chapter 2); the value net is a way of identifying the players in a game (Chapter 5); causal mapping techniques are designed to capture actors' causal belief systems (Chapter 9); and leadership questionnaires are used to assess styles or behaviours of leaders (Chapter 11). The tools that are used in strategy are plentiful and our purpose here is not to review them or explain how to use them (see Ambrosini with Johnson and Scholes (1998) for some practical advice) but to show that many derive from theory.

Most perspectives also give some guidance about strategising. For instance the resource-based view of the firm suggests that sources of competitive advantage are to be found inside the firms and that managers should protect, nurture and leverage these sources. Industrial organization economics on the other hand suggests that what matters most is the structure of the industry and therefore managers should ensure that they monitor and try to manipulate the structural forces that surround them. Transaction cost economics explain how firms can choose an efficient structure that will minimize costs. Game theory shows why it is essential for firms to observe the players in their industry and how they interact in order to achieve the most favourable position. Institutional theory warns that managers need to be aware of the influence of their environment and how it can put pressure on their organization to conform to the rules of the game, and hence that managers may not be as free as they think to make changes and be creative. Chapter 9 highlights that managers' rationality is often limited and they may rely on simplified representations of the world around them. Managers should be aware of this, as how they think and make sense of their world has an effect on the strategic decisions they make. The leadership and entrepreneurship perspectives stress the importance of vision and leadership in an organization, as well as how important it is to understand the entrepreneurial process in order to recognize opportunities and the need for change, and to translate vision into action. The military perspective is perhaps the most prescriptive perspective as it gives precise guidelines for competing. It suggests that in order to win, organizations must have clear objectives, strong values, and leadership. They should also assess their competitors' strengths and weaknesses, to attack competitors with speed and surprise, and act to stretch competitors' resources without stretching their own.

In light of the above, strategic management theories cannot be accused of being normatively free, and, looking at what strategy consultants typically do confirms this. The consultants' role is characteristically about guiding and facilitating the strategy process, to provide managers with some direction and rigour in their decision process. To do so, consultants use theoretical frameworks and tools, and one of the tasks is to ensure that these theory driven frameworks are understood in the context of the daily reality of the business it is going to be applied to.

Obviously consultants must themselves understand their 'tool kit'.[1] They need to be able to communicate to the managers they work with that while frameworks and research-driven prescriptions are valuable aids to making sense of what is going on in the organization and environment, they are not designed to provide precise answers or magical solutions. They are there primarily to help organize the thinking of individuals. They are valuable as mechanisms to help managerial teams engage in and remain focused on the strategy debate, as well as to help them make decisions that will improve their organization's performance. For many managers, strategizing or being involved in strategic decision making for the first time can cause them to feel suspicious, nervous or anxious about the potential outcomes. The use of frameworks allows the debate to proceed in a way that captures rational, objective data as well as instinctive, subjective nuances. Collecting data within a framework can act as a base point from which to step away from their normal or traditional areas of focus and, with confidence, consider more creative ideas and options. They can then come back to the theories and test the strategic fit of their new ideas.

Models facilitate the organising of information and help to make sense of things in a way that is not easily achieved without any support. Frameworks are dynamic tools. Theories and frameworks can be imagined to be rather like the pieces of a jigsaw. To begin with, there is a box full of bits, and the strategy team need to be helped to understand how to create the picture that becomes the finished jigsaw; that is, the strategy. The frameworks are used rather like interlocking jigsaw pieces to demonstrate the relationship between one part of a strategy and another. The only difference with a jigsaw is that this is not a fixed picture, – as it is built, the picture keeps evolving. The frameworks are very much part of the building process and help to test the validity of the data and its influence on the picture. The important thing about frameworks is how they link together and relate to each other in order to build up to the complete picture. Sometimes it is necessary to select a particular technique to get a particular response.

Theories can help the team to reframe the organization's behaviour and its ability to adapt to change. They can provide insights into how and why things are always done in a certain way in the organization. Because organizations are 'living', 'emotional' organisms functioning in a complex, diverse and volatile environment, it is often difficult for managers to deal with strategic issues without help from theories. Dealing with strategic issues can be 'messy' and 'fuzzy', and the use of frameworks can help alleviate this and bring discipline and understanding. For instance frameworks can help reveal taken-for-granted assumptions, explore relationships between different areas of the organization, surfacing paradoxes in the environment and managers' behaviours and so on. Tools are useful as long as they are used critically and in the right context.

In conclusion one can assert that what matters most for managers are not theories *per se*, but how they are used. It is in their judgement and interpretation of the theory and the data they collect that managers can add value to the strategy process. Theories cannot give solutions or definitive answers, but they will inform management judgement and decision making. They help managers think.

Note

1. We would like to thank Simon Carter (Visiting Fellow, Strategic Management Group, Cranfield School of Management) for his contribution to this part of the chapter.

References

Ambrosini, V. with G. Johnson and K. Scholes (1998) *Exploring techniques of analysis and evaluation in strategic management* (London: Prentice-Hall).

Lewin, K. (1945) 'The research center for group dynamics at Massachusetts Institute of technology', *Sociometry*, 8, pp. 126–36.

Whetten, D. A. (1989) 'What constitutes a theoretical contribution?', *Academy of Management Review*, vol. 14, no. 4, pp. 490–495.

Index